T. S. (Timothy Shay) Arthur

Strong Drinks: Cures And The Cure

T. S. (Timothy Shay) Arthur

Strong Drinks: Cures And The Cure

ISBN/EAN: 9783742834140

Manufactured in Europe, USA, Canada, Australia, Japa

Cover: Foto ©Andreas Hilbeck / pixelio.de

Manufactured and distributed by brebook publishing software (www.brebook.com)

T. S. (Timothy Shay) Arthur

Strong Drinks: Cures And The Cure

T. S. Arthur

THE CURSE AND THE CURE.

By T. S. ARTHUR.

Author of "*Three Years in a Man-Trap*," "*Danger*," "*Woman to the Rescue*," "*Cast Adrift*," etc., etc.

HUBBARD BROTHERS,
Philadelphia, Cincinnati, Chicago and Springfield, Mass.
N. D. THOMPSON & CO., St. Louis, Mo.: A. L. BANCROFT & CO.,
San Francisco, Cal.

Entered according to Act of Congress, in the year 1877, by
HUBBARD BROS.,
In the Office of the Librarian of Congress, at Washington, D. C.

E. STANLEY HART, Electrotyper and Printer, 38 Hudson Street, Phila.

PART I.

WHAT SHALL WE DO TO BE SAVED

FROM THE

DEMON OF DRINK?

PUBLISHERS' PREFACE.

IN the FIRST PART of this important work we have one of those intensely wrought temperance stories for which the author is so distinguished. In the conception and execution of this story, he has taken higher ground than usual, and lifted the subject of temperance into the region of spiritual laws and forces. Rarely has the insidious growth and overmastering power of appetite, or the desperate and prolonged struggle of an enslaved man for freedom, been more powerfully exhibited than in the hero of this story—a man of education, social standing, high honor and the tenderest home affections. We follow him in his downward course, step by step, with an almost breathless interest and suspense—glad and hopeful for every new effort that he makes to overcome his pitiless enemy, and disappointed and sorrowful at each successive failure—until manhood is eclipsed, love extinguished and honor a thing of the past; and we turn away from him at the prison door, our hope as dead as his own. But the man is not lost. No; there is ONE who can save to the uttermost all who come unto Him. And by Him this man is saved, and made a power for good in the salvation of many who had once been in the same fearful bondage from which, in the name and by the power of God, he had been able to get free. Can any one who reads what befell this man in the cell where society had shut him away as a foul and guilty thing, caring little whether he lived or died, do so with dry eyes? We think not. It is something to stir the heart profoundly. In this story, the author deals not alone with the curse of strong drink, but with the means of cure, and shows that even with the lowest and the vilest, reform is possible.

But it is in the SECOND PART that he addresses himself to the more serious purpose of his work. It is because the majority of the people are ignorant of the specific action of alcohol on the nerves, membranes, blood-vessels and vital organs, that so many indulge in its use. Under this head he gives the latest and most carefully-conducted experiments of physiologists and scientists, from which it has been clearly demonstrated that alcohol invariably acts as a poison when taken into the body, and that its habitual use always lays the foundation for disease, often of a fatal character. This chapter is a most important one, and should be read by every young man, and by every moderate drinker in the land. Its well-authenticated statement cannot fail to arrest the reader's attention, and deeply impress him with the dangers that always attend the use of alcoholic drinks. It is also shown how mental failure always keeps pace with the physical deteriorations which attend the regular drinking of alcoholic beverages; that no man can do his best, mentally or physically, while under their influence, and that their continued use steadily lessens the intellectual vigor and blunts the moral faculties.

In treating of the means of reformation and cure, the author shows what has been done and is now doing in Inebriate Asylums and Reformatory Homes; and also through what is known as Gospel Temperance Work—giving, in this connection, a brief history of the Woman's Crusade, of The Woman's National Christian Temperance Union, and the establishment of Reform Clubs, Temperance Coffee-Houses and Friendly Inns.

The concluding chapters on the failure and disgrace of license, and the salutory effects of Prohibition, should be carefully studied. In the exceedingly interesting and important letter addressed to the author by Hon. Neal Dow, the reader will find a complete history of the "Maine Law," and the results which have followed its enactment. Its testimony to the value of Prohibition is conclusive and incontrovertable.

CHAPTER I.

HE came in so noiselessly that I heard neither the opening nor shutting of the door, and only became aware of his presence when I felt his hand on my shoulder.

Shall I ever forget the face into which I looked? A face so marred since I had seen it last; so pale, so exhausted, so helpless and despairing, that I was not only shocked by the sight but filled with inexpressible pain. The hand which he had laid upon me was trembling violently.

"Why Granger!" I exclaimed, as I started to my feet. "What does this mean?"

I saw the muscles of his face quiver and spasms run about his lips, as he made an effort to reply.

"It can't be possible that you—"

I held back, from an instinct of delicacy, the words that were coming to my lips.

"Have fallen so low?" he said, in a husky, shaking voice, finishing the sentence which I had left incomplete. Then, with a steadier utterance: "But it is all too sadly true, Mr. Lyon. The devil of drink has seized me, and I cannot get free from the grip of his terrible hand!"

"Don't say that, my friend. You must resist this devil and, like all other devils, when met by resistance, he will flee from you."

A short, bitter laugh, and then: "He isn't one of that kind."

But, surely, Granger, you will not give up your manhood to the vice of an appetite?"

"Vice! That's a little, easy sort of a word, and doesn't seem to mean much, does it?"

He was sitting, now, and I standing just in front of the chair he had taken. As I looked at him steadily, I saw more distinctly than at first the ravages which intemperance had made upon his finely-cut, and once handsome features. I had not met him before for many months.

"To the *demands* of an appetite? Let me make the proposition stronger," said I.

"Vice, demand, curse; anything you choose. It's all the same."

"But the will-power is above them all—can break the bonds of appetite, and let the man go free."

I saw a change begin passing over his face.

"Free! What would I not give to be free!"

"Resolve, and it is done! In a man's will lies his strength. Neither Heaven nor hell can move him if he will not. Set your will against this appetite, and will shall be master."

He looked at me with a gathering wonder in his eyes, as though a new thought were dawning upon his mind. His mouth became a little firmer; and he raised his almost crouching form to an erecter attitude.

"If he will not—will not."

"Just so, my friend. If he will not, all hell cannot move him. Self-mastery! Every man has this power. I have it; you have it. It is the common inheritance of all men."

"An inheritance sold, alas! too often for a mess of pottage," Granger answered, bitterly. "And when once sold, has it not gone hopelessly out of our possession?"

"No. Freedom to will is a birthright which no man living can wholly alienate. He may at any time re-assert his right of inheritance. You can do it now—can set your heel on this serpent of appetite, and crush it beneath your tread. Be a man, Granger! Let the higher things that are in you hold the lower things in subjection. Let reason and judgment rule the appetites and passions, as a master rules his servants. This is the common order of life. God has given us reason as a ruler; and we must see that no usurper gain a foothold in our kingdom."

As I spoke I saw the signs of strength and confidence coming into Granger's eyes.

"It is because you have let the sensual betray and dethrone the rational that you are in so sad a plight to-day. Will has gone over to the wrong side."

"It shall come to the right side again, Mr. Lyon!" His voice had a clear ring. "I see just how it is.

Will went over to appetite instead of standing firm by the side of reason."

"Yes; you state the case exactly as it stands," I said. "It was an abuse of freedom, so to speak. You were not compelled to drink: for appetite has no power above solicitation. It cannot move your hand, nor place a glass to your lips. Only the will has power over the actions, and so nothing can be done without consent of the will."

"I see! I see!" More light and strength coming into his face. "It all lies with myself."

"All," I answered. "There is no help for you outside of your own will. You stand self-centered, or equipoised, with freedom to act in the direction of any force that draws you, be it good or evil."

"Thank you for all this. I see wherein my peril lies, and also the line of a new defence. I *will* control this dreadful appetite! I *will* be a man."

"But, remember," I said, "that eternal vigilance is the price of safety. Appetite is subtle, as well as strong. It is an enemy that never really sleeps."

"I know, I know! But is not safety worth eternal vigilance?"

There was in his countenance the glow of a rising confidence.

"Ah, my friend," he added, as he took my hand and held it tightly, "what would I not do or suffer to be free from this awful slavery; from this bondage to death and hell!"

"And the way is so plain and so easy," said I,

with all the encouragement I was able to throw into my voice. "Just to will to be free; and then to stand up as a man. To say to appetite, 'So far and no farther!'"

"It was my good angel who led me here, and who put these hopeful words into your mouth, my dear old friend!" He spoke with much feeling. "I haven't been home since yesterday. I was in no condition to meet my family last night; and am in little better condition this morning. You see, I've not lost all shame and all consideration."

"You will go home now?"

"Yes."

I saw a shadow drifting over his face.

"Where are you living?"

"Away up town; but not as we used to live."

"Shall I go with you?"

He did not reply at once; but the shadows were deeper on his face.

"If you will." There was a returning depression in his voice; and I saw that his nerves, which had grown steady under the pressure of new thoughts and purposes, were giving way again. He drew a hand across his forehead. It was trembling.

"You remember Helen?" he said.

"Oh, yes. How is she?"

There was something like a gasp, or quick catching of the breath. Then, with an effort to control his feelings: "Not as when you saw her last. Ah! sir, what a cruel devil this drink is!"

"Cruel as death," I responded, falling in with his thoughts.

"As death? Oh, no! Death is an angel of mercy; but drink is a devil! My poor Helen!"

What grief and tenderness were in his voice as he uttered the name of his wife.

"For her sake, Granger."

"For her sake!" He spoke with a sudden intense earnestness, while a strong light flashed into his eyes. "If I were to see a wild beast rushing down upon her, do you think I would pause to question about consequences to myself? Not for a single instant! What would I not do, and bear, and suffer for her sake! Ah! sir, she has been a good wife to me. So patient, so true, so tender always. And I have tried so hard, and fought so hard, for her sake."

"And now let the new life you are going to lead find its highest strength in these three words—For her sake. Let the steady will and the better manhood be for her sake. Hold the brief sentence ever against your heart; set it ever before your eyes. For her sake, my friend!"

"Yes, for her sake, God bless her!" His voice shook, and I saw tears coming into his eyes.

"What higher strength than this. Surely you will stand as a rock against which the maddest billows of temptation must break and dissolve into foam and spray."

"For her sake I will stand! For her sake, and

for the sake of my wronged and humiliated children. What a wretch I have been! To fill the lives of those I love with shame and sorrow; and for what? Just to gratify an appetite!"

"Which, if you *will* to deny, must always stand denied. Keep ever in your thought the true order of life, which is the subjection of the sensual to the rational. If the sensual is suffered to rule, then will anarchy and violence reign in the kingdom; but if reason keeps her seat of power, order, and peace, and happiness will prevail; and the sensual will be as a staff in the hand of Aaron, and not as a biting serpent on the ground."

"Ah! yes, it is growing clearer and clearer. All danger lies in this infirmity of the will, in this hearkening to the lying voice of a serpent, instead of to our God-given reason."

Granger was lifting himself with a more assured air, and there was a growing strength in his face.

"I must go home now," he said, rising.

"And I am to go with you?"

Did I betray a doubt in my voice? Perhaps; for away back and almost out of sight in my mind lay a doubt of the new-born strength of this man's will. It might endure until he reached his home, or it might yield to enticement by the way. He had not yet recovered his manhood. Was still weak, and must walk for a time with unsteady steps. All this I felt rather than thought.

He set his eyes on me with a keen look just for an instant before replying.

"If you care to see what a poor and wretched home it is."

"I care to give you what help and strength lies in my power." I took my hat as I spoke, and we went out together.

I had not seen Alexander Granger before for nearly a year. He was a lawyer of fine abilities, and in the first ten years of his practice at the bar had risen steadily into notice, and been connected, as counsel, with many important cases. But, unhappily, his social nature led him too often out of the ways of safety. It was the old, sad story which has been told so many and so many times. Just in the very prime of his life, the subtle power of drink began to bear him down. If he had taken alarm at the first warning he received of the establishment and growth of this power, and broken free from it in a single resolute effort, all would have been well. But here again it was the old story repeated. He had faith in his own manhood; in his ability to go just so far and no farther; to keep on the edge of danger and never step across. And he held to this, even in the face of one lapse after another, until he became the slave of appetite.

It took years for all this; for he had a strong, tough brain, and great physical energy; and his steadily increasing practice at the bar held him in earnest work, and for a long time out of the sphere of apparent danger. But no brain can do its best under the stimulant of alcohol. There must always come a loss of clearness. There may be an increased activity, but this very activity, where the reason is obscured and interests at the same time imperilled, leads too often to disaster. It happened so to Granger. In the very height of his popularity he lost a case of great importance. His client did not know that on the previous night he had been over-free with wine at a supper from which he did not get home until after the small hours began; and that before coming into court to make his final argument, he had been compelled to steady his nerves with a glass of brandy. No, they did not know this; but what they did know was, that he failed to bring out with logical clearness the strong point in their case, and the one on which they chiefly relied. Considered as a mere forensic display, it was one of the most brilliant ever heard in the court-room, and men listened to it breathlessly, admiring its fine periods, its exhibition of learning, and its wealth of imagery and illustration; but, while it extorted admiration, it failed in the chief essential of a legal argument, working no conviction on the minds of the twelve men with whom the decision of the case rested.

It was Granger's first great failure. Did no suspicion of the real cause intrude itself upon his thoughts? Yes; but it was thrust out as false and unworthy. His head was never clearer, nor his mind more active. So he declared to himself in his quick rejection of the very truth it so much concerned him to know. But the incident troubled him; and in the face of his effort to look away from the real cause of failure, and to count it as nothing, he made an almost involuntary resolution to abstain from any free use of stimulants for some days before arguing another important case; and for more than a year he acted upon this resolution.

But his wine at dinner, his exchange of drinking courtesies with friends, and his indulgence at suppers and social parties, gradually depraved his appetite, and it grew to be more and more exacting. For awhile only a single glass had been taken with his dinner. Then there was an occasional second glass, and in time two glasses became the regular custom. A third glass now and then marked the steady growth of appetite. So it went on, with a slow but sure increase, until it was no unusual thing for Granger to drink half a bottle of wine every day with his dinner; and to finish the bottle before going to bed.

Fame and fortune were just within his reach. He was regarded as the ablest of all the rising men at the bar of his native city, and many of the best cases were coming into his hands, when the evidences of blight and failure of power became visible. After losing the case to which I have referred, he was on guard for a long time; but the steadily increasing use of stimulants wrought its natural result on his brain, and his second great failure in court was due in all probability as much to a complete abstinence from drink as the first was to its use and the unhealthy excitement that followed.

This loss of mental clearness in consequence of a loss of the usual brain-tonic, was a fact far more patent to Granger's mind than had been the other fact of loss of mental clearness through unusual stimulation, and he resolved not to risk another experiment of the kind, but rather to give his nerves a firmer tone by an extra glass on the eve of every specially important effort in court. It is surprising how men who are clear-seeing as to cause and effect in almost everything else, can be so blind about the ultimate result of repeated and increasing stimulation on that wonderful and delicate organism, the brain. It shows how subtle, and strong, and self-deceiving is the sensual side of our nature, if, instead of holding it in strict subordination to reason and the laws of order, we give it the rein, and submit even partially to its rule.

After this second important failure, and Granger's clear apprehension of the proximate cause, he did not again venture on complete abstinence as a safe preparation for entrance upon a legal conflict in which large interests hung on victory or defeat. But, for all this, he was never able to bring to his cases the clear logic and force of argument for which he had once been distinguished. He had, in fact, reached his highest point of success and reputation; and as the causes which had checked his upward movement were still in force, and his power of resistance waning, it was not long before the downward change became apparent to all.

And now, his nearest friends began to warn and to expostulate. But only after some disgraceful fall from sobriety, was heed taken, and efforts at reform made. It was the old story, as we have said. Falling, falling slowly. Then a pause and a rallying of strength, and an effort to move upwards again. And then a yielding to the downward drag. He did not at this time show himself to the world as a common drunkard; and the people who met him on the street, at his office, or in the court-rooms, rarely saw him so much under the influence of liquor as to betray the fact in any marked way; and yet, all could see that he was becoming the slave of drink, and that his utter ruin was only a matter of time, unless there should come a total change in his habits.

Down, down, the descent becoming more rapid. Sudden stoppages, as one strong influence after another was brought to bear upon him; solemn promises, and pledges of reform; firm standing for brief periods; and then, down, down again! And thus it went on for years; and there came loss of an honorable position at the bar; loss of practice; loss of social status; moral weakness and degradation; poverty and wretchedness. And still, there were intermitted struggles with the enemy, and efforts to rise into a true manhood. A sad, sad history, running through years of increasing disaster, humiliation and sorrow, until he had reached the level on which the reader finds him.

Yet, as has been seen, some hope and strength were yet remaining; some feeling of self-respect, and an unextinguished love for his unhappy wife and wronged and suffering children, for whom he would have braved any physical peril—even death itself.

CHAPTER II.

"I HAVE taken a dozen pledges," said Granger, as we passed into the street; "but they are as flax to fire when this thirst seizes upon me."

"Because," I answered, "they are only external bonds; and if the inner force be against them, they will break should the force be stronger than the bond. There is safety only in the strength of an internal integrity. The will must be strong and true. If, to change the figure of speech, the will be set to guard the door, no enemy can make a breach unless the will be corrupted. So long as the will is true, the man is safe. No, no. Put no trust in pledges nor promises. They are things outside of you, so to speak. Mere bonds, weak or strong, as the case may be. You must trust in yourself—in the strength of your will—in your manhood and self-centered power. Here is your only true abiding. The pledge may be well enough as a rallying point where a first stand is made against the enemy; but the man must fight it out to the bitter end, and that in himself and by himself. There is no other hope. No arm but his own can save him."

We walked in silence for almost the distance of

a block before Granger made any reply. He was, evidently, pondering what I had said.

"No arm but his own arm?" He stopped, and turning, fixed his eyes steadily on my face, with a look in them that I scarcely comprehended.

"If a man fight not for himself, who shall fight for him? This enemy is within, and the man himself must cast him out. I cannot fight the battle for you; nor can any one else. It is your own strong right arm that must bring the victory."

"Is there no help in God?" There was an eager thrill in his voice as he put the question.

"Of course," I replied, a little coldly. "But we must be careful not to confound things. A false, or irrational trust, is worse than no trust at all, for it will surely betray. God helps those who help themselves; who use in right and orderly ways the strength He gives to every man. I know of no means by which to get help from God but in the right use of the faculties with which He has endowed us. They are, of course, God-given, for He is our Maker. But He does not live for us, nor work for us, nor fight for us. All these we must do for ourselves."

I saw the light go slowly out of his face as he dropped his eyes to the ground, and moved forward again. Something like a shadow and a chill came upon my own feelings, and my mind seemed to pass into an obscuring cloud. Had I spoken truly? Was there no other help in God but this that I had said?

It was all very clear to me while I was speaking; but, somehow, my strong assurance was all at once broken, and I felt as one drifting to sea. I had been laying out this man's course for him, and now I was in doubt myself.

"You may be right about it, Mr. Lyon," Granger said, after another long silence. "But it seems to put God so far away. To take from Him all pity, and tenderness, and love. He will help me if I try to help myself; but, unless I do this, He will not so much as reach out His hand, though the billows be going over me!"

Even above the noise of the street I heard the sigh that came with the closing of this last sentence.

"Is not His hand always reached out?" I answered; "and is it not because we refuse to take hold of it that we are not saved?"

"I don't know." He spoke in a dreary, depressed tone of voice. "If one could see the hand, and be sure it was God's."

"What is the hand of God but the power that is within us from Him? The power to will and to do what is right; to stand fast in the front of temptation; to walk securely in the strength He gives us? We grasp His hand when we use this power."

"Doubtless it is so; but our poor eyes have become very dim-sighted."

He was silent again, and I began to feel troubled about his state of mind, lest a depressing sense of weakness should destroy that confidence in his own strength of will with which I was seeking to inspire him.

"We may be very sure of one thing, Mr. Granger," I said, repeating my former proposition, "the true order of life is the government of reason. This must rule over all the lower things of sense. The appetites and passions must be held in complete subjection. God is with us, and in us; gives us of His strength, and keeps us in safety, so long as we maintain this true order of life. If we will not maintain it, He cannot do it for us; and the same law must rule in restoration and cure as in normal order. We must take the strength God is always giving, and use it for ourselves. We would be only machines if He merely lived in us as the mainspring of all our actions."

"No help, no love; only laws of order. No pitying face, nor tender voice, nor bending form. No quick, grasping hand as we send out the despairing cry, 'Save, Lord, or we perish!'"

"Don't let us talk any more about this, Mr. Granger," said I. "It is troubling you and confusing your mind; and now, above all things, you need to be calm and clear-seeing, for it is clear-seeing that makes safe walking."

We were not far from his home now, and in a few minutes were at the door. What a poor little home it was as compared with that luxurious one in which I had many times been a guest in former years. Little better than that of an humble day-laborer. I felt a chill and a heart-ache as my eyes looked upon it, and I remembered the beautiful home in which Mrs. Granger had once presided. She was a woman of more than ordinary culture and refinement. In stature below the common height, with regular though not strikingly handsome features. Her eyes made the fine attraction of her face; they were large, and, in color, of a dark hazel, with a perpetual changing of aspect and a restlessness of movement that was very peculiar. But you saw, in all these changing hues and aspects, that they were true eyes, and beautiful as true.

Granger took a latch-key from his pocket as we paused at the door.

"Shall I go in?" I asked. "It might not be pleasant for Mrs. Granger."

He did not answer, but threw the door open, and made a motion for me to enter. There was a narrow hall, covered with a worn and faded carpet. From this we passed into a small parlor, in which were a few articles of furniture, remnants of better days. There were no pictures on the walls beyond a few photographic likenesses and two fine miniatures of Mr. and Mrs. Granger. Once they possessed many rare paintings. Plain Holland shades hung at the windows. Though everything was in order, there was a certain chill and desolateness in the atmosphere of the room that struck me sensibly. It might have come from the contrast I saw between this and the large and luxurious parlor in which I had last met this unhappy family.

But I had scarcely time to notice my surroundings, or to question my state of feeling, before quick feet were heard on the stairs, and in a moment afterwards Mrs. Granger stood at the parlor door with wide-open, eager, questioning eyes; now fixing them upon me, and now upon her husband.

"Mr. Lyon; you remember him."

I reached out my hand as her husband gave my name. A faint tinge of color rose to her pale face. Ah, how changed and wasted!

She did not repeat my name, and I was not certain that she recognized me. For a moment only did her eyes rest on me; then they went swiftly to her husband. I saw a throb in her throat, and a flush and thrill quickening on her face.

"There is going to be a new order of life, Mrs. Granger," said I, breaking the silence and pantomime. "And the old days are coming back again."

"A new life, Helen! Yes, a new life, God helping me! And the old better days again."

I saw the lips that had been closely shut, fall apart, and the large eyes grow larger. There was a statue-like stillness; then a faint, smothered cry, and a dropping down of the quivering face on Granger's breast. My eyes were dim with sudden tears, but I could see the husband's arms fold themselves closely about the small, light form of that true, patient, long-suffering one in whose heart love had never failed.

I would have gone out and left them so, but that might not be well; so I waited for this first strong tide of feeling to ebb. They were still standing— Mrs. Granger's face hidden on her husband's breast, and his arms clasping her tightly—when the sound of other feet on the stairs was heard, and in a moment after a beautiful girl stood, with startled eyes, at the door of the little parlor.

"Oh, it's father!" she ejaculated. Then on seeing me, she shrunk back a step or two, with a timid air, the blood rising to her temples.

"Is anything the matter?" she asked, in a panting voice, as a scared expression came into her face.

"Yes, something good," I answered, quickly.

On hearing this, Granger withdrew one of his arms from about his wife, and holding it out toward the girl, said: "My daughter!"

Gliding past me with a rapid motion, she threw herself within the extended arm, and mother and child lay held in a single strong embrace.

So I left them, passing out with noiseless feet. For stranger eyes all this was too sacred; and I felt that it was best for them to be alone.

Next day I called at Mr. Granger's office, and found him at his desk, busy over some law papers. Things about him had a look of new-made order, as if there had been a recent general setting to rights; and something in his personal appearance gave the same impression. There was a bright flash in his eyes as he lifted them in recognition, and I saw a marvelous change in his face; and, indeed, in his whole aspect.

"All right," I said, cheerily, as I grasped his extended hand.

"All right, thank God!"

"And right once for all," said I, in a confident tone.

"Yes; once for all. Somehow," he added, "I feel stronger than I have ever felt before; more self-centered, and with a firmer grasp on the rein. The fact is, Lyon, you gave me a new thought yesterday, and I've been looking at it and holding fast to it ever since; and the more I look at it, and the longer I keep hold of it, the more assured do I feel. I see, as I never saw before, where the danger lies. It is the weak will that betrays."

"Always," I made answer. "If the will be true and strong, the man is safe. Appetite can do nothing if the will be firm in denial. Never forget this. In the hour of temptation, it is the 'I will,' or the 'I will not,' that determines everything. There is not a devil in hell subtle enough to betray a man if he meet him with the all powerful 'I will not!'"

"I believe you, my friend."

There was, I did not fail to notice, more confidence in Granger's words than in his voice; and this gave me a slight feeling of uneasiness.

"Hold on, as with hooks of steel, to your faith in

yourself—in the strength of your God-given manhood. If the tempter comes, say 'No!' as you will always be able to say. It is the weak, the doubting, the half-hearted who fall."

As we talked, a gentleman named Stannard came in. On seeing the change in Granger's appearance, he said: "Been turning over another new leaf, I see. Glad of it from my heart. And now, friend Granger, what is to be the first writing thereon?"

"*I will not,*" was the firmly spoken answer.

"Good as far as it goes."

"What more?" asked Granger.

"*God being my helper.*"

"Is not God's strength in every true 'I will' or 'I will not?'" said I, speaking before Granger had time to answer, for I was afraid of some confusion being wrought in his mind.

"There is no good thing that does not come from God," was the calmly-spoken answer. "In Him we live, and move, and have our being."

"No reflecting man will deny that. But the grave and practical question is, how does God bestow His good things? What are the laws of order by which He acts with men?"

"Love is His great law," said Mr. Stannard.

"We all believe that; but love works through orderly means. If a man wilfully close his eyes, God cannot make him see. If he shut himself away in a dungeon, God cannot give him light. If he 'will not,' God cannot save him, though all day He stretches forth His merciful hand."

"No one will question that, I presume," was answered. "But now we have the other proposition under consideration. It is the 'I will not' of our friend here as set against temptation. Now, under what law is he to get God's help?"

"It will come to him in his effort to do right."

"'Ask and it shall be given unto you. Seek and ye shall find. Watch and pray, lest ye enter into temptation. Come unto me.' These are the Lord's own words; and do they not mean that we are to do something more than what your answer indicates. Will all the help needed come without the asking?"

"As if," I said, with a slight tremor of feeling in my voice, "as if God held back for man's formal asking? As if His infinite love were not forever yearning to save? and forever flowing with divine strength into every effort to fight against evil. It is in man's will where he is truly potential; and he must set his will against allurement, and stand in the strength of his true manhood."

"But suppose the will has become so sickly and depraved that it cannot receive a just measure of life and strength from God? When an organ in the human body is diseased it is no longer able to do its proper work, though the heart be perpetually sending for its use a due portion of healthy blood. If the will were in order, we might trust to the will;

but, alas! it is not. It is diseased; and without help from the Great Physician, will fail in the work of its office. Nay, nay, friend Granger, put no faith in your '*I will not,*' unless you write also on the leaf of the new page you have turned, '*God being my helper.*' If this be not done all your good purposes will avail, I fear, but little."

"Anything to give our friend strength," I replied. "It will do no harm for him to write as you say; only let him not lose faith in himself because of his trust in God. It is just here that the danger lies. It is the clear-seeing, as I have said to him, that makes the safe-walking. If we do not know the way, we are all the while in danger of stumbling."

"'I am the way, and the truth, and the life,'" said Mr. Stannard. "If we go to Him, shall we be in any danger of losing our way? I think not."

As we talked, Granger looked first at one of us and then at the other, hearkening carefully to what we said, and evidently weighing the import of our words. That all was not clear to him, was evident from his manner. I dropped the argument, in fear that his mind might get confused, and that, while in this unsettled state, his old enemy might rush in upon him and bear him down ere he had time to arrange his order of defence.

Mr. Stannard had called on a matter of business, and on becoming aware of this, I withdrew from the office and left him alone with Granger. I carried away with me an uneasy feeling. Mr. Stannard was a man for whom I had great respect. He was a prominent church member, and active in Christian work; and so far as my knowledge of him went, his life among men was blameless. But my philosophy of religion differed in some essential points from his. We both held to the necessity of a pure life; but were not in agreement as to the means whereby this purity of life was to be attained. He held to the power of grace, through faith, as the only means whereby man could be saved—at least, so I had understood him—I to man's innate force of will, into which strength would flow from God the instant his will moved in a right effort. My fear now was, that Mr. Stannard might undo the work I had attempted, and destroy Granger's faith in himself, leaving him to a blind confidence in some outside help which might never come. This was the ground of my uneasiness.

I did not see Granger again for several days; and then our meeting was in a public thoroughfare, and for a few moments only. His face was clear and bright, and his air manly and assured.

"All right!" I said, as I took his hand.

"All right," he responded, giving me a strong returning grip.

"Standing fast by 'I will not.'"

"Standing fast," was his answer, a slight change in the expression of his countenance.

It was on my lips to say: "Don't forget that the

will is the man; and that all hell cannot move him if the will stand fast." But I held the sentence back from an impulse I did not quite understand. So we parted, each going his way.

CHAPTER III.

"MRS. GRANGER was in church this morning," said my wife, on coming home, a few Sundays afterward.

"Ah! How did she look?"

"The sight of her brought tears into my eyes. How much she has changed. And she looked so poor and humbled."

"Was any one with her?"

I did not put the question that was in my thought; but the one I asked would bring, I doubted not, the answer I wished to hear.

"Yes; a sweet young girl—her oldest daughter, Amy, I presume. The beautiful child has grown almost to a woman since I saw her last."

"No one else?"

"No."

Though I had not been to church myself, and had not much faith in Sunday religious services, judging of them by their influence on a majority of my church-going acquaintances, I could not help feeling regret at the fact of Mr. Granger's absence. Somehow, the impression took hold of me that it would have been better and safer for him to have gone to church; and the fact that he had not accompanied his wife left on my mind a vague sense of uneasiness. Where had he gone; and what were the influences which had been around him on this day of freedom from daily work and the thought and care of business?

"Mr. Granger was not there," said I, wishing to be altogether sure about the matter.

"No." Then, after a little silence, Mrs. Lyon said, "I was sorry not to have seen him with his wife."

It was on my tongue to express the regret I was myself feeling, but as my wife and I were not wholly in agreement on the subject of church-going, I did not care to commit myself so far as to give an assent to her view of the case; and as I did not respond, the subject was dropped.

After dinner I took a walk, and as I could not get Granger out of my mind, nor rid myself of a certain feeling of responsibility in regard to him, I concluded to extend my ramble as far as the neighborhood in which he lived and make him a call. My ring brought his wife to the door.

"Is Mr. Granger at home?" I asked.

I saw a slight shade drop across her face as she answered: "No; he has gone to take a walk in the Park." Then, after a moment, "Won't you come in, Mr. Lyon?"

I accepted the invitation. As I took a seat in the plain little parlor, and looked at Mrs. Granger, I was painfully impressed with the changes a few years had wrought in her appearance. Such lines of suffering as had been cut into her brow and around her lips! Such wasting and exhaustion! It was very sad.

"I met your husband a few days ago," said I, speaking at once, so that there might be no embarrassing pause, "and was glad to see him looking so well."

She smiled faintly; but not with the bright, almost radiant smile I was hoping to see.

"Yes; he is doing very well." Her voice lacked heartiness, I fancied.

"And is going to stand this time," said I, speaking confidently.

"God grant it!" A reverent earnestness coming into her manner.

"He has found a new element of strength."

She met my remark with a look of inquiry, keen and searching.

"A true faith in himself—in his manhood—in the native force of his own strong will."

"There is no sure help but in God, Mr. Lyon."

I seem to hear now her slow utterance of this sentiment, and the strong emphasis given to the words, "*No sure help but in God.*"

"God is in every manly effort to do right," I answered. "He gives strength to the will that sets itself against evil enticement. We trust in Him when we trust in the power He gives us."

"What my husband says; and it may all be so in some way that I do not clearly understand."

I made an effort to explain myself more clearly; but, when I was done, she answered with simple earnestness: "It is better to look to God than to ourselves, Mr. Lyon. I am sure of that. Every hour, every moment, even, we need His help and care, for the enemies who are against us are very malignant, very subtle, and very strong. I should have a safer feeling about my husband if he had a little less confidence in the strength of his own will, and more in that Divine power which I believe can only be had for the asking."

"As if God would stand away, coldly indifferent, and let a striving soul perish because there was no formal asking. Such a thought, in my view, dishonors Him. Would a father wait for his child to call for help if he saw him drowning?"

"No; and I do not think that God ever holds back from saving in the sense you seem to mean, Mr. Lyon. If a father were reaching after his drowning child, and calling to him, 'Give me your hand, my son!' and his child were to refuse the offered help, and trust to his own strength, how could the father save him?"

She waited for my reply, looking at me steadily. What answer could I make? The question seemed to open a window in my soul and let in beams of light; but they were not yet strong enough to make her full meaning clear.

"Well, what more?" I queried.

"Our Heavenly Father is all the while reaching out to save His perishing children, and His voice, tender with compassion, and earnest with love, is forever crying, 'Son, give me thy heart!' And if the heart be not given, how can the soul be saved?"

Mrs. Granger's further question almost startled me. It gave a deeper significance to "being saved" than I had yet comprehended.

She went on: "They that dwell in God dwell in safety. Of that we may be sure. Can this be said, confidently, of any others? Ah! sir, where so much is at stake it will not do to risk anything in doubtful trusts. A man's will may be very strong; but if the Spirit of God be within him, he will be far stronger—nay, invincible in the face of legions of enemies. God is as a walled city about his people, and as a rock of defence. He is a sure refuge in the day of trouble."

Her face had kindled, and there was something in the earnestness of her manner, and in the assured tones with which she spoke, that seemed to bear me away and set me adrift. I had nothing to say in opposition. What could I say? There was truth in every word she had uttered; and if I had questioned or cavilled in anything, it would only have been as to the exact meaning and practical application of the truths she had spoken. And after all, might she not have a clearer insight than myself into the mystery of God's ways with man?

"You must try to get Mr. Granger to go to church with you. It will be best for him, I am sure," said I, speaking with a stronger conviction of the truth of what I said than I was willing to admit even to myself.

"If you would only urge him to go, Mr. Lyon. He has great confidence in your judgment, and will be influenced by what you say. You have helped him greatly; helped not only to lift him to his feet again, but to set them going in the right way. Only, Mr. Lyon—and you will excuse me for saying it—you are leading him, I greatly fear, into a state of false security. We may differ about this. But, sir, the safest way is the best way; and I am sure that he who goes to God under a sense of weakness, and prays for strength, will be stronger in the hour of temptation, and safer under the assaults of his enemies, than he who relies solely upon himself."

"Not solely upon himself," I returned. "I did not mean that he should so understand me. We have no life that is absolutely our own; and no strength that is absolutely our own; all are from God. Still, the life and strength that God is perpetually giving we must take and use as if it were our own. I meant no more and no less. God gives the strength to fight; but we must overcome. He does not work for us, nor fight for us, nor save us; for doing so would be to destroy what makes our very life. We must do all this for ourselves; using the power He is forever giving to all who will use it."

"And especially to all who call upon Him in truth," said Mrs. Granger. "It may be very clear to you, sir," she added, "how one may stand fast in the strength God is always giving. But, if I read my Bible aright there is a sphere of safety higher and surer than this—a more absolute getting, as it were, into the everlasting arms; and I shall never feel at ease in regard to my husband until I feel sure that these everlasting arms are round about him."

I left the house more thoughtful and serious than when I went in, and took my way to the Park, hoping that I might meet Mr. Granger; for, somehow, his wife's sense of insecurity in regard to him had left a like impression on my own mind. The afternoon was clear and bright, and many thousands of people were in the Park, walking, driving and recruiting themselves in many ways; some, I regret to say, making too free use of the restaurants at which, in defiance of Sunday laws, but under license from the Park Commissioners, some of them church-going men, all kinds of intoxicating drinks were dispensed to the people.

I was sitting on the lawn near the largest of these restaurants, from which could be seen the beautiful river, placid as a lake, and the city with its spires and domes in the distance, when I saw Granger in company with two men, one of whom I recognized as a lawyer of some standing at the bar, and the other as a respectable merchant. They were crossing the lawn at the distance of twenty or thirty yards from where I was sitting, and going in the direction of one of the small refreshment tables that stood in front of the restaurant. On reaching this table, they all sat down and one of them beckoned to a waiter, who, on receiving his order, went away. In a little while he returned with two glasses of some kind of mixed liquor and a bottle of soda water. My relief was great when I saw this, for I naturally inferred that the soda water was for Granger; and in this I was right. When they had finished their glasses, one of them took from his pocket a segar-case, and after each had lighted a segar and smoked for a little while, they got up and went leisurely strolling down one of the avenues, taking a homeward direction.

Two or three times I had been on the point of joining them, but the fear lest it should prove to Granger an embarrassing intrusion, restrained me from doing so. I was troubled at the occurrence. This was going into danger; taking unguarded rest on the enemy's ground; inviting temptation. It was scarcely possible, I saw, for Granger to sit drinking with his friends, though he took only soda water himself, without the odor of their glasses drifting to his nostrils with its enticing allurement for his denied appetite. Nor could he do so, without a mental contrast of their freedom with his restraint. In any view of the incident that I could take, it gave me only regret and concern; and I felt grieved almost to anger with the two friends who, knowing as they did the man's weakness, and the great deep out of which he had just struggled, should so set temptation in his way as to make his fall again not only possible, but imminent.

CHAPTER IV.

I DID not feel easy in my mind until I had called at Granger's office on the next day. I found him all right and busy at work. His eyes brightened as he saw me, and he said, with genuine heartiness, as he grasped my hand: "I was so sorry you called yesterday without finding me at home. Helen told me of your visit. I had gone out for a stroll in the Park."

While I was hesitating whether or not to say that I had seen him there, he added, with a shade of pride and self-confidence in his voice: "I had an opportunity to test the native strength that lies with every man, yesterday, and to prove the power of a resolute 'I will not.'"

"Ah? What were the circumstances?" I wished to get his own story, and so gave no intimation of what I had seen.

He replied: "I met two friends while walking near Belmont, and they invited me to join them in a drink. My first thought was to say No; but not wishing to be disagreeable, I said, 'All right,' and we went over to Proskauer's. I had just a little fight with myself as we walked along; but it was soon over, and will stood firmly on guard. 'What

"Soda-water for me."—*Page 47.*

will you take?' asked one of them, as we sat down in front of the restaurant. 'Claret punch,' said the other. 'And you?' looking at me. Will was all right and on guard, as I have said, and 'Soda water for me,' came without a shade of hesitation in my voice. I never felt in greater freedom nor more at ease and assured. Thank you from my heart, friend Lyon; you have helped me to get the full mastery of myself."

"If a man only will to overcome in the day of temptation, his victory is sure," said I, with renewed confidence; for, was not the proof of this before me? "I am glad for your victory," I continued. "It not only gives you increased assurance of safety, but makes clear to your mind wherein this safety lies. It is within ourselves that we must look for help and strength. God is always giving us the power to live right and to dwell beyond the reach of our enemies; but He does not use that power for us. This we must do for ourselves."

"All as clear to me as the sun at noonday," Granger replied. "And how strong I feel in this consciousness that if *I will not*, all hell, as you have said, cannot move me. To stand self-centered is to stand sure."

But for all his confidence and my own, I did not feel that Granger was wholly safe. If there had been no such thing as infirmity of the will, no sudden assaults of the enemy in unguarded moments, no alluring enticements of the flesh, nor subtle reasonings of the sensual principle, which is so ready to say when forbidden fruit is at the lip, "Ye shall not surely die," I might not have doubted. But I could not rule these considerations out of the question. They were ever existing sources of danger and causes of anxiety; and I knew but too well that the history of moral defection was the history of their dominion over the will of man.

"But, after all," I could not help saying, "is it not safest for us to keep as much as possible out of the way of temptation?"

"Yes," he answered, in a tone that was almost indifferent. "Safest, of course, to be in a sheltered embrasure than out on the battle-field. But the skill to fight, and the power to resist assault, cannot be gained while one lies beyond the reach of danger. We must be brave and strong, and ever ready for the fight; not so much seeking to avoid conflict, as to be armed and ready, and quick to strike when the foe appears. Does any man know his strength until it is tried? Is any man really strong until he has met temptation and come out victorious?"

There are truths which become changed into fallacies because not considered in relation to other truths; or because of their too limited or too general application. In the case of Granger, while I could not deny the abstract truth of what he had been saying, I felt that he stood in great danger of letting it be to him little more than a betraying fallacy.

I saw him frequently after this, and observed him

closely. How fast the old strength, the old working force and the old ambition were returning. And with all, how strong he seemed to be in the new power which he had gained.

"My 'will not' is my sword and shield," he said to me, many weeks after his new life began. "If my enemy assault me from a distance, I catch his arrows upon this shield; if he fall upon me suddenly, I defeat him with this sword."

Time passed, and still Granger's feet were standing on solid ground. Business came flowing in, and men who had important cases were again employing him as counsel. He did not keep out of the way of temptation as much as I thought prudent; but his "I will not" held him above the force of all allurement.

At home, the new aspect of things was like the coming of spring after a long and desolate winter. The poor, little, ill-attired house was changed for one larger and more comfortable, and furnished in a style more befitting the tastes and habits of his wife and children. Old social relations were in many cases restored, and Mrs. Granger was seen now and then in public places with her husband. Heart-ache, deprivation, toil and humiliation had made sorrowful changes in her face, and shadowed her beautiful eyes; but slowly the new spring-time which opened upon her life wrought its sweet changes, until you began to lose sight of the winter's ravages, and to find in their stead the pleasant signs of a fast-coming and bountiful summer.

For a whole year Granger held his ground, walking safely amid temptations that assailed him on the right hand and on the left. His profession brought him into familiar association with men who not only used wine freely themselves, but made its offer to their friends a social courtesy. Still, his steady refusal to touch or taste was maintained. "I will not" continued to be his tower of strength.

"I am prouder of this self-mastery," he said to me one day, "than of any achievement in my life. In the strength of this asserted manhood, I stand as a rock, unmoved, though the billows dash madly against me."

"He that ruleth his own spirit is better than he that taketh a city," I replied. "The greatest of all heroes is the man who conquers himself."

"Say, rather, he who, single-handed, meets the infernal crew who would drag him down to death and hell, and beats them back," he replied.

There was a proud flash in his eyes as he lifted himself to a statelier bearing.

"Have you seen Mr. Granger recently?" asked my wife, not many weeks afterwards. It was on Sunday, and we were sitting at the dinner-table.

"No; why do you ask?" Something in Mrs. Lyon's voice gave me a feeling of uneasiness.

"I saw Mrs. Granger at church this morning, and she looked as if she had just come out of a spell of sickness."

"Was she at church last Sunday?"

"Yes."

"Did you observe anything unusual in her appearance then?"

"No."

"Was her daughter with her to-day?"

"Yes; and she looked almost as wretched as her mother. There's something wrong, I'm afraid. Oh, if Mr. Granger should have taken to drinking again, would it not be dreadful?"

My knife and fork dropped from my hands, and I half rose from the table, so pained and startled was I by this suggestion.

"Oh, no, no, that cannot be!" I replied, as I made an effort to compose myself. "Mr. Granger is too strong, and too well established in his reformation."

"From what I have heard you say," returned my wife, "I have been inclined to think him too self-confident. The boastful are not always the farthest removed from peril; and Granger has shown a weakness in this direction. His 'I will not,' in which you and he have put so great faith, may have proven his stone of stumbling."

"Why do you say that?" I demanded, in a voice meant to be assured, but into which came a betrayal of weakness and fear.

"A man," replied my wife, "who has such a fast faith in his 'I will not,' as Granger possesses, may fall through over-confidence in the power of self-mastery."

"How?"

"He may trust it too far."

"I do not get your meaning. What is it?"

"Your friend is offered a glass of wine. The sight and the odor kindle into a sudden flame the old desire. He is conscious of strength, and with an emphatic mental 'I will not!' turns from the tempting glass. But, suppose, in his conscious, self-centered strength, as you call it, he should say, 'I will not taste but a single glass,' what then? Is he not as sure of himself after a single glass as he was before? Can he not say, 'So far and no farther?'"

"You know that he cannot," I replied, almost sharply, for her suggestion had struck me like a blow. "That single glass would not only break the strength of his will but give to appetite a new and stronger power."

"But, suppose, in his self-confidence, he did not believe this? When we are well and strong we make light of over-strain, and the unseen but subtle influences of miasma. Don't you see the perpetual danger in which he would stand?"

I did see it as I had not seen it before, though many times fears and misgivings had troubled me.

"But about Mrs. Granger and her daughter?" I asked. "How did they look?"

"I only saw them for a moment or two in the vestibule of the church. At the first glance I scarcely recognized Mrs. Granger. There did not seem to be a particle of color in her face, which was pinched, as we see it in those who are suffering acute pain. She did not look up at any one, and had the manner of a person who wished to shrink away without attracting observation. Depend upon it, there is something wrong with her husband."

"Something wrong with her husband!" It had the sound of a knell in my ears.

After dinner, I called at Granger's residence and asked for him, but was informed by the servant that he was not at home. I then inquired for Mrs. Granger, who sent word that she was not feeling well, and asked to be excused. The servant's manner was repressed and mysterious. I went away with a heavy weight pressing on my heart, and taking a car rode out to the Park, thinking it possible that I might find Granger there. I spent the whole afternoon in the neighborhood of Belmont, but saw nothing of him. In the evening, I called at his house again, but was told, as before, that he was not at home. There was a look in the servant's face, as she made this answer, which led me to doubt its truth.

I made it my business to go to the lawyer's office as early as ten o'clock on the following day. He had not yet made his appearance. I returned at twelve; but he was still absent. Then I visited the court-rooms and inquired for him there; but no one remembered to have seen him within the last two or three days. Late in the afternoon, I again visited his office, but the door was still locked.

On the next day, and on the next, my efforts to

find Granger were no more successful. He still remained away from his office. A week passed without my seeing him. I had again and again called at his residence, only to be informed that he was not at home.

Sitting in my office late one afternoon, I heard the door open, and turning, saw this man for whom so great a concern was lying on my heart. Was it all a dream, then, this year of reform and restoration?—a bright, but cheating dream? As I had seen him, debased, nerveless, wretched, a year ago, so I saw him now. Eyes blood-shotten,—dress soiled and disordered,—face shorn of all manliness, and marked in every lineament with debauchery and excess!

"Oh, Granger! Granger!" I cried out, the sorrow and pain which I felt going into my voice. "And has it come to this? All your strength gone—all your manhood trodden into the mire?"

"All gone," he answered, in a moody, dogged kind of way, as he shut the door and came a step or two forward. I saw that he was considerably under the influence of drink.

"I had hoped better things of you than this, Mr. Granger," said I, with a measure of rebuke in my voice.

"And I had hoped better things of myself," he replied, as he sat down, or rather, dropped heavily into a chair. "But I rather guess we reasoned without our host, friend Lyon,—built on a sandy foundation; and when the winds blew, and the rain fell, and the floods came, down went the house, and the fall thereof was great. Ha! Isn't it so? Don't you remember that talk we had with Mr. Stannard —about the new leaf I had turned, and the writing that was to go thereon. You and he differed about it, I remember; and I took your view of the case. But, d' you know, I've always had a notion that he was nearest right."

"Then, in Heaven's name, try his way!" I exclaimed. "Anything to save you from this dreadful sin and debasement."

"That is, go and join the church." He gave a short, ironical laugh. "Nice subject for the church!" And he looked down at himself. "But, see here, Lyon," his manner changing, "I'm all cleaned out. Look!" and he held his pocket-book open. "All gone, you perceive. Had more than a hundred dollars when—when—I got on this confounded spree! Lend me a twenty. I want to buy a clean shirt, and get a bath, and fix myself up before going home."

"Will you fix yourself up and go home?" I asked.

"Of course I will. But I can't meet Helen and the children looking like this. I'd rather go and jump into the river."

I hesitated, not feeling sure of him. He was under the influence of drink; and the word of a man in this condition can rarely, if ever, be trusted.

"Honor bright, Mr. Lyon. I'm not going to deceive you. I've set my foot down, and don't mean to drink another drop."

"Here are ten dollars," I said, taking a bank-bill from my pocket-book; "but before I give it to you, I must have your word, as a man of honor, that you will not spend a dollar of this money for liquor."

"My word and my honor, Mr. Lyon," and he placed his hand over his heart.

In the next moment he was reaching out eagerly for the bank-bill, which I let him take, though not without many misgivings as to his proper use of the money. He rose immediately and made a movement to leave the office.

"Not yet, Mr. Granger. Sit down again. I wish to have a little more talk with you."

"I'll call in to-morrow," he replied, not resuming his seat, and showing considerable eagerness to get away. "Haven't been home since day before yesterday, and they're getting worried about me. Good-afternoon!"

And before I could make a movement to intercept him, he was gone.

CHAPTER V.

I FOUND Granger at his office on the next day. He was writing, and did not turn to see who had come in until I had waited for some moments. His color heightened as he recognized me. There was a look of shame in his face, and considerable embarrassment in his manner.

"Good morning," said I.

"Good morning," he responded, in a dull, cold way. There was not the slightest invitation to friendly confidence. I felt him pushing me off almost as distinctly as if his action had been physical instead of mental.

"Just looked in to see how you were," I remarked. "All right, I hope?"

He turned a little from me, not making any reply. While I was still in doubt as to what it were best for me to do or say, a client came in to consult him on business, which gave me an opportunity to retire from the office. I was glad of this, for I was not sure as to Granger's real state of mind; nor half so confident as I had been a year before that I could give the wise counsel a man in his condition so greatly needed. That he had faithfully tried the prescription which I gave him then, I knew; and there was this to be said in its favor, by its help he had stood firm for a whole year—and was not that a great deal? True, but why had he gained nothing in moral and spiritual power during all this rule of the will over his sensual nature? He should have been stronger, more self-centered, more really invincible at the end of a year than at the beginning; and yet, the will off guard, in some moment of assault, and he was again in the hands of his enemy.

One conclusion forced itself upon me. This man's condition was worse than before he made his resolute and, for a time, successful effort to reform. The will-power, in which he had trusted so confidently, had failed in strength and vigilance, and left him a prey to inrushing appetite. Even if faith in himself were not destroyed, it must be a weaker faith and less able to contend with appetite, which, through another victory, had gained a new force.

All this, as I dwelt on the subject, grew clearer and clearer to my mind. I could see how a resolute will might hold a man above consent in any and every temptation by which he might be assailed; and I could also see how, if the will betrayed the man, and he fell, he would be weaker for the fall, and more easily overcome in a new temptation. What then? What hope for him? There would be an inflowing of strength from God with every subsequent effort the man might make to get free from the dominion of evil; but would not the reception of this strength and the ability to use it, be in a steadily diminishing ratio; and would not the power of appetite increase with every indulgence?

My faith in man's will had received a shock. There was an element of weakness somewhere. Why should God fail to give the requisite strength when the effort was sincere? Did he indeed govern, as many taught, by mere arbitrary laws; affording help to the weak and perishing only in the degree of their compliance with certain legal conditions? Or, were the conditions not arbitrary but essential and in the very nature of things? If God be good and wise—loving and compassionate—ever seeking to save to the very uttermost, must not this be so? God is love—love. Heart and soul held to this. But, how was the sustaining strength of this love to make itself a living force in man? How? I could not see it clearly. Once it had been very clear; but my thoughts were in confusion now.

I had reached the door of my own office, and was about entering, when a sudden movement in the street attracted my attention. People were running together, in an excited manner.

"Only a drunken row," said a man who was standing near me.

"That all." And I passed into my office.

Only a drunken row! I had dismissed the incident as of little account when I was startled by the sound of tramping feet and dissonant voices at my very door; and in a moment after, three men entered bearing the body of a man, deathly pale, and with the blood streaming from a wound in his head. I recognized him as a well-known and prominent citizen.

A doctor was sent for, and after the wound was dressed, the gentleman was removed to his own home.

Only a drunken row! An effort was made to keep the affair out of the newspapers, but not with entire success. In one afternoon sheet this account appeared:

"ASSAULT ON A PROMINENT CITIZEN.—A dastardly assault was made this morning on our esteemed fellow citizen, Harvey Leonard, Esq., by a ruffianly fellow named Groot. It occurred just in front of Egbert's saloon. Mr. Leonard had just left the saloon, when Groot dealt him a severe blow from behind, knocking him down. In falling, his head struck the curbstone, and he received an ugly wound above the temple. Mr. Leonard was carried into Frederick Lyon's office, where the wound was dressed by Dr. Gerhard. He was then taken to his own home. We learn that the immediate occasion of this assault was a political argument into which Mr. Leonard permitted himself to be drawn by Groot, and in which both of them—they had been drinking rather freely, we are sorry to say—got angry and called hard names. Mr. Leonard had the best of the argument, and Groot revenged himself, after the ruffianly fashion, by knocking him down. He may thank his stars if he doesn't have to stand a trial for manslaughter; for no one can tell what may be the result of a severe concussion of the brain. When removed to his home, we understand that Mr. Leonard was in a half-cometose state."

I had just read this account of the affair, and was thinking of the mortification Mr. Leonard's family must suffer should it happen to meet their eyes—there were grown-up sons and daughters—when, to my surprise, Mr. Granger entered my office. He smiled faintly as he came in, the smile dying off slowly, and leaving his face very grave.

"I want to have another talk with you, Lyon," he said. "This is a shocking affair of Leonard's, isn't it?"

"Shocking and sad," I replied.

"I know this Groot. He's peaceable enough when sober, but a devil incarnate when drunk. They say that Leonard is in a dangerous condition."

"So the *Telegraph* intimates."

"I don't know when anything has given me such a shock. It might have happened to me as well as to Leonard. Why, only a few evenings ago I had some sharp words with the fellow. I can remember the glitter of his angry eyes. He would have struck me down if he had dared. Liquor makes fiends of some men who are as quiet and peaceable as lambs when sober. I've often thought of that. Can you explain it, Mr. Lyon?"

"I have no settled theory of my own on the subject; but in a book which I read not long ago, I saw an explanation that set me to thinking."

"What was it?"

"The writer had been speaking of the terrible transformations wrought in men by drink. How the once tender and considerate husband became changed often into a cruel fiend. How the loving father grew indifferent or brutal towards his children; the good citizen a social pest; and the esteemed neighbor an offence. How in everything the order of life was changed; the goodly tree that once gave such generous fruit becoming as a thorn or bramble. He then said:

"'We marvel at these awful transformations, wondering how inebriation can change men into fiends; how alcohol, a mere substance in nature, and without moral force, can, through its action on the brain, evolve a new moral quality—intense, destructive and infernal. The fact no one questions, for it stands all the while confronting and challenging us in a thousand terrible and disgusting forms; and yet, for all this, men dally with the subtle agent of hell, giving it a lodgment in body and brain, and suffering it to gain a large and still larger action among the vital forces, which it never touches but to work disorder. They see how it hurts their neighbors; but, strangely enough, do not fear for themselves.

"'There is a truth about this matter which few

consider—a truth that, if well understood, would hold thousands upon thousands away from that so-called moderate indulgence in alcohol which so often betrays to utter ruin. We speak of man as having rational freedom. The seat of this freedom and rationality is the brain, the physical organism through which it acts and influences the outer life. If the brain is hurt or disturbed, the mind's healthy action is at once lost; and it is remarkable that an evil force seems to get possession of the will as soon as the rational equipoise is lost.

"'Whatever disturbs a man's rational equipoise, gives evil forces a power over him which could not otherwise be obtained. Clearly, then, to disturb the brain's healthy action by the introduction of alcohol, through the blood, into that wonderfully delicate organ, is for a man to change so far the true heavenly order of his life, and to open the door for an influx of disorder and evil. The change may at first be very small, and the disorderly action scarcely perceived; but is it not clear to the dullest mind that, if the introduction of alcohol into the brain be continued day after day, and with gradual increase, the time must come when the man's rational control of himself will be lost? And when this takes place, he becomes subject to infernal influences.'"

"This goes deeper than I had thought," said Granger, as I stopped speaking, "and involves more than I can now understand or admit. So much is true, at least, that when the brain is disturbed by drink, a man comes under baleful influences, and is far more inclined to evil than to good. He is quick to take offence, and too ofter grows passionate, cruel and pitiless, hurting even his best beloved. Ah, what a cursed slavery it is!"

A painful agitation disturbed his face.

"And the hardest to break of any into which a poor mortal can unhappily fall," I said.

"Is there any hope, Mr. Lyon?" An anxious, half-terrified look had come into his eyes, as of one who had felt himself borne helplessly away. "I am almost in despair. My will, in which I thought myself so strong, has failed, and I cannot trust it again. It is weaker for my fall, and must grow weaker and weaker every recurring fall. Do you know anything about inebriate asylums?"

He asked the question abruptly, and with the manner of one who had forced himself to do something from which he had been holding back with a strong reluctance.

"There are the Sanitarium at Media, and the New York State Inebriate Asylum at Binghampton," I answered.

"Do you know anything about either of them?"

I did not.

"Did you ever hear of any one being cured at an Inebriate Asylum?"

"Oh, yes."

"Who? Can you find me the man?"

"No case has come under my personal observation; but I remember reading in a New York paper not long ago a very strong report on the good work which had been done at the State Asylum."

"Do you know anything about the treatment?"

"Only in a general way. The patient is removed from old associations, and out of the reach of temptations which he had become too weak to resist; brought under the influence of new social, moral and intellectual conditions; and this for a period of time long enough to give him back the mastery over himself which had been lost. I remember, now, hearing a gentleman who had visited the Sanitarium at Media, say, that Dr. Parish regarded the cultivation of the finest qualities of the head and heart in his patients as the true basis of a permanent recovery. He relied on that self-culture which promotes self-respect, a sense of moral obligation, and the development of a true manhood; and when this consciousness was realized, he considered the foundations laid for permanent safety."

The eager expression which was on Granger's face as I began my answer to his question, had left it by the time I ceased speaking.

"All a delusion," he replied. "If they can offer a man no other help, the number of their saved will be few."

"They are many, I have been told."

He shook his head doubtfully and gloomily.

"New associations," said I, "the cultivation of new tastes, more vigorous thinking in the right direction, a better understanding of the pathology of drunkenness, and above all, the formation of better habits, must help a man and give him a new advantage in the struggle with appetite. These he will gain while under treatment in an asylum."

"Have I not had nearly all of these for a year, standing by their help and that of my strong will in the very face of temptation? And yet there came an hour in which they were as threads of flax in a candle flame! You don't know anything about the wild rush this passion of drink will sometimes make upon a man. It is like the sweep of an irresistible flood.

"Look here!" He drew from his vest pocket a slip of paper. "I cut this out of a newspaper today. It has frightened me. God only knows where I am drifting! It may be to a fate as dreadful. This slip of paper gives, briefly, a few facts in the life of a man who once stood high as a clergyman, and afterwards represented his State in Congress. But drink cursed him and he fell to the lowest level. Recovering himself, he enlisted in the temperance cause and became not only one of its warmest champions, but rose to the head of the Order of Good Templars in the State of Indiana. But he died ere he had reached his fortieth year and from congestion of the brain, caused by a relapse into intemperance!"

"Sad enough! Does the slip give his name?"

"Let me read it: 'Schuyler Colfax, in a recent

letter referring to the death of J. J. Talbot, of Indianapolis, says: "He has made hundreds of eloquent and touching appeals for temperance all over our State within the past two years, but told me that the appetite would sometimes become so insatiate as to almost defy control, though he prayed on bended knee for strength to resist it. I remember the terrible picture of his own experience copied in the enclosed article. He delivered it here, to a crowded audience, hundreds of whom, like myself, were in tears, and he uttered it in desponding tones that seemed almost like the wail of the lost, and as if he felt his impending doom was inevitable.'"

"The extract referred to by Mr. Colfax, is as follows: 'But now that the struggle is over, I can survey the field and measure the losses. I had position high and holy. This demon tore from around me the robes of my sacred office, and sent me forth churchless and godless, a very hissing and by-word among men. Afterward I had business, large and lucrative, and my voice in all large courts was heard pleading for justice, mercy and the right. But the dust gathered on my unopened books, and no foot-fall crossed the threshold of the drunkard's office. I had moneys ample for all necessities, but they took wings and went to feed the coffers of the devils which possessed me. I had a home adorned with all that wealth and the most exquisite taste could suggest. This devil crossed its threshold and the light faded from its chambers; the fire went out on the holiest of altars, and, leading me through its portals, despair walked forth with her, and sorrow and anguish lingered within. I had children, beautiful, to me at least, as a dream of the morning, and they had so entwined themselves around their father's heart that, no matter where it might wander, ever it came back to them on the bright wings of a father's undying love. This destroyer took their hands in his and led them away. I had a wife whose charms of mind and person were such that to see her was to remember, and to know her was to love. * * * For thirteen years we walked the rugged path of life together, rejoicing in its sunshine and sorrowing in its shade. This infernal monster couldn't spare me even this. I had a mother who for long, long years had not left her chair, a victim of suffering and disease, and her choicest delight was in the reflection that the lessons which she had taught at her knee had taken root in the heart of her youngest born, and that he was useful to his fellows and an honor to her who bore him. But the thunderbolt reached even there, and there it did its most cruel work. Ah, me! never a word of reproach from her lips—only a tender caress; only a shadow of a great and unspoken grief gathering over the dear old face; only a trembling hand laid more lovingly on my head; only a closer clinging to the cross; only a more piteous appeal to Heaven if her cup at last were not full. And while her boy raved in his wild delirium two thousand miles away, the pitying angels pushed the golden gates ajar, and the mother of the drunkard entered into rest.

"'And thus I stand: a clergyman without a cure; a barrister without brief or business; a father without a child; a husband without a wife; a son without a parent; a man with scarcely a friend; a soul without a hope—all swallowed up in the maelstrom of drink.'"

Several times, as he read, the voice of Mr. Granger gave way and he had to pause in order to recover himself. His hand shook so that he was obliged to lay the slip of paper down on my table to keep it steady. His eyes were wet and his face strongly agitated.

"Such a devil is the devil of drink!" he said, bitterly, shutting his teeth hard and clenching his hands. "Cruel as hell; pitiless as the grave!"

"And knowing that he is so cruel and so pitiless, Mr. Granger, why place yourself for an instant in his power?"

He put his hand to his collar and drew it away from his throat, as if he were choking.

"The case seems well nigh hopeless." There was a mournful despondency in his voice.

"Say not so. That of Mr. Talbot is largely exceptional. There must have been with him an inherited appetite."

I was looking at Mr. Granger, and noticed a change pass over his face, which had become suddenly pale. There was a startled expression in his eyes.

"A what?" he asked, a little breathlessly.

"An inherited tendency."

"You don't imagine there is anything in that, Mr. Lyon?"

"Undoubtedly there is," not at the moment thinking of any application by Mr. Granger of my remark to his own case. "The law of transmission is well established. Children not only inherit the physical likenesses and peculiarities of their parents, but their mental and moral qualities also. A depraved appetite in a father will, if indulged, be surely transmitted to his child."

"What hope for the child, then?"

"All hope, if he hold the appetite as a wild beast sleeping. It cannot hurt him while it sleeps. But let him beware how he awakens it with a taste of blood on its tongue. No inherited evil can hurt us until we give it a new life in ourselves. Until then it is only potential."

No light came back into Granger's countenance. There was about him a statue-like stillness and a fixedness of look, as though he were gazing at something strange and almost fearful.

"This gives the case a new aspect, Mr. Lyon." There was a forced quiet in his voice as he said this, turning to me as he spoke. I saw another change in his countenance, which now bore signs of conscious weakness. He gave me the impression of one who had folded his arms in the face of danger, all confidence in effort gone. "A man may repent and be saved from the curse of his own transgressions, but if the sin of his father be laid upon him, what hope is there of salvation?"

The truth flashed on my mind. Here was a case of inherited appetite; and the victim's first suspicion of the fact had destroyed in him, for the time being, all remaining faith in the value of resistance.

"The case is only the harder," I replied; "but not desperate. There must be a more vigilant watch and ward; a more earnest and never-ceasing conflict; a daily death-grapple with the foe, if need be. And is not freedom from his infernal power worth all this?"

"Worth it? Aye! Worth all a man may do or dare!"

There swept into his face the flush and strength of reviving confidence.

"Did the criminality of this thing never strike you?" I asked, determined to try the force of a new incentive.

"Criminality?" He gave a kind of start, and the warmer color which had come into his face died out.

"Nor the perpetual danger in which one who lets the devil of drink get possession of his brain stands of becoming a criminal before the law? The deeds of a devil are very apt to be devilish."

He set his eyes on me with a fixed stare, waiting my farther speech.

"Your profession makes you familiar with the causes of crime," I continued, "and you know that over seventy per cent. of the crimes and vicious acts which the law punishes by fines, imprisonments or death, are caused by inebriation."

He still gazed at me without speaking.

"Groot is an inoffensive man while sober, but a brutal fiend when drunk. When sober, he would not have injured a hair of Mr. Leonard's head—drunk, he made a cowardly and murderous assault upon him."

Granger drew a deep, quivering breath, but made no reply. I went on.

"No man who takes this devil into his brain, so giving him the control of will and action, can tell what may be the consequences. When he gets back into himself again, there may be blood upon his hand! Whose blood? Is the insane drunkard careful in his discriminations? Is the beloved wife, or sweet young daughter, or innocent babe, in no danger? What say the records of our courts?"

I paused, for the face of the lawyer had become intensely agitated, and there were beads of sweat on his forehead.

"This criminal aspect of the case," I resumed, seeing that he made no response, "is one of the most serious that drinking presents; and is not the man who, to gratify a mere appetite which he knows, if indulged, will destroy his moral sense, and induce temporary insanity, as guilty of the crimes he may commit while intoxicated as if he had committed them sober? A good citizen will see to it, that he does not wrong his neighbor; and a good husband and father that his wife and children have care, protection and love. Is he a good citizen, or husband, or father, who voluntarily transforms himself into a cruel and destructive demon? The crime and responsibility of this thing cannot be escaped, Mr. Granger, and I press upon you, in all solemnity, this view of the whole sad question. If you go away from here, and, before reaching your home, suffer appetite to draw you back again into the vortex from which you are trying to escape, and on the outer edge of which you are resting now, who can tell whether to-morrow may not find you at the bar of justice, with crime written on your forehead!"

Granger started to his feet and threw up his hands with a bitter cry, then clasped them tightly across his forehead. He stood for several moments in this attitude, his manner that of one in swift debate.

"No, Mr. Lyon, not that—not that!" he said, huskily, as he turned to me. "Not a criminal!"

He sat down again, as if from sudden loss of strength. I saw that he was trembling.

"I trust not, Mr. Granger. But there is no more

immunity for you than for another. These drink-devils are no respecters of persons. If you let them in you become their slave, and no one can tell how soon, nor how deeply, they may lead you into crime and disgrace."

He gave an involuntary shudder. After this, we talked more calmly. The idea of criminality became a central one in his mind. It had never before occurred to him. He was a man of sensitive honor; and this thought of crime against society, and against his family, wrought with him strongly. Not alone the crime of violence, as at first presented, but the crime of robbery towards those who had a claim on him for services and protection. I was careful to go over the ground with him as widely as possible; and especially to dwell on the great crime against wife and children which a man commits who robs them through the waste and self-wrought incapacity of drunkenness.

Granger sat with me for a whole hour, gathering up motive for a new struggle with his enemy, and setting his mental forces in array. The idea of criminality in drunkenness took, I was glad to see, a deeper and deeper hold upon him. He was very severe on himself, in referring to the wrongs his family had once suffered; and did not hesitate to call his conduct towards them an aggravated crime.

"You have helped me to my feet again," he said, holding my hand tightly, as he was about leaving my office, "and may God bless you; not for my sake only, but for the sake of my wife and children. A criminal! No, no, no! A good citizen, an honorable man; Alexander Granger will be all these—but not a criminal! Good-bye! I am your debtor more than can be estimated in any count of gold. Good-bye, and again, may God bless you!"

CHAPTER VI.

MY confidence in Granger's ability to control his appetite by means of the new moral element which had been summoned to his aid, was not as strong as I could have wished. A serious ground of fear lay in the fact, which had been fully admitted, of his father's intemperate habits, for I clearly understood the subtle power of all transmitted inclinations; especially when by indulgence these inclinations are lifted above the region of latent impulse and become a living force, the hereditary and the acquired acting in the same direction. How powerful had been their action in the case of Mr. Granger, was manifest in his sudden fall after a whole year of abstinence. In this renewed struggle, was he not weaker, and these combined forces stronger, than before? I could not get my mind free from the depressing effects which were wrought in me by this view of the case.

But my anxieties were apparently groundless. Granger stood firm again; and I had cause for renewed and stronger hope in the permanence of his reformation in the fact that he was less boastful as to his strength, and more careful to keep as far away from temptation as possible. I made it a duty to see him frequently, and to give him all the moral support in my power. There were times when he talked to me very freely about his old life, and about the latent force of the old serpent of appetite on which he had set his heel.

"I am painfully conscious," he said to me, one day—it was several months after his sudden fall, and quick recovery of himself again—"that appetite is only held down by force; and that at any moment it may give a vigorous spring and seek to throw its slimy folds around me."

"And for this cause you are always on guard," I replied.

"Always."

"Herein lies your safety. You are stronger than your enemies; but, to be safe, must never unbuckle your armor nor lay aside your shield."

"Always a soldier; always in front of the enemy; always standing on guard! It is a hard life for a man to live. How I long, sometimes, for peace and rest and safety!"

"Better to stand always in full armor than to give the slightest advantage to your cruel foes. You know too well what falling into their power means."

"Alas! too well. But," he added, with a serious contraction of the brows, "is there no time in the days to come, when these enemies shall be wholly destroyed or cast out? Am I never to dwell in safety?"

He looked at me with strong and eager questionings in his eyes.

"Sometime, I trust." My reply had in it no assuring quality.

"Sometime! When? In this world, or only in the next?—in Heaven, if I ever should be so fortunate as to get there?"

"Your enemies will grow weaker the longer you hold them down; and will you not be a steady gainer in strength for every day and year you keep this mastery over them? Every day and year dwelling more and more secure?"

"What do you understand by dypsomania?" he asked, abruptly.

"It is a term used by some medical writers to designate what they regard as confirmed inebriety—when the will-power is completely overthrown, and the demands of the diseased organism for alcoholic stimulus becomes so great that the man is literally crazy for drink," I replied.

"What do they say about it?—the medical writers, I mean."

"They give but little ground for hope of cure in one so demented."

"Demented? Ah! I can well believe it. Crazy for drink! I have seen men so."

"When this condition is fully developed, these writers say, the brain has become deteriorated in quality, and its functions impaired. All the higher faculties are more or less weakened. Reason, judgment, perception and memory lose their vigor and capacity. The will becomes feeble and powerless. All the moral sentiments and affections become involved. Conscience, a sense of accountability, and of right and wrong, are all deadened, while the lower propensities and passions are aroused, and acquire a new strength. Another effect has been observed: No influence can frighten or deter the miserable subject from indulging his passion for drink. To gratify it, he will not only disregard every consideration of a personal nature affecting his standing in society, his pecuniary condition, or the well-being of his family, but the most frightful instances of disasters and crimes, as the consequences of drinking fail to have any effect upon him. A hundred deaths from this cause, occurring under the most revolting circumstances, fail to impress him with an adequate sense of his own danger. He would pass over the bodies of these wretched victims without a thought of warning, in order to get the means of gratifying his own insatiate thirst. Such, according to medical testimony, is the dypsomaniac; or, as some say, the subject of confirmed alcoholism; and he is considered as morally insane."

"Fearful!" ejaculated Granger; "and we tamper with a substance that can work such ruin to the souls and bodies of men."

"There is something mysterious in the action of this substance on the human body and its functions," I replied. "So seductive and pleasant in its first effects—so enticing and so alluring; yet so deadly and destructive in the end. An almost invisible bond at the beginning and, and light as a spider's thread, but at the last an iron fetter."

"I met with an extract from a medical journal to-day that gave me a startling impression of insecurity," said Granger. "As you intimated, there must be something occult and mysterious in the way alcohol works its insidious changes in the human economy. We know, alas! too well, that here effect does not cease with the removal of the cause. The thirst, which increases the more it is indulged, is not extinguished by prolonged denial. The man never gets back to his normal state—to a point where a single glass of liquor will produce no more desire for a second glass than did the first he drank in youth or early manhood. One would suppose that, after a longer or shorter period of abstinence, the man would regain his old condition, and be able to taste wine or spirits without immediate danger. That the appetite, if indulged, would have only gradual increase as before. But all experience and observation testify that this is not so, and the extract from a medical journal to which I have just referred professed to give the pathological reason."

"And what is the reason so given?" I asked.

"It startled me, as I have said," he answered. "The statement alleges that a physician of some eminence made careful examination, by dissection, of the blood and internal organs of persons who, before death, had used intoxicating drinks freely, and found in these subjects an enlargement of the blood globules, as well in the brain as in the other organs, so that they stood, as it were, open-mouthed, athirst always, and eager for drink."

"But," I said, "abstinence from alcoholic beverages must, in time, change this condition, and the blood globules shrink to their old dimensions."

"The fact does not bear out the inference. It is farther stated, that the physician referred to, after clearly ascertaining the existence of this morbid change, had the opportunity to dissect the brain of a man who, after being a drunkard for many years, reformed and lived soberly until he died. His surprise was great when he discovered that the unnaturally large globules of the blood had not shrunk to their proper size. Though they did not exhibit the inflammation seen in the drunkard's brain, they were enlarged, and ready, it seemed, on the instant, to absorb the waited-for alcohol, and resume their old diseased condition. The conclusion to which the physician came was given in the brief article. He believed that he saw in this morbid state of the brain the physical part of the reason why a man who has once been a drunkard can never again as long as he lives, safely take one drop of alcoholic liquor. He thought he saw why a glass of wine put a man back instantly to where he was when he drank all the time. He saw the citadel free from the enemy, but undefended—incapable of defence—its doors wide open, so that there was no safety except in keeping the foe at a distance, away beyond the outermost wall."

"If this be true, every reformed man should know it," I said. "The statement is remarkable, and great pains should be taken to ascertain, by repeated examinations, whether it hold good in other cases or not. That there is a change in the physical condition of inebriates, we all know; and we also know that this change is permanent. But whether it be in the blood globules or not, the fact itself should stand as a perpetual warning to men who have at any time been the slaves of this appetite. And I do not think, Mr. Granger, that you should find in the philosophy of inebriation here educed anything to discourage you, but rather a new motive for keeping your foe at a distance, away beyond the outermost wall, as has been said."

"But the citadel incapable of defence—its doors wide open! Think of that, Mr. Lyon!"

"Yes; but the enemy dislodged, and driven over the frontier—held in the far distance, and the man able, if he will, to hold him there forever."

"Ah! yes, yes. The old story. No safety but in eternal vigilance." Granger spoke as one who felt weary and despondent.

"But safety. Don't forget that, my friend! Peace and safety. Rich harvest-fields, and secure abiding. Are not these worth all the vigilance one may give?"

"Yes, yes; his eternal vigilance!" He roused himself as he spoke. "What a weak coward I am! But I know my enemy, and the vantage ground he holds."

"The vantage ground is yours, instead," I made reply. "Don't forget that; and let each new revelation you get of your enemy's strength, alertness and malignant hate, only act upon you as a new motive for watchfulness. Let the resolute will that held you safe for a whole year, add its strength to the new motives and considerations which are influencing you now."

He withdrew his gaze from me, and remained in thought for a considerable time.

"You are not a church-member?" lifting his eyes to my face. I noticed a new quality in his tone of voice.

"No; I have never connected myself with any religious society."

"Why not?"

"It might be difficult to assign a reason that would be entirely satisfactory to any but myself, seeing that I am a reverent believer in Holy Scripture and in the divinity of our Lord and Saviour Jesus Christ. But I do not find in the sphere of worship, in the ordinary range of preaching, and in the practical illustrations of Christianity seen in the lives and conversation of most of the church-members I happen to know, anything to awaken a desire to cast in my lot with 'God's people,' as they are in the habit of styling themselves. They have too much cant of Sunday piety and too little week-day charity to suit me. The teachings of Christ are very explicit, and no man is a Christian, let him profess what he may, who does not live according to His divine precepts. To be a Christian, means a great deal more than to be called by His name; as so many really seem to think. To join a church, and take part in its worship and ordinances, doesn't make a Christian. It *may* make a self-deceiving Pharisee or hypocrite; which is to be in a more dangerous spiritual condition than that of honest unbelief. I have too deeply-seated a reverence for these things to enter into them lightly, or to make of them a stepping-stone to influence and respectability, as I fear is so frequently the case."

Mr. Granger drew a long sigh as I stopped speaking, and I saw a disappointed expression in his face.

"Have you thought of joining the church?" I inquired.

"Oh, yes! I've thought of everything." He spoke with a slight disturbance of manner. "But the question has always been, 'What help will the church give me?' and so far the answer has not been satisfactory. That case of Mr. Talbot, about which we talked once, has been a source of considerable discouragement. He was a clergyman, you know, in the church, and one of its teachers; and yet the church did not save him from drunkenness."

"And you remember," I added, "that he used

often, as he said, to pray to God on bended knees for strength to resist the demon of drink, but all without avail."

"Yes; I remember it." His voice despondent, and a gloom settling over his face.

What did this mean? The truth began to dawn on me. There had been one reserve of hope left in the mind of Granger. When all else failed, he would go to God for help; and in my seeming depreciation of the church as a means of rescue, had I not well nigh destroyed this hope?

"You do not believe in the value of prayer?" He put the question sharply.

"I must reject the Bible if I reject the value of prayer. It is full of exhortation to pray. 'Watch and pray, lest ye enter into temptation,' are the words of our blessed Lord himself. But you will notice that the first injunction was to 'watch;' this is the man's part. If he be not watchful—ever on guard and ready to resist the tempter—his prayers will be offered in vain. In the clergyman's case, prayer on bended knees could not have been supplemented with a due degree of watchfulness. In far too many cases prayer goes for nothing, I fear. Is a man secure from robbers if he only pray for protection, and give no care to the bolting and barring of his house? Or saved from drowning, if he put to sea in a leaky vessel, trusting that God will keep the wretched craft afloat through the agency of prayer? There must be praying and working, asking and doing; the putting forth of our utmost strength, at the same time that our cry for help goes up. This is my idea of effective prayer."

There came back into Granger's face a more assured expression.

"I see reason in that," he said. "And yet," after a pause, "how much easier just to cry out, as Peter did, 'Save, Lord!' and be saved without an effort to bear yourself above the engulfing water."

"Did Peter make no effort?" I asked.

"None. He just cried out, 'Lord, save me!'"

"What was he doing?"

"Trying to go to the Lord over the angry waters."

"Walking, as steadily as he could, on the turbulent billows. Walking, you see; trying to get to Jesus; doing his best. And this means, I think, that we must do something in the way of going to the Lord besides mere looking toward him and calling upon Him. We must endeavor to walk—that is, to live right—and the first step in right living is to 'cease to do evil.' He who thus tries to go to Christ, over the tempestuous waves of sin that leap about his feet, will, when his 'Save, Lord,' breaks out in a half-despairing cry, find himself grasped by one who is mighty to save."

The strength of his countenance increased.

"You have given me some light. Help does not come to effortless weakness."

"Not the help that saves a man from the wretchedness that sin has brought upon him. He sinned freely, and God did not hold him back from sin with a force greater than his will, for that would have been to destroy in him all that makes him human, his rationality and his freedom. As he sinned freely, breaking God's laws, so he must repent and return freely. He must come back of himself, as did the Prodigal Son; but God will see him afar off and run to meet him, and throw His loving arms about him and rejoice over him. But, in all this, He will not touch his freedom; will do nothing for him in which the man does not, as it were, do the things for himself, God being his helper."

I saw Granger's countenance begin to fall again.

"If I could only see it clearly," he answered. "If I only knew just how God saves to the uttermost all who come unto Him."

"Don't let us talk any more about it just now," I replied; "it is disturbing your mind, and that isn't good. Hold fast where you now stand; resist all allurement; give no place to the enemy, and while keeping vigilant watch, pray for help from God. You will be safer for this, I am sure."

He sat silent for a little while, and then, as he arose, said, speaking as if to himself: "Except the Lord build the house, they labor in vain who build it; except the Lord keep the city, the watchman waketh in vain."

I did not think it well to make any reply. He stood for a few moments, as if waiting my response; but as I gave none, he wished me a good-day and retired.

CHAPTER VII.

I HAD been drawn, in this interview with Granger, a little away from my old mooring ground of thought, and I sat for a long time in deep reflection, trying to get many things clear that were veiled in obscurity, and to discover just where I was drifting. This question of prayer as an agency of strength and salvation to weak, repentant, sin-burdened souls, was one, I could see, of infinite importance. There was, with a large class of pious people, a loose way of talking about prayer, and a manner of praying that was, to my mind, not only irreverent, but foolish and utterly valueless. Of all the Sunday services, the prayers to God, especially those that were extempore, had been most distasteful to me, and oftenest the repelling influence that kept me away from church. There was a familiar way of addressing God, and of using His name in vain, that shocked me, for my reverence for the Divine Being, a reverence implanted in childhood, has always been very strong, and I have never been able to pronounce any of the names by which He is called without a falling inflection of the voice which has become instinctive.

I did not, as a consequence, have much faith in

the prayers that I usually heard in public, too many of which were mere bits of effective oratory, instead of a humble submission of the will to God. How often, as I listened wearily to one of these long prayers, full of vain repetitions, has the divine sentence, " God is a Spirit, and they that worship Him must worship Him in spirit and in truth," come into my mind, causing me to wonder that the preacher had forgotten it.

And now there pressed in upon me the question, in what does the power of prayer consist? Does it change the Lord's attitude toward man, or only man's attitude toward God? Does it bring down the sunlight into a darkened chamber, or only open the windows that its beams may enter? How it might change man's attitude toward God, I could, in a measure see; but not how it could change the unchangeable, render the All-Loving more tender and compassionate, or make the Infinite Father more concerned for His sin-sick, lost and perishing children, for whom He had bowed the heavens and come down.

I saw that in the right understanding of this subject lay momentous things; and I was anxious to reach a true perception of all that was involved in prayer as a means of divine blessing and favor. My thinking did not get me far beyond a rejection of the idea that any change in God's purposes toward man could be wrought in Him by prayer. If He were infinitely wise and infinitely loving, He must not only know better what external condition was best for a man than the man could know for himself, but in the orderings of His providence must so arrange all things that he would be kept there until his changing state required, for his good, a new position in life.

But in what way did prayer change man's relation to God? I felt that the truth lay here, but was not able to see it clearly; and I thought and thought until I grew weary and perplexed, and for relief of mind turned myself away from the subject.

Several months passed after this interview with Mr. Granger, and though we met occasionally, the subject about which we had talked so earnestly was not renewed. I learned through my wife that he came to church with his family now and then; and the fact always gave me pleasure, for I had a growing impression that there was a sphere of safety about the church, and especially for one like Granger. There was in the very fact of his going to church an acknowledgment of weakness on his part, and a certain looking to God for strength and protection. And I had an old and well-settled conviction which had come up with me from childhood—inwrought, I doubt not, through my mother's teachings—that in any and every turning of the soul to God, no matter how little the turning, it must receive a measure, large or small, of strength to resist the evils to which we are all so much inclined.

I had been going oftener to church myself of late, and though my reason did not give assent to all the preacher said, and I was shocked now and then by his irreverent way of addressing God, and his too frequent and needless use of Divine names in order to give force to a sentence, or to make an oratorical climax, I was still able to gather into my thoughts many things that gave me light for clearer seeing, and strength for steadier walking in the path of life. I was growing less captious and critical—less annoyed at what I did not like, and more earnest to obtain whatever good was to be had in the religious services that were held on Sunday. I found myself taking a new interest in the lessons which were read from the Bible, many passages from which struck my mind with a singular power, and left an impression of deeper import than I had ever before seen in them. I often found myself pondering one and another of these passages, and giving to them an application which altered my thought of God and of His ways with the children of men. I noticed changes in my states of mind, when listening to the Word of Sacred Scripture—I had for some years neglected reading it for myself—that occurred to me as remarkable. There sometimes fell upon me a deep tranquillity, as if I had passed from the unrest of this world into the peace of Heaven. And there would come, at times, states of self-forgetfulness, and a desire to give my life for others. I often dwelt on these things, wondering what they meant.

Was there not a power in the Word of God, which did not appear in the sense of its letter, but which flowed into the mind with that sense as a soul into the body?

The Word of God! What does this mean? The question came to me one day with such force and distinctness, that it seemed as though spoken by a living voice. The Word of God! Could that be like a man's word; limited, feeble, finite? Was there any ratio between them? I thought of the many loose interpretations which I had heard; of the contentions and angry discussions about the meaning of this and that expression in the letter; of the divisions and uncharitableness, and persecutions even, which were so sadly rife in the Christian world, and all because men vainly imagined that human reason was equal to the comprehension of Divine wisdom; and set the metes and bounds of their narrow doctrine about a Revelation from God in which were divine and infinite things that must remain forever above the reach of man's unaided reason; and which only the Spirit of God can make known.

I marvelled often at the low range and dull platitudes of the pulpit, at the stereotyped vagueness of exhortation, and at the small influence of preachers. There were exceptions, of course; but how few! With the Word of God as the basis of Christian teaching, and especially with the Word of the New Testament, in which our Lord himself, in the human nature which He assumed in the world and made divine, gives in no hidden forms of speech, the laws of spiritual life, through the keeping of which alone man can be saved; with all this, how strange to hear from the men who have been chosen to stand as watchmen on the walls of the city, so little about keeping the commandments in their inmost spirit as the only way of salvation. "He that keepeth my commandments, he it is that loveth me.'

A dull, rambling sermon, or one in which the preacher showed how much more he knew about history, philosophy, poetry and art than he did about divine things, would send me home disheartened, and with a disinclination to go again, which sometimes held me away from church service for weeks. But there was in me a growing hunger and thirst for things spiritual. I wanted to gain a clear and more rational idea of God's relations to and dealings with man, and a knowledge of the exact way in which He saved him.

The better influences of church-going on my own mind gave me encouragement for Granger. I felt sure that he would come within a sphere of protection; that, somehow, he would be brought into new associations as to his spirit, and be less in danger when exposed to assault.

"I haven't seen Mr. Granger at church for three or four Sundays," said my wife, one day. "I hope there is nothing wrong with him again." I saw a shade of concern creep into her face. "He's been attending quite regularly in the past few months."

"I saw him on the street only a few days ago," I replied. "There was nothing wrong about him then; at least nothing that I observed."

And yet, as I said this, I remembered that I had noticed in him something that left a vague question in my mind. But it had passed away and been forgotten until my wife's remark brought it back again.

"I fancied—it may only have been fancy," Mrs. Lyon said, "that Mrs. Granger's face looked more serious than usual."

"Only a fancy," I replied; but still I felt a weight of concern settling down upon my feelings. It remained with me all day and troubled me as I went to my office on the next morning. I had made up my mind to see Granger during the forenoon, but pressing business kept me at my office until two o'clock, when I returned home to dinner.

"Have you seen Mr. Granger?" asked my wife, as I came in. There was an air of suspense in her manner.

"No. I intended calling on him, but had an unusually busy day."

"If I'm not very much mistaken, I saw him," she said.

"Where?"

"Going into a saloon on Sansom Street."

"No; you must have been mistaken."

"I wish I could think so; but if the man I saw

entering a saloon, as I passed down Twelfth Street, was not Mr. Granger, then there was a remarkable likeness in the general appearance of the two men."

"Did you see his face?"

"Only for an instant. He was at the door of the saloon just as I came in sight of him, and in the next moment had disappeared. His manner was that of one who wished to avoid observation. I am almost sure it was Mr. Granger."

I had but little appetite for my dinner. In the afternoon I called at the lawyer's office, but did not find him there. Next day I met him on the street. His manner was not quite as frank and cordial as usual; but beyond this I saw no change in him. It was plain that my wife had been mistaken. My first impression was one of relief; but a feeling of complete confidence did not return, and there was a weight on my heart which I could not throw off.

Granger was not at church on the following Sunday. His wife and daughter were in attendance as usual, and there was now no mistaking the fact that a portion of light had gone out of their faces. In the afternoon I called to see him, but he was not at home. About ten o'clock on the next day I dropped into his office, and found him with a segar in his mouth reading a newspaper. He had, apparently, just arrived, for his green bag lay unopened on the office table. He started up on seeing me, coloring a little, and extending his hand with what seemed to me an excess of cordiality. I looked for the color to recede from his face until the skin was restored to the old healthy clearness, but either my eyes deceived me, or the ruddy tinge did not fade out entirely.

Granger was not completely at his ease, though evidently trying to be so. I remained for only a short time, as my call was not a business one. Our conversation did not pass beyond the common-place topics of the day.

"Call in again. I'm always glad to see you," he said, with the same excess of cordiality which he had shown on meeting me.

I was far from feeling satisfied.

"How is our friend Granger?" I asked of a mutual acquaintance not many days afterwards.

"Not doing right, I'm afraid," he answered.

"Why do you think so?"

"I've seen him two or three times of late when I fancied him the worse for drink."

"May you not have been mistaken?"

"Possibly."

"Why did you fancy he had been drinking?"

"There are signs which one rarely mistakes," he replied.

"If he should get off again," I said, "there will, I fear, be little hope for him."

"Very little. But he's been down and up a great many times, you know."

"Yes; but in the very nature of things he must grow weaker with every fall."

"Of course."

"What is to be done about him? It's dreadful to see a man going headlong to destruction. Is there no way to save him?"

"None that I know of. When this appetite is once established with a man, his case becomes almost hopeless. Every step he takes is downward. He may stop now and then, and hold himself back against the downward drag, but when he moves again the course is still down, down, until the gulf of ruin is reached at last. Is it not frightful?"

I felt a chill creep through my veins There seemed in his words a prophecy of utter ruin for Granger.

"He has stood firm, with only a single brief fall, for nearly two years," I said.

"And he might stand to the end, but not if he dallies with the fatal cup," was answered. "No man in whom the appetite for drink has once been formed can ever taste and be secure. Only in perfect abstinence is there perfect safety. The old appetite lies sleeping, but not dead. Rouse it with a glass of wine, or beer, or spirits, and it will spring upon the man with the old intense life, and he will be as a feeble child in its grasp. If Granger is indulging again, he will fall again. He may, through a resolute will, hold himself for a little while above excess; but every glass he takes is food to the old desire, which will grow stronger and stronger until its mastery is again complete."

"It doesn't seem right to hold ourselves away from him in so momentous a crisis—to leave him in the sweep of the current and not make an effort to save him," I said.

"I doubt if anything can be done. At your first approach, he will either take offense, or utterly reject your intimation that he has been indulging again. I know these men. Lying seems to be one of the fruits of drinking. Liquor is almost sure, earlier or later, to take the truth out of a man— especially in anything that relates to his cups, so long as he yields to indulgence. Men will assure you, even asking God to witness the truth of what they say, that they have not taken a drop of liquor for weeks, when its odor from their lips is rank in your nostrils. I know of nothing that so takes truth, and honor, and all that is good and true and noble out of a man, as this alcohol. It is a very hell-broth!"

I could not rest. To stand away from Granger in this new peril, would, I felt, be little less than criminal. How to approach him without giving offense was the question I had to consider. The opportunity soon came.

CHAPTER VIII.

A DAY or two afterwards, as I stood talking with a friend in the Continental Hotel, I saw Granger pass into the bar. I moved to a position from which I could observe him. He called for a glass of ale, and drank it off at a single draught. His manner was slightly nervous and a little hurried. I threw myself in his way as he left the bar, and noticed a start of surprise when his eyes rested on me.

"Ah! Lyon. Glad to see you!" The salutation was given with heartiness. But he did not look me steadily in the face. We walked out into the street, both silent until we reached the pavement.

"I'm sorry about this, Granger," I said.

"About what?" He affected not to understand me.

"You cannot use ale and be safe. You know this as well as I do."

His lips closed tightly, and his brows fell. We walked for a little way, neither of us speaking.

"Come round to my office, and let us have a talk about this matter," said I, as we reached the next corner.

"Not to-day." He drew out his watch and looked

at the time. "I have an engagement with a client. But don't give yourself any trouble about me, Lyon, I'm all right."

"But to-morrow may tell a different story," I replied. "No, no, Granger! You must not go a step farther in this way. A precipice lies just beyond!"

"Another time; but now I must hurry to my engagement." Saying which, he left me abruptly.

My concern was great. That he could stand secure feeding his old, fierce appetite with a glass of ale now and then, I knew to be impossible, and he knew it as well—only, subtle desire was pressing for indulgence, and blinding him with false assurances.

I did not see him again for two or three days, though I had twice called at his office. At last I found him in. It was late in the afternoon, and I could see from the color of his face that he had been drinking, though not to excess. He received me with the old friendliness of manner, and without any sign of embarrassment.

"You've come for that talk with me, I suppose," he said, smiling, and with a twinkle in his eyes. "All right. You see I'm not down in the gutter, for all the prophecy that was in your face the other day."

There was a certain lightness of tone and manner about him, that in view of the subject to which he referred, almost shocked me. He must have noticed this, for he added, in a more serious voice: "I know how you feel, Mr. Lyon, but let me assure you that I am in no danger of falling back into that wretched slough from which you helped to extricate me. I have too vivid a remembrance of its suffocating mire and horrible foulness ever to let my feet go near its treacherous margin again."

"What and where are the margins of this dreadful slough?" I asked.

He did not answer.

"I saw you on one of these margins, your feet in the very slime of the pit, only a few days ago."

A smile broke over his face.

"Your way of putting it. But, seriously, Lyon, I am not in the danger you think. How long do you suppose it is since I've been using a little ale every day? More than two months. I was getting run down from too close application to business, and the doctor said I must have a tonic. 'Take a glass of stout or bitter ale with your dinner,' he said. Of course that couldn't be. My wife would have been frightened to death."

"Did the doctor know anything of your previous life?" I inquired.

"Can't say about that. He may or he may not."

"Your regular family physician?"

"No. Haven't had a regular doctor in the family for three or four years."

"And you have followed his prescription?"

"Yes; only I don't take the ale with my dinner. I've felt like another man ever since. Can do more work with less exhaustion. Have a clearer head, and more elastic feelings. The ale simply gives a needed tonic, which the system absorbs, and there the matter ends."

"You think so?"

"I'm sure of it."

"With all your sad experience, Mr. Granger, to take so fearful a risk!"

"I know how the thing looks to you, Mr. Lyon; and I know how it stands with me. I am not taking this ale to gratify an appetite, but simply as a tonic, which my system requires. Here lies my safety. I am not off guard for a single moment. I am not only using the will-power which held me secure so long, but motives of good citizenship, and love and duty towards my family are more powerful than ever. If appetite attempts to lift its head again, I shall set my crushing heel upon it. I am standing in the strength of a true manhood."

"Have you forgotten," I said, "that testimony of a physician in regard to the enlargement of the blood globules in the habitually intemperate?"

Granger made a slight gesture of impatience as he replied: "Nothing in it. I've talked with half a dozen physicians and scientific men on the subject."

"But, apart from that particular theory," I said, "the fact remains, as you know, that in a man who has once been intemperate, certain changes in the state of the body have been wrought, which remain permanent. Whether this change be in the blood-globules or not, the imminent danger of the man, should alcohol be introduced into his blood, is just the same. The truth or falsity of the physician's theory in no way touches the essential facts in the case."

As I spoke, I saw a quick, startled motion of his eyes, but it was gone in an instant.

"Have you forgotten Mr, Talbot?" I asked.

"Such cases are exceptional," he replied, with a toss of the head. "We don't meet with them once in an age."

"The history of intemperance is the history of such cases," I replied. "You are deceiving yourself. Thousands and thousands of such men go down to dishonored graves every year. My dear friend, you are taking a fearful risk!"

Granger drew a little away from me with a slightly offended air.

"We shall see," he answered, somewhat coldly, and then changed the subject. I tried to come back to it again, but he pushed it aside with so manifest a purpose not to continue the discussion that I had nothing left but silence.

Every day I looked for his fall. But it did not come suddenly, as I had feared. The usual business hour found him at his office with each new morning, and his presence in court was as prompt and as regular as usual. But there was not an observant friend or acquaintance who did not see the steady change that was in progress. It was slow, but sure. The man was most warily on guard; limiting his appetite—holding it down—saying to it, "I am your master. So much and no more. Enough for tonic and strength, but nothing for indulgence." And yet, from a single glass of ale a day, the concession to appetite had reached, at the end of three months, to as many as three or four, by which time the strong will, and the motives of interest, honor and affection, in which he had entrenched himself, were beginning to show signs of weakness.

I met him one day about this period of his declension. It was in the court-room. I had been drawn thither through my interest in a case in which he appeared as counsel for the defendant, a man on trial for his life—an old man, gray-headed, bent and broken—one of the saddest wrecks I had ever seen. This man had once been a successful merchant, and the possessor of considerable wealth. I well remember the time when he occupied a handsome residence on Walnut Street, and when his wife and daughters moved in the best social circles of our city. But his head was not strong enough for the wine that proved his betrayer, and in the very prime and glory of his manhood he began to fall. Methodical habits, and the orderly progression of a long-established business, kept him free from losses in trade for some years after his sagacity as a merchant had left him. But the time came when the tide began to turn adversely. Younger partners, who had new ideas of business, were impatient of slow gains. Into their hands came a larger and a larger control of things, and the opportunity for speculation. As in all other kinds of gambling, trade speculations lead surely to ultimate losses. Winning is the exception; loss the rule. It took only a few years to bring the firm to bankruptcy.

The merchant never recovered himself. Capital gone, and brain and body enervated by intemperance, he did not even make a struggle, and at the age of fifty-five dropped out of useful life, and became a burden, a shame and a sorrow to his friends and family. An income in her own right of a few hundred dollars possessed by his wife, saved them from utter poverty. There were two beautiful daughters, as refined and intelligent as any you meet in the most cultivated circles. Alas for them! The pleasant places in which they had moved saw them no more.

Ten years later, and the broken merchant, in a frenzy of delirium brought on by drinking, struck down his wife with a blow that caused her death. A trial for murder was the consequence, in which Mr. Granger conducted the defense. One of the saddest and most painful features of this trial was the appearance in court of the two daughters as witnesses, and the evidence they were compelled to give. I can see them now, with ten years of sorrow and humiliation written in their pale, suffering faces, as they stood in the witness-box, tearful and reluctant. Pity made even the lawyers tender and considerate in pressing their examination; but enough came out to give the heart-ache to nearly all who were in the court-room. It was one of the most painful scenes I had ever witnessed.

When all the evidence was in, and Mr. Granger's turn came to address the jury in behalf of the prisoner, the pause and expectation became breathless. The poor old white-haired man bent toward him with a helpless, anxious face, and the two daughters sat pale with suspense, their eyes riveted on the man who was to plead for the life of their father.

"Gentlemen of the jury." His subdued voice, in which a slight tremor was apparent, made deeper the silence of the hushed court-room. It was genuine emotion that came thrilling in his tones, not the art of the pleader. There was a waiting and a holding of the breath for his next words. Turning slowly, he looked at the old man and at the two white-faced women—his daughters—and stretching out a hand toward them, said, his voice still lower than at first: "The most sorrowful thing I have seen in this court-room since my admission to the bar!"

There is no form of words by which to convey any true conception of the pity and deeply moving pathos that were in his voice.

"The most sorrowful thing, gentlemen of the jury!" turning partly round to the jury-box. "I need not tell you what it means. The pitiful story has been fully rehearsed. You know it all. There was once an honorable merchant, a tender husband, a loving father. The city was proud of him. His name was the synonym for high integrity and generous feeling. His home was the dwelling-place of all sweet affections. But an evil eye fell upon the merchant and his happy home. The locust and the canker-worm found their way into his garden of delight. Leaf withered and flower faded, and singing birds departed. Under the spell of this evil eye, the generous merchant lost his wealth and his fine sense of honor, the husband his tenderness and devotion, the father his love. A demon had taken possession of his soul, subsidizing all its noble powers, and making them the ministers of evil instead of good. Shall I tell you the name of this demon?"

He paused for a few moments. Then with a slow utterance and deep impressiveness: "It was the demon of strong drink! You all know him. You cannot walk the streets of this great city—this Christian city—without feeling his hot breath strike into your faces a hundred times an hour! His wretched victims are everywhere about us; and the homes he has ruined may be counted by tens of thousands all over the land. Where has not the blight of his foul breath fallen? Whose home is free from the curse of his presence?

"Look!" He turned to the prisoner and his daughters. "All that the demon has left! Ah, gen-

"All that the Demon has left."—*Page 108.*

tlemen! he is a pitiless demon, and without respect of persons.

"And now what shall I say for my poor, unhappy client? For this man whom the devil of drink has held in chains for these many, many years, and made the creature of his infernal will. Who wronged and beggared his family—the man, or the devil that was in him? The man was kind, and tender, and loving. The man cared for his wife and his children, and would have given his very life, if need be, for their safety. Years of unselfish devotion to those he loved bear him witness. You have heard the testimony of his daughters; and I think your eyes must still remain half-blinded by the tears with which their touching story filled them. No, no! It was not the man who dealt that cruel blow. He would never have laid on the dear and precious head of his faithful wife a stroke as light as that of a feather's fall. It was the devil who did it, and not the man. The devil of drink.

"No, gentlemen! You cannot find the man guilty of murder. He was only a passive instrument, with no more responsibility for crime than the club with which a ruffian fells a citizen, or the pistol with which an assassin does his fatal work. It was the devil who did it. Ah! if the law could only reach this devil!"

The jury retired on the conclusion of Granger's plea, and were not out for half an hour. The evidence had been very direct and clear. The prisoner had developed in the past year an irritable and malignant spirit, and would grow violent and threatening when his wife refused him money. It was proved that he had struck her several times, and that she had once carried the marks of a blow in her face for many weeks. In the evidence bearing on the cause of her death, it was shown that her husband had been wrought into a paroxysm of insane anger by her refusal to give him money, and that in his blind passion he had knocked her down. The blow was a violent one. When her daughters, who had heard the heavy fall of her body, reached the room and attempted to lift her from the floor, she was dead.

At the end of half an hour, the jury came in with a verdict of guilty of murder in the second degree, and a recommendation to mercy. Granger had remained in the court-room while the jury was out, taking part in another case that came up for trial. I saw from his manner that a strong impression, from which he had not been able to break free, had been left on his mind by the incidents of the trial just closed. The two daughters of the prisoner remained in the court-room, waiting for the verdict in their father's case. More than once I noticed Granger's eyes resting upon them with a pitiful, almost sad expression. Was he thinking of his own daughter and their mother, and of the demon that might desolate their home and drag them down to a fate like this?

When the verdict came, and the wretched prisoner was removed, under a sentence of three years' incarceration in the penitentiary, I saw Mr. Granger go out with the two daughters, who moved through the crowd with bent heads and slow, uncertain steps. What a heartache the sight gave me! As I reached the street, I observed him enter a carriage with them and drive away. I was touched by his considerate care and kindness.

"Ah," I said to myself, "if he will but take this awful lesson to heart, and cast out once and forever that devil of drink to which he made, a little while ago, such an eloquent and telling reference."

I felt a strong hope that this would be so. That the incidents of this trial, and his absorption into it as counsel, would make so deep an impression on Granger as to cause him to start back in alarm from the brink of the precipice on which he was standing, and over which he might at any moment plunge. That he had been strongly moved was very evident. It was not possible for him to look on the wrecked and ruined family of the old merchant, or to contemplate the awful tragedy which had been enacted, without a shudder at the thought of such a catastrophe reaching his own home. He was dallying with the devil of drink, who might at any moment bind him hand and foot, as he had once before bound him, and make him again the creature of his will.

It was about eight o'clock in the evening, two

days after the trial, that I was informed by a servant that a lady was in the parlor and wished to see me. She had not given her name. On going down I was met by Mrs. Granger. I saw the worst at a single glance. It was written, alas! too plainly in her face.

"I would like to have some talk with you, Mr. Lyon," she said. Her voice was low and steady; but I could detect an under thrill of feeling held down by a strong effort.

"I am entirely at your service," I replied, using the first form of speech that came into my mind. "And if I can be of any use to you, command me freely."

"You know about my husband." The firmness went out of her voice.

"What about him?" I had neither seen him nor heard anything in regard to him since the day of the trial.

"Haven't you heard?"

"Heard what, Mrs. Granger?"

"That he has—" She could not finish the sentence; her voice breaking in a sob, that was followed by a low, shivering cry.

"I am pained beyond measure to hear of this," said I. "How long has it been?"

"It has been coming on him for two or three months past, and I've been in awful dread. Little by little, day by day, his old appetite has gained strength. What the end must be, I knew too well."

"I saw him in court on the day of that murder trial. He was all right then."

"He has never been right since. It was late in the evening before he came home. His condition I will not describe." Tears, in large drops, were falling over her face.

"Has he been to his office since?"

"I think not," was answered. "He goes out in the morning, and does not return until late at night. If I ask him a question, or venture a word of remonstrance, he gets angry. Oh! sir; this must not go on. I am helpless. He will hear nothing and bear nothing from me. It was not so once. But you are his friend, Mr. Lyon. He has great respect for you; and I know of no one who has more influence over him."

"Any and everything in my power shall be done," I replied. "My regret is that I did not know of this earlier." I let more of hope and encouragement go into my voice than I really felt.

"Oh! sir. If you will only do your best for him." The poor wife looked at me with a pleading face.

"Is he at home now?" I asked.

"Oh, no, no. I haven't seen him since morning, and it may be after midnight before he returns. Oh! isn't it dreadful, dreadful, Mr. Lyon, the way this fearful appetite takes hold of a man! I thought, when he told me about that poor, old, broken-down merchant, who, in a fit of drunken insanity, had killed his wife, and whom he had to defend on a

8

charge of murder, that he would take the terrible lesson to heart. The case had drawn largely on his sympathies, and his pity was great for the daughters who were to appear in court and give evidence that might send their father to the gallows. I have rarely known a case to affect him so much. And to think, Mr. Lyon, that he should go from this trial, with all its warning incidents fresh in his mind, and give himself into the power of the very agency which had wrought so fearful a ruin that the very sight of it sent a shudder through his soul! There is something awful and mysterious in all this, sir! It passes my comprehension."

"And not yours only, ma'am. It is one of the dark problems men find it difficult to explain. Into all hurtful and disorderly things, evil forces seem to flow with an intenser life than into things innocent and orderly. There is violence, aggression, destruction or slavery in every evil agency. And it is never satisfied under any limitation; it must have complete mastery, or work complete ruin."

"A terrible thought!" Mrs. Granger shivered as she spoke.

"Will you try to find him to-night?" she asked, a moment afterwards.

"Yes. I will go in search of him at once."

She arose to depart.

"Wait for a moment; I will see you home first."

"No, no, Mr. Lyon. I'm not afraid. Don't lose

an instant. I want my husband found as soon as possible."

And she went quickly from the room, passing into the street before I could make another effort to detain her.

CHAPTER IX.

I WAS not successful in my search for Mr. Granger, though I visited many of the principal saloons, and met with several persons who knew him; but no one whom I questioned had seen him during the night. It was nearly twelve o'clock when I gave up the search. I was debating with myself whether to return to my own residence or to go, even at this late hour, and ascertain whether he were at home or not, when, on passing a small court in which a tavern was located, a sudden sound of angry voices struck my ears. As I paused I saw a man thrust out of this tavern with violence. He fell with a dull, heavy sound on the pavement; and was kicked as he fell. The door shut in an instant afterwards, and the man was left to all appearance unconscious or dead.

I found a policeman in the next block, and after giving information as to what I had seen, was turning to leave him, when he detained me, saying that if the man had received any serious injuries I might be wanted as a witness. I took out a card, and writing my address on it, asked if that were sufficient. He said yes. I had gone from him for only a few paces when the possibility that the man I had seen might be Granger flashed through my mind, arrest-

"He fell with a dull, heavy sound on the pavement, and was kicked as he fell."—*Page 116.*

ing my steps, and causing me to turn about and hurry back to the scene of the outrage of which I had been a spectator. The policeman was trying to raise the man from the ground; but the latter was either so stupified by drink, or so stunned by his fall on the pavement, as to be unconscious of any effort to arouse him. What was my pain and horror to see, as the face was turned to the light, the features of Alexander Granger. There was a great bruise on one of his temples from which drops of blood were creeping out; and his mouth was swollen as from a blow, and bleeding.

By this time two or three men had come out of the saloon; and I noticed that one of them, on seeing the policeman, dropped quietly from the court and disappeared around the corner. The others assisted to bear the unconscious man into the tavern. It was a low, vile place; and the keeper a vicious-looking fellow, in whose eyes you saw the cruel instincts of a wild beast. He it was, as we learned, who had thrust Granger out; but he denied having kicked him as he fell. The cause for this violence was a drunken dispute. An argument about something had arisen, and the brutal logic of the bully had been used against the lawyer, who was too much under the power of drink for prudent self-restraint. His words had been answered by blows; and the blows had been very hard.

A physician was sent for, but before his arrival, Granger had partially regained his consciousness.

An examination of the wound on his head showed nothing very serious. His mouth, however, had become dreadfully swollen; and the upper lip exhibited so bad a cut that it had to be closed with a few stitches and bands of adhesive plaster.

"There's a very sharp pain just here, doctor," said Granger, after the lip had been dressed, placing his hand to his side as he spoke. "I wish you'd see what it means. There's something wrong, I'm afraid."

"Wrong! I should think there was," replied the doctor, as soon as he had made an examination. "Here's a rib broken!"

A groan escaped the lips of the suffering man. Increasing pain was lifting him out of his drunken stupor.

"He had better be taken home at once," said the doctor. "I cannot attempt to set the broken bone here."

"Oh, no. Don't take me home!" Granger answered, quickly. "The station-house. Anywhere. But not home." His countenance was strongly agitated.

"To my house, then," I said.

"No! no! no! It's considerate of you, Mr. Lyon, but I will not be taken into any gentleman's house while in this condition. Why can't the bone be set here?"

"For reasons I will not attempt to explain," said the doctor, speaking with decision. "I think, sir," addressing me, "that you had better order a carriage and have him removed to his own house. I will accompany you, or you can send for his family physician. In any case, take him home. The fracture is, I fear, a bad one, and will require careful treatment."

Another groan came from Granger's lips. "If I were only dead!" he ejaculated.

A carriage was sent for. While waiting for it to come, Granger sat with closed eyes; his face now almost deathly pale, and with beads of sweat standing all over it. He made no resistance when the carriage arrived, and entered it in silence, accompanied by the doctor, a policeman and myself.

We were some ten or twelve blocks from his residence, and it took over twenty minutes to make the distance, as the driving had to be very slow. When we had come within a few hundred yards of his dwelling, he asked to have the carriage stopped for a few minutes until I could go and break the news.

Leaving the carriage, I went rapidly in the direction of his house. A light was burning in one of the upper windows. What should I say? How should I break this news to his poor, waiting wife? As I drew near, I noticed a shadow on the wall of the chamber in which the light was burning; a moving shadow as of one restlessly walking the floor. As the sound of my hurrying feet broke the silence I saw the shadow grow still for a moment, and then quickly disappear. I had scarcely rung the bell ere the door was drawn swiftly open, and Mrs. Granger's pale, almost rigid face met mine.

"Mr. Granger! What of him? Oh! Mr. Lyon, have you found him?" She had caught hold of me in her eagerness and suspense.

"Yes, yes. I have found him," I replied.

"But where is he? Why didn't he come home with you?"

"He is coming. He will be here in a little while," I said, trying to speak in a voice that would allay her excitement.

"In a little while! What's the matter, Mr. Lyon? Don't deceive me! Don't keep anything back! Am I wanted?"

I felt her hand close on my arm with a tight grip.

"No—no, Mrs. Granger. You are frightened for nothing. You are not wanted. Your husband will be home in a few minutes. I came first to tell you and relieve your mind."

At this moment the sound of approaching wheels was heard.

"Is that Mr. Granger?" she asked, her face as white as ashes.

"Yes," I replied.

I saw that the whole truth had not occurred to her. She stood still, waiting until the slow-moving carriage was at the door, and not stirring until she saw the policeman step first to the pavement. Then there was a start and a repressed cry. Next came the doctor, and then, with the help of the policeman, Granger was assisted from the carriage. It was too dark for his wife to see his face until the light of the entry-lamp fell upon it as he was supported up the steps to the door.

She did not faint, nor cry out in wild terror as she saw that bruised, pain-stricken face; but, as if she had received a blow, staggered back a step or two, but quickly recovered herself, coming forward and saying, breathlessly, and in a hoarse whisper: "What is it? What's the matter?"

"Nothing very serious," the doctor answered. "Your husband has had a fall, and there's a rib broken. But he'll be all right in a short time. We must get him up to his own room with as little delay as possible."

In a moment all signs of agitation disappeared.

"This way," said the wife, calmly, moving back along the hall, and then going lightly up-stairs and leading the way to the chamber in front. How tender and pitiful she was in every word and act; yet with no sign of weakness. Love and duty had lifted her into a sphere of calm self-possession.

I wondered as I observed her that night, moving about with a quiet, almost cheerful bearing, acting in concert with the doctor, ministering to her husband, giving and taking directions with the coolness and self-poise of an experienced nurse, what it meant? I had expected a painful scene, with outbursts of uncontrollable mental anguish; and my surprise was, therefore, the greater at what I saw.

It was between two and three o'clock before I left Mr. Granger. By this time the broken bone had been properly set, and he was not only free from pain but sleeping quietly.

I did not see him for several days, though I made frequent inquiries, and learned that he was doing well. A brief notice of the assault from which he had suffered found its way into the newspapers, but his name was not mentioned. No effort was made to arrest and punish his assailant, for that would have been to make his own disgrace public.

It was nearly a week afterwards that I received a note, asking me to call upon him. He was greatly changed, and looked broken, subdued and troubled. His lip was still considerably swollen and very sore. The wound had not healed readily, and the probabilities were that a disfiguring scar would be left. He held my hand tightly for some moments before speaking.

"I want to have another talk with you, Lyon," he said, his voice trembling a little. "I shall be out again soon, and then—" He stopped, with a strong movement of feeling in his face. "And then? God help me, Lyon! Is there no hope—no escape—no way of safety?"

His agitation increased. I did not reply. What could I say? He saw the doubt in my face.

"There must be help somewhere. Men *are* saved from this curse."

"A man may be saved from any evil if he will," I replied. "But if he will not, as I have said to you many times, even God cannot save him. If you had kept away from the enemy's ground, he could never have enslaved you again. You were free to pass over or to remain within the lines of safety. Of your own will you passed over."

"Poor, weak fool!" he murmured, bitterly. "Poor, silly moth, flying into the candle!"

"Let the days of weakness and folly pass forever. Let there be no more parleyings with the enemy— no more venturing upon his domain."

He shook his head gloomily.

"Of what value are all my good resolutions? Will they save me in the future any more than they have saved me in the past? Are they stronger to-day than they were last year or the year before? There must be something more, Mr. Lyon. Something stronger to lean on, or I am lost!"

"Lean on God," I answered. "Look to Him."

There was no brightening of his face.

"God helps those who try to get free from the sin that doth so easily beset them."

"Does He? Haven't I tried? Doesn't He know that I have tried? But where is the help?"

"It cannot come to you except in your reasserted manhood; and it will come if you stand fast in that manhood. God's strength will be your strength."

He sighed heavily.

"Mr. Gross was here yesterday, and I had a long talk with him about the New York Asylum at Binghampton. He thinks very favorably of the course pursued there, and spoke of several cases where patients have come home radically cured. He promised to send me the last report of the superintendent. If I thought any good would come of it, I'd drop business and everything else and go under treatment there."

I said nothing to discourage the idea. There might be influences brought to bear upon him at this institution which would help to give him the mastery over himself. I could not tell.

At a subsequent visit, I found that the promised report had come into his hands, and that his mind was fully made up to leave for Binghampton as soon as he was able to travel, and spend as long a time there as the resident physician and superintendent thought his case required.

"It is a disease," he said, as we talked the matter over; "and as clearly defined as any other disease; and, moreover, as subject to remedial agencies. The best minds in the medical profession have given to this disease a most careful study, and it is known what organs are affected by it, and the exact character of the affection. Its treatment is based on true scientific and pathological principles, and so conducted as to give the patient a just knowledge of the means whereby he may retain his health after a cure has been made. He is not left to grope in the dark, every moment in danger of falling over some unseen stumbling-block which may have been cast in his way."

I did not share in the new hope which had come to Mr. Granger, but was careful not to offer a word of discouragement. There might, as I have said, be influences brought to bear upon him at the asylum which would prove lasting. It was worth the trial at least.

And the trial was made. Four months were spent by Mr. Granger at the institution in Binghampton, where the treatment for intemperance as a disease was at the time up to the highest skill and intelligence of the medical profession. The treatment was moral as well as hygienic and sanatory. The first thing gained for the patient was his removal from the tainted atmosphere of common society, in which are perpetually floating the germs of the disease from which he was suffering. This was a most important gain, for it took him out of the region of exciting causes. His next gain was in the sanatory care and treatment given by the institution to its patients, through which a steady return to sound physical health was secured. Supplementing this was a thoroughly intelligent hygienic system, through which the health so regained was steadily improved and strengthened.

The moral and religious influences under which he came were of the most salutary kind. Free from the morbid action of alcohol on the brain, his intellect and moral perceptions were clear once more. He could see and feel with a new intensity the obligations that were resting upon him as a man, and the awful responsibility to which he must be held if he did not keep them. There was a quickening of his higher, purer and better feelings—of honor, and a sense of duty—of all the tender social affections. Love for his wife and children, and shame and sorrow for the wrong and suffering he had brought upon them, grew deeper and deeper as the cure went on. He wrote to me several times while in the institution, and his letters were of the most satisfactory character. He had gained wonderfully in health, and felt, he said, no desire for alcohol whatever, and was sure that he should never touch it again.

In the first letter that I received from him, he spoke of the incidents attendant on his arrival at the institution. I give a portion of this letter:

"On the second day," he wrote, "as I was sitting by myself, feeling strange and ill at ease, a little, old man, with a large head, clear blue eyes, and a kind, cheery face, came into the parlor, and seeing me, bowed with a courtly air, and said a pleasant 'Good morning.' My response was somewhat cold and distant, for I was greatly depressed in spirits, and could not rally myself on the instant. He passed through, and as he left the room I felt my heart going out, as it were, after him. In about ten minutes he came back, and, drawing a chair, sat down by me, with the remark, 'This is one of our perfect days. Have you noticed the peculiar softness of the sky?' I tried to rouse myself to meet, in a becoming way, his kind advances; but did it, I fear, almost ungraciously. It was only a little while, however, before the frank and genial warmth of his manner had completely won me, and I found myself talking with him as with a pleasant friend. Almost before I knew it, he had led me to speak of myself, and of my past life. There was about him something that inspired confidence. I felt that no idle sentiment of curiosity, but a genuine interest in my welfare, had drawn him towards me, and that he was seeking to gain my friendly feelings, that he might do me good. He had not spoken half a dozen sentences before I recognized in him a man of culture, and saw in his bearing the true grace of a courtly gentleman. It was not long before we were walking the floor of the parlor, his arm drawn within that of mine, deeply engaged in a conversation, which we kept up for over an hour. At its close, I felt that I had found a new friend, as it has proved, for this quiet, intelligent, refined and gentlemanly old man is none other than our chaplain."

Again he wrote: "In Dr. Bush, our chaplain, about whom I spoke in one of my letters, we have a man of rare fitness for the office he holds in this institution. I never pass an hour with him without feeling stronger for the interview. He said to me, a day or two ago, 'In God and good health lie your only help and sure dependence. You must keep the body sound, avoid all dangers, and take no risks. With regular living, and healthy surroundings, and a mind full of faith and hope in spiritual realities, this sad disorder, with which you have been afflicted, will, in time, die out.' In his unobtrusive and wise way, he moves about among the patients, holding them in conversation by such themes as touch their tastes and habits of thinking most readily; but always at some point turning their thoughts to spiritual things, and pointing them to Christ as their surest refuge. He has great influence over all who are here, and there are some who appear to rest on, and cling to him as if all the strength they were receiving actually came through his agency. The more I see and know of him, and the more I talk with him, the stronger grows my conviction, that the saving power of the work that is being done here is largely due to the influence this good man has with the inmates."

In a letter written nearly two months after he entered the asylum, Mr. Granger said:

"I had a long talk with our chaplain yesterday, and he related many deeply interesting incidents connected with his office in the institution. He has a large correspondence, I find, with persons who have been patients here; and his influence with many of them is still very strong. He encourages them to write to him freely, and to tell him about their surroundings and peculiar trials and temptations, in order that he may send helpful advice and wise counsel, if there should be need therefor. I notice that while he speaks minutely of cases, he rarely mentions names. But I refer to him now because of some things which he said that reminded me of a conversation I had with you. The line of thought he pursued was very similar to yours, though some of his premises and conclusions were different. 'All of our power to resist temptation and to live true and orderly lives,' he said, 'comes from God. The gift of strength is from above; the will to use it lies within ourselves. If we will not use this strength, God cannot help us in times of difficulty, nor save us in times of danger. But, into our right endeavor, if it be resolutely made, will come a divine power that shall enable us to stand as a rock, though the floods of temptation beat never so strongly against us. And here, my friend,' he added, laying his hand upon me, and speaking with great earnestness, ' let me impress upon you this thought, that it is only in the maintenance of true order in our natural and physical lives that we come into such a relation to spiritual laws and forces that they can protect and save us. A true spiritual life cannot be established in any one so long as his natural life remains in disorder. If you want God's help in the new life you are now living, you must, while asking spiritual aid, do your part in the work of establishing sound physical health. Praying will avail nothing if you do not this also. When you go away from here you must make it a religious duty to avoid over-strain in your work, and the consequent nervous exhaustion that will surely follow. All the laws of physical and moral health must be strictly observed; and you must be especially watchful lest you get over, unaware, upon the enemy's ground. If duty calls you there, go with armor and sword, and you will find no armor so impenetrable, and no sword so keen and effective, as the armor of God's Holy Word, and the truths that lie sheathed in its precious sentences. Use these when the tempter assaults you, and he will turn and flee.' You can see how good and helpful all this is. 'Right thinking is one of the surest ways to right acting,' we often hear him say. 'If men would go right, they must know right,' is another of his apt sentences. And he never tires in his efforts to supplement the medical, social, sanatory and moral agencies of cure that are so effective in many cases under treatment here, with the soundest common sense advice, and the tenderest, most heart-searching and deeply solemn ministrations of a devoted spiritual friend and teacher."

At the end of three months, Granger considered his cure so complete that he wished to return home and resume the practice of his profession, which was suffering greatly on account of his absence. In this he was opposed by the superintendent, who urged him to remain longer; in fact, not to think of leaving the institution until he had remained there for at least six months. The superintendent understood his case better than he understood it himself, and knew that he was very far from being cured. Treating intemperance as a disease of the physical organism, manifesting itself in a species of moral insanity, and understanding enough of the pathology of drunkenness to know that it wrought changes of condition of singular permanency, and left a most remarkable sensitiveness to exciting causes, he understood the great value of time in the work of strengthening the system, so that it might, when exposed to assault, be able to resist the encroachments of disease. But he was not able to induce Mr. Granger to remain at the institution for a longer time than four months.

I met him soon after his return home. Four months under the new influences to which he had been subjected had wrought in him a marked change. I had never seen him in better physical health. His eyes were strong and bright, his complexion clear, his muscles round and tense. You saw that life, mental and physical, had gained a higher strength.

"I'm a new man, Lyon," said he, confidently, as he grasped my hand at our first meeting. "A new man," he repeated, "morally, mentally and physically. The lost has been found; the sick man restored to health; the dead is alive again."

There was a certain overglow of enthusiasm about him to which I could not heartily respond. He observed this, saying: "Wait and see, my friend. This isn't the old, sick, miserable body that I took away, with its relaxed pores standing open to drink in every disease that floated in the air. Here is healthy blood, and firm flesh, and high vital action; and what is more, reason and will have regained strength and dominion. I have found my lost manhood."

"And may God give you the strength to keep it," I made answer, speaking from a conviction which I could not repress, that only in God's help was there any sure hope for this man.

"He has given it already," he replied. "And I am taking it and using it. He is always giving; and we faint and fall by the way only because we do not take of the measure we need. This is your doctrine, I believe, Mr. Lyon."

"Yes," I returned, but not with any heartiness of manner.

"Not skeptical here, I trust," said Granger, with a slight lifting of his eyebrows.

"No. All our strength must come from God. In Him we live and move and have our being. The only question is, how are we to get this strength? And I will confess to you, Mr. Granger, that my mind is not so well settled on this point as it was a year or two ago. I had great faith in a man's will then. It is weaker now. And, if I must say it, out of your experience has come many of my doubts and questionings."

"Indeed." A shade of surprise in his manner.

"You remember that turning over of a new leaf a long time ago, and what Mr. Stannard said to you in regard to the writing thereon? About the 'I will not,' and 'By the help of God?'"

"Yes."

"And how I said that we received God's help only when we made an effort to do the right. That His strength flowed then into our endeavor, and only then?"

"Yes; and you said the truth."

"But you did not find it so, Mr. Granger."

A deeper shade of surprise on his face. "I did not use the strength. That was all."

"Why not?"

"The will failed, I suppose."

"Ah! There it is. The will to take the strength was lacking."

"Yes." A falling away from its firmness in his voice.

"I've thought a great deal about this in the last few months, Granger, and I'm afraid there's some error in my reasoning about God's ways with man. That in our efforts to do right, or resist evil, a divine strength sufficient for our day will not always come. It seems to me that it ought to come; but does it come? What is your experience?"

"I have had the strength to resist, as you know, and have stood in that strength for long periods of time," he answered.

"True; but it failed at last. Now God's power

should never fail; and I have a conviction that it never does fail. What then?"

He did not answer me.

"There is one sphere of safety into which I think it will be wise for you to come," said I.

"What is that?" he asked.

"The sphere of the church."

There was no warm response in his face.

"So far as my observation goes," he replied, "church people are no better than others."

"More the shame for them," I answered. "But it is possible that your observation in this direction has been limited."

"Well, as you know, I've never taken much to religion. I'm not one of that kind. I go to church with my wife occasionally, but never get much interested. Now and then I hear a sermon that sets me to thinking; but, for the most part, I find it dull work."

"I inferred, from some things said in your letters, that you had become deeply impressed with the value and necessity of divine help," said I. "Did not Mr. Bush, the chaplain of whom you spoke so warmly, urge you to join some church, and to come within the sphere of its saving influences?"

"Oh, yes. He spoke to me with great earnestness on this very subject. But a man may trust in God, even though he be not a church-member. Christianity means justice, and honor, and right living; and I find as much of this outside as inside of the churches."

"The Church," I replied, "has been established by God. It is His kingdom on the earth; and its laws are divine truths revealed to us in Scripture. These laws, as you know, are very pure, and based on love to God and the neighbor. It is nothing against the Church that some of its members do not comprehend the spirit and meaning of its laws; nor live in a true conformity thereto; and nothing against its power to protect us from evil, if we come within the sphere of its influence."

"You may be right in all that, Mr. Lyon; are right, no doubt; and I intend going to church with my family more regularly than heretofore."

"Do so by all means. I had a long talk with Mr. Stannard only last week on this very subject of church-going; and one or two things that he said have made a strong impression on my mind."

"Mr. Stannard is one of the best men I ever knew. If all professing Christians squared their lives by their doctrines as he does, Christianity would mean something," remarked Granger. "What did he say?"

"If for no other reason, he said, we should go to church to hear the reading of the Bible."

"We may read the Bible at home, if we will," Granger replied.

"True; if we will," I returned.

"And, then," he rejoined, "you know one may read the Bible every day, and a dozen times a day for that matter, and it will do him no good unless he obey its precepts."

"A knowledge of the law must go before obedience. This is as true of divine as of human laws. But I wish to bring to your attention one or two things said by Mr. Stannard in regard to the power of Holy Scripture, and the sphere of safety into which it must bring every one who receives it into his thought reverently, and lets it dwell there. They were new to me. Being the Word of God, the presence of any portion thereof in the thought, must, he said, bring, in a certain sense, God within us, and consequently nearer with His divine power to the enemies of our souls who are ever seeking to gain dominion over us; so enabling Him to fight in and for us by the power of His Word."

Granger sat reflecting on this for a considerable time.

"If that be so," he said, at length, "there is a saving power in the Bible beyond what I had thought."

"And a use in going to church beyond what you and I had imagined."

"Yes."

"For the reading of the Bible makes up a portion of the services, and the sphere of reverence and attention which we find in worshipping assemblies adjusts the mind to hearing and opens it to deeper impressions. The Word gets a firmer hold upon us and remains longer with us. We take it away in our memories; and when in temptation, can bring it out therefrom as a weapon—the sword of the Spirit—with which to fight our enemies.

"Mr. Stannard said," I continued, "that God's Holy Word is sufficient for us under any circumstances of temptation; and that we have only to resist the devil as our Saviour resisted when led of him into the wilderness to be tempted, and he will depart from us."

"How did He resist?" asked Mr. Granger.

"By the utterance of truth from Scripture; and the power of this Divine Word was so great that the devil could not stand before it."

"Yes, that is so. 'It is written,' was the Lord's answer. I never thought of its meaning before."

"In the very way that strength for victory came to Him as He met the hosts of hell on the plane of His infirm human nature, will it come to us and give us the victory also, said Mr. Stannard. From this view of the case, the value of public worship is evident, and I am sure, Mr. Granger, that you will stand safer within than without the sphere of the church."

"You may be right," he answered. "Nay, I am sure you are right. I must see Mr. Stannard and have a talk with him. He is one of the men in whom I believe."

CHAPTER X.

FOR awhile Granger went regularly to church; but after a few months his place in the family pew was often vacant.

"I don't see you at church as much as usual," said I, on meeting him one day.

"Well—no," he replied, speaking with some hesitation of manner, "and I don't know that I've any valid excuse for staying away. But, the fact is, Mr. —— is so intolerably dull and prosy, I get tired to death. He doesn't seem to think at all; but just to open his mouth and let what happens to be in his memory come out. Old stereotyped forms of speech, and sentences that mean anything or nothing as you choose to interpret them, make up the staple of his sermons. You don't get an advanced idea from him once in a month."

"Go somewhere else. To hear Mr. ——, for instance. But don't stay away from church."

"I've been to hear Mr. —— a number of times. But one tires of mere picture-painting, though the artist have rare skill in his line. He says many beautiful things in an eloquent way; and so do the orators and the poets. But a poor, tired and tempted soul will get little help from his preaching. It is pleasing and popular; but after that is said, about all is said. Ah, my friend!" his brows drew closely together, and his voice fell to a serious tone, "your churches and your preaching are all well enough for easy-going, good sort of people, with a kind of natural heavenward drift; but they don't do much in the way of getting hold of us restless, challenging, hardened fellows, who want to know about the reason of things; and who, unhappily, are in the drag of a current that is bearing us down, down, down, it may be, to eternal ruin!"

There came a stern, almost angry expression into his face.

"You mustn't feel in that way Granger. It isn't good. The preachers may not be all we could wish; but they are, for the most part, sincere men, and in the effort to do the best they can for the salvation of souls."

"Oh, yes. No doubt of it. But it rarely happens that I find one who can feed my hunger."

Was it his own fault or the fault of the preacher? Was he not hungering again for the flesh-pots of Egypt, and loathing the manna and the quails? I had my fears. What had been done for him during his four months at the asylum? It was a question of momentous interest. Had there been a cure, or only a temporary suspension of diseased action? Did he not stand in as much danger to-day as before he placed himself under treatment? Was not his fall again only a matter of time?

These questions pressed themselves on my mind and gave me much concern. Think as closely and as earnestly as I could on the subject, I was not able to see wherein lay his immunity. He was back once more in an atmosphere tainted with disease. Predisposition had not been eradicated, and old exciting causes were acting again. As time went on, and the fine health he had brought home with him from the asylum gave place to the exhausted nervous condition which is sure, sooner or later, to follow excessive devotion to business, would not the old hunger for stimulants arouse itself and become irresistible?

The more I considered this view of the case, the more my concern increased; and I felt that something far more radical must be done for Granger than had yet been accomplished, ere his reform was a thing assured. His drifting away from church influences was, I feared, only an indication of the awakening of old desires, and the turning of his thoughts downward to the things in which they had once found gratification.

I was much relieved on the Sunday following to see Granger in church. He sat for most of the time during the services in an attentive attitude; and it struck me that his manner was unusually subdued and serious. I noticed that while a particular lesson from Scripture was read, that his eyes were not taken from the clergyman for a single moment. It was the one hundred and twenty-first Psalm: "I will lift up my eyes unto the hills, from whence cometh my help. My help cometh from the Lord, which made heaven and earth. He will not suffer thy foot to be moved: he that keepeth thee will not slumber. Behold, he that keepeth Israel shall neither slumber nor sleep. The Lord is thy keeper: the Lord is thy shade upon the right hand. The sun shall not smite thee by day, nor the moon by night. The Lord shall preserve thee from all evil: He shall preserve thy soul. The Lord shall preserve thy going out and thy coming in from this time forth, and even forever more."

Other passages read or chanted during the services, seemed as if especially designed to meet his case, and lead him to put a higher trust in God. "They that trust in the Lord shall be as Mount Zion, which cannot be removed, but abideth forever. As the mountains are round about Jerusalem, so the Lord is round about His people from henceforth even forever." "The Lord is nigh unto all them that call upon Him, to all that call upon Him in truth. He will fulfil the desire of them that fear Him: He also will hear their cry, and will save them." "Like as a father pitieth his children, so the Lord pitieth them that fear Him. For He knoweth our frame; He remembereth that we are dust."

I did not get an opportunity to speak to Granger after church, but I was struck with the seriousness of his face as he passed along the aisle. His eyes were cast down, and he did not notice any one as he moved with the crowd.

"What do you think of Granger's case?" I asked of Mr. Stannard, not long after this.

"I greatly fear for him," was replied.

"He has kept himself straight since his return from the asylum."

"Yes; but the saving power of such institutions has its limits. They are good as far as they go, and have helped to restore many men to good citizenship. I say nothing against them. I wish their number were increased. But there are cases in which they rarely, if ever, make permanent cures; and Granger's is one of them. The appetite for drink has taken too deep a hold. For him, I fear, there is no help in man. Only God can save him; and if he does not go to God, humbly and prayerfully, his case is next to hopeless."

"I am sorry you take so gloomy a view of the matter, Mr. Stannard. Will not God help him unless he pray to Him?"

"Can He help him if he does not?"

"I don't know. There's something just here that I do not clearly understand."

"Can a mother feed her babe, though her breast be full, if it turn its mouth away? It may be fainting with hunger, and the mother's heart may be full of love and pity, but if it will not touch the paps what can she do? Prayer is not an arbitrary service, but an attitude of the soul. A simple turning of the spirit, conscious of its own weakness and sinfulness, to the source of all goodness and strength, and accepting what God is ever seeking to give; but which He can only give to those who truly desire to receive. God is always coming to us and seeking to save us; but unless we turn to Him, and look to Him, our rescue is impossible. It is in ourselves that we are lost; and if we will not come out of ourselves, wherein are all our pains and desolations, how can God save us?"

"I don't know. The way ought to be made very plain and easy."

"It is plain and easy. Only to turn from self to God. Only to take the hand that is forever reaching down. Only to ask and receive," Mr. Stannard replied. "God cannot give to those who will not take."

"Yes, yes; all doubtless true. But how shall one turn from self to God? How grasp the hand that is forever reaching down? How take what God perpetually desires to give?"

"Only when a man feels that in and of himself he can do nothing, and that unless help come from above he must perish, can he really turn from self to God. Before that he trusts in his own strength; and so long as he does this, divine strength cannot be given."

"Why not?"

"Can a man use what he will not take? So long as one trusts in himself, he does not use the strength of another."

"And so, until a man feel this utter helplessness, God will not reach down and save him?" said I.

"Of what avail is God's offered hand if the man will not take it? Of God's strength if the man will not use it? Not until he is in utter despair of himself does he really accept help from above. Until then he trusts to an arm of flesh, and not to the all-conquering and all-sustaining power of God. In the very moment that a man comes into this state of despair and lifts thought and desire heavenward, he prays effectually; takes hold of God; gets his feet upon a rock; comes within the sphere of Divine protection; is saved from the power of his enemies. Forever saved? Yes, if he keeps his hold upon God and remains within the sphere of His divine protection. How shall he maintain this hold? Only through steady looking and right living. He must cease to do evil, and learn to do well. Must make the laws of God the laws of his life. If this be not done God cannot make him to dwell in safety."

"For a man like Granger, you think, there is no security but in the church?"

"Unless he dwell in God, he cannot dwell secure; and the church is God's kingdom on the earth."

"Does not Scripture say that the kingdom of God is within us?"

"Yes. God's kingdom is a spiritual kingdom, and can have no real existence but in the souls of men. But it is internal and external, because man is internal and external; and has its internal sanctities as well as it external ceremonials and forms of worship. The laws of this kingdom are the precepts of the Holy Word; and only those who keep these precepts in the heart and life are really the subjects of this kingdom. All such are free from the power of hell; for God dwells in them and around them."

"Must, then, a man join the church to come into God's kingdom?"

"I think he will find that kingdom by the way of a church door more easily than in any other way. We are none of us so strong that we can afford to do without the help that comes from association with our fellow-men. God did not make us to stand alone, but in mutual dependence. This is as true in spiritual as in natural things. And so the church to be a power with men must be external as well as internal."

"You may be right about all this," I made answer. "Certainly I should feel more confidence in Granger's reformation if I knew that he was oftener at church. I was glad to see him there last Sunday. But I have felt more concerned for him since then than usual. The reason may appear to you a little strange."

"What is it?"

"I have never seen his face so serious, nor his manner so absorbed, as they were during the services of the morning. While the lessons from Scripture were read, his eyes were scarcely turned for an instant away from the minister. In all the church there was not, apparently, a more deeply interested listener."

"A reason for hope rather than concern," said Mr. Stannard.

"That depends on the cause of this unusual sobriety of demeanor," I answered. "My thought has been, that the long repressed appetite is beginning to assault him once more; and that, day by day, the conviction is becoming stronger and stronger in his mind that it will, sooner or later, acquire the mastery again. His coming to church, and especially his demeanor at church, may be the signs of his sense of weakness and danger; an effort to gain help from higher influences—a half-desperate reaching out of his hands in the dark for something to which he may cling when the waters that are moving upon him rise higher and gain the force of a resistless flood."

"If this be so he is turning to the Strong for strength, and seeking help where it can alone be found."

"But don't you see, that if this be so, Mr. Stannard, how desperate the case may be? The floods are rising against him. He feels that his strength is going. He is half-blind—half-desperate. Will he take hold of God? If not, what then? Ah! sir, I cannot but feel a low shiver of suspense as I realize, in thought, this awful crisis for a human soul."

"In which it has only to cry out as it turns from self to God; 'Save, Lord, or I perish!' to be lifted from the flood."

"But if it fail in this? If it cannot, or will not?"

"There is no such thing as cannot for a tried and tempted soul. It can look to God, and take hold of God, if it will."

"But," I said, pressing the question, "if it will not?"

The light went out of Mr. Stannard's face and it grew very sober.

"It was because of this 'I will not,'" he replied, "that the Lord, in His tender mercy, bowed the heavens and came down into our very debased humanity, that we might see Him as a Divine Man, and feel the warmth of His compassion, and know Him as our friend and Saviour, and that He might inspire in us the 'I will,' by which He could lift us back again into the pure and happy life which we had lost."

"But if this cannot now be inspired into the soul of Mr. Granger," said I, "what then? Must he fall in his hour of trial and darkness?"

"If the external strength which he has acquired be not sufficient for him—the considerations of honor and good citizenship; of worldly ambition and prosperity; of love and regard for his wife and children; of personal well-being and happiness,—and he will not take God's strength instead, what shall save him? I know not. But let us hope that he is going to God in the right way. I believe that he is."

"Ah! if one could know! I feel that another great crisis has come to our friend. If he should not pass it safely, he may fall never to rise again."

"He can never fall so low," was answered, "that God's love will not be still reaching down and seeking to save him. All day long He will stretch out His hands to him; all day long call after him in tones of love and compassion, 'Son, give me thy heart!' and it will not matter how low he may fall, nor how far away he may wander into the desert of sin and shame, the moment he hearkens to that voice and turns from himself to God, he will be in the fold of safety. It is a good thing for Granger that he is feeling his own helplessness, and beginning to look for help from above. He may not find it now, because he may not be ready to give his heart to God; but if, trusting in his own strength, he should fall again, God will not forsake him, but still go after him, and it may be find him so weak, and helpless, and despairing, that he will no longer hold back, but throw himself into the loving arms of his divine Saviour. Then will be born in him a new life from above; and if he live this life he shall never fall again; for it is a heavenly life. Not a mere life of faith and feeling, but of love to God and good will to man, that continually shows itself in a keeping of the commandments in the spirit as well as in the letter."

"It is your belief, then," said I, "that until Mr. Granger becomes a religious man there is very little hope for him?"

"Very little, I fear."

"He must unite himself with the church?"

"It would be better for him. But joining the church will not make him a religious man. That is the effect of an internal change, not of an external relation. There must be a new spiritual birth before there can be a new man. 'Marvel not that I said unto thee, Ye must be born again.'"

"Ah! if we knew just what that meant," I said.

"That which is born of the flesh is flesh," said Mr. Stannard. "Let us rise higher in our thought. The new birth is in the soul. It has been down into the world, where it has gone by way of the senses, and has lived the life of the world, which is a selfish life, and evil because selfish. The more intense this life, the more opposite to the life of Heaven has it become. Now, unless a new life be born in the soul, it can never come into Heaven, which is a state of love to the Lord and the neighbor. How this life is born is the great and important question. Let me make it as clear to your understanding as lies in my power. This new birth is effected by means of Divine truth cast into the mind as a seed, and the new spiritual birth has its beginning in the very moment that a man endeavors earnestly and by the help of God to obey this truth. For to do is to live. If the doing is in obedience to

Divine truth, which teaches that a man shall not only love God, but cease to do evil, then the new man, a weak and almost helpless infant as yet, begins really to live and grow; and the Divine sphere is round about it, and all the powers of Heaven are arrayed for its protection. It is absolutely safe, this new-born child, so long as it takes the sincere milk of the Word, and lives thereby. But in danger the moment it turns itself away therefrom, and attempts to feed on the husks that can only sustain the lower life of selfishness and sin. The spiritual man cannot subsist on these. It must have heavenly food or it will die."

"Then it is not the instantaneous washing and purifying of the old natural man, but the birth of a new spiritual man, which must live and grow until it attain the full stature, as the apostle says, of a man in Christ Jesus?"

"The natural man is for this world. The spiritual man for Heaven. We must come into the Kingdom of Heaven as little children, not as full-grown spiritual men. He called a little child and set him in the midst of them, and said, 'Verily I say unto you, except ye be converted, and become as little children, ye shall not enter into the Kingdom of Heaven.' First a weak child, with the angels that do always behold the face of my Father close about Him; afterwards a strong spiritual man, ruling in righteousness over all the lower things of natural life, and bringing them into heavenly order—establishing the kingdom of God in the natural man, and doing the will of God in the earth as it is done in Heaven."

"Taking this view," I said, "is not the confident state of mind we so often see in young converts one of false security, and attended with great danger? We hear them speak with the assurance of strong men."

"While yet only babes in Christ. Yes, this state is one of false security, and, therefore, its dangers are great. No wonder that so many stumble—that so few keep to their first love. They use strong meat instead of milk; try to lift themselves to the stature of full-grown men, and to walk with long strides; are bold and confident. But being only little children, they fall; having no root themselves, they endure but for a while, and when tribulations and persecutions arise because of the Word, by and by they are offended."

CHAPTER XI.

I HAD left my office a little earlier than usual in the afternoon, and was on my way homeward, when, on turning the corner of a street, I saw Mr. Granger just in advance of me. He was walking slowly, with his head bent slightly forward. Quickening my pace, I soon joined him. As I laid my hand on his arm and spoke, he gave a start, and when I looked into his face I saw the color rising. There was something in his eyes that gave me a feeling of uneasiness. His manner was more repressed than cordial.

We walked together for the space of a few blocks, and then our ways parted. We had not, in our efforts to talk, touched upon any subject in which we found a mutual interest; and therefore our brief intercourse had been marked by constraint. What followed our separation I learned long afterwards, and from the lips of Mr. Granger himself. I give the story in his own words:

"I had been fighting the old appetite desperately," said he; "fighting it for weeks, and being often on the very eve of defeat and surrender. But the awful condition into which I would be cast if I fell into the enemy's power held me to my post. I saw my home desolated, my wife broken-hearted, my children beggared—and I so loved them! I saw myself cast down again, and to a lower depth of misery and degradation than any into which I had yet fallen. The horror that was before me was appalling, and all the while I felt the peril increasing—my enemy growing stronger, and my power of resistance weaker.

"And now it seemed as if all hell were against me. I could not look this way or that—go here nor there, but temptation met me face to face. Men who knew nothing of my past history, and some who knew it too well, invited me to drink. At dinners, at social gatherings, at private interviews with clients, at friendly meetings on the streets and in offices and stores, the glass was offered or the invitation to drink given. I wearied of saying no, and began to feel ashamed of the weakness that so often brought on me a look of surprise when I pushed the extended cup aside. In the street I could not walk for half a square without encountering a saloon which gave to appetite a reminder through the sense of sight or smell. You may think it strange, but I have gone out of my way again and again, in order to avoid passing a certain drinking saloon, the very sight of which, more than any other, quickened my desire for liquor.

"Stronger and stronger became the pressure of the downward current, and my sense of danger greater. I looked this way and that for help, but saw no way of escape. All faith in my own manhood was fast leaving me, and I knew that the time must come when some stronger sweep of the waters would bear me away.

"It was this feeling that drew me to church sometimes. But I went, always, under a kind of protest, and while there too often set my thought against what I heard, instead of opening my mind to the sacred influences of the place. I shall never forget the last Sunday on which I attended worship—I tried to stay away, and made many excuses to myself for remaining at home. But none of them prevailed. As I entered the church doors on that morning, I was conscious of a new feeling. As if I had stepped from an arena where I had been fighting for my life, into a place of rest and safety. My heart was touched and opened. The lessons from the Bible particularly impressed me; and many of the divine words seemed as if spoken for my assurance. I felt, as I had never felt before, that by the help of God I might stand fast; and I resolved to go to Him and ask Him for aid and succor.

"I went out in the afternoon, saying to my wife that I was going to see Mr. Stannard. I wanted to have a talk with this good man about religion and the church, for I had great confidence in him. But I did not do as I intended; and here was my fatal error. When only a short distance from his house, I met a couple of friends riding out, and weakly yielded to their solicitations to go with them for a drive in the Park. As I entered the carriage I was sensible of an opposite impression to that which I had felt in the morning. Then it seemed to me as if I had passed from strife and peril into a place of safety; now, from a sphere of safety into one of danger. But it was too late for me to recede. The carriage was in motion again and I once more adrift on a current too strong for my steadily lessening powers of resistance.

"A drive for an hour in the Park with pleasant friends, and then an invitation to drink at one of the restaurants. I took only ginger ale; but the smell of their stronger liquors was in my nostrils, and I felt an almost irrepressible desire to taste them. The very act of drinking with these friends, though what I took might only be a harmless beverage, had an evil influence on me.

"I would see Mr. Stannard in the evening, I thought, as I entered the carriage; but when evening came, my state of mind had undergone so complete a change, that the very thought of religious things was distasteful. For the two or three days that followed, it seemed as if I could not turn to the right hand nor to the left without temptation. It was not greater than usual, perhaps; only I was weaker and more open to assault. The day at whose close I met you, as I was on my way homeward, had been marked not only by many incidents of warning, but by an unwonted number of solicitations. I was weary and exhausted from incessant conflict;

and what was worse, my mind was losing its balance. I could not hold it to the high considerations of honor, and duty, and love, which had hitherto influenced me. A cloud came down over it. Clear-seeing was gone. I felt only an irresistible craving. It was as if an evil spirit had taken possession of perception and feeling, and held them to a single thought and desire; the thought of liquor and the desire to drink. Was I not for the time insane and irresponsible? Could I help the fatal plunge I made?

"You remember our brief meeting. Scarcely had we parted when a client for whom I was conducting an important suit, laid his hand on me, saying: 'Ah! This is fortunate, Granger. I missed you at your office. Some new facts, of great importance in our case, have come into my possession, and I wished you to have them with as little delay as possible.' He drew his arm in mine and we walked for a short distance, trying to converse. But the noise and confusion of the street interrupted us. As we were passing a drinking saloon, he said: 'Come; we'll get a quiet corner in here, and talk this matter over.' I went with him passively. We found a quiet corner. 'What will you have?' he said. I made a feeble effort to get to my lips the words, 'Nothing for me,' but failed, and in their stead, as if my organs of speech were controlled by another, answered, 'Not particular. Anything you please.' Beer was set before me, and I drank. You know the rest."

His client did not find him at his office on the next morning, nor in the court-room when the trial of his case, which had been opened on the previous day, was continued. The new facts which had been given to Granger were not put in evidence, and the associate counsel had, in his absence, to meet the issue without them. The result proved disastrous— the case was lost. But that was of small consideration in comparison with the loss of the man who had been tempted at the moment when the power to resist was almost gone.

How rapid the fall which came. It was an almost headlong plunge. The whole man seemed to give way. For over two weeks it was a perpetual debauch with drink, and the end came only when the over-strained nerves and organs gave way, and he was prostrated by sickness. His recovery was followed by a speedy relapse into intemperance. As far as could be seen, there was no longer any effort on his part to resist the demon of appetite, or to struggle against the stream that was bearing him down. In every conflict with this demon he had in the end been beaten, and with each new rally there had been loss of strength. What hope of victory in any new battle? He felt that there was none, and weakly abandoned himself to his fate.

Alas for the swift descent! Friends fell away from him. Clients removed their cases from his hands. Business forsook his office. More than half his time was spent in drinking-saloons, or in sleeping off the effects of drunkenness. Scarcely six months had elapsed when, in passing his residence on Spruce Street one day, I saw a bill on the door. The house was for rent. In the following week he moved away, his family dropping again out of the old circles.

Occasionally, after this, I met him on the street. The change in his appearance was sad to witness. Excessive drinking had swollen and distorted his face, robbing it of its fine intelligence. All the fire had gone out of his eyes. Meeting him on one occasion, I took his hand and said: "Granger, my dear man, this is all wrong. You will kill yourself."

A strange gleam shot across his face, and there was a brief disturbance in his manner. Then, with a short laugh, he replied: "All right. The sooner it's over the better."

"No, no. It's all wrong. Come round to my office. I want to talk to you."

"No, thank you. It won't be of any use; and besides, I've an engagement."

"It's never too late to mend," I urged. "Never too late to stop—"

"You don't know anything about it," he said, with some impatience of manner, interrupting me. "When the devil of drink gets you fairly in his clutches, there's small chance left. Good-bye, and God bless you!" There was a break in his voice in the closing sentence.

Turning from me abruptly, he walked away. I heard, not long afterwards, that in order to keep her two younger sisters at school, his oldest daughter, Amy, a beautiful young girl, who made her appearance in society about a year before, had assumed the duties of a teacher in the seminary where they were being educated, and that Mrs. Granger was trying to get music scholars.

Next it was said that Granger had become abusive to his family. I could not believe this, for I knew something of the natural tenderness of his heart, and the strength of his old love for his wife and children. Even while under the influence of drink, I did not believe that he would be anything but personally kind to them. How great, therefore, was my surprise and sorrow, when, a few months later, the fact became known that his wife had left him on account of ill treatment, and was living with her three daughters in the family of a relative.

Granger still had his law office, and was occasionally in court as counsel in some petty larceny or assault and battery case, picking up a fee here and there, and managing to get money enough to supply the demands of his insatiate and steadily increasing appetite. But the time came when even this poor resource failed. When few, if any, were found willing to trust even the most trifling case to a man who might stand up in court on the day of trial so much intoxicated as to be unable to tell on which side of the case he was pleading.

In less than two years from the date of his last relapse into drunkenness, Granger had fallen so low that to get money for drink he would stoop to any meanness or falsehood. All shame, all sense of honor, all regard for the truth, had died out of him. He had become a miserable beggar, making his daily round among the law offices and through the court-rooms, soliciting the loan of a trifle here and a trifle there from old friends and acquaintances, and taking rebuffs, curses, stern rebukes and pitiful remonstrances with but few signs of feeling. Promises of amendment he would make without limit. If the asked-for loan were withheld under the plea that he would spend it for drink, he would not hesitate about making the most solemn asseveration that he had taken no liquor for days, and only wanted to get something to eat, not having tasted food for twenty-four or thirty-six hours, as this or that period happened to come to his lips. One lie with him was as good as another, so that it served his purpose. And there had been a time when he would have felt his high sense of personal honor tarnished by even a small prevarication! So had the robber demon of drink despoiled the man! And not of honor alone; every moral sense had been stolen away, drugged into sleep, or wrested from him.

I saw a crowd in the street one day, and crossed to see what it meant. As I came near, I observed a slender girl, who had been drawn into the group of men and women, moving back hastily, as if

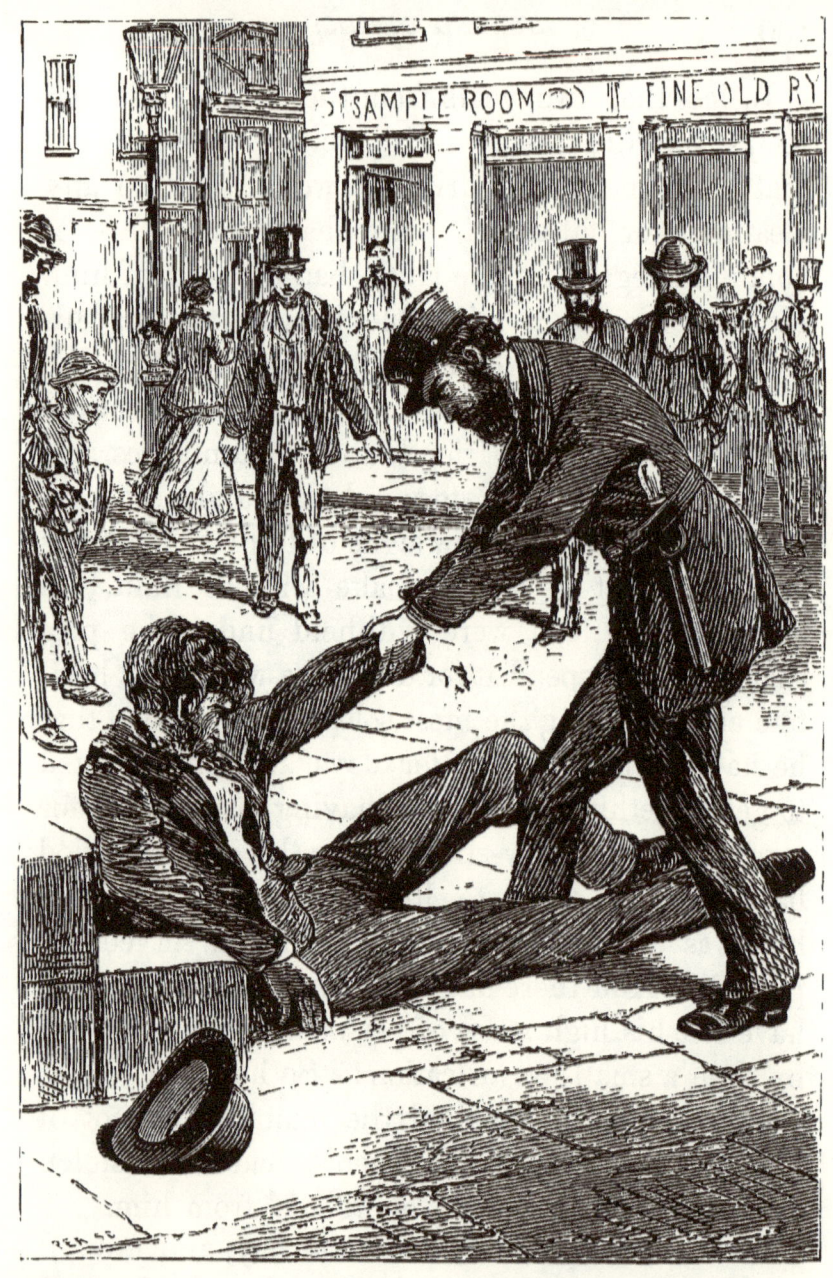

"I saw Alexander Granger sitting on the pavement and leaning back against a door-step so drunk that he could scarcely hold his head up."—*Page 6.*

shocked by what she had witnessed in the centre of the crowd. A white, almost terror-stricken face met my view as she turned. I was impressed by something familiar in its contour and expression. I saw it only for an instant, for the young girl fled past me as one affrighted and went hurrying down the street. For a moment or two I stood looking after her swiftly-retreating form, wondering where I had seen her. All doubts were settled when, on pressing forward, I saw Alexander Granger sitting on the pavement and leaning back against a doorstep, so drunk that he could scarcely hold his head up; while a policeman was endeavoring to lift him to his feet. The girl was his daughter, Amy.

A few hours afterwards, as I stood on the steps of my own residence, about to enter, the door was drawn open from within and I met the face of Granger's daughter again. The whiteness had not yet gone out of it. She gave a little start at seeing me.

"Miss Granger, I believe," said I, with kind familiarity in my voice, extending my hand at the same time. I felt a tremor in the small, soft palm that was laid in mine for an instant and then withdrawn. Tears were coming in the poor girl's eyes, and I saw that her lips were quivering. I stepped aside that she might pass, and in a moment she was gone.

Inside the door my own precious daughter, just Amy's age, met me, and laid her loving kisses on my lips. I could not trust myself to speak because of the tearful pity that was in my heart for the worse than fatherless girl who had just gone over the threshold of my happy home.

"What did Amy Granger want?" I asked, as, with an arm about my daughter, we went from the hall into the parlor.

"She's trying to get a place in the Mint, and she called to ask mother about it, and to see if you wouldn't sign her application."

"Why, of course I will. Did she leave it?"

"Yes. And she asked mother to ask you if you didn't know somebody else who would help her by signing it."

"Poor child!" I said, pityingly. "To be so robbed and wronged! Of course I'll do all in my power to help her. I'll see the Director of the Mint myself, and if there's a place vacant, I'll not leave a stone unturned but she shall have it."

"There's something so sweet about her," said my daughter. "So refined and modest, and gentle. Oh! it must be very hard. What an awful thing this drunkenness is! Why, father, dear," and the sweet girl drew her arms about my neck and laid her cheek against mine, "I should not have a moment's peace if you drank wine or beer every day as some men do."

"You'd have cause for trouble, my darling, if that were so," I replied, "for no man who uses them can be regarded as safe. I know of a dozen ruined homes that were once as secure and as happy as ours. It was drink that desolated them. And I know of many more that are in danger, and towards which ruin is walking with slow but steady steps."

She held her arms more tightly about my neck. When she lifted her cheek from mine her eyes were wet with tears.

My efforts to secure a situation in the Mint for Miss Granger were not successful, another applicant for the vacant place getting the appointment. But my interest and that of my family were thoroughly awakened in behalf of the girl, who not only desired independence for herself, but an opportunity to help her mother and younger sisters. The best that could be done for her in the beginning was to secure the position of attendant in a photograph gallery at four dollars a week. It was accepted with thankfulness. Mrs. Granger, who had commenced giving lessons in music even before her separation from her husband, continued in the profession of teacher, and had scholars enough to give her a moderate income and keep her above absolute dependence on the relatives who had so kindly offered her a home in her sore extremity.

It was three or four months after we had succeeded in getting a place for Amy Granger, that, on coming home one day, I found her mother waiting to see me. I did not know her on first coming into the parlor, a year or two had so changed her, and when, on my entrance, she arose and introduced herself, I could scarcely believe it possible that the wife of Alexander Granger was before me.

"I've called to see you on account of my daughter," she said, after being seated again. Her manner was much embarrassed; and she was evidently trying to hide the distress from which she was suffering.

"What about Amy?" I asked.

"You were very kind in getting her into that photograph gallery," she answered, "and we were all so grateful."

"She hasn't lost her situation, I hope?"

Yes, she had lost it; I saw this in the mother's face.

"How came it?" I asked. "Didn't she give satisfaction?"

"Oh! yes, sir. It was all right so far as that went; and they had increased her pay to five dollars a week. But—" I saw the tears flooding her eyes as the quaver in her voice checked her speech. "Amy couldn't come and tell you herself," she resumed, as she recovered her self-possession. "It was too hard for the poor child. But she wanted me to see you."

"Tell me all about it," I said, kindly. "I'm sure it was no fault of hers, poor child!"

"Indeed it was not, Mr. Lyon. It made her sick. She was in bed for two or three days; and she looks as if she'd come out of a long spell of sickness."

"She mustn't take it so to heart," I replied. "No doubt it can all be made right again."

"Oh! no, sir. She can't go back there any more."

"Why not, Mrs. Granger?"

"Because—because—" her voice breaking and quivering again. Then she recovered herself and said, with firmer speech: "It's on account of her father."

"It can't be possible," I spoke with some indignation, "that his misdeeds should stand in the way of her honest efforts at self-support! No one could be so cruelly unjust toward her as that."

Then the truth came out. Let me give the story as it came to me then, and follow out the sequel as it came to me afterwards.

CHAPTER XII.

THE shock of seeing her father in the condition we have described, hurt deeply the sensitive nature of Amy Granger. All affection for him, debased and degraded as he was, had not died in her heart. Memory held too many sweet pictures of the old, dear home which she had lost, and of the tender and loving father who had once been the light and joy of that home. She could never walk the street afterwards without a nervous fear of again encountering him. From this she was spared for several months after obtaining the place of an attendant in the rooms of a photographer.

But one morning, just as she was at the entrance of these rooms, she met her father face to face. He had slept in a station-house, and had just been sent forth, exhausted from want of food, and with every nerve unstrung for lack of stimulants, wretched in feeling and loathesome in appearance. The shocked and half-frightened girl glided swiftly past him, and fled trembling up the stairway leading to the gallery in which she was employed, hoping that he had not recognized her. But in this she was mistaken. Scarcely had she reached the second floor ere she heard him following her up the stairs, shuffling and stumbling by the way. Retreating to the back part of the room, she stood breathless and frightened, until the awfully marred and distorted face of her father looked in upon her from the door. The sight almost broke her heart. But in an instant all thought of herself was forgotten. The love which had been trampled upon, bruised and broken, and wounded almost to the death, lifted itself into the agony of a new life, and threw out its arms wildly. In this poor dismantled wreck of humanity, storm-beaten, helpless and deserted, she saw the father on whose breast she had once lain in sweet confidence. All the happy past came back in a moment; pity and tenderness flooded her soul. Starting forward, she laid her hands on him, saying in tones of the deepest compassion: "Oh, father! father!"

Weak, nerveless, helpless as a sick child, Granger caught hold of his daughter with a half-despairing eagerness, and held on to her as a drowning man to some new and unlooked-for means of succor.

"Yes, it's your poor father, Amy," he said, in a deep, rattling voice, scarcely a tone of which she recognized. "All that's left of him."

He shivered; for the morning was cold, and his garments were scant and thin. What could she do or say? Before her bewildered thoughts could untangle themselves, he gave the prompting words.

"I haven't had anything to eat since yesterday, Amy." His voice shaking as he spoke.

The child's pocket-book was in her hand ere the

sentence was finished. All it contained was fifty cents. As she took the money out, Granger caught it from her fingers, saying: "Oh, thank you dear! You were always such a good girl."

The little crumpled bit of paper was scarcely in the man's possession ere he turned away and went stumbling down the stairs, his daughter listening in painful suspense, every moment expecting to hear him fall. But he reached the street in safety, and made his way to the nearest bar-room he could find.

When Amy, who had kept all this from her mother, reached the gallery next morning, she found her father already there and awaiting her arrival. His appearance was, if possible, more wretched and disgusting than on the day before. He was sitting near a table on which were a number of fancy photographs, stereoscopic views and small card-cases and frames. The sight of him sent the color out of his daughter's face, and the strength out of her limbs.

"Oh, father! father!" she said, speaking in a low voice, as she came up to where he was sitting. "It's hard for me to say it, but you mustn't come here any more. I shall lose my place if you do."

She saw something like a frightened look in his eyes as he got up hastily.

"I'll go, then. I'll go right away," he answered, in an abject manner. "But just give me a little something with which to get my breakfast. I haven't had a mouthful since yesterday."

She gave him the trifle of change that was in her

pocket-book, which he clutched with the same trembling eagerness he had shown on the day before, and as hurriedly made his way to the street. The only witness of this scene and that of the preceding morning, was an errand boy.

"Is that man your father, Miss Granger?" asked the lad, as Amy turned from the door.

She could not answer him.

"'Cause, if he is, you'd better not let him come here any more. There'll be trouble for you if he does. I thought 'twas your father, and so kept mum until I could speak to you."

"What do you mean?" asked Amy, as she turned a scared face on the boy.

"I don't like to tell you, miss. But he stole one of them small morocco cases. I saw him slip it into his pocket."

The poor girl dropped into a chair, white as a sheet. Everything grew dark about her, and it was only by a strong effort of the will that she kept from losing her consciousness and falling to the floor.

"You are not well, dear," said Amy's mother, as she looked into the face of her daughter on the morning after Granger's first visit to the photograph gallery.

"My head aches a little," was the evasive answer.

Mrs. Granger was sitting in the room about an hour after Amy left home, when she heard some one come in and ascend the stairs. The footfalls were so light as scarcely to give a sound. She waited, listening; but no one came to her door. Listening still, she perceived a faint rustling of garments as of some one passing up to the rooms above. Then the door of Amy's room was opened and closed almost noiselessly; and all was still again. What did this mean? She had a vague sense of mystery and fear. For several minutes she sat with ear bent, and heart beating heavily.

"Who came in just now and went up stairs?" she asked of one of her younger daughters who entered the room where she was sitting.

"I heard no one," answered the child.

"Go and see if Amy has come home."

The child did as requested, but came back in a few moments, with a frightened look in her eyes, and said: "Oh, mamma! Amy's lying on her bed; and she won't speak to me."

Mrs. Granger found her daughter as the child had said. Her face was hidden. She looked as if she had fallen across the bed in utter prostration of strength.

"Why, Amy, dear! What's the matter? Are you sick?"

There was no movement or reply.

Mrs. Granger bent over her daughter and tried to lift her face so that she could look into it; but Amy's only response was a slight resistance and continued hiding of her face.

"Amy, my child! Why don't you speak to me? Has anything happened?" The alarmed and anxious mother pressed her questions rapidly; but no reply coming, she drew her arm beneath the head of her daughter and lifted and turned it so that she could look into the hitherto hidden face. It was pale and rigid, with signs of intense suffering about the closely-shut mouth. A long time passed before Mrs. Granger could gather from the unhappy girl the story of her father's visits to the gallery, and the shame and disgrace which they had brought upon her.

Many days passed ere Amy was able to rise out of the deep prostration of mind and body into which she had been thrown, and to turn her thoughts to the work and duty that were still before her. She could not go back to the photograph rooms. That question did not have a moment's debate, either with herself or her mother. It was to get my advice and help in this new and most distressing state of affairs that Mrs. Granger had called upon me, as mentioned in the preceding chapter. My sympathies were strongly excited, and I assured her that I would do all in my power to assist her daughter in getting another place.

Meanwhile the proprietor of the photograph gallery, who had met Amy on the stairs as she was hurrying away and noticed the pallor and the wild look in her face, had made inquiry of the lad as to the meaning of her disturbed condition. On learning the truth, he became greatly incensed towards Granger—not so much because of the petty theft which had been committed, as on account of the humiliation and suffering which he had brought upon his innocent daughter. Under the heat of his sudden indignation he started out, and by the aid of a policeman, succeeded in finding the miserable man in one of the saloons not far distant. On searching him the stolen article was discovered on his person. His arrest and commitment by an alderman quickly followed. As no one willing to go bail for him could be found, he was sent to the county jail, where he had been lying for two or three days when the fact of his imprisonment first became known to me through Mr. Stannard, a gentleman to whom brief reference has already been made.

"Have you heard about poor Granger?" he said, as we met one morning on the street.

"What about him?" I asked.

"He's in Moyamensing."

"For what?"

"Theft. He stole some trifle from a photograph gallery, and was arrested and sent to prison."

"Better there than living a life of drunken vagabondism on the street," I replied.

"I heard through the prison agent that he was seized with mania soon after his commitment, and had a hard struggle for his life. But he came through after suffering the tortures of hell, greatly prostrated in mind and body."

"Poor wretch! It would have been better had he not come through," I made answer, with less of feeling in my voice than was really in my heart. "A curse to himself and to all who, unhappily, have any relationship with him, why should he continue to cumber the ground?"

I spoke more bitterly than I felt, for I had old remembrances of this man which drew upon my sympathies, and softened my heart towards him. There came to me, even as I spoke, a strong and pitiful contrast between what he had been in the days of his proud and honorable manhood, and what he was now, debased, ruined, homeless, sick and in prison.

"God knows best. With Him are the issues of life." Mr. Stannard drew his arm in mine as he spoke. "And now, friend Lyon," he continued, "as, in God's providence, this man and his dreadful condition have been brought so clearly before us, may we not regard the fact as an indication that it is our duty to make another effort to save him? He has reached a lower deep than any to which he had hitherto fallen. May not the awful sense of loss and degradation which he must feel, quicken into life a new and more intense desire to get free from the horrible pit into which appetite has cast him? And may not He who alone is able to save, find now an entrance which has been hitherto closed against Him?"

I was near my office when I met Mr. Stannard. As he drew his arm in mine we moved onward and were soon at the door.

"Come in. I shall be glad to talk with you about Granger. If there is any hope of saving him, I am ready to do all that lies in my power."

We sat down together and gave his case our most earnest consideration. As for myself, I saw little if anything to encourage a new effort to rescue this fallen man. I had read and thought a great deal about the evil of drunkenness in the last year or two, and was satisfied that, in cases of what medical men define as confirmed alcoholism, a permanent cure is rarely if ever effected. It was a disease that might be arrested for a time through the complete removal of exciting causes; but one which, if predisposing causes were once fairly established, could never be radically cured.

"If there were no bar-rooms and no social drinking customs," I said, as we talked, "we might hope to reform a case like this. But one might as well send a man who had just recovered from intermittent fever back again into the miasmatic region from which he had escaped, as a reformed drunkard into the business and social world of to-day. There would be small hope of escape for either of them."

Mr. Stannard drew a deep sigh, but did not answer.

I continued: "What makes this case of Granger's so discouraging, is the fact that every possible agency of reform has already been tried. You know that he was in the New York Inebriate Asylum for several months."

"Yes, I am aware of that."

"He came home vastly improved; and I had great hopes of him for awhile. But old associations and old influences set themselves against him from the very day of his return home. It was a continual pressure; a continual dropping; a continual allurement. After awhile the old appetite, which had not been extinguished, began to show signs of life. You know the rest. He was not cured. And, from all I can learn of this disease of drunkenness, no one is ever so thoroughly cured as not to be in perpetual danger of relapse. We may take Granger out of prison, and set him on his feet again; but will he stand? Nay, will he not surely fall? If I could only see a reasonable hope. But to my mind there is none."

"There is always hope in God," said Mr. Stannard, his voice low but steady and assured.

My heart did not give a quick response to his words.

"No man ever falls so low that Christ cannot lift him up and save him," he added.

"I believe that," was my answer. "But how does He save? How, for instance, can He save a man like Granger? How can His Divine power reach him, and lift him free from the curse of the terrible appetite which has enslaved him? Men look to God, and pray to Him, and yet are not saved. Granger went to church for awhile, and tried to get a higher strength, but it did not come. Why? Did

God hold himself away from him because faith was halting and blind? Did He make the measure of this poor man's feeble mental effort the measure of His mercy? I cannot believe it."

"And you must not," Mr. Stannard said, gently, "He knoweth our frame, and remembereth that we are dust. Are not His words explicit—'Him that cometh unto me I will in no wise cast out.' Running through all the Divine Word, is there not a perpetual invitation to look to Him and come to Him for refuge, for safety, for strength, and for salvation?"

"But how is a man to come, Mr. Stannard?"

"We begin to come the moment we repent of our sins and look to the Lord for strength to resist and put them away. We come nearer when we obey His command, 'Cease to do evil.' Then, and only then, do we put it into the Lord's power to save us. 'His name shall be called Jesus, for He shall save His people from their sins.' But if the people will not quit the evil of their doing, how can He save them from the love of evil doing—which is the true salvation? 'Behold I stand at the door and knock. If any man hear my voice and open the door, I will come in to him.' Now what is it that shuts the door against God? Is it not sin; the love of self and the world; the indulgence of evil passions and appetites? He cannot dwell in a heart where these abide. They must be cast out, and then God's temple in the human soul is prepared for His entrance."

"But," I said, "who can cast them out but God? Is not this the doctrine of the church?"

"None but a Divine power," Mr. Stannard answered, "can remove the love of sinning. But first man of himself must open the door which evil-doing has barred against God."

"How can this be done?"

"There is only one way. He must cease to *do* evil because it is a *sin against God*. Beyond this he has no power over his corrupt nature. He cannot change his inner vileness into beauty, cannot make himself pure, cannot by good deeds enter the kingdom of God. Over the external things of thought and act he has power, but the Lord alone can change his inner affection—take away the heart of stone and give the heart of flesh. But, ere this can be done, man must not only repent of his evil deeds because they are sins, but actually cease from doing them. In the moment that he does this from a religious principle—that is because to do evil is contrary to the Divine Law, and therefore a sin against God—and looks to the Lord to deliver and save him, in that moment he opens the door of his heart for the Lord to enter, and the Lord, who has been knocking there by His Divine Word and commandments, will surely come in. And so long as he shuns evils as sins in the external of his life, is just, and merciful, and humble, God will abide with him and in him, and he shall walk as safely in the midst of temptation as the three Hebrew children in the fiery furnace, because the Son of God is with him as He was with them."

"Not of faith alone, nor of works, nor of merit," I said.

"No, but of obedience. And in the degree that obedience becomes perfected, will love become perfected. In the degree that a man shuns in thought and act the evils that in any way hurt his neighbor or do dishonor to God, in that degree will the Lord remove from his heart the desire to do them, and give the affection of good in their place."

"Going back now to Mr. Granger," I said, "why, when he put away the evil of drinking for so long a time, was not the desire for this sinful indulgence taken away? Did he not open the door for the Lord to come in?"

"We open the door at which the Lord stands knocking when we see and acknowledge the evils in our lives that hold the door bolted and barred against Him, and cease to do them because they are sins."

"Because they are sins?"

"Yes. If we cease to do evil from any other consideration, we do not open the door."

"I am not sure that I get your meaning," said I.

"Take the case of Granger. Why did he shun the evil of drinking?"

"Because he saw that it was ruining him."

"That it was a sin against himself rather than against God," said Mr. Stannard.

"What is sin against God?" I asked.

"Any and everything that man does in opposition to Divine order."

"The answer is too general," I said.

"The laws of this order as applied to man are very simple and direct," he returned. "Thou shalt love the Lord thy God with all thy heart, and thy neighbor as thyself. Now, in Mr. Granger's case, did he make an effort to control his appetite for drink because its indulgence was a sin against the true order of his life and turned him away from all just regard for God and his neighbor—thus a sin against God Himself—or, did his thought reach only to himself and to his worldly loss or gain?"

"I scarcely think his motive went as far as you suggest."

"If it did not, how was God to save him? If it was not the sin of intemperance that troubled him, but only the consequences of that sin, there could be no true repentance and humiliation before God. And here let me say, Mr. Lyon, that no man can be saved from any particular evil, as, for instance, that of drunkenness, unless at the same time he resist and endeavor to put away all other sins against God. The whole man must be reformed and regenerated. Everything forbidden in the Word of God must be put away through the Divine strength given to all who earnestly try to keep the commandments."

"I see your meaning more clearly," I replied.

"There must be a new and better life in the whole man."

"If not how can God abide with him and in him?"

"Coming back again to the case of Granger," said I, "and regarding it from your standpoint, is there any possibility of a permanent reform?"

"Yes."

"You speak confidently."

"Because I have faith in the Great Physician of souls. There is a Divine healing power which all men may have if they will."

"Nothing but a Divine power can cure him. Of that I am satisfied."

"Shall we not, then, seeing that he has been brought so low, make an effort to bring him under the care of this Great Physician? I have been thinking about it all day, and our conversation has only given strength to a half-formed purpose to visit and make one more effort to save him."

"Let it be done by all means," I replied.

A gentleman who had known Mr. Granger came into my office at this moment, and when he learned of the utter debasement of the man, and of our purpose to make a new effort to reclaim him, said: "Why not place him in the new Reformatory Home recently established in our city?"

"Reformation without regeneration will avail nothing in his case," returned Mr. Stannard. "The best reformatory agencies known have been tried, but their influences proved only temporary. He was at Binghampton, you know."

"Yes, I am aware of that. But the institution to which I refer, is not an asylum for the treatment of drunkenness as a disease, but a Christian Home in which, while all the physical needs of the inmates are rightly cared for, an effort is made to bring them under religious influences, and to lead them to depend on God for safety."

"Is there an institution like that in our city?" asked Mr. Stannard, with much interest in his manner. "I never heard of it before."

"It is scarcely a year old," was replied. "But already the results obtained are quite remarkable."

"Too short a time to predict much on results," I said. "The reformation of a drunkard that dates back no farther than a year, gives little ground for confidence."

"Much depends on the basis of the reformation," remarked Mr. Stannard. "Here, it strikes me, is the true basis, and I am ready to hope much. But what is the name of this institution and where is it located?"

"You will find it in the very centre of our city. They call it the Franklin Reformatory Home for Inebriates; and from what I have heard through one of the managers, whose heart is very much in the work, I am led to believe that in its treatment of drunkenness it has discovered and is using the only true remedy for that terrible disease which no medicine for the body can ever radically cure. Its first work is to draw the poor, debased and degraded inebriate within the circle of a well-ordered and cheerful home, and under the influence of kind and sympathetic friends. All these have been lost to him for years; so utterly lost that all hope of their recovery has died in his heart. He is a stranger to gentle words and loving smiles;—used only to rebuke and blame; to scorn and contempt; is alike despised of himself and the world. But here he finds himself all at once an object of interest and care. His hand is taken in a clasp so warm and true that he feels the thrill go down into his heart and awaken old memories of other and dearer hand-clasps. His lost manhood and sense of respect are found again. New purposes are formed and old resolves—broken, alas! so many times—renewed once more. He finds himself encircled by sustaining influences of a better character than he has known in many years. Hope and confidence grow strong.

"But in lifting the fallen man to this state of life, the Home has done only its first and least important work of reformation. If it were able to do no more, 'Failure' would ultimately be written on its walls. It is organized for deeper and more thorough work—is, in fact, a Church as well as a Home, and has its chapel and its formal worship. When the man is restored and in his right mind, an effort is made to lead him into the conviction that in and of himself he cannot successfully resist the appetite from whose slavery he has just escaped. That only in the Divine power and protection is there any hope for him, and that he must seek this Divine power and protection through prayer and a living and obedient faith in Christ, who saves to the uttermost all who come to Him and keep His sayings. He must become a new man. Must be saved not only from drunkenness, but from all other evils of life. Must become sincere, and humble, and just, and pure, as well as temperate. So becoming steadfast and immovable."

A light had kindled in Mr. Stannard's face. Turning to me, he said: "There is hope for our poor friend. He may yet be saved. Is there not a providence in this thing?"

"I might say yes, if I believed in special providences," I returned.

"What kind of a providence do you believe in?" Mr. Stannard asked.

"In a general overruling providence," I replied.

"Of a providence, for instance, that takes care of a man's whole body, but not of his eye, or ear, or heart, or any individual fibre, or nerve, or organ of which his body is composed. That takes care of a nation, but not of the individual men composing that nation. To have a general providence, Mr. Lyon, you must have a particular providence; for without particulars you cannot have that which is general. Believe me, that God's care is over you and me and every one, specially and at all times. It would be no providence at all if this were not so. Let us think of it as round about us continually, and that if it were intermitted for a single moment, we would perish. Let us think of it as the infinite Love which is forever seeking to save us, and forever adapting the means to this eternal end."

"You think more deeply about these things than I have been in the habit of doing, and may be nearer right in your views than I am in mine. I waive, for the present, all controversy on the subject. As for Mr. Granger, let us get him into this Home, and give him another chance. I believe in the church, and in the power of God to save men from their sins. And I believe more in this Home, from what I have just heard of it, than in any and all of the reformatory agencies in the land."

"Because it is a church, a true church, seeking to gather poor lost and abandoned ones into the fold of Christ?"

"Yes, if you choose to give that form to the proposition," I replied.

"Is it not the true form? Can the Church have any higher mission than the one to which this Home has consecrated itself?"

"None," was my answer. "And yet the Church scarcely reaches out its hand to the perishing inebriate. Nay, draws back from him her spotless garments, and leaves him to perish in the mire from which her hands might have raised him."

"The Church learns but slowly," Mr. Stannard replied, speaking with a shade of depression in his voice. "It has been too busy with creeds and hair-splitting differences in doctrine, and with rituals, and robes, and things external, to give itself as it should to charity. A better day is not far distant, I hope. If, as has been said, the Church is the heart and lungs of common society, and if society is terribly diseased, spiritually as well as morally, is not the Church at fault and responsible? A healthy heart and healthy lungs should make a healthy body. Before the Church can heal the world she must be healed herself. She must rise into the perception of higher and diviner truths, and come down into the world with a more living power. It is difficult to tell which has the larger influence over the other to-day, the Church or the world. I sometimes fear it is the world, the Church is so pervaded with its spirit, and fashions, and ways of doing things, with its pride and its vanities. But here, in this Home of which we have been speaking, we have, thank God, the beginning of a real, earnest, working Church that knows the gospel of salvation, and is seeking by its power to lift up the fallen, to heal the broken-hearted, and to set the captive free."

Mr. Stannard had warmed as he spoke, and now there was a glow on his fine countenance. So interested had we all become in the Home about which we were talking, that his suggestion that we should make a visit and learn for ourselves what was being done there, met with a hearty concurrence, and we started at once to see and make ourselves better acquainted with the character and work of the new Institution.

CHAPTER XIII.

ON the day following I met Mr. Stannard, by agreement. We had made arrangements for placing Granger in the new Home as soon as we could get him released, and thus give him another opportunity to recover himself. All my interest in the man was reviving, and hope gaining strength every moment. Our visit to the Reformatory Home had been most satisfactory. We found the organization far more perfect than we had anticipated, seeing that the Institution was yet in its infancy. After spending an hour with the president, who happened to be there when we called, and obtaining from him all the information desired, we made such preliminary arrangements as were necessary for the admission of Granger, and left with the new hope for the fallen man, we were about making an attempt to rescue, growing stronger in our hearts every moment.

Before going to the prison, we called on the district attorney, who, on learning our purpose, gave an order for Granger's release, saying, as he did so: "I wish, gentlemen, that I could feel as hopeful as you seem to be in regard to the result. But I'm afraid the case is beyond cure. Poor fellow! Our bar lost one of its brightest representatives in his fall. He was a splendid orator. I can hear his voice, now, ringing out in some of his grand periods. Ah, if he had but let drink alone!"

"If men would only take warning by a fall like this," said Mr. Stannard.

"Few fall so rapidly or so low," returned the district attorney. "Some men are weak in the head where liquor is concerned, while others can drink on to the end, always maintaining a due moderation."

"And every man who drinks believes that he can always hold himself to this due moderation."

"Yes, that is the case with most men; but a few get over the line before becoming aware that they have touched it."

"To find, like the too venturesome bather when struck by the undertow, that return is next to impossible."

We went from the district attorney's office direct to the prison, and were taken to the cell where Granger was confined. He was lying on his bed, apparently sleeping, but moved and turned towards us as we entered. At first I though there had been a mistake. Could that wasted, haggard face, and those large, deep-set, dreary eyes be the face and eyes of Alexander Granger? It seemed impossible. But he had recognized us at a glance, as I saw by the quick changes in his countenance, and made an effort to rise; but sunk back weakly on his hard pallet, a feeble moan coming at the same time through his lips.

"My poor, unhappy friend!" I said, in a voice of tender sympathy, as I sat down on the bed and took one of his hands in mine.

All the muscles of his face began to twitch and quiver. He shut his eyes closely, but could not hold back the shining drops that were already passing through the trembling lashes.

I waited a little while before speaking again, but kept tightly hold of his hand.

"Sick and in prison. My poor friend!" letting my voice fall to a lower and tenderer expression.

He caught his breath with a sob. Tears fell over his cheeks. All the muscles of his face were shaking. I waited until the paroxysm was over. How weak and wasted he was! As I looked at him, my heart grew heavy with compassion.

"There is still a chance for you, Mr. Granger," said I, putting hope and confidence in my voice.

There was no response; not even a faint gleam on his wretched face.

"Will you not try again?"

"It won't be of any use, Mr. Lyon. It's very good of you; but it won't be of any use." He spoke feebly and mournfully, moving his head slowly from side to side.

"It will be of use. I am sure that it will," I said, with still more confidence.

"You don't know anything about it, Mr. Lyon."

His voice had gained a steadier tone; but its utter hopelessness was painful.

"Here is Mr. Stannard," I said. "You remember him."

"Yes. It's very good of you, gentlemen. But I don't deserve your kindness."

"We are here as your friends," said Mr. Stannard, coming close to the bed. "We are going to help you to get upon your feet again, and to become a new man."

He shook his head gloomily.

"I've done trying. What's the use of a man attempting to climb a hill when he knows that his strength must give out before he reaches the top, and that he will get bruised and broken in the inevitable fall. Better die in the ditch at the bottom, as I shall die."

He had raised himself a little, and was leaning on his arm.

"You have been sick," said I, wishing to take his mind away from the thought which was then holding it.

"Yes, worse than sick. I've been in hell and among devils."

"But have escaped with your life."

"I'm not so sure. It's about over with me, I guess. You see there's not much left to go and come on."

He held up one of his thin, almost transparent hands, but could not keep it steady.

"Yes, worse than sick, I've been in hell and among devils."—*Page 190.*

"Don't say that. There's to be a new life within and without."

"Not for me. Not for Alexander Granger. Do you know what I am here for?" A dark cloud falling on his face. "For stealing!—for petty larceny! You see it's all over with me. The very shame of the thing is burning my life out. A thief! No, no, gentlemen. Even if I were able to stand against appetite, I could not bear up under a disgrace like this."

"It was not Alexander Granger who committed this crime," answered Mr. Stannard, "but the insatiate demon who had enslaved him and made him subject to his will. Let us cast out this demon and give the true, generous-hearted, honorable man back to himself and society again. It is for this that we are here, Mr. Granger."

He shook his head. "If, in the full vigor of manhood, I was not able to overcome and cast out this demon, what hope is there now?' It were folly to make the effort. No, no, gentlemen. I give up the struggle. All that is worth living for is gone. An utterly disgraced and degraded man, what is left for me but to die and be forgotten? And I shall be better here, dying sober, than in the gutter or the station-house, dying drunk."

His voice trembled, and then broke in a repressed sob.

"There is One who can and who will save you, even from the power of this strong appetite which has so cursed you, my friend," said Mr. Stannard, speaking with a gentle persuasion in his tones, and at the same time laying his hand softly on Granger's head. "He is very near to you now—a loving Shepherd seeking for His lost sheep in the desolate wilderness, where it is ready to perish."

Then, kneeling, with his hand still on Granger's head, he prayed in a low, hushed voice:

"Loving Father, tender Shepherd. This Thy poor wandering sheep is hungry and faint and ready to die. His flesh has been torn by the thorn and bramble; the wild beast has been after him, and the poison of serpents is in his blood. No help is left but in Thee, and unless Thy strong arm save him he will surely perish. Draw his heart toward Thee. Give him to feel that in Thee alone is hope and safety. In his helplessness and despair, let faith and trust be quickened. Thou canst save him from the power of this demon of drink. Thou canst set him in a safe way, and keep him from falling again. Give him to feel this great truth, that if he cast himself at Thy feet and cry from his sick and fainting heart, 'Save me, Lord!' Thou wilt hear and save."

Can I ever forget the almost despairing cry for help that was in Granger's voice as he repeated the words, "Save me, Lord!" throwing his hands above his head as he spoke, and lifting his eyes upwards? A strange thrill ran along my nerves.

"He will save you," said Mr. Stannard, as he rose from his knees. "Trust in Him, and He will give you strength to overcome all your enemies. Though your sins be as scarlet, He will make them white as wool. They that trust in the Lord shall be as Mount Zion which cannot be removed, but abideth forever. As the mountains are round about Jerusalem, so the Lord is round about His people."

I saw a change in Granger's face. It was growing calmer and stronger.

"There is a new life before you, my friend; and if you will look to God, and trust Him, and keep His words, you can live that life in safety. Will you try?"

"If I thought there was any use in trying. But what can I do? Where can I go?"

There was a pleading expression in look and voice.

"Will you try?"

"Yes, God helping me." He spoke with a kind of trembling earnestness.

"We have a carriage outside," I said. You will go with us?"

"How can I go? I'm a prisoner."

"A prisoner no longer. We have brought you a release."

"Is this only a dream?" he said, looking at us with a gathering doubt in his face. "But I am sick and weak. I cannot walk. I can scarcely stand. I am not fit to go anywhere."

He was taken to the carriage we had in waiting, supported by two of the keepers. But few words passed as we drove into the city and over the rattling streets to the institution where we had arranged to place him. He was very weak, and almost in a fainting condition when we reached our destination. Beyond the door our care of him ceased; but we left money to procure clean clothing with which to replace, after he had received a bath, the poor, tattered and unclean garments that were on his person.

"If this fail, all fails," I said to Mr. Stannard, as we came away.

"I do not believe it will fail," he replied.

"I would gladly share your confidence, but confess that I do not. The influences under which he will now come, are, I can see, more favorable than any that have heretofore been brought to bear upon him; but there has been so great a physical and moral deterioration that I fear he can never get back the strength required for safe standing and sure resistance.

"He is stronger, in my opinion, to-day than he has been at any time in the last ten years."

"I scarcely see the ground of your confidence," said I.

"Stronger because all faith and all trust in himself are dead. He had given up the struggle when we found him in prison—given up to die, and his 'Save me, Lord!' came from the depths of his utter despair. There will be no more trust in himself, I think; no more matching of his weakness against the giant strength of an enemy before whose lightest blow he must surely fall. But a complete giving of himself into the care and protection of One who is not only mighty to save, but who saves to the uttermost all who come unto Him. Herein lies the ground of my confidence."

"In such a giving up, Mr. Stannard, what becomes of the manhood? Is it wholly lost?"

"It is in this surrender of ourselves to God that a higher and truer manhood is born. What is it to be a true man? To let the appetites and passions rule; or the reason, which, enlightened from above, can see and determine what is just, and pure, and merciful. Does the man possess himself so long as he lets the lower things of his nature rule over the higher?—his appetites and passions over his rational? The whole order of man's life has been reversed by sin. He has turned from God to himself, and vainly thinks that true manhood consists in self-dependence and self-assertion; as though his inmost life were his own, and not the perpetual gift of God. And so he tries to get as far away from God as possible, and to make a new life for himself; and as this new life begins in self, it is in the nature of things, a selfish life, and separates him from God and his neighbor. And he lives this life down in the lower regions of his mind, where sensual things reside—the appetites, the passions and the concupiscences. Is it any wonder that, so living, these sensual things should gain dominion over him—a dominion that nothing short of Divine power can break? Herein lies the loss of true manhood, which can only be restored when we are willing to sell all that we have of self in order to buy heavenly treasures. Granger is not going to lose, but gain his manhood."

"Ah, what a gain that would be!" I felt oppressed with the inflowing pressure of new thoughts. I was beginning to see, dimly, how two men might pray to God to be delivered from evil, and the prayer of one be answered, while that of the other proved of no avail. Until a man is ready to give up his selfish life, and turn wholly from the evil of his ways, how can God help him to live the new and diviner life which will give him power to hold all the appetites and passions of his nature in due subjection and control. I saw for the first time an exact parallelism between spiritual and natural things. A vessel must be emptied of one substance before it can be filled with another. So must a soul be emptied of evil and selfishness before it can be filled with love to God and the neighbor. There must be poverty of spirit before the riches of Divine grace can be given. "Blessed are the poor in spirit: for theirs is the kingdom of Heaven." The text flashed upon me with a new and deeper meaning than it had ever before brought to my mind.

CHAPTER XIV.

ON the following day I went to see Granger at the Reformatory Home. I found him in a clean, well-furnished and cheerful room. He was in bed, looking very pale; but his eyes were clear and bright, and he welcomed me with a smile that played softly over his wasted features, and gave them a touch of their old fine quality. A book lay open on the bed. I saw that it was a copy of the New Testament. His manner was very subdued, and he did not speak until after I was seated; and then not until I had asked how he was feeling. His answer almost gave me a start, it was so unexpected. He spoke in a low but even voice.

"As if I were standing just inside the gate of Heaven."

I waited for a few moments before replying, for I scarcely knew what to say; then remarked: "I am glad you feel so comfortable. This is better than the station-house or the prison."

The light went out of his face, but came back quickly.

"But for you, my kind friend, I should now be dying in the cell from which you and good Mr. Stannard brought me yesterday. It was God who sent you; and it seems as if I shall never be done thanking Him. My poor heart broke all down when Mr. Stannard prayed for me. It seemed as if God were all at once bending right over me, and when I cried out to Him in my helplessness, I had a feeling as if His arms were reached out and I taken into them. And I believe it was so."

"May they ever be round about you," I replied, scarcely able to keep my voice steady, for I was not prepared for this, and it affected me strangely.

"Nothing less can save me from the assaults of my enemy," he said, his countenance growing more serious.

I remained with him for half an hour, and when I left, my confidence in this new effort at reformation was greatly increased. An incident of the visit gave me large encouragement. As I sat talking with him there came a rap on the door, and then a lady, in company with the matron of the Institution, entered. I knew her well by sight. She was related to a family of high social standing; and while a woman of refinement and intelligence, and an ornament to the circle in which she moved, was largely given to good works. Her hand as well as her heart were in many charities. She had often met Mr. Granger and his wife in their better days, and was among those who had been deeply pained at his downfall. A member of the Auxiliary Board of Lady Managers, she had learned on her visit to the Home that Mr. Granger was there, and all her interest was at once awakened. To save him and restore him to his family and society, was something to be hoped for, and prayed for, and worked for; and she lost no time in seeing him, and letting him feel the warmth of her interest in his welfare.

I was talking with Granger, as just said, when this lady, whom I will call Mrs. Ellis, entered his neat little chamber. He knew her, of course, and I saw a slight tinge of color steal over his pale face as she came to the bedside.

"I am right glad to see you here, Mr. Granger," she said, with an interest so genuine that it affected me.

"And I am glad to be here, Mrs. Ellis," he replied, in a voice subdued but earnest. "It is like coming out of hell into Heaven."

"May it indeed be as the gate of Heaven to your soul," she responded. "If that be so, all will be well with you again. And I pray for you that it may be so. Only look to the blessed Saviour and trust in Him, and you shall be as Mount Zion, which cannot be removed."

She remained only for a few minutes, but said as she was going out: "You are now among true friends, Mr. Granger, and they will do everything in their power to help you. Take heart; it is all going to come out right again."

He was much affected by this brief visit, and after Mrs. Ellis had left the room said, in a half-wondering tone of voice: "I can hardly understand it all. What is she doing here?"

I explained to him that she was one of the Lady Managers of the Institution, through whose constant care and supervision the highest comfort of the inmates was secured. That the presence of these ladies in the Home, as visitors and supervisors, enabled them to gain an influence with the inmates that was very helpful. They made themselves acquainted, as far as possible, with the nature of their domestic relations, if they had families, and if their families were in destitute circumstances, visited them and did whatever lay in their power to help them. Many desolate homes had already been made bright and happy through their agency.

Granger listened with half-closed lids while I spoke of all this. A deep sigh was his only response when I ceased speaking. His thoughts had evidently drifted out of the room in which he was lying, and gone far away from the Home. I did not break the spell of thought that was upon him, but waited until he came back to himself again.

"It seems still as if I were only dreaming," he said, lifting his eyes at length and looking at me with a kind of wistful earnestness. "As if I would awaken at any moment into the old, dreadful life."

"You may dream this dream to the end if you will," I replied.

"God keep me from waking!" He gave a slight shiver as he said this.

At my next visit I found Granger well enough to be down stairs. He was in the reading-room talking with an intelligent-looking man, whose face I recognized as one with which I was familiar. I did not at first know this man, but when he reached out his hand and called me by name, his voice brought him to my recollection. He had once been a merchant, standing at the head of a firm doing a large business; but wine, the mocker, had betrayed him, and he had fallen into hopelessly dissolute habits. When I last saw him he was staggering on the street.

"Why, Lawrence!" I exclaimed, in pleased surprise. "You here?"

"Yes, I am here, friend Lyon. And here is our old friend Granger. You remember him."

"Of course I do," taking the hand of Mr. Granger as I spoke, who gave me back a silent pressure.

I looked at the two men, wondering at the change which had been wrought in them; noticing, as I have had occasion to notice many times since, the quick restoration of the face, after drink is abandoned, to something of its old, true character.

We sat down and had a long talk. Mr. Lawrence informed me that he had been there about five weeks, and was now holding the position of bookkeeper in the store of one of the directors of the Home, but still boarded in the Institution, as he felt that he needed all the help it could give him. He had been separated for over two years from his wife, who was now living in a distant city; but he had already written to her, telling the good news of his reformation, and of his purpose, by God's help, to keep himself forever free from his old habits.

"And here's a letter from her that I received to-day," he said, as he took an envelope from his pocket, with an almost child-like exhibition of pleasure. "And she writes that she'll be here in two weeks. She was always so good and so true, and she stayed by me until it was of no use. Poor Helen!"

I did not wonder at the dimness that came over his eyes; nor at the break and gurgle in his voice.

"But it shall never so be again," he went on, after a little pause. "I trusted in myself, and did not care for God. He was never in my thoughts. But I have found a better way since I came here, and One who will keep me in that way if I look to Him—walking always by my side. So long as I put my trust in Him, I shall be safe, but not for a moment longer."

I was looking at Granger, and saw that his gaze was fixed intently on Mr. Lawrence. His eyes were a little dilated and there was a shade of sadness on his countenance. He did not take any part in the conversation. When an opportunity came for us to be alone, and I could ask more particularly about him, his manner changed and brightened; but was more subdued than on the occasion of my previous visit.

"You are looking so much better," I said, "and are feeling, of course, as well as you look."

"I hope so," he answered, quietly. Then, after

a slight pause: "If one could only stop thinking sometimes."

"Right thinking is the way to right acting," I replied, speaking in an aphorism, because I was not sure as to what was in his thought, nor how my answer might be taken.

"If it were as easy to do right as to think right, living in this world would be safer than it is. But that is not what I meant. It is the trouble of unavailing thought to which I refer. Ah! if I could only stop this kind of thinking for awhile. If I could only bury the past out of sight!"

"If your future be as the verdure of spring and the fruitfulness of summer, the past will ere long be covered, as the earth after a desolate winter is covered with greenness and beauty. The influx of life into what is orderly and good is quick and strong. You are already beginning to feel this influx, my friend. May it have steady increase."

A man came into the room where we sat conversing, and, after taking a book from the library, went out. I noticed that he had an intelligent face, and an air of refinement, but looked wasted and broken as though just risen from a severe illness.

"That is Dr. R——," said Granger. "He had a large practice in our city a few years ago, but lost it on account of intemperance. His family was broken up at last—wife and children being compelled to leave him. This breaking up of his family and separation from his wife and children so affected him that he quit drinking and started off for a western city, in order to get away from old associations, there to begin life anew, and make for his family another home into which the old blight and curse should never come. But this change did not take him out of the sphere of temptation, nor diminish the strength of his appetite. He fought allurement and desire for awhile, and then yielded, little by little at a time, still fighting, but steadily losing the power to resist, until he was down again. That was five years ago. Falling and rising; now struggling for the mastery over his appetite, and now in its toils again; now taking his place in respectable society, and now rejected and despised; never standing firm for longer than a few months at a time—the years since then have passed. Two weeks ago he came drifting back to his native city, a poor, helpless, broken wreck, with a vague impression on his mind that he was being impelled hither by a force he could not resist. He came, as a drifting wreck, wholly purposeless. Let me tell you the story of what followed, just as he told it to me. I give you his own words as near as I can remember them. He said:

"'A man in Pittsburg, to whom I told a plausible story, in which was not a single word of truth, got a pass for me on the railroad to this city, and gave me two dollars with which to get something to eat on the way. The first thing I did, after parting from him, was to buy a bottle of whisky. With this as my companion, I took my seat in the second-class car to which my pass assigned me and started on my journey eastward. The bottle was empty before half the distance had been made. It was filled at one of the stopping places, and emptied again before the trip was completed. So drunk that I could not walk steadily, I was thrust out of the car by a breakman on the arrival of the train at midnight, and sent into the street homeless and friendless. I still had forty cents in my pocket, and might have procured a night's lodging, but I preferred the station-house to a comfortable bed, in order that I might have the means of getting my drink in the morning. When morning came, I made a narrow escape from a commitment to the county prison for drunkenness and vagrancy, but got off with a reprimand and a warning. At a cheap restaurant I spent fifteen cents for a breakfast, and ten cents for something to wash it down. In less than an hour afterwards the remaining fifteen cents had disappeared, and I was the worse for three glasses of bad whisky.

"'Aimless and miserable, I wandered about for the whole of that day; spending the greater part of my time in bar-rooms, in the hope of being asked by somebody to drink. My thirst was growing intense. I was beginning to feel desperate. Late in the afternoon I went into a saloon and going up to the bar, called for a glass of whisky, making a motion with my hand as if I were going to take money from my pocket. The bar-keeper eyed me sharply for a moment or two, and then gave me the liquor for which I had called. It was at my mouth and down my throat with the quickness of a flash. I knew by the man's face that he would kick me out of the saloon, but what cared I for that! My fumbling in my pockets, and turning them inside out, and my calling on God to witness that I had money when I came in, did not save me. I was collared and dragged to the door, and then kicked into the street. As I fell on the pavement, a crowd of boys jeered me, and when I attempted to rise, pushed me over. A friendly policeman saved me from their farther persecutions.

"'I was not drunk. The glass of whisky which I had taken did nothing more than give a little steadiness to my nerves. As I arose from the pavement, assisted by the policeman, I saw on the opposite side of the street a face that made my heart stand still. A young girl had stopped, and was looking across at me with a half-startled, half-pitiful expression. It was my own daughter, whom I had not seen for five years. A little girl of twelve when I last saw her, she was now a tall and beautiful young lady in her eighteenth year. Her dress was plain, but very neat, and she looked as if she might be on her way home from some store, or office, or manufactory, in which she was earning a livelihood. Scarcely had I recognized her, ere she turned and went on her way. But it seemed as if I could not let her go out of my sight. As though some strong invisible chords were drawing me, I started after her, keeping so close that her form was always in view. So I followed, now within a few paces, and now farther behind, lest she might turn and recognize me, until we had gone for a distance of seven or eight blocks. Then she passed lightly up to the door of a house, and after ringing the bell, turned her face while she stood waiting, so that I could see it again. It came to me like a gleam of sunlight. But in a moment after the sweet vision was gone, and I stood in outer darkness.

"'I lingered about the neighborhood until the fast failing twilight was gone. Night shut in; the lamps were lighted, and the hurrying sound of homeward feet became almost silent. And still I lingered. Inside were, I believed, the wife and children I had once so loved and tenderly cared for; and I stood on the outside, an alien to the love which had once been given me in lavish return. Twice I ascended the steps and laid my hand on the bell, but turned each time and went back without ringing it. I will go away, I said, and make myself more fitted to come into their presence. But where was I to go? Friendless and penniless, soiled and tattered, who would take me in? And then there rushed upon me such an overwhelming sense of helplessness and degradation, and of the utter folly of any new attempt to lead a better life, that the very blackness of despair came down upon my soul! Better die! said a voice within me. Better take the chances of the life to come than the certain misery of this. God is more merciful than man. I hearkened to this voice. A single plunge in the river, and all would be over. I felt the waters closing about me, and the rest and peace of their dark oblivious depths. I was sitting on the curb-stone with my face buried in my hands, when this purpose was reached, and was about rising to put it into execution, when a hand was laid on my shoulder, and a voice, whose tones sent a thrill through me, said: "You seem to be in trouble, my friend." It was the voice of a man whose family physician I had been more than ten years before, and its sound was as familiar to my ears as if no time had intervened since I heard it last. I could not move. A great weight seemed holding me down. "Are you sick?" The voice was even kinder than at first. "Yes," I replied. "Sick with an incurable disease."

"'He did not speak again for several moments. Then he said, in a voice full of mingled compassion and surprise; "Dr. R——! Can it indeed be you?" "All that is left of me," I returned, not looking up or attempting to rise. "Sick, but not with an incurable disease, Dr. R——," he said, after a brief pause. "There is a Physician who can cure all manner of sickness. He can make the lame walk, the deaf hear, the blind see, and bring even the dead to life. Come to this good Physician, my old friend, and be healed of your malady."

"'How strange and new this sounded—almost as

much so as if I had never before heard of this Physician; and in fact, so far as any conscious need of Him was concerned, I never had. Sickness of the soul and the healing of spiritual diseases had been to me little more than figures of speech; and my idea of a Physician of souls had rarely lifted itself above the thought of a vague symbolism that might mean anything or nothing. But now there was in it something tangible; the impression of a real personality; and my poor, despairing heart began to turn and lift itself, and to feel in its dead hopes the feeble motions of a new life. And when he said again, "Come, my old friend, come to this good Physician," and drew upon my arm, I got up from the curb-stone on which I was sitting, and stood cowering and trembling in my shame and weakness, dimly wondering as to how and where this Physician was to be found. "And now, doctor," he said, "do you really wish to be saved from the power of this dreadful appetite?" "I would rather drown myself than continue any longer in this awful bondage," I replied.

"'And then I told him how I had made up my mind to gain deliverance through the desperate means of suicide. "My poor friend," he answered, "there is a safer and better way. Come with me."

"'I did not hesitate, but went with him. As we walked, he told me of this Christian Home, and said that if I would enter it and make use of all the means of reformation to which it would introduce me, I might hope to be restored to myself, and gain such power over my appetite as to hold it forever in check. And here I am, with new hopes and new purposes, and a trust in God for deliverance and safety, that my heart and my reason tell me shall not be in vain.'"

After Mr. Granger had related Dr. R——'s story, he said: "If that man can be saved, and if I can be saved, through trust in God, no one is so fallen that he may not be lifted up, and his feet set in a secure way." Then, after a slight pause, he added, in a subdued and humble voice: "But in and of myself I cannot hope to stand. When I forget that, my imminent peril is nigh."

CHAPTER XV.

AFTER two or three weeks, the change in Mr. Granger's appearance was so great that I found it difficult to realize the fact that he was the same man whom we had, a little while before, taken from the county prison. Nutritious food was rapidly restoring muscular waste, and giving tension to shattered nerves. Sound sleep was doing its good work also. While above all, and vital to all, was a new-born trust in God, and a submission of himself to the Divine will and guidance.

I could see the steady growth of a new quality in his face; the expression of which was becoming softer, yet not losing the strength of a true manliness. The old, confident ring did not come back to his voice; though it gained in firmness, and you felt in its tone the impulse of a resolute will.

Up to this time I had said nothing to Granger about his wife and children, nor had he referred to them; but I knew, from signs not to be mistaken, that they were hardly for a moment absent from his thoughts; and I was sure that his heart was going out to them with irrepressible yearnings. It could not be otherwise, for he was a man of warm affections.

Nor had I said anything of this new effort at reformation to Mrs. Granger, whom I had seen twice since she told me of her husband's visit to the photograph rooms. I had been trying ever since to find another place for Amy, but so far was not successful. Why should I keep the good news away from her any longer? I had withheld it so far, in fear lest the hope and joy it must occasion might too quickly be dashed to the ground. But now I was beginning to have a more abiding faith in this last struggle upon which Granger had entered; because of the new and higher elements of strength it was calling into exercise.

For several days I debated the question, and then dropped a note to Mrs. Granger, asking her to call at my office. She came promptly, hoping that I had succeeded in finding a situation for her daughter. I had not noticed before how much her beautiful hair had changed. It was thickly sprinkled with gray. A shadow lay in her large brown eyes, which had lost much of their former depth and brightness. There was an earnest, expectant manner about her as she came forward. I saw that she was troubled and anxious, and half-regretted having sent for her, not knowing, of course, how she might be affected by the information I was about to communicate.

"Any good word for Amy?" she asked, with an effort to keep her voice from betraying the suspense from which she was suffering.

"Nothing certain, as yet," I replied. "But there's something else that I wish to talk with you about."

Her large eyes widened a little. She asked no question, but kept her gaze fixed upon me.

"Have you heard anything from Mr. Granger since Amy was at the photograph rooms?"

She shook her head, but did not remove her eyes from my face.

"You did not know that he was arrested and sent down to prison?"

A slight negative movement of the head, and a close, hard shutting of the lips.

"I heard of it, and went with a friend to see him."

A start, a catching of the breath, and a receding color.

"I think he must have died within twenty-four hours if we had not taken him from the cell in which we found him. Utterly broken down in body and spirits, he had given up in despair."

The eyes of Mrs. Granger dropped swiftly from my face. I saw a strong shiver run through her body. Then she was motionless as a statue.

"Mr. Stannard and I went to see him," I resumed. "We had an order for his release, and took him to the new Reformatory Home in Locust Street, where he has been ever since."

Mrs. Granger raised her eyes and looked at me again. No light had come into them. If anything, the shadow that lay over them was deeper. I was disappointed at this apparent indifference, and at her failure to ask me any questions in regard to her husband.

"Mr. Stannard and I feel very hopeful about him."

She shook her head in a dreary way. "There is no hope," she murmured, in a dead level voice. "It was kind of you and Mr. Stannard, and you meant well. But it will be of no use. If you had brought me word that he was dead, I would have felt thankful to know that his helpless, hopeless, wretched life was over. It is hard for me to say this, Mr. Lyon, but I can say nothing less. He is in the hands of a demon whose strength, as compared with his, is as that of a giant to a new-born infant."

"Is not God stronger than any devil?" I asked, speaking with quiet earnestness.

There was another quick, half-wondering dilation of her large eyes, and a swift change in her countenance. She waited for me to go on.

"There is no sin from which God cannot save a man," said I.

"Except, I have sometimes thought, the sin of drunkenness; it so utterly degrades and destroys the soul. It seems to leave nothing upon which men, or angels, or even God Himself can take hold."

She spoke with some bitterness, but with more of doubt and sorrow in her voice.

"Many men," I replied, "who had fallen quite as low as Mr. Granger, have been saved from this dreadful sin and curse by means of the Institution where we have placed your husband, and are back in their old social places again, and restored to their once broken and deserted families."

A death-like paleness swept suddenly into her face. She reached out her hands and caught the table by which she was sitting, holding on to it tightly, and trembling violently.

"Have you not heard about this Franklin Home?" I asked.

She shook her head, her lips moving in a silent No.

"It is a Christian home," I said. "All its inmates are brought under Christian influences. There is daily readings of the Scripture, and also family prayer in the chapel of the Institution. Every Sunday evening religious worship is held in this chapel, and in the afternoon of Sunday there is a Bible class. First and last the inmates are taught that only by God's grace and help can they ever hope to overcome completely the sin of drunkenness. They must fight this, as well as all other evil habits and inclinations, shunning them as sins against God, and looking to Him for the strength that will give them the victory; so seeking to be saved from all sins, and coming thereby completely within the sphere of His Divine protection."

The manner of Mrs. Granger was that of one who did not clearly understand what was being said to her. There were rapid changes in her face, lights and shadows passing swiftly across it.

"For over three weeks your husband has been in this Home, and the improvement is so great as to be almost marvelous."

She laid her head down upon my office table, and I saw that she was weeping.

"I have never had so great faith in your husband's efforts at reform as I feel now. He has passed below the limit of self-confidence; has lost all faith in himself; knows that he cannot stand in his own strength; that only God can help and save him."

I heard the office door open, and turning, saw Mr. Granger. As I uttered his name in a tone of surprise, his wife sprang to her feet, and turned toward him a face from which the color had gone out suddenly. The two gazed at each other for some moments, standing a little apart, their startled faces all convulsed.

"Helen! Oh, my poor Helen!" came trembling from Granger's lips, as he saw the sad changes which a few sorrowful years had wrought upon her. There was an involuntary reaching out of his hands; but he held himself away. His voice was inexpressibly tender and pitiful. Still, very still, she stood; then I saw a slight movement, and then, with a low cry, "My husband! my husband!" she sprang forward and laid her head on his bosom, his arms at the same moment gathering tightly around her. I went out and left them alone. When I came back, they were gone.

I was concerned about this. Granger had been, I felt, too short a time at the Home to be safely removed from its influence. I was not one of those who believed that in an instant of time a sinner was washed white and clean, and lifted wholly away from temptation and danger. To be born again, converted, renewed by the Spirit, had for me a different meaning. I had thought much about these things of late, and held many conversations with Mr. Stannard, whose mind to me seemed peculiarly enlightened. I believe that man must be a co-worker with God. That there was no washing until after repentance and the putting away of evils as sins; and that the "every whit clean," when applied to young converts, was a fallacy, and in consequence a snare; that "He that overcometh, the same shall be clothed in white raiment," and none others. I believed that a change of heart was a gradual thing, progressing with the new life of obedience to Divine laws, and that as obedience was continued and perfected, the new spiritual man became stronger and stronger, until at last able to stand firm, though all hell were in battle array against him.

Only a few weeks since we had lifted this man out of the mire and clay; only a few weeks of the new and better life. Was he strong enough to leave the safe harbor in which he had been anchored for so short a time, and try the open sea again? I did not believe it. My fear was, that he had gone home with Mrs. Granger, and that he would not return again to the Institution in which we had placed him. If this were so, I should tremble for his safety.

In the evening I went to the Home, and, to my great relief, found Mr. Granger in the reading-room. The whole expression of his countenance had changed. There was a light in it which I had not seen before. He grasped my hand and held it firmly for a few moments without speaking.

"Coming out right very fast," said I.

"Yes, faster than I had dared to hope," he replied.

"Did you go home with your wife?"

"No. We walked together for an hour after leaving your office, and then I came back here. I am too weak yet for any great trial of my strength. It is easy enough to stand with all these helps around me; but I must grow stronger in myself before I attempt to walk alone. And then I cannot be a burden to my poor wife, who is already overtaxed in her efforts to keep a home for our children. As soon as possible I must get something to do that I may come to her relief."

"Will you open a law office again?"

"Law is my profession. I have no skill in anything else. It is my only way of return to business and profit. Yes, just as soon as I feel strong enough to make the effort, I shall endeavor to get into practice. In passing along Walnut Street to-day, I saw several small offices to let, any one of which would suit me. My great drawback will be the want of a law library."

"Don't let that trouble you," I replied. "There are plenty of old friends in the profession who will gladly let you have the use of books until you are able to buy for yourself. As soon as it is seen that you are in real earnest about getting on your feet again, you will receive a warm welcome and the grasp of many helping hands."

Within six weeks from the time Granger came out of prison, he had a desk in the office of a prominent lawyer, whose large practice enabled him to throw considerable business in his way from the very start. He still remained at the Reformatory Home, where, for a moderate price, he had a well-furnished room and excellent board. He not only identified himself with the Institution, but became deeply interested in the work of reform. He had, himself, been a cast-away on the desolate shore where so many thousands are wrecked every year; and he knew all the pains and horrors of such disasters. His pity and his sympathy drew towards him every new inmate of the Home, and prompted him to do all that lay in his power to encourage, comfort and help him to begin that new and higher life, in which, as he never failed to urge, true and permanent safety could alone be found.

"Have you ever attended religious services at the Home on Sunday evening?" Mr. Stannard asked, one day. It was about two months after Mr. Granger's admission. I had not.

"Come round to-morrow night. It will interest

you. Rev. Mr. S—— is going to preach to the men."

I went, and, to my surprise, found a little chapel, which held about two hundred, so well filled that only a few seats remained. There were quite as many women as men; wives, mothers, sisters or friends of the inmates. A little way back from the reading-desk I noticed Mr. Granger, and it almost took my breath when I saw his wife sitting on one side of him and his daughter on the other. There was reading from the Bible, and one or two hymns, in which the whole congregation joined heartily. Then a most excellent sermon from one of the leading clergymen of the city.

It was a long time since I had been so much impressed as by the services of this evening. I sat where I could look into the faces of nearly all who were present. Just in front of me was Mr. Granger, and beside him his wife and daughter, all attentive listeners to the discourse. Not far from them I recognized the person of Dr. R——. He sat between two women, also, and I had no doubt from the way they leaned towards him, or turned now and then to look at him, that one was his wife and the other the daughter whom he had followed for so many blocks in the street, too sorely conscious of his degradation to dare even to speak to her. And Mr. Lawrence, who had written to his wife and received the promise of her speedy return, was there likewise; and by him sat a woman with a calm, strong, true face, and I saw, with a throb of feeling, which sent the moisture to my eyes, that she was holding one of his hands tightly in one of hers.

There were nearly a hundred men present who had been, or were now, inmates of the Institution; and wives, sisters and mothers almost as many more. Sad, indeed, was the writing on nearly all of the faces into which I gazed; but light mingled with the shadows. There were men before me who had been drunkards for over ten and twenty years—some for even a longer time—and women who had borne the awful sorrow of the drunkard's wife for periods quite as long.

What followed touched me most of all. After the benediction was said, and the congregration began slowly to retire, I saw little groups of twos and threes and fours gathering here and there, standing or sitting, and soon comprehended what it meant. Here you saw a husband and wife, who had lived apart for years, sitting close together in earnest conversation; and there wife and children gathered about a husband and father who had long been lost to them, but was now found again. What light, and even joy, were to be seen in the faces of many, the women's faces especially. And it was affecting to notice some of the children—little girls more particularly—holding tightly to their father's hands, sitting close to and leaning against them, or looking up lovingly into their faces. There were many tender re-unions that night in the little chapel, above whose reading-desk a silken banner held the inscription, "BY THE GRACE OF GOD, I AM WHAT I AM."

I made my way, as soon as the crowd had cleared a little, to where Mr. Granger and his wife and daughter were standing together. They looked very happy—yes, "happy" is the word—and greeted me with much cordiality.

"Is this the first time you have attended worship in our chapel?" Mr. Granger asked.

"The first time," I replied. "But I feel as if it was not going to be the last. I have heard people speak of the 'sphere of worship,' but never knew what it meant until to-night."

"It is because," he answered, "there are very few in the congregations that assemble here on Sunday evenings, who do not feel that their only hope is in God, and that without His grace they cannot stand for a moment."

"Who are all the people I see around me?" I asked.

"About thirty of the men are present inmates of the Home. Nearly all the rest were formerly inmates, and are standing firm. They come here on Sunday evenings; and those who have families bring their wives, and many their children. If one absents himself from these Sunday evening services, there is a feeling of concern in regard to him; for experience has shown, that the first sign of danger is a manifest indifference to the things of religion. I never look at that banner above the reading-desk, without a new sense of my entire dependence on God for strength to walk safely in the midst of temptation; and I am sure that its silent admonition has wrought a like influence with many others. It is by God's grace that I am what I am."

Mrs. Granger's large eyes were fixed on her husband's face while he spoke; and I saw something of their old charm coming back into them. A soft smile was hovering like a faint gleam of sunshine on her lips. We moved back the chairs amid which we were standing, making with them a small circle, and sat down together.

"My last night in the Home," said Granger, after a brief silence. His voice had lost some of its steadiness.

"Indeed!" I betrayed a little surprise.

"Yes." He turned towards his wife, looking at her tenderly. We are going to set up our household gods again."

The smile grew warmer on her lips.

"We have taken a little home, and are going to make a new start in life; and there is going to be in this home what was never seen in the old home. Shall I tell you what that is, my good friend to whom I owe so much?"

I waited for him to go on. Hushing his voice, and speaking reverently, he said: "A family altar."

Before the silence that followed was broken, we were joined by the president and two or three gentlemen who were active in the management of the Home. While I was talking with them, Mr. and Mrs. Granger, with their daughter, drew away, and a little while afterwards I saw them separate at the door of the chapel.

On the next day Granger left the Institution, and went back into the old common life, to try, amidst its thousand enticements to evil, the new sources of strength in which he was now trusting for safety.

CHAPTER XVI.

STILL in the very prime of manhood, the springs of action were yet strong. An orderly life soon restored Granger to a measure of the old vigor, and it was not long before cases of importance began to come into his hands. And now my concern for him began to grow again. If the engrossing cares of his profession, and the worldliness that creeps in so easily through the door that prosperity opens, should draw him into religious indifference, and inspire him with self-confidence, would not the old peril return?

One thing gave me much assurance. Granger had identified himself with the cause of temperance, and made frequent public addresses. He took an active part in all the movements designed to effect restrictive legislation, and was the author of several able articles in which the magnitude of the liquor traffic, and its attendant evils were set forth with startling boldness.

Had the family altar been set up? Yes. I put the question direct about six months after he had left the Institution in Locust Street. He laid his hand quietly but firmly on my arm as he replied: "In my home and in my heart."

His countenance softened, and his eyes grew tender. I learned then for the first time that he had become much interested in church work, and had been chiefly instrumental in the establishment of a mission school in a destitute part of the city; and that he did not confine his efforts alone to the poor children who were gathered into this school, but endeavored to reach with good influences their parents, many of whom were sadly degraded, and most of them intemperate. On expressing my gratification, he merely said: "I would make a poor return for all the good I have received, if I did not try to do something for others. The heart that closes itself to gratitude, closes itself to higher and diviner things. If the love of God be in a man, it must prompt him to help and save others; and his love is spurious—of himself and selfish—call it by what name he may, if it does not do this."

"What about that old appetite?" I asked on another occasion. It was six months later. "Does it trouble you?"

"No."

"Has it been extirpated?"

He looked at me for a few moments, a serious expression gathering on his face, and then replied: "It would be about as safe for me to put a pistol to my head as a glass to my lips. Appetite is not dead; it has only been removed from the seat of power, and made passive and subordinate. I give it no opportunity. I resist its slightest effort to rise, and hold its indulgence as a sin which I dare not commit."

"When its motions are felt, how do you resist them?"

"As I would resist a temptation to steal or commit murder or any other sin against God. I turn my thought from the image or allurement, and hold myself free from action. If temptation presses, I lift my heart and say, 'Lord, deliver me from evil;' and He does deliver me."

"Do you often have these temptations?" I asked.

"Their assaults are growing less and less frequent, and less and less violent. But I make it a rule to keep away as far from the enemy's ground as possible. Invitations to public dinners, where liquor is served, I rarely, if ever, accept. And I am as chary of private entertainments, where wine is too often more freely dispensed than water. Nothing would tempt me to go inside of a drinking saloon, unless it were in order to save some fallen brother, and then my good purpose would be a panoply of defence."

"Do you never expect to have this appetite wholly removed?"

"What may come in the future is more than I can say. But safe abiding to the end is what I desire, and I do not mean to fail through any overweening confidence in the utter extinction of this appetite."

"Do you not believe that God will take it away in answer to prayer—take it away by an act of grace, and without any resistance to the demands of appetite, or co-operation of any kind on your part?"

"No, I do not believe anything of the kind. I have met with some who held such a view, and who spoke confidently as to themselves; but I have always regarded them as being in more danger than others. I cannot understand how it is possible for God to save a man who makes no effort to save himself. I have seen quite a number of cases in the last year, where men professed to be cleansed from all sin, drunkenness included, in a moment of time, and simply in answer to prayer. It did not take a great while to make it manifest that the old Adam was about as strong in them as before. Some of them led better lives, and were able to keep free from drunkenness; but it was not because their evil inclinations had been removed in answer to prayer and faith, but because they began fighting them, and looking to God as they fought, and overcoming through the Divine power that is given to all who will take it. Regeneration is a slow and gradual work; not the sudden creation of a new spiritual man with all of his affection in Heaven. This higher life is not attained through faith and prayer, but through combat against the evils that are in the human heart. The Church is militant.

"'Must I be carried to the skies
On flowery beds of ease,
While others fought to win the prize,
Or sailed through bloody seas?

> 'Sure I must fight, if I would reign;
> Increase my courage, Lord.
> I'll bear the cross, endure the pain,
> Supported by Thy Word.'

"Fight against what? The world, the flesh and the devil. Where? In our hearts; for nowhere else can they assail or do us harm; and with God on one side, and the Divine power of His Word from which to take sword and shield, we may be invincible if we will—Christian soldiers, fighting our way to Heaven; not weak spiritual babes, borne thither in supporting arms, and of little use when we get there."

Granger had been thinking, living and growing more than I had thought. I saw in clearer light the ground of his safety. He was not a mere professor, trusting for salvation in some ideal purification, or resting satisfied in simple church-membership; but an earnest inner-living and outer-working Christian man, who could give a reason which other men's reason might apprehend for the hope that was in him.

From this time my concern for Granger decreased; for I understood better wherein his strength lay. He was living a new life, obedient to Divine laws, in the higher and more interior regions of his mind; and this new life, or new spiritual man, born from above "of water and of the Spirit"—was ruling over the old natural life and holding it in orderly subjection. With him, reason and faith had become harmonized.

He was not walking blindly, nor in any false security, trusting in some dogma he could not understand; but in a clear spiritual light—a thinking as well as a believing Christian. With him, faith was the "*evidence* of things not seen;" and this faith, or evidence, had two foundations to rest upon, the Divine Law, and the reason which God had given him for the apprehension of that Law. "A blind faith is worth nothing—is no faith at all," he would say. "Is, in fact, spiritual blindness. But Christ came to open the eyes of the spiritually blind that they might see, and discern the weightier things of His law—judgment, mercy and faith—in the keeping of which salvation is alone to be found."

"The whole theory of religion is embraced in this simple precept," he once said to me: "Cease to do evil because it is sin, and therefore contrary to the Divine Law. When a man does this, he makes an effort to obey God; and obedience is higher than faith and more effectual than sacrifice. Just as soon as a man begins to shun the evils to which he is inclined, because to do them would be sin, God begins in him the work of purification, and gives him strength for still further resistance. This is true saving faith; for it is the faith of obedience—the faith that looks humbly to God, trusts in Him and seeks to do His will. The first effort may be very feeble, but if it be a true effort, Divine strength will flow into it; and then he will have an almost immediate sense of deliverance, followed by a season of rest and peace. The dangers of this first state are many. In the parable of the Sower, our Lord has declared them. Only they 'which, in an honest and good heart, having heard the Word, keep it, and bring forth fruit with patience'—the fruit of right living—can attain to the kingdom. Too many err in mistaking this first delight, when the springing blade feels the refreshing airs and warm sunshine of heaven, for the later harvest time. With them the good seed has fallen in stony places or among thorns. Alas! that we have so many of these."

Mr. Granger's interest in the cause of temperance grew as he continued to devote all the time he could spare from his profession to the work of its extension. When, two years after his reformation, that remarkable movement known as the "Woman's Crusade," began in Ohio, and spread with the rapidity of a prairie fire from town to town and State to State, until it reached almost every city and hamlet in the land, he gave it such aid and approval as lay in his power. I was surprised at this, and said so frankly.

"It is a mere outbreak of wild enthusiasm," I remarked, "and will die as suddenly as it has flamed up. And, moreover, those who are engaged in it are acting in violation of law, and order, and the sacredness of individual rights."

He waited for a little while before answering me, and then said: "I have watched this movement, and thought about it a great deal, and I must own that it has stirred my heart profoundly. There is something deeper in it than I am yet able clearly to comprehend. That its effects are marvelous no one can deny—and good as well as marvelous. If praying with and for saloon-keepers, in or out of their bar-rooms, will induce them to abandon their deadly traffic, then I say 'God-speed!' to those who see in this way of fighting the common enemy their line of duty. If praying will shut the doors of all the saloons in a town, by all means let prayer be tried."

"But is it really prayer that does the work?"

"Prayer is certainly the chief agency. No one can question that."

"You believe, then, that because a praying band of women kneel down in a saloon and pray to God to turn the heart of the keeper away from his evil work and lead him to abandon it, that God answers their prayers and converts the saloon-keeper?"

"You have the facts of such conversions before you; and they are not a few. How will you explain them?"

"I confess myself at fault. But I do not believe that God was any the less inclined to convert the saloon-keeper, and lead him to abandon his work of destroying men, soul and body, before the women prayed, than He was afterwards."

"Perhaps not. Indeed, I am sure He was not. God's love for the human race is infinite, and cannot therefore gain any increase through man's intercession. If He waits to be entreated, it is for the entreaty that shall change man's attitude towards Him, not His attitude to man. And herein I take it lies the value and the power of prayer."

"But how can the prayers of a band of women change a saloon-keeper's attitude towards God?" I asked. "He doesn't pray, but actually sets himself against prayer. Instead of looking to God, he rejects Him."

"All that is effected by prayer we cannot know," Granger replied; "for its influence is in the region of things invisible to mortal eyes. We understand but little of the laws that govern spiritual forces; but that they are as unerring in their operations as any law of nature, we may safely conclude."

Mr. Stannard joined us here, and, learning the subject of our conversation, said: "If you will reflect a little, I think you will see that there must be a kind of spiritual medium or atmosphere on which our thoughts and feelings pass in some mysterious way from one to another, as light and sound are transmitted by our common atmosphere. Let us suppose, by way of illustration, that a mother is thinking intently of her absent son, and her heart at the same time going out lovingly towards him. Or, let us suppose that she feels deep concern for his spiritual state, and is praying earnestly that he may turn from the evil of his ways and give his heart to God. Now, will not her thought of her son reach him on some medium of transmission too subtle to be perceived by our grosser senses, and so make her present to his thoughts? And will not the loving concern which is affecting her so deeply reach him at the same time, and open his heart to the heavenly influences which have been waiting, it may be for years, at the shut door, for an opportunity to come in? God has not changed. He has not waited for the mother's prayers to reach Him before He will save her son; but the mother's prayers have affected the son, and revived, it may be, old states of innocence, or reverence for God, or thoughts of love and duty into which angelic impulses might flow, and the Spirit of God take hold, and through them quicken the sleeping conscience.

"There is a doctrine, which, if true—and I think it must be true—throws a strong light on this subject, and explains the phenomena of what are regarded as answers to prayer. It is this: From infancy up to mature years, the Lord continually provides for the storing up in the memory of pure, and true, and innocent things—such as various states of innocence and charity; of love towards relatives, brothers and sisters, teachers and friends; of mercy toward the poor and needy, and kindness towards all. When infancy is passed, and the mind begins to open, then, as far as it is possible to be done, the Lord provides that some precepts of life be stored up, as duty to the Lord and the neighbor, and also knowelge of faith. These remain protected in the inner memory, as the things by which the Lord can operate with man after he arrives at the age of freedom and rationality; and it is by means of these that He lifts him out of his inherited evil affections, and leads him heavenward."

"A most important doctrine, if true," I said. "But I am not able to see how it explains the phenomena of answers to prayer."

"Suppose," replied Mr. Stannard, "we take the case of a saloon-keeper in whose memory, hidden away and covered up for years, have lain some of these innocent, and tender, and merciful states, stored there in childhood through the loving care of a mother. The Lord has been very watchful over them; and has kept them hidden and safe in some closely-sealed chamber, lest the evil things of his evil life should destroy them. Not one of these states has been lost; not a good or true precept erased from the book of his memory—they have only been kept away from his consciousness while he immersed himself in evil, so that they might not be rejected and lost. This man is in his bar-room. The door opens, and half a dozen women enter. The moment he sees them, his anger flames out, and he launches frightful oaths and vile imprecations against them. But the women are in earnest. They believe in the power of prayer, and are going to try its influence here. As they pass into the saloon, the clear, sweet voice of the leader swells out, and for the first time in a dozen years, it may be, there breaks on the man's ears the words, 'All hail the power of Jesus' name!' It does not need the chorus of voices that take up the words and music to drown his imprecations. They have already died on his lips. What a strange feeling has come over him! Where is he? In the old village church, listening to his mother's or sister's voice in the choir? The Lord has ever been very near to him, though unseen and unknown, waiting for an opportunity like this. How still he stands, listening and bending a little forward towards the singers! And now, in the strange hush that follows, the women kneel, and one of them lifts her voice, speaking to God reverently, and asking Him to touch and soften the heart of this man, who has forgotten the loving precepts of his mother and the God whom she served, and who has given himself to the work of destroying his fellow-men. 'Have pity on him, Lord!' she says, in pleading tones; 'for the hurt to himself will be deeper than the hurt to his neighbor. By the memory of his mother's love, of his pure and innocent childhood, of the prayers that came once from his sweet, baby lips, touch and soften his heart, and turn it to higher and better and holier things.' Do you wonder, as the women rise, and commence singing 'Nearer my God to Thee,' that the bowed head of the saloon-keeper is not raised; that his eyes are dim, if not blinded by tears? Do you wonder that conviction of sin strikes him to the heart; or that, under these influences, quickened and strengthened by the Spirit of God, which has found an opportunity in this stirring of old memories and revival of old states, he is filled with such a horror of his old life, and such sorrow for the evil he has done, that he resolves, through God's help, to be a new and a better man?

"Now, what did prayer effect in this case? Did God soften and change the heart of this man in answer to the prayers that were offered in his saloon; or, were these prayers the agency by which God's Spirit was able to reach his heart and vivify the remains of innocent, and good, and holy things which, through the Divine mercy, had been stored up in childhood and youth, and kept hidden away and safe from destruction? I cannot comprehend how the first could be. The last is clear to my apprehension. The first makes God seem worse than indifferent. Souls may perish by myriads if no one will make intercession for them. He will not stoop to save unless supplication be offered. But in the latter view, He is forever bending down, merciful and compassionate; forever reaching out His hands; forever providing the means of salvation; forever seeking to save that which is lost. Prayer becomes a more powerful agent, in so far as its rationale is seen. Faith is not diminished, but made stronger. We need not ask God to be gracious; to turn away His anger; to be pitiful and compassionate—for He is as much more loving, and pitiful, and compassionate, than any man or angel, as the infinite is greater than the finite. But we may feel sure, if we pray from the heart for submission to the Divine will; for patience, and humility, and strength for duty and self-denial, that our prayers will be answered, in the degree that they are offered in spirit and in truth."

"But our prayers for others," said Mr. Granger; "what form of intercession shall we use for them? How shall we make them avail for good? This is now the important question."

"Let each pray out of the fullness of his heart," Mr. Stannard replied. "If it be with those whom we seek to influence and turn from evil to God, the effect will be more marked, and often attended with more favorable results than when we pray for the absent and the unseen. Our voices and tones, and the words we speak, are heard by those for whom we thus pray, and more quickly penetrate the locked chambers of the soul, where the Lord has been keeping the remnant of precious things which has been left from infancy and childhood, and by the quickening and life of which, He can save their souls from sin. And let us not fail to pray for the absent in whom our interest has been awakened; for our beloved ones; for any and all towards whom our hearts are yearning. And, as we pray, let us think of them intently, so that we may come nearer to them in spirit, and our thought of God bring the thought of Him into their minds, so that He may be able to stir in their hearts the motions of a better life. The Lord is not waiting for our prayers to avail with Him that He may do this; but for our prayers, it may be, as the only means by which the doors of their hearts can be opened to let Him come in."

CHAPTER XVII.

THE "Crusade," as it was called, went on; and for awhile the whole country was in a state of wondering excitement. Thousands of saloons were closed, and in many towns the traffic in intoxicating liquor ceased altogether. Brewers, especially in some of the larger western cities, took the alarm, as well they might, for the sale of beer had diminished so rapidly that the fear of ruin began to stare them in the face. At Cincinnati, Chicago and St. Louis, so heavy a loss was suffered in the internal revenue from malt liquors that Government officials became much disturbed in consequence.

And still the Crusade went on. But now the surprised and discomfited enemy began to rally his scattered forces. In some of the smaller towns he had fought desperately; but only with partial success in a few cases. Except in the larger cities, he had been sorely hurt, or vanquished altogether. But here, he was able to make his first sure stand, and to begin striking back with an effective force that restored his confidence. The aid of the press was invoked; appeals made to the law; fines imposed, and the interference and protection of local governments demanded. Praying in saloons was declared to be a nuisance, if not a crime against social order; and the assembling of women in the streets for singing and prayer was forbidden because it led to riot. In Cincinnati, Cleveland and other cities, disgraceful attacks were made by brutal men on some of the praying bands; and in a few cases Christian women were arrested and sent to prison.

Almost as suddenly as this strange, intense and irresistible impulse had risen, gained strength and swept over the land, did it seem to die away; and the enemy said it was dead, and made rejoicings over its obsequies. The wise ones who knew from the beginning that it would speedily come to nought, were happy in their fancied prescience. As for myself, the result was scarcely different from what I had anticipated. The thing was abnormal, in my view, and could not last. Merely an impulse—wild and strong—which must die from exhaustion. But my sympathies had been all on the side of the movement; and there were times when the irresistible strength of its onward rush had led me to question whether some new spiritual force had not been evolved, through the agency of these praying women, which was destined to sweep this fearful curse of intemperance from our land.

But the seeming collapse of the movement left my mind free to drift back among former ideas and impressions, and even to take up the belief that as a result of this wild impulse, there would follow a corresponding indifference and supineness.

16

"What do you think of the woman's movement now?" I asked of Mr. Granger, who had made several public addresses while the excitement was at its height in our city, and in act, as well as speech, given it both aid and sympathy. "I was afraid of this," I added, before he had time to answer my question.

"Afraid of what?" he inquired.

"Of its utter collapse. A little while ago, and it was the great sensation of the day. The columns of our most influential and most widely-circulating newspapers were teeming with its marvels and its achievements. To-day, there is scarcely to be found in any of them so much as a paragraph an inch long to tell of its dying throes."

"And yet," he answered, speaking with an earnestness that surprised me, "this woman's movement was never so strong, and deep, and effective as it is to-day."

"I do not see the evidence," I replied.

"There is more real strength in unobtrusive, thoughtful, well-organized effort, than in the impetuous sweep of high-wrought impulse," said Granger. "In this great pioneer movement, this wild rush of wronged, and in many cases, heart-broken and desperate women, as, losing faith and hope in man, they sprang upon their deadly foe with a bitter cry to God for help, there came to them a revelation of the true sources of their power. The Lord answered them in the still, small voice, that grew clear, and sweet, and full of comfort and assurance as the noise of the whirlwind which had rent the mountain grew silent on the expectant air. In prayer they had found a weapon which, if rightly used, would make them invincible. Should they throw it away in despair, because in the very first great trial their hands had struck a little wildly, and the maddened foe seemed pushing them in consequence to a small disadvantage? Not so. They had heard the still, small voice, and knew it to be the voice of their Lord. If the prayers of a few hundreds, or a few thousands of Christian women could effect so much, what might not be done through the united prayers of tens and hundreds of thousands of such women, going up in concert from every city, town, village and neighborhood in the land? Here was a question full of significance and large with promise; and this is the question to which some of the best and most thoughtful women of our country are giving an earnest consideration to-day. But their hands are not resting while they consider it; nor is the sword by which they mean to have the victory lying idle in its scabbard. Neither prayer nor work among saloon-keepers and their families, and among their wretched victims, has ceased because the press no longer makes record of the fact; nor are the results less wide and cheering because the general public remains unadvised."

"Have you evidence of all this?" I asked, not concealing my astonishment.

"Abundant."

"And the work of praying in saloons still goes on?"

"No. That has ceased almost entirely. It was only a pioneer movement—a first wild rush upon the enemy and trial of his strength and resources. He is not only able to guard himself in this direction, but to weaken and divide the forces of his assailants if the advance is made upon him here. Organization, drill, discipline, wise generalship, a knowledge of the laws that govern in attack and defence; all these are in progress and being gained now."

"While the enemy, warned by his brief discomfiture, will entrench himself more securely," said I.

Granger smiled. "In war the resources of attack gain perpetually on defense. To be invincible is to be exceptional. Our women are already getting their siege guns in position, and organizing their sappers and miners. Their spies and scouts are busy; weak places are being discovered, and new modes of assault adopted. Let me give you a single instance connected with the present state of the war in our own city, which has never been intermitted. There was a certain saloon-keeper who had repulsed a praying band with considerable rudeness. He had a wife and two young daughters, and a son in his twelfth year; his family living a short distance from his bar-room. A committee of twelve women were selected to visit in the neighborhood, and do what lay in their power as well to repress the evil of intemperance as to guard the young from its fatal allurements. To visit and pray in saloons was no longer in their programme; but to reach the saloon-keepers and get them to abandon their traffic was; and to the work of doing this with the one I have mentioned they set themselves in sober earnest. Their first business was to learn all about him; the character of his family, and the nature of his home relations. He was not a bad man, the neighbors said, and, when he did not drink too freely, was kind and indulgent. A visit by a single one of the ladies was now made. At first, the wife was cold and distant; but the visitor was a woman with so much of the magnetism of Christian charity in her soul, and withal, so wise and prudent of speech, that it was not long before the heart of the saloon-keeper's wife opened to her, and the mother's hidden concern for her boy and two young daughters became manifest. After a brief, carefully-worded prayer, the visitor went away, but not without asking if she might not call again, and receiving an invitation to do so.

"At her next visit, she got farther down into the woman's heart and confidence, and was able to speak to her with some freedom about the danger that was in the path of her son—a danger it was scarcely possible for him to escape if his feet continued therein. The mother wept at the picture of peril the lady drew, and said: 'Oh, if my husband were in some other business.' The boy, a fine-looking lad, came in while they were talking about him. The lady took his hand and spoke to him kindly, then drew her arm about him and asked if he went to Sunday-school. On his saying No, she told him that she had a class of nice little boys, and would be glad to have him among them. He was pleased with her notice, and touched by her gentle kindness. On the next Sunday the lad presented himself at school, and was taken into the lady's class. He was very attentive and orderly, and promised to come again on the following Sunday. True to his promise, he was there, conducting himself with as much decorum and attention to his lessons as at first. A juvenile temperance meeting was held at the close of the school, and all who were not already members invited to join. A little to the surprise, and greatly to the lady's delight, the boy came forward and enrolled his name, receiving a card on which a pledge not to drink intoxicating liquors, or to give them away or traffic in them, was printed. At the bottom he wrote his signature.

"Naturally a little anxious to know what effect had been produced at home by this, and what the prospect of the boy's being able to keep his pledge, the lady called to see the saloon-keeper's wife near the close of the week, when she heard the following story:

"'When John told me what he'd done, and showed me his pledge, I was so glad! And I kissed him, and I said: "You must keep it forever and forever,

John." And he said that that was just what he meant to do. I kept it from his father; for I didn't know just how he'd take it. It seemed like a reflection on him. "John," says his father, on Monday morning, as he was leaving, "come along. I want you in the bar to-day. Peter's going on an excursion, and I can't be left all alone." John's face became right pale. He hadn't moved when his father got to the door; on seeing which, he called out sharply: "Did you hear me?" "You'll have to go, John," said I, in a whisper; for, you see, my husband's quick, and I was afraid for the boy. So they went out, and I was dreadfully troubled about him. It was, maybe, an hour afterwards that John returned. He had a scared kind of look about him, as he came in. "What's happened? Why have you come home?" I asked. "Father sent me home." "What for?" "Well, you see, mother, when Peter went, father told me that I must tend bar in his place; and then I said: 'I'm sorry, father, but I've taken the pledge and can't drink, nor give liquors away, nor sell it to anybody.' 'How dare you! you young villain!' he cried out; and I was afraid he'd knock me down, he looked so strange and wild like. Then he got red, and pale, and I thought once he was going to strangle, he breathed so hard, and then, as a customer came in, he said: 'Off home with you!'"

"'I didn't see anything of my husband until late that night,' continued the saloon-keeper's wife. 'He was alone in the bar and had to stay till business was over. I was sitting up for him, but John was in bed. He didn't say a word; but I noticed that he hadn't been drinking, and that gave me a little heart. In the morning he met John at the breakfast-table. I had been dreading this meeting. He didn't speak to him, but two or three times, as he sat eating in a silent, moody sort of way, I saw him steal a curious look at the boy's face. He hadn't half-finished his breakfast, it seemed to me, when he pushed his chair away, and says he: "John, I want you!" and went out of the dining-room into the passage. John got almost white, but went out and shut the door after him. I felt dreadfully, for I didn't know what was going to happen. In about a minute John came back alone. The color was all over his face now, and there was a great light in his eyes. "Father says it's best now that it's done, and that he'll expect me to keep it." I was such a happy woman, and cried for joy.

"'And that isn't all, ma'am,' she went on. 'Somehow my husband can't get over it; and he's spoken so kind to John ever since, and only last night he said: "Jane, I wish I could see my way clear out of this business. I don't like it at all." Oh, if he only could get out of it!'

"'Let us pray that the Lord will make all plain before him,' said the lady visitor. And then she knelt down with the woman and her two young daughters, and prayed for the husband and father with such earnestness of supplication that it seemed to them that God must and would hear and answer her prayers. And even while she prayed, led home by a Providence that was in this work, and governing its issues, the man stood at the very door of the room in which the petition went up, and heard every one of its carefully-chosen and reverently-uttered sentences. Did he enter the room all broken down? No; he went quietly away, giving no sign, but with an arrow of conviction in his heart. God had found a way of entrance, and was uncovering old memories and quickening old states, and calling to him from away down among the innocent things of his childhood. And he was hearkening, and repenting, and desiring a truer and better life than the one he had been leading. It was not long before the change came; for the good will is never long in finding the good way. In the work of destroying the souls and bodies of men there was one less; and in the work of service and restoration one more. Nay, might I not say many more—for the duplication and increase of every man's good or evil work is often very great."

"And is there much of this kind of work going on?" I asked.

"Yes," he replied, "and it is being gradually shaped into a system. Mistakes are being corrected; and the blind enthusiasm of too impetuous and strong-willed leaders repressed. The quiet intrusion that takes the enemy off guard is surer of victory than the open attack for which the blast of a trumpet has given warning to be ready. A besieged city that is proof against assault, may be reduced to capitulation through the cutting off of supplies. All this is being seen and understood. If neither by direct effort with a saloon-keeper, nor indirectly through his family, he can be induced to give up his hurtful business, then a thorough work of temperance reform will be inaugurated in his neighborhood, and the profits of his business be reduced, and if possible destroyed, through the loss of custom."

"Temperance men and temperance organizations have been trying to do this very thing for over fifty years," I replied, "and the sale of liquor has increased instead of diminishing. So long as you have the saloons you will have the customers. My faith in this thorough work of temperance reform of which you speak, is not, I am free to say, very great. I well remember the rise and progress of that first great tidal wave of reform, known as Washingtonianism, which went sweeping over the land. Hundreds of thousands took the pledge in a brief period, and we looked for a great percentage of diminution in the traffic, if not its destruction altogether. But taverns and bar-rooms went on flourishing as of old. As that great wave began to subside, another, and a feebler wave, that of Jeffersonianism, succeeded, and broke upon the rock-bound shores of license, and usage, and appetite, with scarcely a manifest impression. Then the work of a more general organization began, and the order of the Sons of Temperance was established, and set itself to the task of resistance. The promise was very great. It looked as if we were going to have, in every town and neighborhood, and in every city ward, a working force of temperance men, whose leading end and effort would be the extirpation of intemperance from their midst. But it was not so. Good work was done in many places; and thousands were protected and saved through pledges and associations, but the lodge meetings fostered a love of social ease and enjoyment, and steadily diminished the aggressive force of the organization. Then the Good Templars came to the front, and associated women in the work and administration of the order. But the same general causes which had wrought their enervating effects on the Sons of Temperance, were in operation with the Templars and kindred organizations as well. Love of office and of power and influence crept in, as they usually do where there are titles and honors and distinctions, and were of more account with many than the high purpose of the order itself. And so the work of temperance languished, and the enemy went on increasing in strength and confidence. What better promise now? What is to make this movement any more permanent than those which have gone before it? Human nature is the same. Enthusiasm will die of exhaustion, and the weariness in well-doing, which is sure to come, sooner or later, make idle the hands that are now so busy.

This reform work is so slow. We scarcely perceive its progress, and are often in doubt whether the movement be retrograde or onward. I must own to having more faith in legal than in moral suasion; in Maine Laws than in pledges."

"You forgot the new element," said Granger.

"What?"

"Prayer."

"Yes, I had forgotten."

"This is a religious as well as a temperance movement."

"True."

"And the effort is not merely to save men and women from the sin of drunkenness, but from all other sins. It is on a higher plane, and nearer the true sources of power. There is less of self in it, and more of God."

Granger spoke with great seriousness; and I saw that he had strong faith in the results of this new effort to organize a force that should have larger success than any which had hitherto set itself to do battle with intemperance.

CHAPTER XVIII.

THE work of "Gospel Temperance," as some began to call this latest effort to weaken and destroy the monster evil which had so long cursed the land, had a steady growth. Pious women in all the churches began to take part in it, and to strengthen its effective agencies. Prayer was incessant, and trusted in with implicit confidence. There was a literal acceptance of the promise, "That if two of you shall agree upon earth as touching anything that they shall ask, it shall be done for them of my Father which is in Heaven." They believed in the faith that removes mountains; and in the Word of Him who said, "Ask and ye shall receive; seek and ye shall find; knock and it shall be opened unto you." And when they met in His name, they had an assurance that He was in the midst of them. They were consecrating themselves to the work of saving souls that were well-nigh lost. Souls so far out of the reach of common Gospel influences, that even the churches had practically ceased to regard them as within the pale of salvation, and knew that God's power to save could be given them in the largest measure; for were not these souls, so fearfully imperilled, as precious to Him as the souls of any in His whole universe?

Never had the poor, degraded, suffering drunkard met, since his sad debasement, with such influences as came to him now. "My brother" fell on his ears in a voice so tender and compassionate, that feelings, which had lain dormant for years, stirred in his heart once more. A hand was laid on him so gently and kindly, that it seemed like the hand of a sister, or a wife, or a mother, felt in the long ago. And when prayer was offered for him, and he felt himself borne up to the throne of grace on the sweet, and tender, and pleading voices of gentle women, he broke all down, and under the suddenly-kindled hope of being rescued from his sin and misery, he lifted his poor, broken spirit to God and prayed for help, and mercy, and forgiveness.

Differ as we may about the philosophy of prayer, and the true sources of its power, of one thing we may be sure, that the ear of God is open to the cry of every sin-sick soul, if it is made in sincerity and in truth. As to the answer, that will depend on the measure of the willingness to receive. The love and the bountifulness are infinite The cry of the lips will bring nothing; the cry of the heart everything it is capable of receiving; and its capacity will always be equal to the displacement of evil in the life, because such evil is contrary to God's will and Word, and obstructs His influent love. The growth in grace, from the first moment the soul turns to God in prayer, and makes its first sincere effort to lead a new spiritual life, will be in an exact ratio to its resistance and conquest of evil on the plane of its natural life in the world and among men.

Prayer, in the hands of these women, wrought marvels. Men who had been drunkards for years, stopped suddenly, professed faith in Christ, joined the church, and became once more good and useful citizens. So quietly was all this done, in the second stage of this Gospel temperance work, that the general public heard little about it, and knew less. But the seed was being sown broadcast, and in due time the promise of an ampler harvest than had yet been seen was apparent on every side. Many men who had become reformed through the ministry of prayer, threw themselves into the work of rescuing the fallen; going from town to town, and by their eloquent appeals, stirring the hearts of the people, and arousing them to a sense of their duty and their danger.

And now, one after another, the slumbering churches began to awake and to recognize the hand of God in this work, and to give it countenance and approval, if not the practical support it yet so largely needed. But the work itself went on chiefly outside of the churches, though in the hands of the most active and earnest Christian men and women connected with the churches; for it was nearer to humanity than to sectarian conservatism, and drew to its aid those who had in them the larger measure of that Christianity which stoops, as Christ stoops, to the lowest and the vilest, if in so doing he may save them.

"I do not understand this strange indifference of the churches," said I, to Granger, one day. "In temperance work, they are doing little or nothing; and they might be doing so much."

"There are signs of better things," he replied. "Let us be patient for awhile. The time is not far off, I trust, when every society that calls itself a church, will have its special praying and working band of women, and an open door for the lowest and the vilest to come in; when the heathen who are perishing in the very shadow of its porches will take precedence of the heathen afar off. We have cheering intelligence from all sides. Almost every day we hear of new workers coming into the field, and of successes everywhere. In some places, from one-third to two-thirds of the whole population have signed the pledge, to the joy of good citizens and the consternation of liquor-dealers."

"If we could have anything like that in our poor, rum-cursed city!" I replied. "But hope is vain. In smaller communities, where each is known to all, and a chain of interest and personal influence holds the people in nearer contact, a common sentiment or impulse may bear them in a single direction. But it is not so here. Set any force you please in motion, and its impression can only be partial."

"We hope for a widely different result," Granger made answer. "Next week a man whose power with the people is almost a marvel and a mystery, will come from the West to our city; and then an effort will be made, through daily and nightly religious meetings, to get up such a temperance revival as has never been seen or heard of in the land."

I smiled at his ardor. He had become almost an enthusiast on the subject of temperance.

"We shall see," was my doubting response.

And we did see. The man came—this new apostle of temperance. He was not learned, but had largely the gift of persuasion; was not so eloquent as ready of speech; not so logical as impassioned; moved his audiences not so much by the clearness of a well-considered argument, as by the force of fact and incident. He was easy of manner, and at home with the people; recognizing in the lowliest and most wretched a brother, and telling the poor drunkard, whose hand he held so tightly, that he knew all about the pit in which his feet were mired, and all about the way of deliverance. "As God saved me, my brother, He will save you," was ever spoken with that sympathy and assurance which gives speech a passage to the heart. From the very commencement of his work, Francis Murphy exercised an influence that to some appeared half-miraculous. The halls in which his meetings in our city were held, were crowded night after night to overflowing, hundreds being unable to gain access. In the conduct of these meetings, there were no particularly remarkable features. They were opened with the reading of Scripture and prayer, followed by singing. Then there would be addresses from clergymen and others, including Mr. Murphy; and speeches and experiences from reformed men—the whole interspersed with the singing of temperance and revival hymns. During the progress of the meetings, and at their close, invitations to come and sign the pledge were given and responded to, very many coming forward each night and taking the pledge of total abstinence; the number soon increasing from hundreds to thousands. Men would enter the hall so badly intoxicated that they could scarcely walk straight, and before leaving sign their names to a pledge, and in many cases keep it. It was not with poor, degraded wretches alone—the outcast and the abandoned—that these meetings had power. Men of standing and education, who were beginning to feel the strength of an appetite that too surely betrays to ruin; lawyers, merchants, physicians; the representatives of all conditions and classes—alike felt the warning or the persuasion that came to them, and alike took heed.

"Will it last?" was my question after the weeks had begun gathering into months.

"Does not my good friend live too close to Doubting Castle?" returned Granger, to whom I had addressed the inquiry. He was already deeply absorbed in the exciting movement.

"Perhaps. But we hear of things being too good to last, you know."

"Things may be too bad to last; but never too

good. It is only the good that is really substantial," he returned, smiling.

"The good will last, of course. But how much is really genuine in all this, and how much factitious? Of the scores who nightly sign the pledge, and are pointed to God as the One who alone can give them strength to keep it, how many do you think will stand?"

"God only knows," he replied, a little soberly, and with, I thought, a slight disturbance in his manner.

"A suddenly inspired good resolution; a cry to God for help; the impression of an inner change which may be nothing more than a feeling; the signing of a pledge—all the work of a minute, it may be; are these to be relied upon with any well-grounded assurance?" I said. "The man is here to-night in the sphere of an excitement that moves him deeply. He sees, as he has not seen for a long time, his sin and wretchedness; the pain and loss to himself, and the wrongs and sufferings of those who love him or are dependent on him. And he sees, too, a way of escape, and hands reached out with a promise of help. He signs the pledge, and tries to look up and pray. Hopeful words are spoken in his ears. He is pointed, in a few words, to Christ as his Saviour. And then he goes out alone, hungry, it may be, and homeless, to sleep in the street or station-house. What hope for him, with his exhausted nerves and gnawing thirst? He wants more than pledge or prayer; he wants good food, shelter and protection; and, until he can stand alone, a hand to hold him up; and if these are not given, it were about as well to let him alone."

As I spoke, I saw the shadows that were falling over Granger's face grow deeper.

"We have not forgotten this," he replied. "We have a relief committee, and are doing what we can. Every Sunday morning, a breakfast is provided. Clothing, as far as we are able to procure it, is distributed, employment obtained, and all the protection in our power to throw about the men who are trying to reform. But the work is taking on dimensions so far beyond what we had anticipated, that we find ourselves without sufficient means for its thorough prosecution. We give our time, our efforts and our money; but we who are active in this movement are few compared with the thousands who stand looking on, wondering, approving, doubting or criticising. 'What is a Sunday-morning breakfast?' said a gentleman only to-day. 'Can a man live on a single meal a week?' But when I asked him to give us money, that we might minister more largely, his answer was that he knew where better to dispense his charity. Perhaps he did, and I shall not judge him. 'It isn't so much praying, as food and clothing and employment that are needed,' said another. 'If there were less talking and canting, and more good, solid doing for these poor wretches, the chances in their favor would be increased ten to one.'

And yet I could not so interest him in their behalf as to get from him either personal or material aid."

There was an undertone of trouble in Granger's voice, which fell to a heavy sigh in the closing words of his last sentence.

"From four to five hundred destitute men seeking aid," he resumed, "and our resources utterly inadequate to the demands that are made upon us—hungry, half-clothed, and in too many cases, homeless men. We may arrest their feet by Gospel means; but if we would turn their steps into the ways of sobriety and hold them there, we must meet and care for them on a lower plane. If we would lift them into spiritual safety, we must get the foundations of natural life secure. An empty stomach, and soiled and ragged and scanty clothing, with idleness superadded, are not, I agree with you, favorable to the growth of true piety. The struggle with this dreadful appetite is hard enough under the most favorable conditions; and, therefore, our work must be regarded as only initiated when, by force of these new spiritual influences, we have been able to draw the unhappy victims of intemperance over from the enemy's ground."

As we talked a man entered—I was sitting in Mr. Granger's office—and came forward in a hesitating, half-embarrassed manner. His clothing was poor and soiled, his person unsightly, and his face that of an exhausted inebriate. He stopped when a few steps from us, and said: "You do not know me."

We both recognized him by his voice. He had been a conveyancer, and a man with some property; but intemperate habits had done for him what they too surely accomplish for nearly all who indulge them.

"Yes, I know you, Hartley," Granger answered, quickly, rising as he spoke, and grasping the man's hand. He held it for some moments, looking intently into his face. "Didn't I see you at the meeting in Broad Street, last night?" he asked, while still holding his hand.

"Yes, I was there."

"And you signed the pledge?"

"Yes, sir. After I heard you speak, I said, if God can save Granger, He can save me, and I'm going to try this new way."

"God can and will save you, my friend," was Granger's warm response. "Sit down and let us talk about it."

He drew Hartley into a chair, and sat down in front of him.

"Now, tell me all about yourself." There was a genuine interest in his voice; and its effect upon this poor wreck of a man, was to send a glow to his face, and cause his dull eyes to kindle. "How is it with you; and what the chances are for getting on your feet again. Tell me all about it. You signed the pledge last night?"

"Yes, I signed at the meeting in Broad Street. And you were standing just in front of me, and looking at me; and I heard you say, 'Trust in God, my brother. Look to Him, and pray to Him, and He will give you strength to keep this pledge.' You said it to me; but I saw that you didn't know me. I wanted to speak to you, and to tell you who I was; and I was pressing forward when some one drew you away, and then I couldn't get near you again. I waited at the door until you came out; but you were talking with a gentleman, and while I hesitated about interrupting you, you passed down the street, and I was left standing alone."

"Where did you go after that?" asked Granger.

"I had nowhere to go. In this whole city, there was no place that I could call my home—no house in which I could claim the right to lay my head. My wife died three years ago; and my only child is with my mother, who lives in a neighboring town. I am alone and friendless."

"No; not friendless," said Granger, his voice struggling with his feelings. "There is One who sticketh closer than a brother. He is your friend."

The poor man looked down at his wretched garments in a way that it was not hard to understand. His face did not brighten perceptibly under this last assurance.

"Where did you sleep last night?" I inquired.

"I would have gone to one of the police-stations, but was afraid of being sent to the House of Correction. You see I had taken the pledge, and in a new way, and I was going to try to keep it, if God would indeed help me, as it kept coming to me that He would. So I walked out to Fairmount, and as the night was dark, I found it easy to hide away in a place where the police wouldn't find me, and there I slept till morning. I got some breakfast, and have been trying ever since to find something to do. But it's no use. I'm not a fit object to be in anybody's place of business."

And again he cast down a dreary look at his unsightly clothing.

"Of course you are not," said Mr. Granger. "I'm sorry you didn't speak to me last night. And now, if you are in real earnest, Mr. Hartley, we'll see if something can't be done for you."

"God knows that I'm in earnest, sir," he said, with a sudden trembling eagerness. "I lay awake so long last night, thinking over my whole life, and many times asking God to help me to live a better one in future. But I'm down so low that it seems as if there was no way for me to get up all by myself. I'm like a man in the sea who will drown unless somebody throws him a rope."

"You shall have the rope." Granger spoke in no uncertain voice.

It was plain from Hartley's exhausted and nervous state, that he was in no condition to enter at once upon any employment. He wanted rest, quiet and protection; with healthy mental surroundings, and a sufficient quantity of nutritious food. We knew of but one place in the city where these could be secured; and there we took him.

Two weeks in the Franklin Home, and you would not have known the man. Even before the lapse of that time he had found employment in the office of a conveyancer who had been with him as a boy, and who now felt a deep interest in the welfare of his old preceptor.

"I have had one of the sweetest passages of my life," said Granger, whom I met a few weeks afterwards. "I was in Chester day before yesterday, where I went to make an address at one of the meetings now being held in that town. In the audience, and sitting close to the platform, I noticed an old lady, and a young girl about sixteen years of age, both plainly dressed, but with something in their faces that caused my eyes to turn towards them frequently. There was a look of subdued and patient trouble in the face of the elder; and a grave quiet in that of the younger. While I spoke their eyes did not seem to be off of me for a moment. During my address I mentioned Hartley's case, referring to him with some particularity. As I progressed, I noticed that the old lady began to lean forward with an air of deep interest, if not eager expectancy; and I fancied that the girl by her side was turning pale. All at once it flashed on me that these might be the mother and daughter of the man whose rescue I was describing, and the impression was so strong that I held back the name of Hartley as it was coming to my lips, and closed my relation of the case with the words: 'Another soul saved through the power of that Divine strength which is freely given to all who will receive it.'

"At the close of the meeting I saw that the two women were lingering in their seats while the audience slowly retired; and that their eyes were turned towards the platform where I remained talking with some members of the committee which had the meetings in charge. They were almost alone when I came down and commenced moving along the aisle. 'May I speak a word with you?' said the elder of the two ladies, laying her hand at the same time on my arm. I saw a quiver in her face. 'What is the name?' I asked. 'Mrs. Hartley,' she replied, softly, and as if half afraid to utter her own name. Then I knew it all, and my heart gave a sudden bound of gladness. Dear old mother. I felt like putting my arm about her and crying out: 'This thy son that was dead is alive again!' But I kept a guard on my lips, not knowing how the good news, if broken too suddenly, might affect her; and taking her hand, said: 'I am glad to meet you, Mrs. Hartley.' 'I would like to ask you a question, sir,' she said, beginning now to show considerable agitation. 'First,' I replied, 'let me ask you one. Have you a son named Lloyd Hartley?'

"Her startled face became white as ashes; and she caught hold of me with a tight grasp of the hand. 'Thank God for his deliverance,' I said, softly.

Her slender form sunk down upon the seat by which she was standing, and her head drooped over her breast. She was very still, and I knew that her heart was lifting itself in thankfulness to God. 'In the strength of Him who conquered death and hell, your son shall stand now as a rock,' said I, bending to her ear. 'He is trusting no more in his own weakness, but in the power of the Infinite and the Almighty. I know what that dependence means; and because of this knowledge I have hope for your son.' 'Blessed be the name of the Lord!' came in a low, tender out-breathing of gladness from her lips. Her head was still bowed and her face hidden. Then, as she reached up one of her hands, she whispered: 'Darling, where are you?' and in a moment after her arm was about the neck of her granddaughter; and the two clung together, weeping silently. And all was so quiet and unobtrusive, that the people passed out scarcely noticing anything unusual until we were left almost alone.

"'I have been praying for him night and day ever since the temperance revival began,' said the happy mother, as I sat with her that evening in her home, replying to her questions, and giving her all the assurances in my power. 'And God has answered my prayers. And when He saves, it is no half work, but a true salvation. I have no hope in anything else. My son has taken pledge after pledge; has made and tried to keep good resolutions over and over again; but only to fall, and each time to a lower and a lower depth. If he had put his trust in God, if he had prayed for grace and strength, and entered, as you tell me he is now doing, upon a Christian life, it would have been far different. It is the Christian life that saves; and it saves from drunkenness as well as from every other sin; for all sin must be removed before there can be a dwelling-place for Christ in the soul.'

"I have felt happier and stronger ever since," Granger continued. "It was really touching to see this mother's confidence. She had been praying and weeping before God night and day for weeks—pleading for this son that he might be turned from the evil of his ways. She did not even know where he was; but she knew that her Lord and Master knew. And now, when, as she believed, her prayers had been answered in his conversion, she rejoiced and was confident. The Everlasting Arms were about him, and he would dwell secure."

"Happy faith!" I made answer. "May its foundations never be removed."

"I think they never will," Granger said. "If her prayers did not avail just in the order of her belief, they still availed, and her son has been brought within the fold; and there is, in the spirit he manifests, something that gives me confidence in his stability."

"Have you told Hartley about this meeting with his mother and daughter?" I asked.

"Oh, yes. And they have been up to the city to see him."

"A happy re-union."

"You would have said so if you had seen them together. Dear old lady! The love, and tenderness, and joy-subdued that were in her face as she sat and looked at her son, to whom much of the old true manliness of expression and bearing has already commenced coming back, was beautiful and touching to witness. It will not be a long time, I think, before there will be one home for them all, and that a happy one."

And it was not long.

CHAPTER XIX.

STRIKING cases of reformation, like the one related, yet varying as to the incidents, were of daily occurrence. Men who had been for years regarded as hopeless drunkards, made a new effort to struggle out of the swift waters that were bearing them to ruin, and caught eagerly at the new means of rescue that were offered. Families long separated were united again; and men who had been dead weights and burdens upon society, became once more good and useful citizens.

"A glorious work!" was heard on all sides. But the men who were in the midst of it—who came into direct contact with the scores and hundreds of wretched creatures who had sounded the lowest depths of misery and degradation, who were homeless, friendless, penniless, and mentally, morally and physically so enervated as to be scarcely capable of an effort in the direction of self-recovery, found themselves confronted with a task of almost appalling magnitude. What was to be done with and for these men, whose idle hands were held out in piteous appeal for work, and whose hungry faces and dirty and tattered garments pleaded mutely for relief? Nightly the great meeting hall was crowded to overflowing, and nightly the increase went on.

"It is one thing," I said to Mr. Granger, as I walked home with him from one of these meetings, "to reap this great harvest, but quite another thing to garner and preserve the grain. I sadly fear that much of it will never be gathered out of the field. The work is too much *en masse*, and too little in detail. The numbers who sign the pledge every night cannot be regarded as a measure of the good that is being done."

"You must bear in mind," he replied, "that all who sign at these meetings are not the utterly destitute and homeless; nor of those who have lost the power to control their appetites. The larger proportion are men engaged in work or business, to whom so strong a conviction of danger has come that they take the pledge for protection and safety. Most of these will find elements of strength and encouragement in their homes and among friends."

"True; but if it be as was said to-night, that there are from four to five hundred of the destitute and friendless class who have signed the pledge, and who must have something more to rest upon than the singing, and talking, and exhortations to stand fast, which they get at these nightly meetings, is it not plain that the loss between the reaping and the garnering is going to be very great?"

"You cannot feel the burden of that thought more heavily than we who are in the heart of this work. But its growth has been more rapid than we had anticipated, and its proportions have already assumed a magnitude for which we were not prepared. The people are looking on and wondering. Crowds flock nightly to witness the progress of the movement; but how few come up to our help. What would it be for a score of our rich citizens to establish for our use a depot of clothing from which we might draw at will, and so be able to take off the rags of such men as we found to be in earnest about reform, and send them forth in sightly garments, that they might be in a condition to apply for and get employment? Or what for the churches in our city—over four hundred in number—to do the same thing?"

"Is nothing really being done to help and save these poor creatures? When the last hymn is sung, and the benediction said, and the lights put out, does all care for them cease? Is there nothing more until to-morrow night—and then only this general work, which merely brings the individual to the front for a little season, and then lets him drift out of sight, his special needs unrecognized and unprovided for?"

"If you will come to my office at three o'clock to-morrow, I will try to give an answer to your question," Granger replied. "I must now take the next car that passes and get home as quickly as I can, as it is growing late."

I called at his office at the hour mentioned.

"There is other Christian temperance work going on in our city besides that remarkable exhibition of it which is known as the Murphy movement," he said. "Work about which the public knows little, but which, in its influence on that particular class about which we were speaking yesterday, is accomplishing a vast amount of good. I am going to answer your question of last evening by showing you a phase of this work—unobtrusive, yet very effective—and when you see it, you will know that, while the hands of the reapers are strong and the harvest great, they who gather and garner are not idle."

I walked with Granger for a number of blocks, talking by the way. As we left his office he remarked: "You might have known that in a work like this the hands of the women would not be idle; nor the spirit that moved the late 'Crusaders' dead. There has only been a change of front, with a more guarded movement upon the enemy, and less expenditure of war material. You do not find them so much in the noisy front of battle, as where the wounded are left on the field or gathered in tent and hospital."

"Do you mean," I asked, "that there is another movement, parallel to this one which is attracting so much attention, now going on in our city?"

"Yes; wholly independent, yet in complete harmony therewith. Two sets of reapers are in the same field; but with one there are better facilities for gleaning and garnering than with the other. Women draw more closely to the individual than men; have more pity, and sympathy, and faith in humanity; more practical trust in God, and a more absolute belief in the power and efficacy of prayer. There is a marked contrast between their meetings and the vast assemblages you have attended. The sphere is quieter, and the services held closer to the order of religious worship. There are fewer spectators, and, I think, a more complete singleness of purpose with those who are giving themselves to the work. What we, as men, are doing, is extra to our common life-work. The largest part of our time and thought is devoted to business or professional duties; and we can give only our odds and ends of leisure to extra public service and the duties of charity. It is different with many of the women who are taking the lead in this Gospel temperance work. Heart and mind are absorbed in it. It is almost as much their daily thought and care as business is to the merchant, or the interests of his clients to the lawyer. We can, by single strong efforts, move the masses in this or that direction; can influence and direct public sentiment, and even set great tidal waves of reform in motion; but for the gathering of results, we have little time, and, it may be, little inclination; and results are too often left to take care of themselves."

We talked until we came in front of a small church in a thickly populated part of the town, when

Granger paused with the words, "In here," and we passed through a small vestibule to a room capable of holding from two to three hundred persons. Nearly every seat was occupied. We were conducted to chairs set in the space fronting the reading-desk, and on being seated I had an opportunity to look at the audience, which was composed of men and women; the men largely outnumbering the women. It took but a glance to tell who and from whence most of these men were. Lives of sin and suffering; of degradation and crime; of abused and wasted manhood had left their disfiguring tokens on nearly every countenance before me. Half a dozen women occupied the small platform, on which the reading-desk stood. They were singing—

> "Jesus, lover of my soul,
> Let me to Thy bosom fly,"

as we entered, most of the congregation taking part. My eyes ran over the strange assembly, looking from face to face, and trying to read each varied expression. With scarcely an exception, you saw a deep, and, in some cases, a most pathetic earnestness. At the close of the hymn, one of the women arose, and said, in an easy, familiar way, but with a tender, penetrating solemnity in her voice: "And with such a refuge, how safe! Jesus, *lover* of my soul. The love of Jesus! Of the all-compassionate and the all-powerful. Think of it! Come to this Saviour, His arms are open to receive you. Comfort, support, defense; all these shall be yours. Under the shadow of His wing you shall dwell in safety."

There was a deep hush in the assembly; a bending forward to hearken, and a profound solemnity on most of the faces. You saw eyes grow wet, and lips move in silent prayer.

"And now," said the gentle speaker, after a pause, "we want to hear from as many of you as can bear testimony to the saving power of Him who has taken your feet out of the miry clay and set them upon a rock. Speak with brevity that we may have a multitude of witnesses."

She sat down and a man, whose face had been holding my eyes for some moments, arose from his seat. What could one with such a countenance have to say about the saving power of Christ, I thought. His voice trembled a little as he began:

"He has taken my feet out of the pit and set them on solid ground; blessed be His name. I've been a dreadful hard drinker. Until six weeks ago, I don't think I had drawn a sober breath for ten years. My wife left me in despair more than three years ago; and then I didn't care for anything. When I heard about the Murphy meetings and what wonderful things were being done, I thought I'd go and see what it meant. Somehow, with the singing, and the way Mr. Murphy talked, I got all broken up, and when he told us that if we'd take the pledge and trust in God to help us keep it, we could stand just as well as he had stood, I said, I'll try. And I did try, and, blessed be God! I've been able to keep my pledge. I don't know how it might have been if I hadn't come to these meetings. I've found work, and I'm trying to make another home. It isn't much of a home as yet—only a single room—but my wife is so happy. And we've got something in that home we never had before. Shall I tell you what it is?"

He paused for a moment, then in a lower voice said: "Our Saviour."

As he sat down, the leader of the music touched the organ keys, and a single verse from a well-known hymn was sung:

> "Saviour, like a shepherd lead us,
> Much we need Thy tender care;
> In Thy pleasant pastures feed us,
> For our use Thy folds prepare;
> Blessed Jesus!
> Thou hast bought us, Thine we are."

As the singing ceased, I heard the voice of a woman in the audience, and turned in the direction from which it came. I saw a worn and sallow face, and a slender form, plainly but cleanly attired.

"I want to tell you," said the speaker, "that I've got my husband again, after having lost him because of drink for years and years. And this time I'm going to keep him, for God has converted his soul. Oh, bless the Lord! Bless the Lord!" her voice rising into almost a passionate outburst.

"Yes, bless the Lord, my sister," responded the lady who had direction of the meeting. "For when He finds the lost ones, He can keep their feet from wandering any more."

Another hymn, and then another short speech. And so for an hour the speaking and the singing went on, the interest not flagging for a moment. Men told of the awful slavery from which they had escaped through the power of God, and of the new strength which had come to them in answer to prayer, with a positiveness that had in it an element of conviction for the intently listening hearers. Some had been standing safe in the midst of temptation for only a few days, some for weeks, and some for months. Many had already united themselves with one or another religious society, and were receiving that protection and strength which comes from Christian fellowship.

"A good Christian brother has been holding on to me ever since I took the pledge," said one. "May God reward him! If he hadn't held so tightly, I don't know what might have happened; I was so miserable and helpless. But I'm getting stronger and stronger, and now I'm trying to help the weak ones."

Said another: "Thank God for these good Christian women. One of them found me not long ago in the hands of a policeman. I'd been drinking in a saloon, and got into a quarrel with the barkeeper, who called an officer. Just as I was dragged out upon the pavement, a woman came by, and she stopped and said to the policeman: 'What's the matter? What's this man been doing?' She spoke so gently, and yet with something so like authority in her voice, that he let go of my collar. 'Drunk and quarrelsome,' he answered, gruffly. 'Oh, I see,' she returned. 'They've made him crazy with drink, and then turned him over to you.' 'Something of that sort,' said the policeman, speaking more respectfully. Then she said, 'Suppose you let me have this case. I shouldn't wonder if I could do a great deal better with it than you can.' The officer stood for a little while looking puzzled; and I was puzzled, too, for the liquor was beginning to go out of my head. 'What will you do with him?' he asked. 'Try to make a sober man out of him.' At this he laughed, and said, 'If you can make a sober man out of Jack Brady, all right. Go ahead and try. It'll be the hardest job you ever took.' But she didn't find it so. I don't know how it was, but the very minute I heard her say that, I made up my mind to stop drinking. The policeman went on, and she stood and talked to me for a good while, and told me about these meetings, and how easy it would be to lead a better life if I would come and try to get help from above. I'd never been talked to like that before. It seemed so strange to have anybody care for me, and to seem so anxious about me. 'Please God, I'll come,' said I. And I did come. It seemed as if I couldn't wait for the hour next day. And when I entered that door, there stood the lady, just where she's standing now, by the reading-desk. She was speaking, and as her voice fell on my ears like the voice of an old friend, my heart began to beat heavy, and I got all into a tremble. Would she know me? I saw her eyes go searching about the room as she talked, but if she was looking for me she didn't make me out. I went up as close to the desk as I could get, and sat there while the singing and talking and praying went on. Not for a minute did I take my eyes away from her. All at once as she looked at me hard I saw her face brighten up, and I knew that she had seen me. In a little while she came and sat down by my side and took my hand, and said, just for my ear alone, 'I'm so glad to see you here, Mr. Brady.' You see she hadn't forgotten my name. 'I've been looking for you ever since the meeting opened. You're going to sign the pledge, of course; and, better still, give your heart to Jesus. And then what a happy man you will be.' And I did sign the pledge, and I did give my heart to Jesus. And I'm one of the happiest men in this room to-day."

As the meeting drew to a close, requests for prayer were sent up in writing, or asked for verbally. A mother asked for prayers for an intemperate son; a wife for an intemperate husband; a sister for two brothers who were in great danger of becoming drunkards; a reformed man that he might find his wife and children, from whom he had not heard for two years; the wife of a tavern-keeper, that her husband might be convicted of sin, and led to abandon his dreadful business; for a sick wife with a drunken husband; for a daughter whose father was intemperate.

While these requests were being made, a young woman—she did not look over twenty-six or seven years of age—arose and said: "My heart is so full, Christian friends, that I can't keep silent. I want to tell what great things prayer can do. I've got a husband and two little children. My husband took to drinking, and it 'most killed me. He was so good and kind before; but now he got cross and ugly, and wouldn't bear a word from me. It was getting worse and worse. He'd stay out late at night and come home so much in liquor that he didn't know anything. One day I said to his mother, 'If Tom keeps on in this way, I shall have to leave him and go home to father.' And then she cried, and said, 'Don't do that, Mary. He'll go all to ruin if you do.' And we both sat and cried for ever so long. While we were crying, a neighbor came in; and she said, 'Why don't you go round to the women's temperance meeting and ask them to pray for him?' I didn't see what good that was going to do; but she talked so much about it that I said to myself, 'It can't do any harm, that's sure.' So I put on my things and came round here, and Tom's mother came with me. I wrote on a piece of paper, 'Prayers wanted for a young husband and father who is being ruined by drink,' and sent it up. And when, singling this out from all the rest, Mrs. W—— said, in her prayer, 'This young husband and father, Lord, who is being ruined by drink, oh, hear the pitiful cry of his wife, and the cry that we are all sending up to Thee now. Let Thy Spirit prevail with him. Quicken in him the desire for a better life; turn him from the evil of his ways,'—it seemed as if the Lord had come down into this room, and as if I had got right hold of Him. After the meeting was over we went home, and my husband's mother waited until he came in to supper. He didn't have much to say; looked kind of troubled about something, I thought. He usually went out directly after supper; but this time he sat for, maybe, half an hour, reading a newspaper. Then he took up his hat and went away. 'Don't stay out late, Tom, please,' said I, as pleasantly as I could speak. But he didn't answer me a word. His mother had gone home by this time, and I was alone with my two little children, and they were both asleep. I had a strange feeling, as if something was going to happen. It might be bad or it might be good—I couldn't tell. My heart was trembling and starting. I couldn't sew; I couldn't do anything, but kept going about, up and down-stairs, so restless and troubled that I didn't know what to do with myself. At last I got down on my knees and began to pray for my husband. And then it seemed as if the blessed Lord and Saviour had come into my little room; and I talked to Him as a friend, and pleaded for my husband, and begged Him to save him from the dreadful appetite that was ruining him soul and body. I felt better after that. But I couldn't settle down to doing anything. Then I got the Bible and read two or three chapters. Tired at last, I laid my face down upon the open book and fell asleep. I had a sweet dream, but a sweeter waking up, for my husband's arms were around me, and I heard his voice saying, 'Mary, dear!' in the old, loving way. 'Oh, what is it, Tom?' I cried out, as I started up. And then he kissed me, and said, 'It's going to be all right again, Mary. I've been down to the Murphy meeting, and signed the pledge, and, God helping me, I'm going to keep it.' And he has kept it so far; and what's better, he's given his heart to Christ, and we've both joined the church. Oh, I'm so happy!"

My eyes were full of tears when this happy young wife sat down.

Then the lady to whom she had referred, made a few impressive comments on the incident just related, adding two or three others as strikingly illustrative of the value of prayer. One of these was quite remarkable, and I was not able to trace, except remotely, the relation between cause and effect. She said: "At one of the Central Coffee-Room Thursday evening meetings at which I was present, a gentleman arose and said, 'I want to ask your prayers for the drunken son of a poor old mother. I don't know who he is—not even his name, nor where he lives. To-night, as I was coming here, I saw an old woman standing on a corner, and she seemed to be in trouble. I stopped and asked what was the matter, and she said, "Oh, dear sir, I'm in great distress. I'm old and poor, and have nothing to depend on but one son, and he's taken to bad habits, and spends nearly everything he earns in drink; and if I say a word to him, he goes on dreadfully. He hasn't been home all day; and there's nothing in the house to eat, and I've been going all about trying to find him." And the poor old mother wrung her hands and moaned so piteously that it made my heart ache. I could do nothing for her but give her a little money and tell her to go home and pray for her son. And now I ask the prayers of all here to-night for the son of this aged mother.' The case was very blind. We did not know even the man's name, nor the name of his mother; how then were we to present him to God? But it was not for us to put limits to the Divine power of saving. So we laid this unknown mother's sorrow, and this unknown man's sin and desolation before the Lord and left the case with Him. Well, on the next Thursday evening the gentleman arose again, and said, 'I have good news from the man whom I asked you to pray for at our last meeting. He has been saved.' What a thrill of joy went through me! 'On the very evening afterwards I met his old mother again. It seemed almost as if she had dropped down in the street before me; and she told me this glad story:

"After I saw you," she said, "I went home and waited for my son, crying and praying, and in great distress of mind. It was about half-past ten o'clock when I heard him come in—he never got home much before twelve—and it gave me a start. Upstairs he came; not stumbling nor unsteady, but every step distinct and firm. When he opened the door, I saw something strange in his face. I didn't know what it meant. Such a light in his eyes, and such a soft, gentle look about his mouth. 'O John!' I cried out, almost catching my breath. Then he said, 'Mother, I've been to one of them great meetings, and I've signed the pledge, and if God will only give me the strength to keep it, I'll live and die a sober man.' Oh, dear, how my poor old heart did leap for joy. Then I got him round the neck, and I said, 'Let us kneel right down here, John, and pray that God will give you all the strength you want.' And down we knelt; and such a prayer-meeting as we had together; it lasted till almost morning."'

"With such instances of the power of prayer for our encouragement," continued the speaker, "and I could give many more that have come under my own observation quite as remarkable, let us not hesitate in our petitions, but come confidently to God. Among the written requests for prayer which I now hold in my hand, is one that has moved me deeply. Three young wives ask your prayers for their intemperate husbands. Three young wives."

Her voice falling on the words in low, pitying cadences. "Think of it! Three young wives; happy brides a little while ago, and with the sweet grace and charm of girlhood still about them! What an outlook upon life for these dear young souls. They have met together, and each has told to the others her sorrow and her fear. They have seen their young husbands drifting, and drifting, and drifting away, every effort to hold them back in vain. They will be lost if some influence, greater than it is their power to exercise, is not brought to bear upon them. And now they ask our prayers. Let us offer them in loving faith; and not for these only, but for all the special cases which have been brought to us this day."

I had heard at one of the revival meetings, a year or two before, a long list of requests for prayer read off very much in the routine way of an entry clerk reading off the items of an invoice; and then the prayers were offered up in a kind of wholesale fashion that struck me as almost irreverent and quite useless.

But the prayer that I now heard affected me very differently. There was in it nothing of routine or dead formality. Mrs. W——, to whom the duty of offering these requests to God had been assigned, felt, it was plain, the troubled heart-beat of those whom she represented in her petitions. Not a single request, written or verbal, was forgotten. Each, in turn, was offered before the Lord, and with such feeling and earnestness and individuality of need and condition, that I was not only surprised at the singular clearness with which she had apprehended each case, but deeply moved by the sphere of her trusting and reverent piety.

At the close of this prayer and the singing that followed, the pledge was offered to those who had not signed, and all who felt the need of spiritual counsel and comfort were invited to go into the inquiry-room.

CHAPTER XX.

"How long has this been going on?" I asked of Mr. Granger as we walked away.

"For months," he replied.

"Are the meetings held daily?"

"Yes."

"And always crowded like this?"

"Always."

"And as full of interest?"

"The interest never flags. You see how entirely in earnest these women are, and how completely they have thrown themselves into this work, which has still another side."

"Another side?"

"Yes. Their faith in prayer is unbounded. Some of them take the Bible promises so literally that they verily believe a mountain could be removed and cast into the sea if prayer and faith were strong enough. 'Spiritual forces are higher and more subtle than natural forces, and spiritual laws above and superior to natural laws,' I once heard one of them say, while speaking of the power of prayer, 'and can suspend or set them aside altogether, as in miracles; and it is because our faith is so weak, and we ask so often amiss, asking selfishly, that marvels are not wrought by prayer which would astonish the world.' She held that if the Christian people of this city would unite in one strong and persistent prayer to God, He would set agencies in motion that would close every liquor-saloon in our midst and cause wickedness to cease. But there are those among them who keep nearer to the earth, and who have faith in other saving means beside that of prayer. Who believe in feeding the hungry, and clothing the naked, and building up and sustaining the natural degree of life, so that the spiritual degree which has just been vivified with grace from above may have an orderly foundation upon which to rest. The other side of this work to which I have referred, has relation to the lower degree of life which rests on the earth, and which must be in some degree of health and order before it is possible for spiritual life to have sustenance and growth."

"Women have a very practical side, and are quick in their perception of wants and means," I remarked.

"Yes; and what is more, are quick to act. When they see that a thing ought to be done, they go about doing it; and often while we are thinking and debating, their will has found the way. You remember how it was at the beginning of the war. Soldiers from the North who were landed from the ferry-boats at the foot of Washington Avenue to await farther transportation, were found hungry and exhausted, sitting on curb-stones and door-steps, or lying asleep on the pavement, no provision having been made for feeding them on the way. What happened? While the men stood looking on, and blaming the Government for neglect of provision at this point, the women had their coffee-pots on the fire, and out from the houses all along the line of the street came quickly smoking cups and pitchers, and plates of bread and meat, and baskets of refreshing fruit. You remember how this thing stirred your heart at the time, and the hearts of all to whom it was told the land over; and how, from this good beginning, the refreshment-saloons were started, giving such abundance of good cheer to the hundreds of thousands of soldiers who afterwards went through our city—the new recruits pressing forward to the battle-fields, and the sick, and war-wasted, and wounded returning home to recover their strength or die."

"Yes, yes. I remember well. And the thought of it after so many years gives my heart a quicker motion."

"Now, as then, the action of the women is direct and practical. They do not stand looking on sorrowfully, and with folded hands, waiting for organized agencies. There are no strong appeals to the public for help, and pauses for response. But instead, an immediate taking hold of and use of whatever means lie close at hand. Food and clothing are gathered and distributed, and cases of destitution and homelessness met and ministered to. If not to the full extent of the need, yet always to the extent of ability."

"That is well," said I. "Prayers are good, but they never take the place of potatoes. A hungry man is a poor subject for religion; and a dirty and ragged one scarcely any better."

"Yes, we all understand this. And it is just here that the great work of reform now going on in our city finds one of its chief impediments," Mr. Granger answered. "What these devoted Christian women are doing is as the first spontaneous efforts which were made by loyal women to feed the hungry soldiers who were passing through our city. There was a great blessing in it, but the blessing was limited for lack of the larger supplies and more perfect organization which came afterwards. So now, much is being done with imperfect means; but, as the work goes on, and its results become more widely known, as interest deepens and sympathy grows broader, I look for that liberal and substantial co-operation which is so essential to its success."

"The ardor that now attends this work," said I, "will it not die out? There is a waste of energy in enthusiasm. Of all excitements, none spend themselves more quickly than religious excitements, because they are so intense. The more permanent forces are quiet and almost unobtrusive. In a few weeks the heat of summer will be upon us, and Mr. Murphy will go away. There will be no more crowded halls, no more Sunday-morning breakfasts, nor stirring appeals and moving invitations. What, then, is to become of these weak, and tempted, and almost friendless ones who have just been lifted from the slough? It troubles me to think of it. Is the entire cessation of these religious temperance meetings for two or three months a well-considered thing? To retire from the field and leave the enemy in full possession after such a series of victories as you have had, can hardly be considered good generalship."

"There is going to be no abandonment of the field," Granger replied.

"I understood differently."

"Do you suppose, for a single moment, that the women who are in this battle are going to ground their arms, or leave the field for any cause? 'How often will you hold your meetings?' I asked of Mrs. W——; and she answered quietly, "Three hundred and sixty-five days in the year.' 'No intermission this summer?' 'None,' she replied. 'How could we leave these hundreds of precious souls, just rescued from the slavery of drunkenness, some of them without homes, or friends, or work, in the very midst of temptation? If any were lost through our neglect, or ease-seeking, would not the stain of their blood be upon our garments? Verily do we believe that God has called us to this work of saving men who, because of their utter degradation through intemperance, have been rejected by society and abandoned by the churches. Helpless, hopeless, lost but for the agencies now raised up in the Divine Providence for their rescue, shall we, to whom has been committed the great responsibility of using and directing these agencies, fold our hands and seek for rest and recreation, while so many feet are only on the unsteady margin of the pit out of which they have been dragged, and so many hands clinging to our garments, lest, if their hold be loosed, they fall again? No, no. There is too much at stake.'"

"Brave, true women!" I responded, with ardor. "In all works of Christian charity they are ever in the advance. But will nothing be done by the men whose efforts have been crowned by such wonderful results as we have seen? Will they wholly abandon the work until their summer vacation is over? The enemy will surely be diligent in his work of sowing tares in their field while they rest."

"Only this great public demonstration will cease," Mr. Granger replied. "But you may be sure of one thing, the enemy is not going to have it all his own way. Faithful guards, and sentinels, and reserve forces will be left, and he will be held to the lines back upon which he has been driven. When the fall campaign opens, we shall have a more thorough organization, and larger means. So far, it has only been as a skirmish along the lines compared to the battles that must be fought. We do not make light of our enemy. He is not to be vanquished by a single fierce onslaught, nor by a single desperate battle. All hell is on his side; and among men he draws his myriads of recruits from the young and the old who have inordinate desires and evil passions, and selfish ends to serve and gratify. Prejudice, and interest, and sensual desire are on his side. He is intrenched behind law, usage, fallacy and appetite. His friends and emissaries are to be found everywhere. In the halls of legislation, in courts of justice, in executive and municipal offices, and, sad to say, often even in the pulpit; though, thanks to the growth of a higher Christianity, his representatives are fast disappearing from the sacred desk."

"No mean enemy with which to engage in battle," said I. "As to the ultimate victory, that is very far off. It will hardly be seen in your day or mine. The battle with hell has been raging for thousands of years, and, for all we can see, will continue for thousands of years longer; and if all hell is on the side of the liquor traffic and intemperance, all hell must be conquered before they will cease. From this survey of the field the outlook is not, I confess, a very hopeful one."

"It is as full of hope as Christianity," returned Mr. Granger. "As that gains in strength and vital power, temperance will have an equal gain, for the very life of Christianity is to reject evil as sin against God. An intemperate man cannot be a Christian man in any true sense, because he is selfishly indulging a depraved appetite which not only hurts his body, but weakens and degrades his mind, and so unfits him for that service of God and his neighbor which constitutes religion."

"Taking this view, intemperance becomes a sin."

"Is it the service of God or the service of self?" Granger asked. "The holding of appetite subject to reason and the laws of health, or the giving of lower and destructive things power over the higher and conservative? Is intemperance a good or an evil? If evil, then it is sin."

"What of moderate drinking—the temperate use, as it is called, of wine and other stimulants? Is there sin in this?"

"Sin is the voluntary doing of anything that we know to be hurtful to the neighbor, or contrary to the law of God," Granger replied.

"Then I may drink wine or beer moderately, and be innocent. There is no law of God which says, 'Thou shalt not drink wine or beer.' And it cannot hurt my neighbor. If any one is hurt, it is myself alone."

"Can you hurt yourself without hurting your neighbor?"

"Not if my neighbor have any claim which this hurting of myself prevents me from meeting."

"Has the body no claim on the hand or foot? Can either of them say, I may hurt myself if I choose—that is my own affair? Depend upon it, Mr. Lyon, there is no man in human society, no matter how weak, or obscure, or lowly he may be, who has not a service to perform, in default of which some other human being—it may be many human beings—must suffer. Society is an organic form, in which we all have our places and functions; and society is sick, and lame, and covered with cancerous sores, only because it has so many idle, useless, self-hurting and vicious members and organs in its great social body. Under this view, no one who selfishly indulges in any practice that diminishes his power to serve those who have claims upon him, can be free from sin."

"I see your broader view and your broader confidence," I returned. "Whatever is gained for Christianity is gained for temperance."

"Any true gain to Christianity is a gain to temperance; for to be a Christian man means to be a temperate man," he said. "There is no such a thing as a tippling Christian, though there may be a tippling professor; for in so far as a man tipples, moderately or immoderately, he is not a Christian—not a free spiritual man, but in bondage to the flesh."

"There are many who would consider such a declaration as uncharitable and unwarranted," I remarked.

"Do you?" he asked.

"My ideal of a Christian man is very high," I returned.

"You would not have him a slave to any corporeal lust or appetite?"

"He could not be; for in so far as one is not

lifted above these, he is not a Christian. Religion can scarcely be worth anything if it does not save a man from the dominion of his animal nature. It must reform and regenerate the external as well as the internal. His very feet, the lowest and most ultimate things of his life, must be washed and made clean."

"I could not express my own views more exactly," Granger replied. As we were parting, he said: "A few friends are to be at my house this evening. I wish you would come round."

"Who are they?" I inquired.

"Dr. Gilbert, from New York, will be there."

"I shall be glad to meet him."

"And Judge Arbuckle and his wife, from Columbus. The judge and I were in the same class at college, and warmly attached friends. It is nearly twenty years since our last meeting. He is a man of fine qualities, both as to head and heart, with decided opinions and considerable force of character. You will enjoy an evening in his company, I am sure; and none the less, I think, from the fact that there is likely to be an earnest encounter between him and Dr. Gilbert."

"Indeed! On what subject?"

"The judge, I am sorry to say, is not a temperance man. He has always taken stimulants, and believes their moderate employment to be useful."

"Has he ever given the subject a careful investigation?"

"I presume not. Law and politics have claimed his closer attention."

"A discussion between him and Dr. Gilbert, if it should happen to arise, is likely to be a warm one."

"It will be earnest, but fair and courteous, for both are gentlemen," said Mr. Granger. "I am glad of the opportunity to bring these men together, for after their meeting, my old friend Arbuckle will, I think, be in possession of facts that must set him thinking in a new direction. As for himself, I do not greatly fear the serious encroachments of appetite; for he is an exceptionally well-balanced man, with a cool, clear head, and finely-strung nerves; and is known for his moderation and conservative force of character. But his example and influence cannot fail to be exceedingly hurtful, especially with young men."

I promised to make one of his guests that evening, and we parted.

CHAPTER XXI.

MR. GRANGER'S law business, which had grown rapidly, was already giving him a handsome income, and his family was again living in a style of comparative elegance. His daughter Amy had developed into a rarely attractive maiden, and was greatly beloved and admired in the circles where she moved. Her quiet grace and dignity were in marked contrast with the free and jaunty manners seen in too many of our young girls, and lifted her above them in the estimation of all who held the sex in any high regard. There were those who sought to win her favor, but as most of the young men whom she happened to meet in society, took part in its drinking customs, she kept herself on guard against their advances and held them at a safe distance. The shadows which intemperance had thrown over her early life rested too deeply on her spirits to be wholly removed; and the pain and humiliation they had occasioned were things that could never be forgotten. To see a glass of wine at the lips of a young man was to lift between himself and her an impassable barrier. She might esteem him as a friend; but she locked the door of her heart against him. If, as happened more than once, a warmer sentiment than friendship had commenced forming, she smothered it out with a quick and resolute hand on discovering the fatal impediment.

But love steals in by unguarded ways, and when once within the citadel of the heart, holds to his advantage and makes vigorous resistance should an attempt be made to cast him out. It so happened that a young man named Pickering, found favor with Amy, and that almost before she was aware of her danger, the citadel of her heart had been taken. Handsome in person, pure in life, and true and manly in his character, Henry Pickering was entirely worthy of the love which she was not able to keep from revealing itself in her eyes.

A few months after their more intimate acquaintance, and when the young man's attitude towards Amy left but little doubt as to his feelings and intentions, they met at an evening entertainment, where liberal refreshments were served. A sudden chill and suspense fell upon the maiden's heart, as, with her hand on Pickering's arm, she began moving towards the supper-room; for the clink of glasses and popping of corks could already be heard. She had never until now met this young man at an evening party; nor had anything occurred in their intercourse so far that gave her any intimation of his attitude towards the too prevalent drinking usages of society. In all her intercourse with him, she had not seen the smallest indication of any indulgence in wine or intoxicating drinks, and there

"Thank you; no wine for me," replied Amy.—*Page 301.*

had come to be with her a tacit and fond belief that he was one of those who kept himself entirely free from their use.

But now the hour of trial and proof had come, and as they entered the supper-room, Amy's breathing became constricted, and her heart beat with heavy, almost suffocating throbs. She took her place a little back from the table, which was liberally supplied with glasses and bottles of wine, and waited for her attendant to bring her some of the refreshments that were being served. This was speedily done. As Pickering handed her the plate which he had filled, he said: "Will you have a glass of champagne, or some sherry?"

"Thank you; no wine for me," replied Amy, with something in her voice that caused the young man to look at her a little curiously.

"You would not have me drink alone?" he said.

"I would not have you drink at all," she answered, a low thrill of feeling in her otherwise steady voice.

Pickering's eyes rested on hers for a moment or two, after which he turned from her slowly, going to the table and filling another plate with salad and oysters. Then he came back to his place by her side; but, as they stood eating, they were turned a little away from each other. The young man, who had been a resident of the city for only a year or two, knew nothing at this time of Mr. Granger's history.

It soon became evident to Pickering that his companion was only making a pretence of eating.

"Let me get you something else," said he. "This isn't to your taste. What shall it be?"

But she replied, as she handed him her plate: "Nothing more, I thank you."

He was looking full into her face now, and saw with concern that the brows were slightly drawn, and the color diminished.

"Are you not feeling well? The room is very warm. Let me bring you an ice?"

But she declined anything more, and promptly accepted the young man's invitation to return to the parlor, where they took a seat near one of the windows through which the fresh, cool air was coming. The whole manner of the girl, as well as the expression of her face, had changed; and Pickering was troubled and at a loss to know the meaning of this change which had come so suddenly.

"I'm afraid you are ill," he said.

"Oh, no, no," Amy replied, endeavoring to rally herself. She was too truthful for any subterfuge.

"If not ill, then something has gone wrong, Miss Granger; and I am concerned to know what it is. Have I done anything to disturb or offend you?"

Amy's eyes, which had been on his face, dropped to the floor, and she made no answer. The young man's thought turned back hurriedly, and went over the brief incidents of the supper-room. Was it the offer of a glass of wine? He would know, and at once put the question: "Do you object to wine?"

"It is a dangerous thing," she replied.

"If carried to excess; but not when used in moderation."

"If never used in moderation, excess is impossible. No man is safe but he who lets it alone."

She spoke in a low, steady voice, in which the young man noticed the same thrill of feeling that was in it when she answered him in the supper-room—"I would not have you drink at all."

"Why, Miss Granger!" Pickering exclaimed, trying to make light of the matter, "I didn't know before that you were a little temperance enthusiast."

"It is not with me a matter of enthusiasm," she replied, speaking soberly, "but of deep feeling and settled principle."

"Oh! I was not aware of this before. If I had known it, I should not have committed the rudeness of offering you wine; and I crave pardon for my unfortunate blunder. You are, then, an advocate of entire abstinence."

"Where the use of a useless thing is attended with such awful perils as attend the use of wine, is not he the wise man who lets it alone?"

"I will not say no, Miss Granger. But your proposition is very sweeping. I might take issue with you on the word 'useless,' but am in no way inclined to do so just now. Intemperance is, I am well aware, the great curse of our land."

"And no one who uses intoxicating drinks of any kind, whether moderately or not, is safe from this curse," said Amy.

"I should be sorry to believe that, Miss Granger. I know of a great many men who take their wine or beer every day; but I do not think them in any danger."

"Not one of them?" Her voice was quiet, but firm.

"All men are not strong alike, nor given to moderation. Some are inclined to excess in everything. There is always danger with such."

"And danger with all who use an article which invites to excess the very moment you take it. It is here, Mr. Pickering, that the great peril lies. No man is safe who admits an enemy within his fortress; and alcohol is always an enemy."

"We were speaking of wine, not ardent spirits," said the young man.

But Miss Granger was better informed than he had supposed.

"What we call wine is, for the most part, only diluted, drugged and flavored alcohol. Without the character and quality given by alcohol, few would care to drink it. It takes more wine than brandy to give the required exhilaration; that is all."

"You are booked on this subject, Miss Granger," said Pickering, his brows arching slightly, and his voice betraying some annoyance.

"Where such grave results attend the use of an article, is it not well to examine carefully the ground of its claim upon our confidence?"

There was no excitement in Amy's manner; yet it did not escape the young man's observation that, hidden beneath her quiet exterior, was a great deal of repressed feeling.

"But the novel thing to me is, the fact that a young lady like yourself should be posted on the subject of making and flavoring wines," returned Pickering, rising into an air of banter. "According to your view of the case, wine-drinking is only another name for whisky-drinking."

"If," replied Amy, not moved from her serious attitude, "the drink we call wine is acceptable as a beverage because of the temporary exhilaration its alcohol produces, may it not be true that wine-drinking is, as you say, another name for whisky-drinking?"

"But is it, as you allege, Miss Granger, that alcohol gives to wine its chief acceptable quality? I have never studied the subject; but it seems to me that you must be in some degree of error."

"I have been in the way of hearing a great deal about these matters, and from those who have conducted their investigations with great care," said Amy, "and I am just as certain, as I am of any other declared result of chemical test and analysis, that wine contains so large a proportion of alcohol as to make its use exceedingly dangerous."

"What proportion?" asked Pickering. His manner had become more serious.

"I have heard it variously stated," was replied; "the percentage running from seven or eight to twenty-five or six."

"So large? I wonder how much alcohol whisky or brandy contains? You are, no doubt, informed as to that also."

"From forty to sixty per cent., I am told."

"Then, if I drink two or three glasses of wine, I get about as much alcohol as if I took a single glass of whisky or brandy?"

"The danger is that such will be the case."

The young man sat with a thoughtful air for a few moments, and then looking up, said, with a forced levity of manner: "This is almost comical, Miss Granger."

"What?" inquired his companion, her clear eyes fixed steadily on him.

"Free-and-easy drinking in the dining-room, and a temperance lecture in the parlor," he replied, with a smile breaking into his handsome countenance.

Ere Amy could reply, the sound of laughing voices was heard at the parlor doors, and half a dozen girls and young men came in from the hall and dining-room in gayer spirits than when they went to the refreshment-tables half an hour before. As one and another returned to the parlor, it was noticeable that a change had come over their spirits.

Many of the young girls laughed and talked in louder tones, and were freer in their manners than before; sometimes to a degree that was unmaidenly; while the conduct of some of the young men was offensive to good taste for its rudeness or folly.

"When the wine is in the wit is out," said Pickering, as, rising, he offered his arm to Amy, and they moved down the parlor and mingled with the company, adding, as they gained the lower end of the room, "We might call this the application to your little sermon."

"And the oftener the wine goes in will the wit go out," returned his companion, speaking for his ear alone, "until in the end it may come to stay out altogether."

"I see how it is, Miss Granger," said the young man. "Your thought has a habit of running to the last result of things."

"Is not that wisest?" she asked.

"Doubtless. But the surprise with me is, that a young lady should have such radical views on the subject of drinking. You are in no danger. Nor are these young ladies, for all the wine they get at parties. A little lightness in the head as you see now, then a night's sleep, and all will be over."

"But what of the young men, their companions?" asked Amy.

Pickering gave a slight shrug.

"Will it be all over, as you say, with them?

Will the appetite be no stronger, and the power to resist its enticements no weaker?"

"I was speaking of the young ladies, and the danger to them," said Pickering.

"Is no one hurt by intemperance but the men who are its victims?" inquired the girl. "If I am not at fault in my observation, there are to be found among them sons, brothers, husbands and fathers. Have women no relation to these men? In their wounding is there no hurt to the sisters and daughters, to the wives and the mothers?"

Pickering felt again the old thrill in Amy's calm but earnest voice.

"If a young or middle-aged man should go home from here to-night the worse for the wine he has taken," she added, after a slight pause, "will there be no shame or sorrow in any woman's heart because of it?"

His ear caught the sound of a faint sigh which followed the closing words that fell from his companion's lips.

"We won't talk about this any more," he said. "The theme is too sombre for so gay and festive an occasion." He spoke with some decision of manner. "And now," he added, in a lighter voice, "let us try a little nonsense, by way of a restorative."

Amy had already said far more than it was in her thought or purpose to say at the outset, and was very willing to let the subject drop, even though far from being satisfied with the young man's utterances on the question, which, if his views were not in accord with hers, must stand as an impassable barrier between them. One thing she had long ago settled in her mind, and that was, never to give her hand in marriage to one who did not wholly abstain from the use of alcohol in any of its forms. She would take no risks here. The danger, in her view, was too appalling. Her answer to the question: "How shall I be saved from the curse of strong drink?" was simple and direct. She would neither touch it herself in any of its covert or enticing forms, nor place her happiness in the keeping of one who did.

At the next meeting of the lovers, for so we must call them, though the young man had not yet made a formal declaration of his sentiments, each felt that a barrier had risen between them. In the meantime, Pickering had, in response to some inquiries about Miss Granger's family, learned something of its painful history, and of the sufferings and humiliation through which the girl had passed. This made clear the ground of her prejudice against wine-drinking. I say "prejudice," using the word as Pickering used it at the time. One thing was plain to him; he saw that there would be little hope of compromise with Amy in regard to the use of intoxicating liquor in any of its forms. If he were not prepared to stand on her ground, so far as this question was concerned, he could hardly hope to stand with her at all.

It was this conviction in the mind of Pickering,

and the doubts and uncertainties as to his real attitude in regard to the use of alcoholic drinks which troubled Miss Granger, that raised the barrier too plainly visible to each on their next meeting. Both studiously avoided any reference to the subject, though it was never absent a moment from the thought of either. For the first time since their more intimate acquaintance, Amy made an effort to hold herself away, and even to close her heart against him. Her reserve was so apparent that it hurt, then piqued, and then partially offended the young man.

"If love," he said to himself, "has no deeper foundation than this, is it worth the name? Is the taking or refusing of a glass of wine to be the test of its quality? The love that I want is a love that can take me for what I am, and trust me all in all; and if she cannot do this, it might as well be at an end between us. To subject myself to any humiliating pledges and restrictions, is simply impossible. I hold my manly freedom too high for that."

An evening of embarrassed intercourse, followed by a cold parting, was the result. They did not meet again for over a week, during which time Amy had striven hard, but vainly, to keep the thought of Pickering out of her mind. With him the effort to banish her image had been no more successful; and as day after day went by without seeing her, tenderness grew in his heart, and the conviction became stronger and stronger that for him life would be nothing if not shared with her. Taking all things into consideration, he was beginning to feel more sympathy with the girl in her extreme views. "It is but natural," he said, "for a burnt child to dread the fire. All that she has seen and suffered must be set down in her favor."

A week of enforced absence was all that Pickering could endure; and when he met the sweet young girl again the ardor of his feelings was too strong for repression. Love looked out from his eyes more tenderly than ever, and betrayed itself more nearly on his tongue. As for Amy, the gladness of heart which she could not repress overflowed and revealed itself in her blushing face. Before they parted on that evening, the lover had spoken, and the maiden, while not consenting in words, had left him in no doubt as to the real state of her feelings.

Not the remotest reference was made to the subject which had, only a little while before, come in between them with its warning shadow and its separating wall. Was it forgotten by either of them? Not so. But their hearts held it away from any present influence. Love's fruition was for the moment too full for the intrusion of any remote questions of prudence. For love's sake all light impediments must disappear when the time came for their consideration.

So they felt; but with each the feeling of confidence had its ground in the fancied concession of the other. If Henry Pickering really loved her, would he hesitate in a matter which she held to be of such vital moment? So the maiden thought, and took the sweet assurance to her heart. "Amy loves me too well to let a mere prejudice or fancy stand between us," said the young man, confidently, to himself.

But they erred in their conclusions. When the young man pressed a closer suit, Amy referred him to her father, and Pickering found that there would be no consent with either unless the question of his attitude to the drinking customs of society was clearly settled.

"Neither myself nor my daughter," said Mr. Granger, "can afford to run so great a risk as is here involved. For myself, I would rather see my child with the angels." He betrayed considerable emotion.

"I must infer from all this," said Pickering, unable entirely to conceal his disappointment and irritation, "that you think me in special danger."

"No; only in the danger that comes to all who walk in dangerous ways," was the seriously-spoken reply. "If we know that robbers lie in wait along a certain road, what immunity from attack have we if we travel that road?"

"Shall we be cowards, then? or, like brave men, fight our way through?"

"If we have no business that requires us to go by that road, we put our courage to a useless test," replied Mr. Granger. "This way of drinking, my young friend, is not an orderly appointed way in life. It leads to no desirable result; has no goal of fortune, or honor, or happiness. They who walk in it are not exposed to the assaults of robbers alone, who waste and plunder their substance, but fatal miasmas lie along the marshes through which it often winds. It has pitfalls in many of its smoothest places, and steep precipices to which the road clings treacherously. If a man propose to go in this way, it is better that he should go alone, Mr. Pickering. Love, surely, will not expose its object, needlessly, to dangers like these."

"Frankly, Mr. Granger, I see more of hyperbole in all this than a statement of what the real danger is," said Pickering.

The irritation that betrayed itself in his manner a little while before was all gone; and though his speech was plain, it was not in the least disrespectful.

"The direful effects that too surely attend on excessive drinking, can scarcely be exaggerated by any figures of speech that our language is capable of forming," answered Mr. Granger. "I am many years older than you, and have seen deeper into this evil of intemperance than it is possible for you to have seen; and such is my dread of its subtle power that I never see a man with a glass of intoxicating liquor in his hand that I do not feel like uttering a cry of warning. Depend upon it, Mr. Pickering, there is no safe way for a young man, as he makes his entry into this world's busy, exciting and, in too many cases, exhausting arena, but that of complete abstinence from beverages in which alcohol is found."

"It certainly has its good as well as its evil effects," said the young man. "Used in moderation, it serves as a restorative in some cases, and as a tonic and vitalizer in many others. And in certain forms of disease it is almost a specific; at least, I have so understood."

"I scarcely think you have studied this subject in the light of more recent investigations and experiences," remarked Mr. Granger.

"In truth, I have not studied it at all. But there are facts which are commonly known and accepted, and these scarcely warrant the complete banishment to which our extreme temperance advocates would subject all kinds of liquor, not excepting beer and the lighter wines."

"There are many inferences, and loose sayings, and unproved assertions in regard to the beneficial effects of alcohol on the human body, as well in health as in sickness," was replied, "but one after another, they are being disproved, until the substance called alcohol has, by the ablest chemists and pathologists, with only an exception here and there, been set over to the side of poisons. It has no food value whatever; and its disturbing and disorganizing effects have become so well known in the medical profession, that even the small number of intelligent physicians who hold to its administration in certain cases, the range of which grows narrower every day, are giving it with great caution and in very small doses."

"Is this really so?" asked the young man, showing some surprise.

"It is just as I have said," replied Mr. Granger. "This whole subject is receiving the most careful attention from the best medical experts; and the day of guess work and loose generalization is over. Nothing will now do for prudent men but rigid analysis and clearly-established fact. Let me urge upon you, in the outset of life, to give this question of the true effect of alcohol on the human system an impartial examination; to challenge a substance that works such fearful havoc among men, and require it to answer in no uncertain speech. If it be a friend of the people, there will be no difficulty in establishing the fact; if an enemy, the case can be made equally clear."

"Thank you for the suggestion, Mr. Granger," said the young man. "There is reason in what you say. I will look into this matter more carefully, and if I find it as you allege, I shall not hesitate about my future attitude."

"If you will come and see us to-morrow evening, I think you will be likely to hear a discussion on this subject that will interest you. A few friends are coming in, among whom will be a Dr. Gilbert, from New York, who has given the subject of inebriation and the action of alcoholic stimulants on the human body, a careful study for many years. He is no temperance enthusiast, as the people are too much inclined to call such men as I am, but a cool-headed observer, who will be satisfied with nothing in relation to this subject which the most perfect methods of chemical analysis and physiological investigation have not settled. You will be impressed with him as a man who knows whereof he speaks."

"Thank you, Mr. Granger. I shall certainly avail myself of the opportunity. It is clear seeing that makes right action. But to act where the judgment is not convinced is never wise. And this is the cause of my hesitation now. I might promise you that I would never take wine or brandy; but if I did not think it wrong, for some clearly-seen reason, to use these articles, my promise would ever after be an annoying impediment, and might be broken. But if my promise rests on principle; if I abstain from prudence and judgment; my attitude towards the drinking customs of society will express my true sentiments, and I shall stand firm on the solid ground of my convictions."

"Which will be far better," returned Mr. Granger.

CHAPTER XXII.

ON arriving at Mr. Granger's, I found a small but select company. There were Dr. Gilbert, and Judge Arbuckle and his wife, whom I had been particularly invited to meet. Mr. Stannard was there also; and a Mrs. K——, one of the representative women who were actively engaged in the work of Christian temperance reform. I had not before seen young Henry Pickering, and was attracted by his face and bearing; and particularly so, as it was plain, from unmistakable signs, that he was more to Amy Granger than an ordinary acquaintance. But I did not fail to observe that there was in the attitude of these young people towards each other a certain reserve that was almost embarrassment. During the conversation that ensued, and which soon drifted into a discussion of the claims of alcohol to have any nutritive or therapeutical value, I was struck by the intentness with which Amy watched the young man's face, as if trying to read his thoughts; and there was, at times, a restlessness in her manner that was particularly noticeable, with occasional swift changes in the expression of her countenance. You saw it light up suddenly when some strong point was made by Dr. Gilbert; and this was always accompanied by a glance towards the young man who was seated by her side.

Dr. Gilbert, whom I had not met before, was a man about fifty, with a quiet, thoughtful face. You saw in his eyes, which were a dark gray, that steady, intent expression which comes of earnest thought. His mouth was firm, its character harmonizing with what you saw in his eyes. You recognized him at once as a man with whom neither fancy nor impulse could have much influence.

Judge Arbuckle was another style of man altogether. He was taller, with a finer muscular development, and a larger head. His eyes were darker, and so was his complexion. All his features broke into a quicker play, and you perceived at once that he was a man of sentiment and feeling as well as of intellect and perception, and that in any direction in which he might throw himself he would display both mental vigor and force of will.

It was curious to see these two men meet in the discussion I had come prepared to hear. But I knew enough of the results of recent investigations in regard to alcohol, to be very well satisfied about the issue, if Dr. Gilbert was as well posted in facts and results as I had reason to believe.

I will not hold the reader in any of the preliminary phases and drifts of conversation into which the company fell, but bring him in contact therewith where the points of interest were clear, and bore with distinctive force on the main subject under discussion, which was the affirmation on one side that alcohol, if used in moderation, was beneficial, and the declaration on the other that its action on the human body, except in some very unusual conditions, was always hurtful.

"I claim," said Judge Arbuckle, "that wine, and in many cases brandy, are necessary articles, both in diet and medicine. They assist nature in the work of digestion, and give tone to weakened nerves. I have seen many lives saved, under conditions of extreme prostration, by the use of spirits. In typhoid fevers, brandy, as you well know, is the physician's sheet-anchor. Without it, three out of every five of his patients would die from simple lack of heart-power, which can only be restored through active stimulation. In sudden attacks of illness, as in faintings, cholics, a suspension of heart-action, or exhaustion from fatigue or cold, there is nothing that will act so quickly as a glass of brandy. I never think of leaving home without a supply; and should regard myself as culpable were I to do so. I can point to scores of instances in which a timely draught of brandy has saved me from a spell of sickness, if it has not saved my life. There is one fact that should never be overlooked. Society is not in a normal condition. It is overworked. There is a strain upon everything, and a consequent exhaustion of strength. Nature, always quick in her instinct of danger, has, at the same time, as quick a perception of the remedy needed; and her indication is unmistakable here. It is stimulation that is required. All men feel this; and the universal resort to stimulants of one kind or another is but the natural and necessary response to the demands of our exhausted and failing vital forces."

The judge spoke with considerable warmth of manner, and with a tone and emphasis which expressed his firm conviction that the assertions he was making were unanswerable.

"Facts and experience are stubborn things, doctor," he closed by remarking; "and these we have in abundance. But men who have pet theories"—he smiled pleasantly as he said it—"are wonderfully skilled in the art of explaining away both."

Dr. Gilbert did not seem to be in any haste to controvert the judge's assertions. His first response came in the form of a question.

"If you were to find a man benumbed with cold, what would you do for him?"

"Pour a glass of brandy down his throat as quickly as possible."

"For what purpose?"

"To heat him up, of course. Heat is life; cold is death."

"Suppose I were to tell you that alcohol lowers instead of raising the temperature of the body."

"I would say that you were jesting."

"And yet the assertion is true."

"Did you ever take a swallow of brandy?"

"Yes."

"Did it make you feel cold or warm?"

"I felt a sense of warmth."

"Burning up even to your face?"

"Yes."

"Is heat cold, doctor?" The judge spoke as one who had closed the controversy in a single sentence.

"Does heat cause the thermometer to fall?" asked Dr. Gilbert.

"I do not see the drift of your question," replied the judge.

"After the most carefully conducted experiments, often repeated," said the doctor, "the fact has been clearly established that alcohol, instead of imparting warmth to the body, actually lowers its temperature."

Judge Arbuckle shook his head in a decided negative. "If I take glass of wine or brandy, I come into an immediate glow. It doesn't do to tell me that I feel cold. Experiment may prove what it can; but it certainly cannot prove this—at least not to my satisfaction. There is such a thing as color blindness; and a like defect may exist in some of the other senses. Feeling with some may be blind also, and mistake heat for cold."

"A young lady blushes," said the doctor, in reply. "You will hardly say that because her cheeks have become hot the temperature of her whole body has been raised; but rather infer that the equilibrium of heat has been disturbed, or that the capillaries have become relaxed and suffused. An impulse of feeling has disturbed the heart's action, and made its beats more violent. Suppose this temporary engorgement of the minute blood vessels of the skin were to take place, with a sense of heat all over the body, would there not be an increased radiation of heat from all the surface, and a consequent lowering of the body's temperature, especially with the interior organs?"

"But what has the blushing of a young lady to do with the colorific or refrigerant effect of a glass of brandy?" asked the judge.

"The phenomenon observed in both cases is due to the same cause," said the doctor. "Alcohol relaxes the minuter vessels so that they are unable to return the blood promptly to the circulation; cutaneous engorgements follow, with an increase of surface heat, and accelerated radiation. The effect on the extremities of the nerves is that of a warm glow, such as is felt during a reaction from cold. Instead of there being an actual increase in the general temperature of the body, as the result of alcoholic stimulant, a reduction takes place, as has been proved over and over again by the thermometer."

"You take me out of my depths here, doctor. I have never given much attention to physiology," answered the judge, a little less confident in his manner.

"But you know what common sense is; and how to deduce conclusions from well-established facts. It is the habit of your mind to weigh evidence. Now, for the sake of the truth, which is as dear to you as to any man living, will you not, for a little while, take the place of a judge in this controversy, and give to the evidence I shall bring against alcohol as an enemy to the human race, the grave consideration it should have?"

"I accept the office to which you so gracefully assign me," replied the judge, smiling. "But as I leave my client without an advocate, I shall claim the right to say a word in his behalf if I think you treat him unfairly."

"As many words as you please. If there is any good in him I should like to know it; but I am free to say, that the more carefully I investigate his claim to be, in any sense, a friend to the human race, except for what service he may give in chemistry and the arts, the more complete are my convictions that he is only an enemy. I cannot find a single thing in which the harm of his presence is not greater than the good.

"But we were talking about the heat-producing quality of alcohol. Now, heat is generated through the union of oxygen with carbon, by which the latter is consumed. There are certain articles of food, such as the fat, starches and sugars, which are known as heat-producing and force-generating, and chemistry is at no loss in regard to them. Their value has been determined with the greatest accuracy. The amount of heat that each of these substances will give when taken into the body has been carefully measured, and is known to all in our profession.

But in regard to alcohol, so long held even by medical men, to be a heat-producer, animal chemistry has not yet been made to detect any evidence of oxidation, the blood showing none of the usual results of this process. And now, since we have been using the thermometer as a test of the internal temperature of the body, in order to ascertain the heating value of foods, or its thermal condition under various disturbing influences, we find that when alcohol is taken there follows a marked reduction of heat. The best medical writers now agree on this subject; and some practitioners have even gone so far as to administer it in fever as a cooling agent.

"Even before science had made this discovery of the non-heat-generating power of alcohol, arctic navigators had learned from experience that the use of spirits lessens a man's ability to withstand cold; and now the extreme northern voyager avoids its use altogether, in order to retain sufficient heat to sustain him under the intense cold to which he is subjected. In the voyage made in search of Sir John Franklin, no alcoholic stimulants were used; and the northern whaler employs them very sparingly or not at all."

"Do you remember," said Mr. Stannard, at this point, "a Pole named Lemonowsky, who, some twenty years ago, gave lectures in this country on Napoleon?"

Some of us remembered him very well.

"I mentioned him because of a lecture he gave on

temperance, the facts of which fully corroborate what the doctor has just been saying. Lemonowsky, who had been an officer in Napoleon's army, stated, that when about leaving home, as a boy, his father placed his hand upon his head, and after declaring that intoxicating drinks were the great curse of mankind, solemnly conjured him never to touch or taste them; and that he gave his father a promise that he never would. And all his life he remained true to that promise. He took the ground, that the use of alcohol in extreme cold, extreme heat or extreme exhaustion, was dangerous, and often fatal, and, in proof of his position, made three statements of remarkable facts which had come within his own observation and experience.

"Lemonowsky accompanied Napoleon in his invasion of Russia. He said, that among his immediate associates in the army were about thirty who, like himself, wholly abstained from ardent spirits, and that while men who drank freely were dying almost like sheep from gangrene and other diseases, brought on from exposure to the intense cold, every one of these thirty abstainers were in good health, and every one came back from that disastrous campaign. In Egypt, when heat was enervating the army, and death rapidly reducing its numbers, the men who refused to drink ardent spirits still retained their health, and suffered from thirst and heat far less than their companions. This intelligent Pole then went on to relate how, after the battle of

Waterloo, and the delivery by the allies of Marshal Ney and many of the officers to the French at Paris, he, with a few others, effected their escape, and put to sea in a boat, from which they were taken while in the British Channel by a vessel bound to the United States. Subsequently this vessel was wrecked in a storm, and Lemonowsky found himself again upon the sea in an open boat, with nine companions and only a small supply of provisions and water. These were soon used up, and for many days they had nothing to eat or drink. When finally rescued, by a vessel bound to Philadelphia, they were in such an extreme state of exhaustion that they had to be literally carried on board. 'Immediately,' said the narrator, 'on being placed in a berth, the ship's doctor brought me a glass of hot whisky and water, and placed it to my lips. But I refused to drink it.' 'You must, or you will die,' he said. 'Then I told him I would die, for I never had and never would drink intoxicating liquor. He got angry, and swore at me, and called me a fool. But I wouldn't touch his whisky. Well, gentlemen and ladies, I recovered; but of the nine who were taken with me out of the boat, and who took the doctor's stimulating draught, hot even though it was, every one died. So, you see, that in extreme cold, or heat, or exhaustion, alcohol, so far from being useful, is one of the most dangerous substances a man can take into his system.'"

"A very striking experience, certainly," said Dr.

Gilbert, "and one that is entirely in the line of legitimate results, as proved by the latest and most carefully-conducted experiments. There was a time when, if I had heard this story of Lemonowsky's, I would have pronounced it a bit of fancy work, or, at least, an exaggeration of an isolated case or two which were but exceptions to a rule, the action of which was all on the other side. But I can well believe, now, that the sturdy old Pole gave truthful evidence of which he knew."

"If I understand the case," remarked Judge Arbuckle; "I am on the bench, you see, and am considering the evidence—the result of some recent experiments, and the evidence of a few isolated facts are held to disprove the beneficial effects of a substance which medical men have used efficiently for generations, and which every head of a family has administered with success in scores, if not hundreds of instances of sudden sickness."

"The new and exhaustive tests to which this substance has been subjected," replied Dr. Gilbert, "have nearly all been conducted within the last ten years, and so conclusive have been the results, that in the International Medical Congress, which met last year in Philadelphia, at which over six hundred delegates from this country and Europe were assembled, a report was adopted in which alcohol was declared to have no food value whatever, and to be so deleterious in its effects on the human organism, as to leave a grave doubt whether, even as a medicine in the most extreme cases, it did not do more harm than good."

"Not unanimously adopted, certainly."

"The facts are simply these. The National Temperance Society sent a memorial to this important Congress, asking from it a public declaration to the effect that alcohol should be classed with other powerful drugs, and that when prescribed medicinally, it should be with conscientious caution and a sense of grave responsibility. That it should declare it to be in no sense a food for the human system, and that its improper use is productive of a large amount of physical disease, tending to deteriorate the human race; and further, to recommend to their several nationalities, as representatives of enlightened science, a total abstinence from aloholic beverages. The consideration of this memorial was referred to the 'Section on Medicine,' in which the questions proposed were discussed with marked ability and earnestness, resulting in the almost unanimous adoption of an elaborate report by Dr. Ezra M. Hunt. In this report alcohol is declared to have no food value, and to be of doubtful utility as a medicine. Indeed, its therapeutic value is limited almost exclusively to that of a cardiac stimulant in certain extreme cases which often admit of substitutions. Of its evil and destructive action on the body and brain, a frightful exhibit is given. This report, as transmitted by the 'Section on Medicine' to the General Congress, was ordered by that body to be sent to the National Temperance Society as an answer to its memorial."

I was observing the face of Judge Arbuckle while Dr. Gilbert was speaking. The grave, almost puzzled expression that came creeping over it, was curious to see. The judge had a respect for science, learning and authority. The testimony of the old Pole, Lemonowsky, went for almost nothing. But here was an International Medical Congress of over six hundred eminent physicians, representing, of course, the highest intelligence of the profession, uttering its grave condemnation, and at a word sealing up the bottle from which he had been drawing his favorite medicament, and declaring its use to be hurtful in nearly every case of administration.

"I don't know, doctor," he said, "whether I am really awake or not; all this is so new and improbable. I shall expect to hear, presently, that a beefsteak has its hidden dangers, and that coffee will poison as surely as arsenic."

"By their fruits ye shall know them; and it so happens that, in regard to alcohol, there is no difficulty about the fruit," returned the doctor.

"None whatever in regard to its abuse," returned the judge. "That is admitted by every one. But we are talking of its moderate use as a beverage, and of its value as a medicine. Take me, for example. I have used more or less wine and spirits for over twenty-five years. Few men enjoy better health.

Except some torpor of the liver, which I believe is hereditary."

Dr. Gilbert looked steadily into Judge Arbuckle's face for a few moments, as if making a critical examination. Then reaching out his hand, he said: "Let me feel your pulse, judge."

There was a deep pause and silence.

"With some slight disturbance of the heart occasionally," remarked the doctor, quietly.

"Very slight. Nothing to speak of," replied the judge, with the manner of one who felt a little disturbed.

"A sinking sensation after exertion, or anxiety, or abstinence from food?"

"Yes, sometimes."

"Which all comes right after a good, strong glass of brandy?"

"Yes."

"You find this occurring oftener than it did a few years ago?"

"Well, yes. I'm getting older, you see, and any organic trouble one may have generally increases with age. But, fortunately, I know what to do, and have my remedy always at hand."

"In some form of alcoholic stimulant?"

"Exactly."

"How often do you resort to this remedy? Every day?"

I saw a change of expression in the judge's face,

and a contraction of his brows, as he replied: "Almost every day."

"Especially in the morning before you have taken food?"

"Yes."

"Well, now, Judge Arbuckle," said the doctor, with a grave smile on his face, "did it never occur to you that the remedy you are taking for the relief of this trouble is the very agent by which it has been produced?"

Judge Arbuckle shook his head in a decided manner.

"And that your torpid liver is only another evidence of organic deterioration produced by this favorite remedy—or shall I say beverage—to which you resort so frequently?"

"Organic deterioration, doctor!" There was a covert alarm in the judge's voice.

"There is no substance used by man which produces so many and such serious organic deterioration as alcohol," replied the doctor, speaking soberly. "There is not an organ, or delicate nerve, or membrane, or fluid, or vessel, that it does not hurt by contact, or deteriorate if the contact be continued. The heart, which is the centre of life, is subjected to an excess of strain so long as it is in the system, because, being a substance that is never digested, or converted into food or force, it hurts and disturbs until elimination takes place. But this strain, or overwork, is the least of the evils which come from the presence of alcohol. The changes and deteriorations of structure, and in the condition of the blood, which take place in consequence of the presence of alcohol, are of a most serious character. Let me try to make this plain. The whole surface of the body, and every particular organ, muscle, nerve, blood-vessel, and even the bones, are enveloped in sheaths or coverings called the membranes. Besides the first apparent use of these membranes, many of which serve as enveloping bandages, by which all the structures are held together in perfect order, they have a still more important use in the animal economy. They are the filters of the body, and without them there could be no building of the structures they line or enclose. The food we take contains all the various things required for the life and health of the body; albumen, caesin and vegetable film for tissue building; fat, sugar and starch for the production of heat and force; water as the general solvent, and salt for constructive and other purposes. These have, after digestion, to be arranged in the body, which is done by the membranes, through which nothing can pass which is not, for the time, in a state of aqueous solution. Water passes freely through them, and so do soluble salts; but the constructive albuminous matter does not pass until it is chemically decomposed. Upon their integrity all the silent work of building up the body depends. If these membranes are rendered too porous, and let out the tissue-building fluids of the blood, the body dies gradually, as if it were being slowly bled to death; if, on the contrary, they become condensed or thickened, they fail to let the natural fluids pass through them, and the result is either an accumulation of fluids in a closed cavity, or the contraction of the substance enclosed within the membrane, or a dryness of membranous surfaces which ought to be freely lubricated and kept apart.

"Now, the most carefully-conducted experiments have educed the fact that upon all the membranous structures alcohol exerts a direct and perverting action. It produces in them a thickening, a shrinking and an inactivity that reduces their functional power. That they may work rapidly and equally, they require to be at all times charged with water to saturation; and an agent that deprives them of any portion of this water interferes with their work, and lays the foundation of structural derangements and deteriorations that are often fatal in the end. Alcohol is an agent which possesses, in a high degree, this power of absorbing water; and as soon as it is taken into the body it begins the work of absorption. Dr. Hunt, in his report to the Medical Congress, says: 'The power alcohol has of drying secretions, and congesting membranes, is unsurpassed by any known remedy in general use;' and Dr. Richardson, in his Cantor Lectures on Alcohol, dwells particularly on this point in his startling exhibit of the destructive effects of alcohol when taken into the human body."

CHAPTER XXIII.

"YOU almost take my breath away, doctor!" exclaimed Judge Arbuckle, affecting a lightness of tone that did not wholly conceal the more serious impression which these charges against alcohol, as an enemy to the animal organism, had produced on his mind. "I was going to ask you in what specific manner this substance affects the heart and the liver; but I'm half afraid."

"The best way to deal with any danger, is to look it steadily in the face, and measure its power for evil," replied the doctor. "Let us take the heart, which, by its propelling force, sends the blood along the arteries. One of the first effects of alcohol is a temporary relaxation or paralysis of the minuter blood-vessels, which shows itself often, as I said a little while ago, in a sensation of heat. This causes the heart to beat more quickly. The vessels throughout the whole body become dilated, and are held in a state of unnatural relaxation and unnatural tension. If the use of alcoholic drinks is continued, the persistent pressure causes, in the course of time, a change in the diameters of these vessels, and the whole marvelous web-work of blood, upon which the organs of the body are constructed, is deranged. Soon the functions of the heart become perverted—for it cannot escape the effects of stimulation. If, to-day, under the excitement of wine or spirits, it gives twenty-five thousand strokes in twenty-four hours more than its usual number, it cannot to-morrow sink back to the old rate without experiencing some disturbance, some feebleness, or some hesitation. And is it not fair to conclude that an organ which, by its own stroke feeds its own substance with blood, must be among the first to suffer from irregular supplies of blood? As stimulation goes on increasing, the heart, whipped to greater efforts, gradually enlarges, as the arm does by excessive use; its exquisite valves, subjected to prolonged strain, are drawn out of their fine proportion; the orifices, through which the great currents of blood issue in their course, are dilated; the minute chords which hold the valves in position and tension are elongated; and the walls of the ventricles are thickened. All this is, of course, very gradual, and nature, ever on the alert for defense or repair, holds her own, as far as possible, against the enemy that is assaulting her, and disputes the ground inch by inch, and for a long time so successfully, that but few outward signs of the evil work that is going on make themselves visible. But the time comes when her power of resistance fails, and when deteriorations of organic tissues begin. The membranous envelope and lining of the heart thickens, becomes cartilaginous, and even bony. To this may succeed degenerative changes in the muscular tissues of the heart, by which the power of contraction may be reduced, or fatty cells may begin to replace the muscular structure. So insidiously do these organic changes progress, that those who are suffering from them are scarcely aware of the mischief until it is far advanced. They are for years conscious of a failure of central power, which they try to restore by the very stimulation that produced the failure, until, in the end, the remedy ceases to act; whip and spur can do no more, and the poor, jaded, overworked heart gives up the hopeless struggle."

"And the man dies," said the judge, in a half-incredulous voice. But his manner was very grave.

"That event may be long delayed; for nature never yields an inch of ground so long as she can defend it, and when forced to retire, usually does it slowly, fighting as she retreats. It often happens that, before the heart gives up the struggle, other vital organs are subdued—the brain, the liver or the lungs. Sometimes paralysis or apoplexy ends the contest. Indeed, death comes from a wide range of diseases, which have their origin in alcoholic deteriorations. No man, who uses the substance habitually is a sound man. He cannot bear exposure, or sudden changes of the temperature, or the subtle invasion of epidemics, near so well as the man who never permits the poison to enter his system."

"You think my torpid liver comes from the

presence of alcohol in my system?" said the judge.

"I have very little doubt of it; for it is on that organ that alcohol most frequently works structural changes," replied Dr. Gilbert. "The liver has a remarkable capacity for holding active substances in its cellular parts. In cases of poisoning from arsenic, strychnine and other substances, we turn at once to the liver as the place of chief deposit for foreign matter. Alcohol finds its way there promptly; and we might say that, with the free drinker of ardent spirits, it is almost continually saturated with it. The effect of alcohol on the liver is to retard free secretion and the passage of fluids. The organ enlarges at first from the distension of its vessels and the thickening of its tissues. Afterwards there follows a contraction of membrane, and a slow shrinking of the whole mass of the organ in its cellular parts. Dr. Richardson, in his Cantor Lectures, to which I have referred, clearly describes this process. Of course, as in other alcoholic poisoning, the change is slow, and the subject of it rarely suspects the cause of his trouble. When the liver has become a shrunken, hardened mass, dropsy in the lower extremities appears, and the case becomes hopeless. Sometimes, in these extreme changes, a fatty degeneration takes place."

I saw the judge glance down at his feet and move them, I thought, a little uneasily, when Dr. Gilbert spoke of dropsy in the lower extremities; and I fancied that the face of Mrs. Arbuckle changed suddenly. There was a pause, which no one seemed for awhile inclined to break.

"If all this be so, doctor," Judge Arbuckle's brows were drawn closely together, "what are we to do with the fact that in typhoid fevers brandy is relied upon almost as much as if it were a specific for that disease? If alcohol is such an enemy to the human body, how can it act as a friend here? Poison is poison, and works destructively, whether he who takes it be sick or well."

"Does your physician make free use of brandy in typhoid fever?"

"He did as late as six months ago," replied the judge. "But now, that we are talking on this subject, I recall the fact that since then one of my neighbors, whose daughter was down with this fever, sent him away and called in another physician, because milk punch was interdicted. My neighbor would not take the risk of any experiments with his child. He had always seen milk punch given freely in typhoid fever, and as Dr. D—— refused to let it be given, on the ground that he had adopted some new theory of cure, he was discharged, and the case given to Dr. L——, who held strictly to the old mode of treatment."

"What was the result."

"It was a very bad attack. I remember it all now. Dr. D—— was severely blamed by the family for his treatment of the case while it was in his hands. He let it sink so low for lack of stimulation, that when brandy was given it was too late to produce any reactive effect."

"And the patient died?"

"Yes."

"Killed by the brandy, most likely. Nature had all that she could do to fight single-handed with her enemy. To give him a recruit was to make his victory sure."

"You speak very confidently, Dr. Gilbert."

"Because I speak from the stand-point of accurate knowledge in regard to the action of alcohol, as well as from the experience and observation of the most enlightened men in our profession. No physician, who has kept pace with the advance of medical science in the past few years, would now dare to risk the life of his patient, or to retard his cure, by giving him alcohol freely in any serious illness. If administered at all, it would be in very small doses, and with an exceeding close observation of its effects. If I had you in my library, I could refer you to the recorded testimony in medical journals, treatises and text-books of the most distinguished and trustworthy members of the profession in this country and Europe, on the subject of the use of alcohol in disease; and with scarcely an exception, it is unfavorable. Where its use is now sanctioned at all, it is under the strictest limitations, and with the greatest injunctions of caution. Prof. Loomis, of New York city, who does not entirely exclude alcohol in his treatment of typhoid fever, says, that in this disease the experience of very few physicians is such as to enable them to determine from the patient's appearance, when the administration of stimulants should be commenced, and that where there is reasonable doubt as to the propriety of giving or withholding, it is better to withhold them. He admits a possible value, but admonishes the physician when prescribing alcohol to his patient in this disease to see him at least every two hours, and to watch the effect with the greatest care. Dr. Hunt, while approving this extremely guarded use, says, that many excellent practitioners rely wholly on ammonia, ethers and foods in such cases."

"The evidence against my client continues to accumulate," said the judge, with something like a grim smile on his face. "Anything more, Dr. Gilbert?"

"The testimony, if all were taken," replied the doctor, "would require this court to remain in session for weeks, and if printed, would fill many volumes. There are a few things more which I would like to say, if you have patience to hear them. The prisoner at the bar, your honor, is an exceedingly dangerous fellow; and it may be well to permit those who know him best, and who understand his hidden and subtle ways, and the evils that are wrought by his hands, to offer still further evidence against him. Richardson says of alcohol, that it dries the liver, the stomach and the lungs; and even steals moisture from the corpuscles of the blood; and more than any other article in common use, initiates degeneration of important organs. A claim has been made for alcohol that it fattens the body, if that be a desirable result. Many beer-drinkers certainly do become fat; but as a substance which contains no fatty material cannot produce fat, investigation may naturally seek for a reason in the pathological effects of alcohol. It is found that the individual so fattened invariably diminishes in physical activity, and in the power of endurance in proportion to his increase of weight; and this is held to be due to a degenerative change in the more actively vital materials of the body, and the slow accumulation of uneliminated carbonacious material. It is really disease and not health; the product of a degenerative and not a normal process. If alcohol can serve the human body no better than this, the body might well dispense with its service.

"As a digester, alcohol has a wide reputation. Men take it before a meal to prepare the stomach for its work, and with and after a meal to assist it in doing its work. Now, what has the medical profession to say on this subject; and what is the result of careful test, analysis and observation? One authority declares that alcohol, when added to the digestive fluid, 'produces a white precipitate, which suspends digestion;' and Richardson declares that of all the systems of organs that suffer from the use of alcohol, two, viz: the digestive and the nervous, are effected most determinately. The stomach, he remarks, being unable, because of the presence of alcohol, to produce, in proper quantity, the natural digestive fluid, and also unable to absorb the food which, in consequence, is but imperfectly digested, becomes affected with anxiety and irritation, or oppressed with nausea, or with a sense of distension, or with a loathing for food, or an unnatural craving for drink. This self-inflicted disease, as it becomes confirmed, is called dyspepsia; and the sufferer, instead of giving up his wine, or spirits, takes pills, or pours into his poor abused stomach floods of effervescing and mineral waters; does, in fact, a hundred foolish things by which he is made worse. Between his drinking and his medicine, he increases his indigestion, until it takes on a chronic form, and all enjoyment of life is over."

"One might infer from all this," the judge here remarked, "that our prisoner at the bar is responsible for all the ills that flesh is heir to."

"His responsibility," replied the doctor, "has a far wider range than most people imagine. The consumption of spirits, wine, ale and beer reaches, annually, in this country, the enormous amount of over three hundred millions of gallons. Is it possible for the people to consume this vast quantity of a beverage containing from two or three to over sixty per cent. of a substance which, in the words of Dr. Hunt, is 'beyond dispute, fraught with the most prevalent and direful results to the physical structure,' without a serious impairment of the public health in the reduction of vital power, and in functional derangements, which lay the foundations of diseases which too often baffle the physician's skill? I say nothing of the ills that afflict our social life, which are more terrible, even, than the ills from which our bodies suffer. One medical writer says of alcohol: 'It helps time to produce the effects of age; it is the genius of degeneration.' Another says: 'Practical medicine tells us that three-quarters of all diseases in adults who drink at all are caused thereby,' and farther, that, 'the capacity of the alcohols for impairment of functions and the initiation and promotion of organic lesion in vital parts, is unsurpassed by any record in the whole range of medicine;' these facts being so fully granted by the profession as to be no longer debatable. But why continue to accumulate evidence? If what I have stated be not sufficient to convict the accused, it would be a waste of time to bring other allegations against him."

Judge Arbuckle's fine face lighted up as he grasped the hand of Dr. Gilbert, and said: "I must declare the evidence to be complete; and confess, at the same time, that I have been too much prejudiced against temperance reformers, as a class, to give this subject the careful and honest investigation it should long ago have received at my hands. We cling to old prejudices sometimes with an unreasoning tenacity, you know. But is the statement just made by you taken from official returns?—the one in regard to the enormous consumption of intoxicating drinks in this country?"

"It is from Dr. Hargreaves' important work, 'Our Wasted Resources,' which ought to be carefully studied by every intelligent man who feels an interest in the welfare of his country, and in the well-being of the people. The statements given are, of course, authentic. And let me refer you, also, to the exhaustive report on 'Alcohol as a Food and Medicine,' made to the recent Medical Congress, by Dr. Ezra W. Hunt, which has been published in a volume of nearly a hundred and fifty pages; and to Dr. Richardson's able lectures on alcohol. These works are candid, honest and thorough, and offer abundant means for an examination of this great subject, on the right treatment and adjustment of which hang such vast results of good or evil. I shall feel that a cause which my judgment approves, and in which my feelings are deeply interested, has gained a large accession of strength, if you, Judge Arbuckle, should, from conviction and principle, range yourself upon the side of its friends. That cause is known as Total Abstinence."

The light which had come breaking into Judge Arbuckle's face, as he grasped the doctor's hand, faded out slowly, a sober, thoughtful, indeterminate expression coming in its stead. "Total abstinence!" Ever since he could remember, these two words had been, in his mind, the synonym for ignorant and meddlesome fanaticism; and he had felt something like contempt for men who could let the glass of generous wine pass them untasted. He must be a poor milk-sop, or cold, mean and unsocial, who could do this, he thought. In standing consciously above this class, in his use of "a beverage fit for the gods," the judge had enjoyed a feeling of superiority, and a sense of more affluent manhood. It is no cause of wonder, then, that his countenance became exceedingly grave and thoughtful. Had these men been the really wise ones? Had they been of the prudent, who, foreseeing the evil, hide themselves, while he, passing on with the simple, had been punished? I saw that a great conflict was going on in his mind; and I saw, too, that his wife was watching him with an intensity of interest which she made no effort to conceal.

"Total abstinence, doctor!" The judge shook his head. "I believe in moderation. And all you have said as to the bad effects of the alcohol contained in wine and spirits, only makes moderation the more imperative."

The judge had risen to his feet. In doing so, I noticed a slight stiffness of movement. He straightened himself up rather slowly, placing one hand tightly above his right hip, and holding it there for a few moments. Then he stepped out and walked across the room. There was, at first, a perceptible limp in one leg; but it was soon gone.

Dr. Gilbert smiled, as he said: "Getting a little stiff, judge?"

"Yes," was answered good humoredly. "We are none of us as young as we were twenty years ago."

"A man ought to be called young at fifty," replied the doctor. "And neither you nor I have gone far, if at all, beyond that age."

"Fifty-one," said the judge.

"In advance of me less than a year. This should be the age of full vigor. Every organ and function in the body, if there has been no overstrain, nor exposure to morbific causes, ought to be in their highest activity. The filtering and lubricating membranes that line and inclose the joints, should be in perfect health; and so should the membranes that sheathe the muscles and nerves, and enfold and line the vital organs. It is too soon for age to impair the action, or to dry the fluids of any part of the body's wonderful mechanism."

"I don't know about that, doctor," returned the judge. "I am acquainted with a great many men who have reached fifty, and there is scarcely one of them who is not beginning to show signs of approaching age."

"What about their habits? Are they strictly temperate men? Total abstinence from alcoholic drinks, I mean?"

"No. They are for the most part, good, generous livers, but not given to excess, except, perhaps, in a few cases."

Dr. Gilbert smiled, as he said: "The effects of arsenic, when taken into the stomach moderately, have been carefully observed and recorded, and are so well known to the physician, that he rarely, if ever, mistakes them: Now, if he were called to see a patient who had been indulging in the moderate use of arsenic, and found all the indications of arsenic poison about him, would he not fairly conclude that it was arsenic, and not old age or anything else that was working the mischief. The case with your friends is in exact parallel with this. The effects of alcoholic poison have been as carefully noted and recorded as that produced by arsenic. We know just what it does in the human body, and how it does it, and what the indications of its health-destroying actions are. And when we see a man who regularly uses alcohol in any of its forms, suffering from the troubles which we know alcohol produces, we naturally assign the cause of his ailments to the poison he has taken. If we find him troubled with sciatica, and know, as we do, that alcohol perverts the membranous coverings of the nerves, and gives rise to pressure within the sheath of the nerve, and to pain in consequence, we natually infer that the origin of his trouble lies in the poison of alcohol. If the neuralgia is in the face, commencing at some point where a nerve passes through an opening in the bone, as near the centre of the chin, or in front of the lower part of the ear, or over the eye, and we know that alcohol thickens, as I have shown, the sheath of the nerve, we do not hesitate to conclude that this thickening has gone on until the bony openings have become too small, and congestion and intense suffering are the consequence. If one of our moderate-drinking patients has any of the troublesome forms of indigestion, we refer the cause to the alcohol contained in his favorite beverage, for we know that alcohol not only retards instead of promoting digestion, but weakens and diseases the stomach. If he is afflicted with insomnia, we see in this most serious condition the result of the relaxation of the blood-vessels of the brain, caused by the presence of alcohol, and their consequent inability to return the blood promptly to the heart; or if his sleep be heavy and apoplectic in character, we know that this relaxation of the blood-vessel is so great as to result in engorgement and danger. If there is fatty degeneration of the heart, or kidneys, or liver, we know that alcohol will do this very thing. If we find Bright's disease, we know that the action of alcohol is to deteriorate the lining membranes of the kidneys, by which they may lose their power to retain and rightly dispose of the albuminous material out of which the tissues of the body are constructed, and let it pass through and be drained from the system, which, in the end, is certain death. I could go on and show how nearly every organic disease with which our poor bodies are afflicted, may have its origin in the deteriorations or obstructions caused by alcohol."

"But, doctor, we have 'tic,' and sciatica, and insomnia, and albuminuria, and all the diseases you mention in persons who make no use of wine, or beer, or spirits."

"Of course we have," was replied. "I did not mean to say that only alcohol causes these maladies. I was speaking of persons who were habitual drinkers; and the conclusion I wished to press was, that as alcohol would produce the diseases from which they were suffering, it was but fair to assume that alcohol was the responsible agent in their special cases of suffering."

"There are hereditary tendencies to many diseases, you know, doctor," said the judge, speaking with the manner of one who was being driven from his entrenchments, and with little more than a suggestion in his voice.

"The greater reason why we should carefully avoid everything that will excite these tendencies," returned the doctor. "If there be one substance which, above all others, in common use among men, disturbs the vital functions, and works unhealthy changes in every particular thing in the body which it touches, will not that substance be sure to give to all hereditary susceptibilities to disease a quickening force? It cannot be otherwise."

The judge returned to his chair; and as he sat down, drew his handkerchief from his pocket and wiped away the perspiration which had collected on his forehead. The expression of his countenance was still more thoughtful and serious.

"Passing from the physical to the mental," said Dr. Gilbert, "and we come to the higher and more appalling forms of disaster which spring from the drinking customs of society. Are you at all familiar with these, Judge Arbuckle?"

"I am aware that many cases of insanity are attributed to intemperance; and I can easily see that confirmed drunkenness must tend to impair the mental as well as the bodily powers," returned the judge.

"Is it not clear," resumed the doctor, "that a substance which attacks and injures every functional structure in the body, must seriously affect that delicate and wonderful piece of mechanism, the brain? The moment you disturb this organ, you disturb the mind. You may hurt the hand, or the foot, or almost any other organ or member of the body, and yet thought may remain clear, and the intellect balanced; but touch the brain—congest its finer blood-vessels, thicken its delicate membranes and impair the quality of the nervous matter they inclose, and a new peril begins. Before, it was only the physical man that was in danger; now it is the rational and the moral man. A deterioration of brain-structure has commenced, which, if not arrested, may terminate in insanity. That it does so terminate we know, for of the inmates of our insane asylums, from fifteen to twenty per cent. have been reduced to their melancholy condition through intemperance. The percentage would be placed much higher, if we included all the cases wherein the brain had been so much injured by alcohol as to be unable to bear the shock of misfortune, bereavement or humiliation, by which the reason has been dethroned.

"Men who are in good health rarely break down and lose their reason in consequence of business disasters, keen disappointments or domestic afflictions. I do not hesitate to affirm—and, as a physician, I know of what I speak—that no man who regularly uses any beverage in which alcohol is present, is, or can be, in perfect health, or in the full and undisturbed possession of his mental faculties. He is, in the degree that he uses this substance, sound neither in mind nor body, and is exposed to more imminent dangers than men who abstain from its use altogether. He cannot endure the same amount of physical or mental strain that he might have done if there had been no impairment of function or faculty. Now, a point that I wish to urge, is this: while we are not responsible, as moral beings, for the sins of our fathers, there is laid upon us, under the law of transmission, a sad heritage of diseased tendencies, both of body and mind, coming down to us through many generations—arrested and modified in one, and intensified, it may be, in another. As we take this legacy, it is only in the form of a latent force. If our lives be strictly in the line of natural and spiritual laws; if we shun excess of every kind, and hold the appetite and passions in check, we may keep that latent force inactive and harmless. But if, on the contrary, we indulge our appetites and passions, and disobey the laws of natural and spiritual health, then we come into the possession of this evil legacy, and into the disorders and sufferings it entails; transmitting it with an intenser vitality, it may be, to the generation that comes after us. Just what this legacy of evil tendencies may be in your case or mine, neither of us can know until we violate some law of natural or spiritual health, impelled thereto, it may be, by its hidden motions. Then it first begins to gain power over us. There may be an inherited taint of insanity, intemperance or consumption, which an orderly life and good health may keep from ever showing itself. But let such a health-disturbing element as alcohol get into the body and brain, and who may foretell the consequences."

CHAPTER XXIV.

DURING the whole of this time, scarcely a remark had been made by any one except the judge and Dr. Gilbert; but all were attentive listeners; none more so than young Henry Pickering and Amy Granger. My attention had been drawn towards them from the first, and the impression soon came to me that the young man's attitude towards the question under discussion had not been altogether such as the maiden approved. But it was plain now, that Dr. Gilbert's evidence, so clearly stated, had made a deep impression on his mind. He turned to Amy, as the doctor closed his remarks, and spoke to her very earnestly for a few moments. The effect was striking. Her face lighted up gradually until it was as if a sunbeam had fallen over it, while her beautiful eyes became almost radiant.

"For one," said Mr. Stannard, the first to break the silence that followed, turning to Dr. Gilbert as he spoke, "I must express my thanks for the clear explanation you have given us of the physical effects of alcohol. We, the people, need instruction on this subject. It is because of our lack of reliable information here, that so many go on impairing health, and laying the foundation of incurable diseases. If this were all; if the use of a substance so destructive to the body did not lead, as you have just intimated, to other and more appalling disasters. Among these, you have referred to insanity. Ah! if there were nothing else, this would be bad enough. But among the evils that it inflicts on our race, insanity, I had almost said, is among the lightest. Of its agency in making criminals, Judge Arbuckle is, perhaps, as well informed as any one present."

The judge, who had been sitting with his eyes bent to the floor, almost started at the mention of his name, his absence of thought had been so great.

"What were you saying?" he asked, glancing towards Mr. Stannard.

"Only that you were probably better informed than any one present as to the direct agency of alcohol in making criminals."

"There is no gainsaying the fact," replied the judge, with much gravity of manner, "that a very large number of the crimes for which men are tried and punished, have their origin, or secondary exciting cause in liquor-drinking."

"Statistics," remarked Mr. Granger, "tell a sad story as to the crime, destitution, suffering and pauperism which spring from this one source. The figures are indeed startling. I have looked at the hundreds of poor wretched creatures who gathered nightly at our meeting on Broad Street, and read in their faces the sad story of their fall and degradation; my thought has gone to the homes made desolate; to the broken-hearted wives and mothers; to the abused and neglected children, that must be counted in as a part of the ruin involved in what I saw before me. At a single glance, I have taken in as many as from three to five hundred of these wretched beings, with faces and forms so marred and disfigured that it made my heart ache to look at them; and for every individual I saw before me, somewhere, away out of sight and observation, were from one to half a score of wronged and suffering ones, who, but for the debasement of these men, might have been living in comfort and happiness. This is the thought that intensifies our pity and stirs our compassion when we look at even a single one of these wrecks of humanity.

"But when we begin to aggregate these human disasters, the result becomes appalling. We take an isolated home. It is the dwelling-place of sweet content. But the demon of drink comes in, and beauty fades, and peace retires, and sorrow, and pain, and unutterable woe take up their abode in the desolate habitation; or it is thrown down and utterly destroyed. How sad we grow over a single case like this, when it comes clearly before us. What, then, is the fearful aggregate? Statistics place the great army of drunkards in this country at six hundred thousand! It may be more, it may be less. Do we place the average too great when we say, that, for every one of these, five persons are hurt in some way—fathers, mothers, wives, children, sisters, brothers or dependents? Three millions of persons involved in the debasement and ruin of these six hundred thousand! What an awful aggregate, when we comprehend just what this debasement and ruin means and involves! Then statistics tell us that, from two to three hundred thousand children are yearly deserted, or orphaned, and sent to poor-houses, or bequeathed to private and public charities, in consequence of intemperance; to say nothing of the little ones who perish from neglect and cruelty. Of the crimes committed, our newspapers and our police, our courts and prison records make perpetual advertisement, until the awful facts become so familiar that the public grow hardened and almost indifferent. In a single year, in the State of New York, according to one of the reports of the Prison Association, not less than from sixty to seventy thousand persons, men, women and children, were committed to the jails of that commonwealth, and seven-eighths of these commitments, according to the estimates of the prison-keepers, were due either directly or indirectly to the use of intoxicating liquors. The estimates of leading temperance writers as to the number of men and women who are yearly sent to prison in consequence of using strong drink, give the figures at one hundred thousand; but taking the returns of New York as a basis of calculation, and they swell to more startling numbers.

"The mortality of drunkenness is another aspect of the case fearful to contemplate. Sixty thousand are said to die annually in this country from the direct effects of inebriety; and where epidemics attack a community, the intemperate, and those who use alcoholic drinks regularly, are the first to yield to their malign influences. A remarkable instance of this is given in a letter written to the *Boston Medical Journal,* in 1853, by Dr. Carnwright, of New Orleans. The yellow fever, he said, came down like a storm on the devoted city, sweeping off five thousand intemperate men, before, so far as he was able to get at the facts, a single sober man was touched by the epidemic. A Liverpool coroner made public declaration, that gin caused him to hold annually a thousand more inquests than would otherwise have been the case; and he said, farther, that he had seen, since holding the office of coroner, so many murders by poison, by drowning, by hanging and by cutting the throat, in consequence of drinking ardent spirits, that he was astonished that the legislature did not interfere to stop the sale of intoxicating liquor. It was his belief, that from ten to fifteen thousand persons died annually in that metropolis from the effects of gin-drinking.

"Looking beyond the questions of health, mortality and personal suffering involved in the use of intoxicants, the loss to the whole people in material prosperity is something startling. If, as has been established over and over again by the testimony of judges, grand juries and prison-keepers, from sixty to eighty per cent. of the heavy cost of maintaining courts, prisons and almshouses, is due to the crime and pauperism engendered by drinking, we have in this item alone a vast drain upon the productive industry of the country. What this drain is may be seen from a single fact. In Ulster County, New York, a committee was appointed to ascertain from reliable sources, the percentage on every dollar of tax paid to the county which was required for the support of her paupers, and the prosecution and maintainance of her criminals; and, after careful examination, it was announced, that on every dollar of tax paid, sixty-three cents was the penalty exacted from·the people for permitting the liquor traffic to be carried on in that county. But this is only a single item. The loss in productive labor suffered through the voluntary or enforced idleness of six or seven hundred thousand drunken men, paupers and criminals, to say nothing of the reduced power of work and production that inevitably attends moderate drinking, as it is called, adds an additional drawback to the general prosperity. There is yet another view of this case. Hundreds of thousands of bushels of grain, instead of going to feed the people, are annually used for the production of beverages which injure the health of all who drink them, and create an army of paupers and criminals. The amount paid for these beverages by those who drink them, is from eight hundred to a thousand millions of dollars every year, or more than the value of all the flour, cotton goods, boots and shoes, woolen goods, clothing, books and newspapers produced in the whole country. A government of the people, by the people, and for the people, can hardly be called, in all things, a wise government, so long as it fosters and protects, by legal enactment, and draws a part of its revenue, from a traffic like this, which offers no good to the people, but mars their industry, corrupts their politics, and sows crime, pauperism, disease and death broadcast over the land. Is it not time that the citizens of this great nation called a halt; and time that every man who holds in regard the well-being of his neighbor, and the happiness and safety of his children, should come out from among the friends of so monstrous an evil, and set himself resolutely to the work of its repression?"

"The work of repression is a very slow and halting work," came in the clear, calm voice of a woman, and I turned towards Mrs. K——, who had been silent up to this time. Judge Arbuckle, who had been listening with a grave, judicial attention to Mr. Granger, almost started at the sound of her voice, and looked at her with a lifting of his eyebrows, and awakened surprise on his countenance. "Its progress, if there be really any progress at all, except in one or two exceptional States," she went on, "is so slow as to be utterly disheartening. I depreciate none of the efforts which are being made to restrict the traffic and warn the people against the use of a substance which yields no single benefit, but curses with unutterable woes every one on whom its blight falls—they all have their measure of good —but, while we wait for the agencies of repression, thousands, and tens of thousands are perishing around us. Shall we stand off and see these wretched men and women so perish while we seek to influence legislation, and wait for a new public sentiment that shall lessen the evil in some far-off time to come? Shall a man, whom an effort on my part might save, die at my door, and I be guiltless?"

"There are many agencies of reform and means of rescue in active operation, as you are well aware, Mrs. K——," said Mr. Stannard. "Our inebriate asylums and reformatory homes are saving a large number of men."

"For every man that is so saved, I thank God, and bless the agency that saved him," was answered. "But what impression can less than a score of such institutions, scattered here and there over the land, excellent as they are, make upon the six hundred thousand drunkards Mr. Granger has just told us about? Are these to be left to perish, while we are trying to establish more asylums for their treatment and cure? There must be quicker, readier and less costly means for more than four out of five of these six hundred thousand, or they are lost forever."

"You, and the noble women who are at work with you in the cause of reform and restoration, are giving us, I trust, a solution of this great problem."

"God is giving the solution," replied Mrs. K——, in a low, subdued voice. "In our blindness we went to Him, and He showed us the way. We called upon Him in our weakness and our despair, and He heard and answered us."

Mrs. K—— spoke with a confidence of manner that brought a look of wonder to the face of Judge Arbuckle, and caused him to lean a little forward in his chair.

"You men may continue to fight this foe of intemperance with carnal aids to warfare, if you will, but we have found in the Sword of the Spirit the most effective weapon that we can use against him," Mrs. K—— continued, a soft smile just touching her lips, to show that she did not mean any discourtesy by her form of speech.

"What do you mean by the Sword of the Spirit, madam?" asked the judge, as he leaned towards Mrs. K——, and looked at her still curiously.

"Prayer and faith," she replied.

"Oh! I see," he returned, with a slight betrayal of amused incredulity in his voice. "Prayer and faith are used as a kind of exorcism by which the devil of drink is cast out."

"If you choose to put it in that form, judge," the lady answered, with a smile still lingering on her gentle lips.

"And you really believe, madam, that prayer will make a drunken man sober?"

"No, I do not believe anything of the kind."

"What then?" asked the judge.

"I believe that God will do it in answer to prayers."

"In answer to your prayer?"

"If," asked Mrs. K——, "there lived in my neighborhood a man who had become miserably drunken; who wasted his earnings in liquor, and neglected and abused his wife and children; and I, pitying his state, and earnestly desiring to save him, should go to the Lord and present his case, and pray that His Holy Spirit might strike conviction to his soul, and give him not only to see the dreadful sin he was committing, but lead him to repentance; and suppose that, after I had so presented him to the Lord, for a single time, or for many times, he should repent, and turn from his evil course, and be gathered into the fold of Christ, what would you say?"

"Have you ever known such a case?" asked the judge.

"Yes; and not only one, but many, each, of course, with its peculiar aspects and incidents, but all quite as remarkable as the one I have given."

"There is something more in this than appears on the surface," remarked the judge. "I do not believe that God was waiting for your prayers before He would lead the man of whom you speak to repentance and reformation of life. What is your view of the case?"

"I know," replied Mrs. K——, "that all things are promised to those who pray, believing; and I know, that after I had prayed, in the case I have instanced, and in many other such cases, God has brought conviction and repentance. Just how it was all done, I do not pretend to know. I am not so much interested in the philosophy of this salvation as in the glorious fact And I am not alone, Judge Arbuckle, in my experiences. Hundreds of pious women in this city, and thousands more all over the land, are saving poor drunkards by scores and hundreds through the power of faith and prayer. If you could be with us in our daily meetings, and see the men whom we are rescuing, and hear them speak of the power of Divine grace in setting them free from the slavery of appetite, your heart would be so stirred within you that you would accept the fact of the value of prayer, and leave the philosophy to be discussed and settled hereafter."

"If you can lead a man to pray for himself, and he then gain, through prayer and intercession, the power to resist and control his appetite, I can see a clear relation between cause and effect," said the judge. "He comes voluntarily into a new attitude towards the Lord, who can now give him grace and strength, because he is ready to receive it. But how the prayer in which he has no part can have any avail, passes my comprehension."

"We who are in the midst of this great Gospel temperance work are so crowded with surprising instances of the effect of our prayers for others—even for men and women whom we have not seen, whose names often we do not know, nor sometimes their places of abode—that doubt is no longer possible," Mrs. K—— replied. "And when, at our daily afternoon prayer and experience meetings, we make requests of God for those who ask for our intercession in their behalf, we do it in full confidence that we shall be heard and answered, though nothing of the result should, in many cases, ever come to our knowledge."

The deep calmness of a settled conviction was seen in the countenance of Mrs. K——, as she spoke.

"We know so little of the spiritual world that lies in and around us," said Mr. Stannard, at this point of the conversation, "and of the laws which govern therein, that we must not be surprised if some of its phenomena are found difficult of explanation. We cannot, knowing as we do, that God is infinite and essential love, and that His compassion is so great that our compassion in its tenderest movements bears no ratio to it whatever, believe that He withholds His saving power from any sin-sick and perishing soul until we ask Him to be gracious. But rather that, in our prayers for and thought of the individual for whom we pray, spiritual forces or influences, whose action is above the region of our knowledge, are set in motion, as the atmospheres are set in motion by the concussions we call sound, and so thought and feeling be stirred and acted upon, and he for whom we pray be led to turn to the Lord, whose ears are always open to His children's cry for help, and whose hands are always stretched out to save."

"Be that as it may," remarked Mrs. K——, "I am not wise enough to say whether Mr. Stannard's view be right or wrong; but this I know, wonderful results follow the prayers we offer to God, and men whom we are asked to pray for to-day—drunken, debased and evil men; husbands, sons, brothers, for whom our prayers are asked by wives, mothers and sisters—often, within a day or a week, present themselves at our meetings, or at other places where Gospel meetings are held, and sign the pledge, and give their hearts to Christ. And so long as we women see these results, we should continue to pray mightily to God."

A few moments of thoughtful silence, and then Mr. Stannard said, addressing Mrs. K——: "I know all about what you are doing in this city, and the great success of your work; and I see in the organization of a kindred work in every city, town and neighborhood all over our country, the largest and most effective agency of temperance reform ever known in our liquor-cursed land. My only fear is, that you may depend so completely on prayer, and faith, and Divine grace, in the work of saving drunkards, that you will fail to use the natural means of reform and restoration that are as essential to permanent cure as the others."

"A woman's instincts are swift and true, Mr. Stannard," was the reply. "We know that a man, with hunger gnawing at his stomach, is in a poor condition for effective praying; that if he be homeless and idle, he is especially exposed to temptation, and the feeble spiritual life he may have found will be almost sure of extinguishment in its foul breath. We know that health must come back to the body, and its orderly life be restored, if we would keep down the old craving desire, and give to spiritual forces an unobstructed sphere of action. While we believe in prayer, and the grace of God, and a change of heart, we believe also in the saving power of natural and physical health, and order as well. The man to be truly saved must be saved within and without. But, with God's grace in his heart, he will find the work of keeping his outer life in order a far easier task than if he tried to do it in his own strength. And herein it is that our work is meeting with such large success. We point the poor, exhausted inebriate, who comes to us in his rags and defilements, to Him who is able to save, and urge him to cast himself upon His love and mercy. To make new resolves and new pledges; but with this difference from the old resolves and pledges, that now prayer is added to the new resolutions, and spiritual strength asked humbly and trustingly from God. We take him to the church-door, and invite him to enter and cast in his lot with religious people; helping him to form a new external, as well as a new internal life. He is thus removed from old, debasing associations, and brought into fellowship with pious people, who take him by the hand, and if he have any ability for Christian work, find him something to do in the Sunday-school, in the prayer-meetings, in the temperance work of his neighborhood, or in anything else that is good and useful."

"And this is what you mean by Gospel temperance," said Judge Arbuckle, his fine face lighting up beautifully.

"It is one of its phases," answered Mrs. K——.

"And the best and most promising phase, I'll warrant you," returned the judge, with rising enthusiasm. "Why this is church work! I'm a good churchman, you see, madam; and believe, with our excellent bishop, that all saving reforms should originate in, and be fostered and carried on by, the church."

"What if the church, in its organized form, neglects, or wholly ignores temperance work—even Gospel temperance work—what then? Shall we wait for the church and let the poor drunkard perish because she neglects her duty?"

"God forbid!" responded the judge. "There is no monopoly in the work of lifting up fallen humanity."

"Nor in soul-saving," said Mr. Stannard. "But

this drift which the subject has taken, brings us face to face with the church and its great responsibilities. It has something more to do than the provision of a Sunday service for the people. The preaching of the Gospel is one thing, and the doing of Gospel work another. The building of stately church edifices, with costly finish and exquisite ornamentation, into which so much of the pecuniary means of a congregation are absorbed, as to leave it too often with a sense of poverty and an excuse for drawing the purse-strings more closely, when suffering or destitute humanity stretches forth its pleading hands, may be all well enough; but worship in a less expensive and ostentatious building, and a more Christ-like concern for the sick and perishing souls that lie helpless, it may be, within the sound of its choir and organ, would, I think, be far better and more acceptable to God."

"You do not approve, then, of the splendid churches and grand cathedrals which, in all Christian countries, have been erected to the honor of God and dedicated to His worship?" said Judge Arbuckle.

"Not if they are built and maintained at the cost of human souls."

"I am not sure that I reach your meaning, Mr. Stannard."

"Let me give an illustration. We will take the case of a congregation which has built for itself a splendid marble or brown-stone church at a cost of one, or two, or three hundred thousand dollars, into which the people come twice every Sunday to hear the service and preaching, and once or twice a week for evening prayers or a lecture. This elegant structure is an ornament to the neighborhood, and the people who have built it feel proud of their fine edifice, and not a few of them contrast it, a little depreciatively, it may be, with the achievements of certain sister churches in the same line, and take credit to themselves for having thrown these just a trifle into shadow. Now, as to the spiritual value of all this—and no good is gained in any church work unless it be a spiritual good—there may be serious doubts. Has the creation of a grand temple for the worship of God wrought in the minds of those by whom it was erected that state of receptive humility which is the dwelling-place of Him who says, 'I am meek and lowly of heart?' Are they humble, more teachable, more self-denying, more self-forgetting, more given to good works than before? What if, like a wise corporation, one of these congregations had invested in their land, building and required church machinery, just one-half of the sum they had in possession, and reserved the other half for working capital? Don't you see how differently the case would stand? Here is a church that cost two hundred thousand dollars. Now, if it had cost but one hundred thousand; and a building just as large and just as comfortable could have been erected for that sum—all the excess is but imposing display and ornamentation—that congregation could have established and maintained, with the other one hundred thousand dollars, a reformatory home for inebriates, like the Franklin Home of our city, and been the means of saving from fifty to a hundred fallen men every year. Or, it could have placed in the hands of its pious women, who, like Mrs. K—— and her sister workers in this Gospel temperance movement, which has already wrought such marvelous results, the money required to give healthy food, and sightly clothing, and safer and better surroundings to the poor, nerveless, appetite-cursed men they are seeking to save. I instance but these; there are many other ways in which the reserved working capital of this church might be used for the good of souls. Think! How would it be if our blessed Lord were to stand some day in the midst of that congregation? Would they hear from His lips, as His eyes took in the richness and grandeur of the temple they had built to His honor, and then, penetrating its stately walls, went searching among the poor, desolate homes, and wretched hovels, and dens of vice and crime that lay in the very shadow of its beauty, and saw His lost sheep perishing there, with none to pity or to succor—would they hear from his lips the words, 'Well done?' I fear not."

"You have struck the key-note of the great question that lies at our door to-day," said Mrs. K——, speaking with a rising earnestness of manner. "Are the churches, established for the salvation of souls, to remain content with one or two Sunday services, and a week-night prayer-meeting or lecture, maintained, in many cases, at an expense of from five to fifty thousand dollars a year? Can you find in any mere secular calling so large an investment with such meagre returns? The theory seems to be that the work of the chuch, as a body of Christian men and women, is limited to Sunday, and may be intermitted for six days."

"Let us be careful that we are not unjust," Mr. Stannard replied. "I stated my case strongly, in order to illustrate my views. Many of our churches are active in good works, and are doing much for the spiritually destitute. They have their mission schools, and visiting committees, and laborers among the poor; but with most of them their usefulness is restricted for lack of means. It takes so much to maintain Sunday worship that but little is left for anything else."

"To seek and to save that which was lost. It was for this that Christ came." Mrs. K—— spoke in a low, earnest voice. "Ah! if our churches all over the land would give themselves to this seeking and saving of the lost—of those who have fallen so low that, to common eyes, their case is hopeless. Would go out into the wilderness, like the Good Shepherd, seeking for and bringing back the lost sheep. These six hundred thousand drunkards, of whom over a thousand die every week; what hope for them if the church comes not to their rescue?—for the church alone can lead them to the sure refuge of Christ. The world knows Him not. Only in a few cases is a human hand strong enough to save. If the larger number be not led to take hold upon Christ, they must perish in their sin and degradation. Think what joy there would be in Heaven, if all the churches in the land, singly, or in union with near sister churches, were to establish Gospel temperance meetings, and draw into them these six hundred thousand men and women—or as many of them as felt their slavery and wretchedness and wished to escape therefrom. The very thought makes my heart stir within me."

The evening had worn away, the hours passing with little heed from any of us, until it was time to separate. The judge had risen to his feet, and Mrs. Arbuckle and Mrs. K—— were moving from the parlor in order to make ready for going away, when Mr. Granger, who had been silent for most of the time, said, in a voice that at once gave him an attentive audience: "I would like, before we part, to say one or two things that have come crowding into my mind this evening. All good work is from the Lord. Every effort, of whatever kind, perfect or imperfect, which has for its end the saving of men from evils and disorders, has in it a heavenly power and the approval of God; and we must, therefore, be careful that, while we magnify the means of salvation, which to us seem most effective, we do not depreciate or throw hindrances in the way of those who labor in different fields, and with methods different from our own. This work of saving the people from the curse of drink, in which we are all so deeply interested, has many aspects, because men differ not only in personal character and temperament, but in their external conditions and the ways of thinking and habits of life, which grow out of these conditions. The influences that will powerfully affect one, may have little weight with another. Our panacea, in which we have such an abounding faith, may fail in many cases where another remedy would work a cure; while cases of failure under a diverse treatment from ours may find a quick restoration on coming into our hands. Let us, then, be watchful over ourselves in this matter, and be readier to give a 'God speed' to methods different, and, it may be, less efficient than our own, than to depreciate them by comparison, or hurt their influences by direct condemnation. Whatever tends, in even the smallest degree, to abate this curse, must be recognized as good work. It may be through restrictive laws, or binding pledges, or social organization, or appeals to the people by the press and the platform, or the opening of cheap coffee rooms. It may be in Christian work and prayer, and direct spiritual help from God through these appointed means, in which I have the strongest faith. It may be in the establishment of inebriate asylums and reformatory homes, where, while seeking to cure by medical, sanitary, moral and religious means, the pathology of drunkenness is carefully studied, and the skill and wisdom of the medical profession brought to the examination and cure of one of the most fearful diseases which man, by self-indulgence, has brought upon himself; involving in disorder, as it does, his physical, moral and spiritual nature. Tolerance of views and harmony of action are what we need in this work. If I think my methods are best, let me pursue them with all zeal and confidence, doing what good I can; only let me be careful not to depreciate my brother's methods, of the scope and value of which I may know far less than I imagine."

"Thank you, Mr. Granger!" came with a hearty utterance from the lips of Mrs. K——, who had turned back into the parlor, from which she was passing when our host began his remarks. "You have said the right thing in the right way. The temptation to magnify our own particular work, because its fruit is so near our hands, is very great. But, apart from this; are not some ways of doing a thing better than other ways? In the work of salvation, is not a Divine Hand more certain to save than a human hand?"

I saw a light break suddenly from within into Mr. Granger's face.

"If we can lead the man, in whom inebriation has almost, if not entirely, destroyed the will-power, to Him who is able to cure him of all diseases, if he will accept the means of cure," continued Mrs. K——, "may we not hope to do more and better for him in this than in any other way?"

"Yes, yes, I believe it, and I know it," replied Mr. Granger. "When all other means fail, this may be held as sure; for God's strength, if we take it and rest upon it, never fails."

"But, after all," spoke out Judge Arbuckle, "is not the work of warning and prevention better than the work of cure? Of all that I have heard this evening, and much of it has been deeply interesting, nothing has impressed me like the evidence brought by Dr. Gilbert against alcohol. It may be only imagination," and he smiled a little dubiously as he said it; "but I've recognized in my sensations more than half a dozen symptoms of its deleterious effects since he described its action on the tissues, nerves and organs of the body." He stretched his arms upwards, then drew them down again slowly, pressed one hand against his forehead, and then held it against his right side.

"The fact is," going on, after a few moments of reflective silence, "I have an unpleasant impression that I'm not quite as sound as I thought myself. This torpidity of liver is something, I'm afraid, more serious than I had supposed. And my head," giving it a shake, "isn't as clear as it ought to be. There's often a heavy, confused feeling about it which I don't like." As he stepped out to move across the room, I saw him limp. "One of my knee-catchers again." The judge made a slight grimace.

"A diminished supply of sinovial fluid," remarked Dr. Gilbert.

"One of the effects of old age," said the judge.

"Anticipated, most likely, by the alcohol in your wine and brandy," returned the doctor. "You know that, of all substances taken into the body, none absorbs water like alcohol, and that its first action on the membranes is to rob them of as much of this fluid as it has the power to appropriate. That more or less torpor and stiffness of the joints and limbs should come in consequence of the continued use of this substance is not at all surprising; nor that the liver, heart and brain, and some of the more important nerve centres, should suffer from disturbances growing out of unhealthy structural changes."

"Not at all—not at all," answered the judge. "The thing stands to reason. What I wish to say, is, that as prevention is better than cure, how more effectually can the cause of temperance be served, than by the most thorough dissemination of the truth in regard to the action of alcoholic drinks in deteriorating the body and laying the foundation for painful and too often fatal diseases? Why, sir, do you think that, if I had known as much about this matter when I was twenty-one years of age, as I do now, that I would have joined the great army of moderate drinkers? No, sir! It was because I believed, with thousands of others, that these enticing beverages were good and healthful, when not taken in excess, that I used them. Now I see that there is a double peril. That, besides the risk of becoming their slave, he who uses them is surely laying the foundation for troublesome, painful, and, often, fatal diseases."

"It is in consequence of the physical deteriorations wrought by alcohol in the stomach and brain," said the doctor, "that appetite increases, and the will so often loses power over it. For this reason, no one is safe who drinks at all; for a double disease—moral, as well as physical—is almost sure to be the result; and this is the hardest to cure of all diseases."

"And yet the easiest," spoke out Mrs. K——, in her clear, sweet voice, "if one will only come to the Great Physician, and be healed by the touch of His hand."

The judge let his gaze rest, for a moment or two, on the speaker's calm face and slightly upturned eyes, and then, as he withdrew them, said, gravely: "Prevention is best, my friends. Don't forget the boys and the young men, while you are trying to save the unhappy fallen. Conservation is in the line of true order. And, remember, that it will cost less of time, effort and money to keep ten from falling than to lift up and restore one who is down. Don't forget to provide safeguards for the ninety-

and-nine, while you are going after the one lost sheep."

"I think," said Dr. Gilbert, as he laid his hand upon Judge Arbuckle's arm, "that we may count you as upon our side of this great question."

"I should not wonder if it were so," replied the judge, "for I regard the argument, so far as presented by you, as complete; and, until I am satisfied that you are in error, I shall take no more risks. Too much of comfort, and use and happiness depend on good health, to put it lightly in jeopardy. My wine may be very pleasant and exhilarating, but if there be really poison in the cup, I must, as a wise and prudent man, let it pass untasted, or acknowledge myself the slave of an appetite that will have indulgence at any cost."

"And you, Henry?" It was the voice of Mr. Granger. He spoke with a quiet cheerfulness that concealed any suspense or concern, if either existed. Young Pickering, who was bending towards Miss Granger, and talking to her, in low tones, turned his handsome face towards the speaker. "On which side of this question shall we count you?"

"On the right side, of course," said Amy, not waiting for her lover's reply, a happy smile rippling over her face as she spoke. His answer I did not hear; but that it was entirely satisfactory, I had the assurance a few weeks later, when the fact of their engagement became known to the friends of the family.

And here our story must end, if so meagre a plot and so light a thread of narrative can be called a story. Whatever interest has been felt in the characters, must give place now to the profounder convictions we have sought to awaken. In the curse and cure of drunkenness lie problems, to the solution of which we must bring neither prejudice, nor passion, nor partisan feeling, but the truth, if we can but find it; and in all questions that concern man's moral and spiritual life, as well as his natural and physical condition, we shall be more apt to find the truth, if we consider the action of moral and spiritual laws, in their connection with the effects that lie lower and more on the plane of common observation, than if we made light of them, or ignored them altogether.

There is one fundamental doctrine of Christianity, without which all the rest must go for nothing. We have it from the mouth of the Lord Himself: "Ye must be born again." Differ as we may about the means of attaining this new spiritual birth, all Christians agree that it involves an inner change through the gift, or grace, or co-operative agency of the Spirit of God, by which man's evil nature, with all of its depraved and debasing appetites, is either taken wholly away, or removed from the centre to the circumference of his life, and there held in complete subjection. There is no condition of depravity or wickedness from which a man may not be saved in this new birth; and there is no power in all hell strong enough to bear him back into his old evil life, if he use the new spiritual strength that has been born in him from above.

On this fundamental law of spiritual life, all Christian believers stand; and it is being more and more widely accepted as the one on which we can most surely depend in our efforts to save men from the curse of drink. It is on this conviction that what is known as the Gospel temperance movement is based; a movement in which the old, tireless workers in the great cause of reform find new hope and encouragement. Heretofore the churches have held themselves, in too many instances, aloof from active participation in the cause of temperance, leaving it to be dealt with by legal enactment, or moral suasion. But now they are beginning to see that this work is really their work, and that to them has been given the special means for its prosecution. In most, if not all, of our inebriate asylums and homes of reformation, the value of spiritual aid is fully and practically recognized; and in some of the larger institutions they have their chaplain as well as their physicians; and we are very sure that where the physician of the body and the physician of the soul unite in their efforts to cure a patient who is sick of an infirmity that has exhausted his body and enslaved his will, his case is far more hopeful that if he were left in the care of either alone.

And now, what need to write another sentence? We cannot make clearer, by any new illustrations, this leading thought of our story, that in coming to God through sincere repentance and earnest prayer, refraining, at the same time, from drink and all other evils of life, as sins, there lies for the inebriate a road to reformation, in which he can walk safely, and which will bear him farther and farther from danger with every step he takes therein. Some have fallen so low—alas, for the number!—that every way except this has been closed; but all will find it the safest, the surest, and the easiest by which to reach an abiding self-control.

PART II.

THE CURSE AND THE CURE.

INTRODUCTION.

IN writing the second part of this book, the author found himself embarrassed from the beginning, because of the large amount of material which came into his hands, and the consequent difficulty of selection and condensation. There is not a chapter which might not have been extended to twice its present length, nor a fact stated, or argument used, which might not have been supplemented by many equally pertinent and conclusive. The extent to which alcohol curses the whole people cannot be shown in a few pages: the sad and terrible history would fill hundreds of volumes. And the same may be said of the curse which this poisonous substance lays upon the souls and bodies of men. Fearful as is the record which will be found in the chapters devoted to the curse of drink, let the reader bear in mind that a thousandth part has not been told.

In treating of the means of reformation, prevention and cure, our effort has been to give to each agency the largest possible credit for what it is doing. There is no movement, organization or work, however broad or limited in its sphere, which has for its object the cure of drunkenness in the individual, or the suppression of the liquor traffic in the State, that is not contributing its measure of service to the great cause every true temperance advocate has at heart; and what we largely need is, toleration for those who do not see with us, nor act with us in our special methods. Let us never forget the Divine admonition—"Forbid him not: for he that is not against us is for us."

Patience, toleration and self-repression are of vital importance in any good cause. If we cannot see with another, let us be careful that, by opposition, we do not cripple him in his work. If we can assist him by friendly counsel to clearer seeing, or, by a careful study of his methods, gain a large efficiency for our own, far more good will be done than by hard antagonism, which rarely helps, and too surely blinds and hinders.

Our book treats of the curse and cure of drunkenness. How much better not to come under the terrible curse! How much better to run no risks where the malady is so disastrous, and the cure so difficult!

To young men who are drifting easily into the dangerous drinking habits of society, we earnestly commend the chapters in which will be found the medical testimony against alcohol, and also the one on "The Growth and Power of Appetite." They will see that it is impossible for a man to use alcoholic drinks regularly without laying the foundation for both physical and mental diseases, and, at the same time, lessening his power to make the best of himself in his life-work; while beyond this lies the awful risk of acquiring an appetite which may enslave, degrade and ruin him, body and soul, as it is de-degrading and ruining its tens of thousands yearly.

CONTENTS OF PART II.

CHAPTER I.
The Curse of Strong Drink, ... 389

CHAPTER II.
It Curses the Body, ... 399

CHAPTER III.
It Curses the Body—Continued, ... 417

CHAPTER IV.
It Curses the Soul, ... 431

CHAPTER V.
Not a Food, and very Limited in its Range as a Medicine, ... 451

CHAPTER VI.
The Growth and Power of Appetite, . . . 471

CHAPTER VII.
Means of Cure, ... 493

CHAPTER VIII.
Inebriate Asylums, ... 503

CONTENTS.

CHAPTER IX.
Reformatory Homes, ... 527

CHAPTER X.
Tobacco as an Incitant to the Use of Alcoholic Stimulants, and an Obstacle in the way of a Permanent Reformation, ... 561

CHAPTER XI.
The Woman's Crusade, ... 569

CHAPTER XII.
The Woman's National Christian Temperance Union, 583

CHAPTER XIII.
Reform Clubs, ... 605

CHAPTER XIV.
Gospel Temperance, ... 617

CHAPTER XV.
Temperance Coffee-Houses and Friendly Inns, . . 630

CHAPTER XVI.
Temperance Literature, ... 639

CHAPTER XVII.
License a Failure and a Disgrace, ... 647

CHAPTER XVIII.
Prohibition, ... 660

CHAPTER I.

THE CURSE OF STRONG DRINK.

THERE are two remarkable passages in a very old book, known as the Proverbs of Solomon, which cannot be read too often, nor pondered too deeply. Let us quote them here:

1. "Wine is a mocker, strong drink is raging; and whosoever is deceived thereby is not wise.

2. "Who hath woe? who hath sorrow? who hath contentions? who hath babblings? who hath wounds without cause? who hath redness of eyes? They that tarry long at the wine; they that go to seek mixed wine. Look not thou upon the wine when it is red, when it giveth his color in the cup, when it moveth itself aright. At the last it biteth like a serpent and stingeth like an adder."

It is many thousands of years since this record was made, and to-day, as in that far distant age of the world, wine is a mocker, and strong drink raging; and still, as then, they who tarry long at the wine; who go to seek mixed wine, discover that, "*at the last*," it biteth like a serpent and stingeth like an adder.

This mocking and raging! These bitings and stingings! These woes and woundings! Alas, for the exceeding bitter cry of their pain, which is heard above every other cry of sorrow and suffering.

ALCOHOL AN ENEMY.

The curse of strong drink! Where shall we begin, where end, or how, in the clear and truthful sentences that wrest conviction from doubt, make plain the allegations we shall bring against an enemy that is sowing disease, poverty, crime and sorrow throughout the land?

Among our most intelligent, respectable and influential people, this enemy finds a welcome and a place of honor. Indeed, with many he is regarded as a friend and treated as such. Every possible opportunity is given him to gain favor in the household and with intimate and valued friends. He is given the amplest confidence and the largest freedom; and he always repays this confidence with treachery and spoliation; too often blinding and deceiving his victims while his work of robbery goes on. He is not only a robber, but a cruel master; and his bondsmen and abject slaves are to be found in hundreds and thousands, and even tens of thousands, of our homes, from the poor dwelling of the day-laborer, up to the palace of the merchant-prince.

PLACE AND POWER IN THE HOUSEHOLD.

Of this fact no one is ignorant; and yet, strange to tell, large numbers of our most intelligent, respectable and influential people continue to smile upon this enemy; to give him place and power in their households, and to cherish him as a friend; but with this singular reserve of thought and purpose, that he is to be trusted just so far and no farther. He is so pleasant and genial, that, for the sake of his favor, they are ready to encounter the risk of his acquiring, through the license they afford, the vantage-ground of a pitiless enemy!

But, it is not only in their social life that the people hold this enemy in favorable regard, and give him the opportunity to hurt and destroy. Our great Republic has entered into a compact with him, and, for a money-consideration, given him the

FREEDOM OF THE NATION;

so that he can go up and down the land at will. And not only has our great Republic done this; but the States of which it is composed, with only one or two exceptions, accord to him the same freedom. Still more surprising, in almost every town and city, his right to plunder, degrade, enslave and destroy the people has been established under the safe guarantee of law.

Let us give ourselves to the sober consideration of what we are suffering at his hands, and take measures of defense and safety, instead of burying our heads in the sand, like the foolish ostrich, while the huntsmen are sweeping down upon us.

ENORMOUS CONSUMPTION.

Only those who have given the subject careful consideration have any true idea of the enormous annual consumption, in this country, of spirits, wines and malt liquors. Dr. Hargreaves, in "Our Wasted Resources," gives these startling figures: It amounted in 1870 to 72,425,353 gallons of domestic spirits, 188,527,120 gallons of fermented liquors, 1,441,747 gallons of imported spirits, 9,088,894 gallons of wines, 34,239 gallons of spirituous compounds, and 1,012,754 gallons of ale, beer, etc., or a total of 272,530,107 gallons for 1870, with a total increase of 30,000,000 gallons in 1871, and of 35,000,000 gallons in addition in 1872.

All this in a single year, and at a cost variously estimated at from six to seven hundred millions of dollars! Or, a sum, as statistics tell us, nearly equal to the cost of all the flour, cotton and woolen goods, boots and shoes, clothing, and books and newspapers purchased by the people in the same period of time.

If this were all the cost? If the people wasted no more than seven hundred millions of dollars on these beverages every year, the question of their use would be only one of pecuniary loss or gain. But what farther, in connection with this subject, are we told by statistics? Why, that, in consequence of using these beverages, we have six hundred thousand drunkards; and that of these, sixty thousand die every year. That we have over three hundred murders and four hundred suicides. That over two hundred thousand children are left homeless and friendless. And that at least eighty per cent. of all the crime and pauperism of the land arises from the consumption of this enormous quantity of intoxicating drinks.

In this single view, the question of intemperance assumes a most appalling aspect. The

POVERTY AND DESTITUTION

found in so large a portion of our laboring classes, and their consequent restlessness and discontent, come almost entirely from the waste of substance, idleness and physical incapacity for work, which attend the free use of alcoholic beverages. Of the six or seven hundred millions of dollars paid annually for these beverages, not less than two-thirds are taken out of the earnings of our artisans and laborers, and those who, like them, work for wages.

LOSS TO LABOR.

But the loss does not, of course, stop here. The consequent waste of bodily vigor, and the idleness that is ever the sure accompaniment of drinking, rob this class of at least as much more. Total abstinence societies, building associations, and the use of banks for savings, instead of the dram-sellers' banks for losings, would do more for the well-being of our working classes than all the trades-unions or labor combinations, that ever have or ever will exist. The laboring man's protective union lies in his own good common sense, united with temperance, self-denial and economy. There are very many in our land who know this way; and their condition, as compared with those who know it not, or knowing, will not walk therein, is found to be in striking contrast.

TAXATION.

Besides the wasting drain for drink, and the loss in national wealth, growing out of the idleness and diminished power for work, that invariably follows the use of alcohol in any of its forms, the people are heavily taxed for the repression and punishment of crimes, and the support of paupers and destitute children. A fact or two will give the reader some idea of what this enormous cost must be. In "The Twentieth Annual Report of the Executive Committee of the Prison Association of New York," is this sentence: "There can be no doubt that, of all the proximate sources of crime, the use of intoxicating liquors is the most prolific and the most deadly. Of other causes it may be said that they slay their thousands; of this it may be acknowledged that it slays its tens of thousands. The committee asked for the opinion of the jail officers in nearly every county in the State as to the proportion of commitments due, either directly or indirectly, to strong drink."

The whole number of commitments is given in these words: "Not less than 60,000 to 70,000 [or the sixtieth portion of the inhabitants of the State of New York] human beings—men, women and children—either guilty, or arrested on suspicion of being guilty of crime, pass every year through these institutions." The answers made to the committee by the jail officers, varied from two-thirds as the lowest, to nine-tenths as the highest; and, on taking the average of their figures, it gave seven-eighths as the proportion of commitments for crime directly ascribed to the use of intoxicating drinks!

Taking this as the proportion of those who are made criminals through intemperance, let us get at some estimate of the cost to tax-payers. We find it stated in Tract No. 28, issued by the National Temperance Society, that "a committee was appointed by the Ulster County Temperance Society, in 1861, for the express purpose of ascertaining, from reliable sources, the percentage on every dollar tax paid to the county to support her paupers and criminal justice. The committee, after due examination, came to the conclusion that upwards of sixty cents on the dollar was for the above purpose. This amount was required, *according to law*, to be paid by every tax-payer as a *penalty, or rather as a rum bill*, for allowing the liquor traffic to be carried on in the above county. What is said of Ulster County, may, more or less, if a like examination were entered into, be said of every other county, not only in the State of New York, but in every county in the United States."

From the same tract we take this statement: "In a document published by the Legislature of the State of New York, for 1863, being the report of the Secretary of the State to the Legislature, we have the following statements: 'The whole number of paupers relieved during the same period, was 261,252. During the year 1862, 257,354.' These numbers would be in the ratio of one pauper annually to every fifteen inhabitants throughout the State. In an examination made into the history of those paupers by a competent committee, *seven-eighths of them were reduced* to this low and degraded condition, directly or indirectly, through intemperance."

CURSING THE POOR.

Looking at our laboring classes, with the fact before us, that the cost of the liquor sold annually by retail dealers is equal to nearly $25 for every man, woman and child in our whole population, and we can readily see why so much destitution is to be found among them. Throwing out those who abstain altogether; the children, and a large proportion of women, and those who take a glass only now and then, and it will be seen that for the rest the average of cost must be more than treble. Among working men who drink the cheaper beverages, the ratio of cost to each cannot fall short of a hundred dollars a year. With many, drink consumes from a fourth to one-half of their entire earnings. Is it, then, any wonder that so much poverty and suffering are to be found among them?

CRIME AND PAUPERISM.

The causes that produce crime and pauperism in our own country, work the same disastrous results in other lands where intoxicants are used. An

English writer, speaking of the sad effects of intemperance in Great Britain, says: "One hundred million pounds, which is now annually wasted, is a sum as great as was spent in seven years upon all the railways of the kingdom—in the very heyday of railway projects; a sum so vast, that if saved annually, for seven years, would blot out the national debt!" Another writer says, "that in the year 1865, over £6,000,000, or a tenth part of the whole national revenue, was required to support her paupers." Dr. Lees, of London, in speaking of Ireland, says: "Ireland has been a poor nation from want of capital, and has wanted capital chiefly because the people have preferred swallowing it to saving it." The Rev. G. Holt, chaplain of the Birmingham Workhouse, says: "From my own experience, I am convinced of the accuracy of a statement made by the late governor, that of every one hundred persons admitted, ninety-nine were reduced to this state of humiliation and dependence, either directly or indirectly, through the prevalent and ruinous drinking usages."

Mr. Charles Buxton, M. P., in his pamphlet, "How to Stop Drunkenness," says: "It would not be too much to say that if all drinking of fermented liquors could be done away, crime of every kind would fall to a fourth of its present amount, and the whole tone of moral feeling in the lower order might be indefinitely raised. Not only does this vice produce all kinds of wanton mischief, but it has also a negative effect of great importance. It is the mightiest of all the forces that clog the progress of good. * * * The struggle of the school, the library and the church, all united against the beer-shop and the gin-palace, is but one development of the war between Heaven and hell. It is, in short, intoxication that fills our jails; it is intoxication that fills our lunatic asylums; it is intoxication that fills our work-houses with poor. Were it not for this one cause, pauperism would be nearly extinguished in England."

THE BLIGHT EVERYWHERE.

We could go on and fill pages with corroborative facts and figures, drawn from the most reliable sources. But these are amply sufficient to show the extent and magnitude of the curse which the liquor traffic has laid upon our people. Its blight is everywhere—on our industries, on our social life; on our politics, and even on our religion.

And, now, let us take the individual man himself, and see in what manner this treacherous enemy deals with him when he gets him into his power.

CHAPTER II.

IT CURSES THE BODY.

FIRST as to the body. One would suppose, from the marred and scarred, and sometimes awfully disfigured forms and faces of men who have indulged in intoxicating drinks, which are to be seen everywhere and among all classes of society, that there would be no need of other testimony to show that alcohol is an enemy to the body. And yet, strange to say, men of good sense, clear judgment and quick perception in all moral questions and in the general affairs of life, are often so blind, or infatuated here, as to affirm that this substance, alcohol, which they use under the various forms of wine, brandy, whisky, gin, ale or beer, is not only harmless, when taken in moderation—each being his own judge as to what "moderation" means—but actually useful and nutritious!

Until within the last fifteen or twenty years, a large proportion of the medical profession not only favored this view, but made constant prescription of alcohol in one form or another, the sad results of which too often made their appearance in exascerbations of disease, or in the formation of intemperate habits among their patients. Since then, the chemist and the physiologist have subjected alcohol to the most rigid tests, carried on often for years, and with a faithfulness that could not be satisfied with guess work, or inference, or hasty conclusion.

ALCOHOL NOT A FOOD AND OF DOUBTFUL USE AS A MEDICINE.

As a result of these carefully-conducted and long-continued examinations and experiments, the medical profession stands to-day almost as a unit against alcohol; and makes solemn public declaration to the people that it "is not shown to have a definite food value by any of the usual methods of chemical analysis or physiological investigations;" and that as a medicine its range is very limited, admitting often of a substitute, and that it should never be taken unless prescribed by a physician.

Reports of these investigations to which we have referred have appeared, from time to time, in the medical journals of Europe and America, and their results are now embodied in many of the standard and most reliable treatises and text-books of the medical profession.

In this chapter we shall endeavor to give our readers a description of the changes and deteriorations which take place in the blood, nerves, membranes, tissues and organs, in consequence of the continued introduction of alcohol into the human body; and in doing so, we shall quote freely from medical writers, in order that our readers may have the testimony before them in its directest form, and so be able to judge for themselves as to its value.

DIGESTION.

And here, in order to give those who are not familiar with the process of digestion, a clear idea of that important operation, and the effect produced when alcohol is taken with food, we quote from the lecture of an English physician, Dr. Henry Monroe, on "The Physiological Action of Alcohol." He says:

"Every kind of substance employed by man as food consists of sugar, starch, oil and glutinous matters, mingled together in various proportions; these are designed for the support of the animal frame. The glutinous principles of food—*fibrine, albumen* and *casein*—are employed to build up the structure; while the *oil, starch* and *sugar* are chiefly used to generate heat in the body.

"The first step of the digestive process is the breaking up of the food in the mouth by means of the jaws and teeth. On this being done, the saliva, a viscid liquor, is poured into the mouth from the salivary glands, and as it mixes with the food, it performs a very important part in the operation of digestion, rendering the starch of the food soluble, and gradually changing it into a sort of sugar, after which the other principles become more miscible with it. Nearly a pint of saliva is furnished every twenty-four hours for the use of an adult. When the food has been masticated and mixed with the saliva, it is then passed into the stomach, where it is acted upon by a juice secreted by the filaments of that organ, and poured into the stomach in large quantities whenever food comes in contact with its mucous coats. It consists of a dilute acid known to the chemists as hydrochloric acid, composed of hydrogen and chlorine, united together in certain definite proportions. The gastric juice contains, also, a peculiar organic-ferment or decomposing substance, containing nitrogen—something of the nature of yeast—termed *pepsine*, which is easily soluble in the acid just named. That gastric juice acts as a simple chemical solvent, is proved by the fact that, after death, it has been known to dissolve the stomach itself.

ALCOHOL RETARDS DIGESTION.

"It is an error to suppose that, after a good dinner, a glass of spirits or beer assists digestion; or that any liquor containing alcohol—even bitter beer—can in any way assist digestion. Mix some bread and meat with gastric juice; place them in a phial, and keep that phial in a sand-bath at the slow heat of 98 degrees, occasionally shaking briskly the contents to imitate the motion of the stomach; you will find, after six or eight hours, the whole contents blended into one pultaceous mass. If to another phial of food and gastric juice, treated in the same way, I add a glass of pale ale or a quantity of alcohol, at the end of seven or eight hours, or even some days, the food is scarcely acted upon at all. This is a fact; and if you are led to ask why, I answer, because alcohol has the peculiar power of chemically affecting or decomposing the gastric juice by precipitating one of its principal constituents, viz., pepsine, rendering its solvent properties much less efficacious. Hence alcohol can not be considered either as food or as a solvent for food. Not as the latter certainly, for it refuses to act with the gastric juice.

"'It is a remarkable fact,' says Dr. Dundas Thompson, 'that alcohol, when added to the digestive fluid, produces a white precipitate, so that the fluid is no longer capable of digesting animal or vegetable matter.' 'The use of alcoholic stimulants,' say Drs. Todd and Bowman, 'retards digestion by coagulating the pepsine, an essential element of the gastric juice, and thereby interfering with its action. Were it not that wine and spirits are rapidly absorbed, the introduction of these into the stomach, in any quantity, would be a complete bar to the digestion of food, as the pepsine would be precipitated from the solution as quickly as it was formed by the stomach.' Spirit, in any quantity, as a dietary adjunct, is pernicious on account of its antiseptic qualities, which resist the digestion of food by the absorption of water from its particles, in direct antagonism to chemical operation."

ITS EFFECT ON THE BLOOD.

Dr. Richardson, in his lectures on alcohol, given both in England and America, speaking of the action of this substance on the blood after passing from the stomach, says:

"Suppose, then, a certain measure of alcohol be taken into the stomach, it will be absorbed there, but, previous to absorption, it will have to undergo a proper degree of dilution with water, for there is this peculiarity respecting alcohol when it is separated by an animal membrane from a watery fluid like the blood, that it will not pass through the membrane until it has become charged, to a given point of dilution, with water. It is itself, in fact, *so greedy for water, it will pick it up from watery textures, and deprive them of it until, by its saturation, its power of reception is exhausted*, after which it will diffuse into the current of circulating fluid."

It is this power of absorbing water from every texture with which alcoholic spirits comes in contact, that creates the burning thirst of those who freely indulge in its use. Its effect, when it reaches the circulation, is thus described by Dr. Richardson:

"As it passes through the circulation of the lungs it is exposed to the air, and some little of it, raised into vapor by the natural heat, is thrown off in expiration. If the quantity of it be large, this loss may be considerable, and the odor of the spirit may be detected in the expired breath. If the quantity be small, the loss will be comparatively little, as the spirit will be held in solution by the water in the blood. After it has passed through the lungs, and has been driven by the left heart over the arterial circuit, it passes into what is called the minute circulation, or the structural circulation of the organism. The arteries here extend into very small vessels, which are called arterioles, and from these infinitely small vessels spring the equally minute radicals or roots of the veins, which are ultimately to become the great rivers bearing the blood back to the heart. In its passage through this minute circulation the alcohol finds its way to every organ. To this brain, to these muscles, to these secreting or excreting organs, nay, even into this bony structure itself, it moves with the blood. In some of these parts which are not excreting, it remains for a time diffused, and in those parts where there is a large percentage of water, it remains longer than in other parts. From some organs which have an open tube for conveying fluids away, as the liver and kidneys, it is thrown out or eliminated, and in this way a portion of it is ultimately removed from the body. The rest passing round and round with the circulation, is probably decomposed and carried off in new forms of matter.

"When we know the course which the alcohol takes in its passage through the body, from the period of its absorption to that of its elimination, we are the better able to judge what physical changes it induces in the different organs and structures with which it comes in contact. It first reaches the blood; but, as a rule, the quantity of it that enters is insufficient to produce any material effect on that fluid. If, however, the dose taken be poisonous or semi-poisonous, then even the blood, rich as it is in water—and it contains seven hundred and ninety parts in a thousand—is affected. The alcohol is diffused through this water, and there it comes in contact with the other constituent parts, with the fibrine, that plastic substance which, when blood is drawn, clots and coagulates, and which is present in the proportion of from two to three parts in a thousand; with the albumen which exists in the proportion of seventy parts; with the salts which yield about ten parts; with the fatty matters; and lastly, with those minute, round bodies which float in myriads in the blood (which were discovered by the Dutch philosopher, Leuwenhock, as one of the first results of microscopical observation, about the middle of the seventeenth century), and which are called the blood globules or corpuscles. These last-named bodies are, in fact, cells; their discs, when natural, have a smooth outline, they are depressed in the centre, and they are red in color; the color of the blood being derived from them. We have discovered in recent years that there exist other corpuscles or cells in the blood in much smaller quantity, which are called white cells, and these different cells float in the blood-stream within the vessels. The red take the centre of the stream; the white lie externally near the sides of the vessels, moving less quickly. Our business is mainly with the red corpuscles. They perform the most important functions in the economy; they absorb, in great part, the oxygen which we inhale in breathing, and carry it to the extreme tissues of the body; they absorb, in great part, the carbonic acid gas which is produced in the combustion of the body in the extreme tissues, and bring that gas back to the lungs to be exchanged for oxygen there; in short, they are the vital instruments of the circulation.

"With all these parts of the blood, with the water, fibrine, albumen, salts, fatty matter and corpuscles, the alcohol comes in contact when it enters the blood, and, if it be in sufficient quantity, it produces disturbing action. I have watched this disturbance very carefully on the blood corpuscles; for, in some animals we can see these floating along during life, and we can also observe them from men who are under the effects of alcohol, by removing a speck of blood, and examining it with the microscope. The action of the alcohol, when it is observable, is varied. It may cause the corpuscles to run too closely together, and to adhere in rolls; it may modify their outline, making the clear-defined, smooth, outer edge irregular or crenate, or even starlike; it may change the round corpuscle into the oval form, or, in very extreme cases, it may produce what I may call a truncated form of corpuscles, in which the change is so great that if we did not trace it through all its stages, we should be puzzled to know whether the object looked at were indeed a blood-cell. All these changes are due to the action of the spirit upon the water contained in the corpuscles; upon the capacity of the spirit to extract water from them. During every stage of modification of corpuscles thus described, their function to absorb and fix gases is impaired, and when the aggregation of the cells, in masses, is great, other difficulties arise, for the cells, united together, pass less easily than they should through the minute vessels of the lungs and of the general circulation, and impede the current, by which local injury is produced.

"A further action upon the blood, instituted by alcohol in excess, is upon the fibrine or the plastic colloidal matter. On this the spirit may act in two different ways, according to the degree in which it affects the water that holds the fibrine in solution. It may fix the water with the fibrine, and thus destroy the power of coagulation; or it may extract the water so determinately as to produce coagulation."

ON THE MINUTE CIRCULATION.

The doctor then goes on to describe the minute circulation through which the constructive material in the blood is distributed to every part of the body. "From this distribution of blood in these minute vessels," he says, "the structure of organs derive their constituent parts; through these vessels brain matter, muscle, gland, membrane, are given out from the blood by a refined process of selection of material, which, up to this time, is only so far understood as to enable us to say that it exists. The minute and intermediate vessels are more intimately connected than any other part with the construction and with the function of the living matter of which the body is composed. Think you that this mechanism is left uncontrolled? No; the vessels, small as they are, are under distinct control. Infinitely refined in structure, they nevertheless have the power of contraction and dilatation, which power is governed by nervous action of a special kind."

Now, there are certain chemical agents, which, by their action on the nerves, have the power to paralyze and relax these minute blood-vessels, at their extreme points. "The whole series of nitrates," says Dr. Richardson, "possess this power; ether possesses it; but the great point I wish to bring forth is, that the substance we are specially dealing with, alcohol, possesses the self-same power. By this influence it produces all those peculiar effects which in every-day life are so frequently illustrated."

PARALYZES THE MINUTE BLOOD-VESSELS.

It paralyzes the minute blood-vessels, and allows them to become dilated with the flowing blood.

"If you attend a large dinner party, you will observe, after the first few courses, when the wine is beginning to circulate, a progressive change in some of those about you who have taken wine.

The face begins to get flushed, the eye brightens, and the murmur of conversation becomes loud. What is the reason of that flushing of the countenance? It is the same as the flush from blushing, or from the reaction of cold, or from the nitrite of amyl. It is the dilatation of vessels following upon the reduction of nervous control, which reduction has been induced by the alcohol. In a word, the first stage, the stage of vascular excitement from alcohol, has been established.

HEART DISTURBANCE.

"The action of the alcohol extending so far does not stop there. With the disturbance of power in the extreme vessels, more disturbance is set up in other organs, and the first organ that shares in it is the heart. With each beat of the heart a certain degree of resistance is offered by the vessels when their nervous supply is perfect, and the stroke of the heart is moderated in respect both to tension and to time. But when the vessels are rendered relaxed, the resistance is removed, the heart begins to run quicker, like a watch from which the pallets have been removed, and the heart-stroke, losing nothing in force, is greatly increased in frequency, with a weakened recoil stroke. It is easy to account, in this manner, for the quickened heart and pulse which accompany the first stage of deranged action from alcohol, and you will be interested to know to what extent this increase of vascular action proceeds.

The information on this subject is exceedingly curious and important."

* * * * * * * *

"The stage of primary excitement of the circulation thus induced lasts for a considerable time, but at length the heart flags from its overaction, and requires the stimulus of more spirit to carry it on in its work. Let us take what we may call a moderate amount of alcohol, say two ounces by volume, in form of wine, or beer, or spirits. What is called strong sherry or port may contain as much as twenty-five per cent. by volume. Brandy over fifty; gin, thirty-eight; rum, forty-eight; whisky, forty-three; vin ordeinaire, eight; strong ale, fourteen; champagne, ten to eleven; it matters not which, if the quantity of alcohol be regulated by the amount present in the liquor imbibed. When we reach the two ounces, a distinct physiological effect follows, leading on to that first stage of excitement with which we are now conversant. The reception of the spirit arrested at this point, there need be no important mischief done to the organism; but if the quantity imbibed be increased, further changes quickly occur. We have seen that all the organs of the body are built upon the vascular structures, and therefore it follows that a prolonged paralysis of the minute circulation must of necessity lead to disturbance in other organs than the heart.

OTHER ORGANS INVOLVED.

"By common observation, the flush seen on the cheek during the first stage of alcoholic excitation, is presumed to extend merely to the parts actually exposed to view. It cannot, however, be too forcibly impressed that the condition is universal in the body. If the lungs could be seen, they, too, would be found with their vessels injected; if the brain and spinal cord could be laid open to view, they would be discovered in the same condition; if the stomach, the liver, the spleen, the kidneys or any other vascular organs or parts could be exposed, the vascular engorgement would be equally manifest. In the lower animals, I have been able to witness this extreme vascular condition in the lungs, and there are here presented to you two drawings from nature, showing, one the lungs in a natural state of an animal killed by a sudden blow, the other the lungs of an animal killed equally suddenly, but at a time when it was under the influence of alcohol. You will see, as if you were looking at the structures themselves, how different they are in respect to the blood which they contained, how intensely charged with blood is the lung in which the vessels had been paralyzed by the alcoholic spirit.

EFFECT ON THE BRAIN.

"I once had the unusual, though unhappy, opportunity of observing the same phenomenon in the brain structure of a man, who, in a paroxysm of alcoholic excitement, decapitated himself under the wheel of a railway carriage, and whose brain was instantaneously evolved from the skull by the crash. The brain itself, entire, was before me within three minutes after the death. It exhaled the odor of spirit most distinctly, and its membranes and minute structures were vascular in the extreme. It looked as if it had been recently injected with vermilion. The white matter of the cerebrum, studded with red points, could scarcely be distinguished, when it was incised, by its natural whiteness; and the pia-mater, or internal vascular membrane covering the brain, resembled a delicate web of coagulated red blood, so tensely were its fine vessels engorged.

"I should add that this condition extended through both the larger and the smaller brain, the cerebrum and cerebellum, but was not so marked in the medulla or commencing portion of the spinal cord.

THE SPINAL CORD AND NERVES.

"The action of alcohol continued beyond the first stage, the function of the spinal cord is influenced. Through this part of the nervous system we are accustomed, in health, to perform automatic acts of a mechanical kind, which proceed systematically even when we are thinking or speaking on other subjects. Thus a skilled workman will continue his mechanical work perfectly, while his mind is bent on some other subject; and thus we all perform various acts in a purely automatic way, without calling in the aid of the higher centres, except something more than ordinary occurs to demand their service, upon which we think before we perform. Under alcohol, as the spinal centres become influenced, these pure automatic acts cease to be correctly carried on. That the hand may reach any object, or the foot be correctly planted, the higher intellectual centre must be invoked to make the proceeding secure. There follows quickly upon this a deficient power of co-ordination of muscular movement. The nervous control of certain of the muscles is lost, and the nervous stimulus is more or less enfeebled. The muscles of the lower lip in the human subject usually fail first of all, then the muscles of the lower limbs, and it is worthy of remark that the extensor muscles give way earlier than the flexors. The muscles themselves, by this time, are also failing in power; they respond more feebly than is natural to the nervous stimulus; they, too, are coming under the depressing influence of the paralyzing agent, their structure is temporarily deranged, and their contractile power reduced.

"This modification of the animal functions under alcohol, marks the second degree of its action. In young subjects, there is now, usually, vomiting with faintness, followed by gradual relief from the burden of the poison.

EFFECT ON THE BRAIN CENTRES.

"The alcoholic spirit carried yet a further degree, the cerebral or brain centres become influenced; they are reduced in power, and the controlling influences of will and of judgment are lost. As these centres are unbalanced and thrown into chaos, the rational part of the nature of the man gives way before the emotional, passional or organic part. The reason is now off duty, or is fooling with duty, and all the mere animal instincts and sentiments are laid atrociously bare. The coward shows up more craven, the braggart more boastful, the cruel more merciless, the untruthful more false, the carnal more degraded. '*In vino veritas*' expresses, even, indeed, to physiological accuracy, the true condition. The reason, the emotions, the instincts, are all in a state of carnival, and in chaotic feebleness.

"Finally, the action of the alcohol still extending, the superior brain centres are overpowered; the senses are beclouded, the voluntary muscular prostration is perfected, sensibility is lost, and the body lies a mere log, dead by all but one-fourth, on which alone its life hangs. The heart still remains true to its duty, and while it just lives it feeds the breathing power. And so the circulation and the respiration, in the otherwise inert mass, keeps the mass within the bare domain of life until the poison begins to pass away and the nervous centres to revive again. It is happy for the inebriate that, as a rule, the brain fails so long before the heart that he has neither the power nor the sense to continue his process of destruction up to the act of death of his circulation. Therefore he lives to die another day.

* * * * * * * *

"Such is an outline of the primary action of alcohol on those who may be said to be unaccustomed to it, or who have not yet fallen into a fixed habit of taking it. For a long time the organism will bear these perversions of its functions without apparent injury, but if the experiment be repeated too often and too long, if it be continued after the term of life when the body is fully developed, when the elasticity of the membranes and of the blood-vessels is lessened, and when the tone of the muscular fibre is reduced, then organic series of structural changes, so characteristic of the persistent effects of spirit, become prominent and permanent. Then the external surface becomes darkened and congested, its vessels, in parts, visibly large; the skin becomes blotched, the proverbial red nose is defined, and those other striking vascular changes which disfigure many who may probably be called moderate alcoholics, are developed. These changes, belonging, as they do, to external surfaces, come under direct observation; they are accompanied with certain other changes in the internal organs, which we shall show to be more destructive still."

CHAPTER III.

IT CURSES THE BODY.—Continued.

WE have quoted thus freely in the preceding chapter, in order that the intelligent and thoughtful reader, who is really seeking for the truth in regard to the physical action of alcohol, may be able to gain clear impressions on the subject. The specific changes wrought by this substance on the internal organs are of a most serious character, and should be well understood by all who indulge habitually in its use.

EFFECT ON THE MEMBRANES.

The parts which first suffer from alcohol are those expansions of the body which the anatomists call the membranes. "The skin is a membranous envelope. Through the whole of the alimentary surface, from the lips downward, and through the bronchial passages to their minutest ramifications, extends the mucous membrane. The lungs, the heart, the liver, the kidneys are folded in delicate membranes, which can be stripped easily from these parts. If you take a portion of bone, you will find it easy to strip off from it a membranous sheath or covering; if you examine a joint, you will find both the head and the socket lined with membranes. The whole of the intestines are enveloped in a fine membrane called *peritoneum*. All the muscles are enveloped in membranes, and the fasciculi, or bundles and fibres of muscles, have their membranous sheathing. The brain and spinal cord are enveloped in three membranes; one nearest to themselves, a pure vascular structure, a net-work of blood-vessels; another, a thin serous structure; a third, a strong fibrous structure. The eyeball is a structure of colloidal humors and membranes, and of nothing else. To complete the description, the minute structures of the vital organs are enrolled in membranous matter."

These membranes are the filters of the body. "In their absence there could be no building of structure, no solidification of tissue, nor organic mechanism. Passive themselves, they, nevertheless, separate all structures into their respective positions and adaptations."

MEMBRANOUS DETERIORATIONS.

In order to make perfectly clear to the reader's mind the action and use of these membranous expansions, and the way in which alcohol deteriorates them, and obstructs their work, we quote again from Dr. Richardson:

"The animal receives from the vegetable world and from the earth the food and drink it requires for its sustenance and motion. It receives colloidal food for its muscles: combustible food for its motion;

water for the solution of its various parts; salt for constructive and other physical purposes. These have all to be arranged in the body; and they are arranged by means of the membranous envelopes. Through these membranes nothing can pass that is not, for the time, in a state of aqueous solution, like water or soluble salts. Water passes freely through them, salts pass freely through them, but the constructive matter of the active parts that is colloidal does not pass; it is retained in them until it is chemically decomposed into the soluble type of matter. When we take for our food a portion of animal flesh, it is first resolved, in digestion, into a soluble fluid before it can be absorbed; in the blood it is resolved into the fluid colloidal condition; in the solids it is laid down within the membranes into new structure, and when it has played its part, it is digested again, if I may so say, into a crystalloidal soluble substance, ready to be carried away and replaced by addition of new matter, then it is dialysed or passed through the membranes into the blood, and is disposed of in the excretions.

"See, then, what an all-important part these membranous structures play in the animal life. Upon their integrity all the silent work of the building up of the body depends. If these membranes are rendered too porous, and let out the colloidal fluids of the blood—the albumen, for example—the body so circumstanced, dies; dies as if it were slowly bled to death. If, on the contrary, they become condensed or thickened, or loaded with foreign material, then they fail to allow the natural fluids to pass through them. They fail to dialyse, and the result is, either an accumulation of the fluid in a closed cavity, or contraction of the substance inclosed within the membrane, or dryness of membrane in surfaces that ought to be freely lubricated and kept apart. In old age we see the effects of modification of membrane naturally induced; we see the fixed joint, the shrunken and feeble muscle, the dimmed eye, the deaf ear, the enfeebled nervous function.

"It may possibly seem, at first sight, that I am leading immediately away from the subject of the secondary action of alcohol. It is not so. I am leading directly to it. Upon all these membranous structures alcohol exerts a direct perversion of action. It produces in them a thickening, a shrinking and an inactivity that reduces their functional power. That they may work rapidly and equally, they require to be at all times charged with water to saturation. If, into contact with them, any agent is brought that deprives them of water, then is their work interfered with; they cease to separate the saline constituents properly; and, if the evil that is thus started, be allowed to continue, they contract upon their contained matter in whatever organ it may be situated, and condense it.

"In brief, under the prolonged influence of alcohol those changes which take place from it in the blood corpuscles, and which have already been described, extend to the other organic parts, involving them in structural deteriorations, which are always dangerous, and are often ultimately fatal."

ACTION OF ALCOHOL ON THE STOMACH.

Passing from the effect of alcohol upon the membranes, we come to its action on the stomach. That it impairs, instead of assisting digestion, has already been shown in the extract from Dr. Monroe, given near the commencement of the preceding chapter. A large amount of medical testimony could be quoted in corroboration, but enough has been educed. We shall only quote Dr. Richardson on "Alcoholic Dyspepsia:"

"The stomach, unable to produce, in proper quantity, the natural digestive fluid, and also unable to absorb the food which it may imperfectly digest, is in constant anxiety and irritation. It is oppressed with the sense of nausea; it is oppressed with the sense of emptiness and prostration; it is oppressed with a sense of distention; it is oppressed with a loathing for food, and it is teased with a craving for more drink. Thus there is engendered a permanent disorder which, for politeness' sake, is called dyspepsia, and for which different remedies are often sought but never found. Antibilious pills—whatever they may mean—Seidlitz powders, effervescing waters, and all that pharmacopœia of aids to further indigestion, in which the afflicted who nurse their own diseases so liberally and innocently indulge, are tried in vain. I do not strain a syllable when I state that the worst forms of confirmed indigestion originate in the practice that is here explained. By this practice all the functions are vitiated, the skin at one moment is flushed and perspiring, and at the next moment it is pale, cold and clammy, while every other secreting structure is equally disarranged."

TIC-DOULOUREUX AND SCIATICA.

Nervous derangements follow as a matter of course, for the delicate membranes which envelope and immediately surround the nervous cords, are affected by the alcohol more readily than the coarser membranous textures of other parts of the body, and give rise to a series of troublesome conditions, which are too often attributed to other than the true causes. Some of these are thus described: "The perverted condition of the membranous covering of the nerves gives rise to pressure within the sheath of the nerve, and to pain as a consequence. To the pain thus excited the term neuralgia is commonly applied, or "tic;" or, if the large nerve running down the thigh be the seat of the pain, 'sciatica.' Sometimes this pain is developed as a toothache. It is pain commencing, in nearly every instance, at some point where a nerve is inclosed in a bony cavity, or where pressure is easily excited, as at the lower jawbone near the centre of the chin, or at the opening in front of the lower part of the ear, or at the opening over the eyeball in the frontal bone."

DEGENERATION OF THE LIVER.

The organic deteriorations which follow the long-continued use of alcoholic drinks are often of a serious and fatal character. The same author says: "The organ of the body, that, perhaps, the most frequently undergoes structural changes from alcohol, is the *liver*. The capacity of this organ for holding active substances in its cellular parts, is one of its marked physiological distinctions. In instances of poisoning by arsenic, antimony, strychnine and other poisonous compounds, we turn to the liver, in conducting our analyses, as if it were the central depot of the foreign matter. It is, practically, the same in respect to alcohol. The liver of the confirmed alcoholic is, probably, never free from the influence of the poison; it is too often saturated with it. The effect of the alcohol upon the liver is upon the minute membranous or capsular structure of the organ, upon which it acts to prevent the proper dialysis and free secretion. The organ, at first, becomes large from the distention of its vessels, the surcharge of fluid matter and the thickening of tissue. After a time, there follows contraction of membrane, and slow shrinking of the whole mass of the organ in its cellular parts. Then the shrunken, hardened, roughened mass is said to be 'hob-nailed,' a common, but expressive term. By the time this change occurs, the body of him in whom it is developed is usually dropsical in its lower parts, owing to the obstruction offered to the returning blood by the veins, and his fate is sealed. * * * Again, under an increase of fatty substance in the body, the structure of the liver may be charged with fatty cells, and undergo what is technically designated fatty degeneration."

HOW THE KIDNEYS SUFFER.

"The kidneys, also, suffer deterioration. Their minute structures undergo fatty modification; their vessels lose their due elasticity of power of contraction; or their membranes permit to pass through them the albumen from the blood. This last condition reached, the body loses power as if it were being gradually drained even of its blood.

CONGESTION OF THE LUNGS.

"The vessels of the lungs are easily relaxed by alcohol; and as they, of all parts, are most exposed to vicissitudes of heat and cold, they are readily congested when, paralyzed by the spirit, they are subjected to the effects of a sudden fall of atmospheric temperature. Thus, the suddenly fatal congestions of lungs which so easily befall the confirmed alcoholic during the severe winter seasons."

ORGANIC DETERIORATIONS OF THE HEART.

The heart is one of the greatest sufferers from alcohol. Quoting again from Dr. Richardson:

"The membranous structures which envelope and line the organ are changed in quality, are thickened, rendered cartilaginous, and even calcareous or bony.

Then the valves, which are made up of folds of membrane, lose their suppleness, and what is called valvular disease is permanently established. The coats of the great blood-vessel leading from the heart, the aorto, share, not unfrequently, in the same changes of structure, so that the vessel loses its elasticity and its power to feed the heart by the recoil from its distention, after the heart, by its stroke, has filled it with blood.

"Again, the muscular structure of the heart fails, owing to degenerative changes in its tissue. The elements of the muscular fibre are replaced by fatty cells; or, if not so replaced, are themselves transferred into a modified muscular texture in which the power of contraction is greatly reduced.

"Those who suffer from these organic deteriorations of the central and governing organ of the circulation of the blood learn the fact so insidiously, it hardly breaks upon them until the mischief is far advanced. They are, for years, conscious of a central failure of power from slight causes, such as overexertion, trouble, broken rest, or too long abstinence from food. They feel what they call a 'sinking,' but they know that wine or some other stimulant will at once relieve the sensation. Thus they seek to relieve it until at last they discover that the remedy fails. The jaded, overworked, faithful heart will bear no more; it has run its course, and, the governor of the blood-streams broken, the current either overflows into the tissues, gradually damming up the courses, or under some slight shock or excess of motion, ceases wholly at the centre."

EPILEPSY AND PARALYSIS.

Lastly, the brain and spinal cord, and all the nervous matter, become, under the influence of alcohol, subject alike to organic deterioration "The membranes enveloping the nervous substance undergo thickening; the blood-vessels are subjected to change of structure, by which their resistance and resiliency is impaired; and the true nervous matter is sometimes modified, by softening or shrinking of its texture, by degeneration of its cellular structure or by interposition of fatty particles. These deteriorations of cerebral and spinal matter give rise to a series of derangements, which show themselves in the worst forms of nervous diseases—epilepsy; paralysis, local or general; insanity."

We have quoted thus largely from Dr. Richardson's valuable lectures, in order that our readers may have an intelligent comprehension of this most important subject. It is because the great mass of the people are ignorant of the real character of the effects produced on the body by alcohol that so many indulge in its use, and lay the foundation for troublesome, and often painful and fatal diseases in their later years.

In corroboration of Dr. Richardson's testimony against alcohol, we will, in closing this chapter, make a few quotations from other medical authorities.

FARTHER MEDICAL TESTIMONY.

Dr. Ezra M. Hunt says: "The capacity of the alcohols for impairment of functions and the initiation and promotion of organic lesions in vital parts, is unsurpassed by any record in the whole range of medicine. *The facts as to this are so indisputable, and so far granted by the profession, as to be no longer debatable.* Changes in stomach and liver, in kidneys and lungs, in the blood-vessels to the minutest capillary, and in the blood to the smallest red and white blood disc disturbances of secretion, fibroid and fatty degenerations in almost every organ, impairment of muscular power, impressions so profound on both nervous systems as to be often toxic—these, and such as these, are the oft manifested results. And these are not confined to those called intemperate."

Professor Youmans says: "It is evident that, so far from being the conservator of health, alcohol is an active and powerful cause of disease, interfering, as it does, with the respiration, the circulation and the nutrition; now, is any other result possible?"

Dr. F. R. Lees says: "That alcohol should contribute to the fattening process under certain conditions, and produce in drinkers fatty degeneration of the blood, follows, as a matter of course, since, on the one hand, we have an agent that *retains waste* matter by lowering the nutritive and excretory functions, and on the other, a *direct poisoner* of the vesicles of the vital stream."

Dr. Henry Monroe says: "There is no kind of tissue, whether healthy or morbid, that may not undergo fatty degeneration; and there is no organic disease so troublesome to the medical man, or so difficult of cure. If, by the aid of the miscroscope, we examine a very fine section of muscle taken from a person in good health, we find the muscles firm, elastic and of a bright red color, made up of parallel fibres, with beautiful crossings or striæ; but, if we similarly examine the muscle of a man who leads an idle, sedentary life, and indulges in intoxicating drinks, we detect, at once, a pale, flabby, inelastic, oily appearance. Alcoholic narcotization appears to produce this peculiar conditions of the tissues *more than any other agent with which we are acquainted.* 'Three-quarters of the chronic illness which the medical man has to treat,' says Dr. Chambers, 'are occasioned by this disease.' The eminent French analytical chemist, Lecanu, found as much as one hundred and seventeen parts of fat in one thousand parts of a drunkard's blood, the highest estimate of the quantity in health being eight and one-quarter parts, while the ordinary quantity is not more than two or three parts, so that the blood of the drunkard contains forty times in excess of the ordinary quantity."

Dr. Hammond, who has written, in partial defense of alcohol as containing a food power, says: "When I say that it, of all other causes, *is most prolific* in exciting derangements of the brain, the spinal cord and the nerves, I make a statement which my own experience shows to be correct."

Another eminent physician says of alcohol: "It substitutes suppuration for growth. * * It helps time to produce the effects of age; and, in a word, is the genius of degeneration."

Dr. Monroe, from whom we have already quoted, says: "Alcohol, taken in small quantities, or largely diluted, as in the form of beer, causes the stomach gradually to lose its tone, and makes it dependent upon artificial stimulus. Atony, or want of tone of the stomach, gradually supervenes, and incurable disorder of health results. * * * Should a dose of alcoholic drink be taken daily, the heart will very often become hypertrophied, or enlarged throughout. Indeed, it is painful to witness how *many* persons are actually laboring under disease of the heart, owing chiefly to the use of alcoholic liquors."

Dr. T. K. Chambers, physician to the Prince of Wales, says: "Alcohol is really the most ungenerous diet there is. It impoverishes the blood, and there is no surer road to that degeneration of muscular fibre so much to be feared; and in heart disease it is more especially hurtful, by quickening the beat, causing capillary congestion and irregular circulation, and thus mechanically inducing dilatation.'

Sir Henry Thompson, a distinguished surgeon, says: "Don't take your daily wine under any pretext of its doing you good. Take it frankly as a luxury— one which must be paid for, by some persons very lightly, by some at a high price, *but always to be paid for.* And, mostly, some loss of health, or of mental power, or of calmness of temper, or of judgment, is the price."

Dr. Charles Jewett says: "The late Prof. Parks, of England, in his great work on Hygiene, has effectually disposed of the notion, long and very generally entertained, that alcohol is a valuable prophylactic where a bad climate, bad water and other conditions unfavorable to health exist; and an unfortunate experiment with the article, in the Union army, on the banks of the Chickahominy, in the year 1863, proved conclusively that, instead of guarding the human constitution against the influence of agencies hostile to health, its use gives to them additional force. The medical history of the British army in India teaches the same lesson."

But why present farther testimony? Is not the evidence complete? To the man who values good health; who would not lay the foundation for disease and suffering in his later years, we need not offer a single additional argument in favor of entire abstinence from alcoholic drinks. He will eschew them as poisons.

CHAPTER IV.

IT CURSES THE SOUL.

THE physical disasters that follow the continued use of intoxicating beverages are sad enough, and terrible enough; but the surely attendant mental, moral and spiritual disasters are sadder and more terrible still. If you disturb the healthy condition of the brain, which is the physical organ through which the mind acts, you disturb the mind. It will not have the same clearness of perception as before; nor have the same rational control over the impulses and passions.

In what manner alcohol deteriorates the body and brain has been shown in the two preceding chapters. In this one we purpose showing how the curse goes deeper than the body and brain, and involves the whole man—morally and spiritually, as well as physically.

HEAVENLY ORDER IN THE BODY.

In order to understand a subject clearly, certain general laws, or principles, must be seen and admitted. And here we assume, as a general truth, that health in the human body is normal heavenly order on the physical plane of life, and that any disturbance of that order exposes the man to destructive influences, which are evil and infernal in their character Above the natural and physical plane, and resting upon it, while man lives in this world, is the mental and spiritual plane, or degree of life. This degree is in heavenly order when the reason is clear, and the appetites and passions under its wise control. But, if, through any cause, this fine equipoise is disturbed, or lost, then a way is opened for the influx of more subtle evil influences than such as invade the body, because they have power to act upon the reason and the passions, obscuring the one and inflaming the others.

MENTAL DISTURBANCES.

We know how surely the loss of bodily health results in mental disturbance. If the seat of disease be remote from the brain, the disturbance is usually slight; but it increases as the trouble comes nearer and nearer to that organ, and shows itself in multiform ways according to character, temperament or inherited disposition; but almost always in a predominance of what is evil instead of good. There will be fretfulness, or ill-nature, or selfish exactions, or mental obscurity, or unreasoning demands, or, it may be, vicious and cruel propensities, where, when the brain was undisturbed by disease, reason held rule with patience and loving kindness. If the disease which has attacked the brain goes on increasing, the mental disease which follows as a consequence of organic disturbance or deterioration, will have increased also, until insanity may be established in some one or more of its many sad and varied forms.

INSANITY.

It is, therefore, a very serious thing for a man to take into his body any substance which, on reaching that wonderfully delicate organ—the brain, sets up therein a diseased action; for, diseased mental action is sure to follow, and there is only one true name for mental disease, and that is *insanity*. A fever is a fever, whether it be light or intensely burning; and so any disturbance of the mind's rational equipoise is insanity, whether it be in the simplest form of temporary obscurity, or in the midnight of a totally darkened intellect.

We are not writing in the interest of any special theory, nor in the spirit of partisanship; but with an earnest desire to make the truth appear. The reader must not accept anything simply because we say it, but because he sees it to be true. Now, as to this matter of insanity, let him think calmly. The word is one that gives us a shock; and, as we hear it, we almost involuntarily thank God for the good gift of a well-balanced mind. What, if from any cause this beautiful equipoise should be disturbed and the mind lose its power to think clearly, or to hold the lower passions in due control? Shall we exceed the truth if we say that the man in whom this takes place is insane just in the degree that he has lost his rational self-control; and that he is restored when he regains that control?

In this view, the question as to the hurtfulness of alcoholic drinks assumes a new and graver aspect. Do they disturb the brain when they come in contact with its substance; and deteriorate it if the contact be long continued? Fact, observation, experience and scientific investigation all emphatically say yes; and we know that if the brain be disordered the mind will be disordered, likewise; and a disordered mind is an insane mind. Clearly, then, in the degree that a man impairs or hurts his brain—temporarily or continuously—in that degree his mind is unbalanced; in that degree he is not a truly rational and sane man.

We are holding the reader's thought just here that he may have time to think, and to look at the question in the light of reason and common sense. So far as he does this, will he be able to feel the force of such evidence as we shall educe in what follows, and to comprehend its true meaning.

NO SUBSTANCE AFFECTS THE BRAIN LIKE ALCOHOL.

Other substances besides alcohol act injuriously on the brain; but there is none that compares with this in the extent, variety and diabolical aspect of the mental aberrations which follow its use. We are not speaking thoughtlessly or wildly; but simply uttering a truth well-known to every man of observation, and which every man, and especially those who take this substance in any form, should lay deeply to heart. Why it is that such awful and destructive forms of insanity should follow, as they do, the use of alcohol it is not for us to say. That they do follow it, we know, and we hold up the fact in solemn warning.

INHERITED LATENT EVIL FORCES.

Another consideration, which should have weight with every one, is this, that no man can tell what may be the character of the legacy he has received from his ancestors. He may have an inheritance of latent evil forces, transmitted through many generations, which only await some favoring opportunity to spring into life and action. So long as he maintains a rational self-control, and the healthy order of his life be not disturbed, they may continue quiescent; but if his brain loses its equipoise, or is hurt or impaired, then a diseased psychical condition may be induced and the latent evil forces be quickened into life.

No substance in nature, as far as yet known, has, when it reaches the brain, such power to induce

MENTAL AND MORAL CHANGES OF A DISASTROUS CHARACTER

as alcohol. Its transforming power is marvelous, and often appalling. It seems to open a way of entrance into the soul for all classes of foolish, insane or malignant spirits, who, so long as it remains in contact with the brain, are able to hold possession.

Men of the kindest nature when sober, act often like fiends when drunk. Crimes and outrages are committed, which shock and shame the perpetrators when the excitement of inebriation has passed away. Referring to this subject, Dr. Henry Munroe says:

"It appears from the experience of Mr. Fletcher, who has paid much attention to the cases of drunkards, from the remarks of Mr. Dunn, in his 'Medical Psychology,' and from observations of my own, that there is some analogy between our physical and psychical natures; for, as the physical part of us, when its power is at a low ebb, becomes susceptible of morbid influences which, in full vigor, would pass over it without effect, so when the psychical (synonymous with the *moral*) part of the brain has its healthy function disturbed and deranged by the introduction of a morbid poison like alcohol, the individual so circumstanced sinks in depravity, and BECOMES THE HELPLESS SUBJECT OF THE FORCES OF EVIL, which are powerless against a nature free from the morbid influences of alcohol.

"Different persons are affected in different ways by the same poison. Indulgence in alcoholic drinks may act upon one or more of the cerebral organs; and, as its necessary consequence, the manifestations of functional disturbance will follow in such of the mental powers as these organs subserve. If the indulgence be continued, then, either from deranged nutrition or organic lesion, manifestations formerly developed only during a fit of intoxication may become *permanent,* and terminate in insanity or dypsomania. M. Flourens first pointed out the fact that certain morbific agents, when introduced into the current of the circulation, tend to act *primarily* and *specially* on one nervous centre in preference to that of another, by virtue of some special elective affinity between such morbific agents and certain ganglia. Thus, in the tottering gait of the tipsy man, we see the influence of alcohol upon the functions of the *cerebellum* in the impairment of its power of co-ordinating the muscles.

"Certain writers on diseases of the mind make especial allusion to that form of insanity termed DYPSOMANIA, in which a person has an unquenchable thirst for alcoholic drinks—a tendency as decidedly maniacal as that of *homicidal mania;* or the uncontrollable desire to burn, termed *pyromania;* or to steal, called *kleptomania.*

HOMICIDAL MANIA.

"The different tendencies of homicidal mania in different individuals are often only nursed into action when the current of the blood has been poisoned with alcohol. I had a case of a person who, whenever his brain was so excited, told me that he experienced a most uncontrollable desire to kill or injure some one; so much so, that he could at times hardly restrain himself from the action, and was obliged to refrain from all stimulants, lest, in an unlucky moment, he might commit himself. Townley, who murdered the young lady of his affections, for which he was sentenced to be imprisoned in a lunatic asylum for life, *poisoned his brain with brandy* and soda-water before he committed the rash act. The brandy stimulated into action certain portions of the brain, which acquired such a power as to subjugate his will, and hurry him to the performance of a frightful deed, opposed alike to his better judgment and his ordinary desires.

"As to *pyromania*, some years ago I knew a laboring man in a country village, who, whenever he had had a few glasses of ale at the public-house, would chuckle with delight at the thought of firing certain gentlemen's stacks. Yet, when his brain was free from the poison, a quieter, better-disposed man could not be. Unfortunately, he became addicted to habits of intoxication; and, one night, under alcoholic excitement, fired some stacks belonging to his employers, for which he was sentenced for fifteen years to a penal settlement, where his brain would never again be alcoholically excited.

KLEPTOMANIA.

"Next, I will give an example of *kleptomania*. I knew, many years ago, a very clever, industrious and talented young man, who told me that whenever he had been drinking, he could hardly withstand the temptation of stealing anything that came in his way; but that these feelings never troubled him at other times. One afternoon, after he had been indulging with his fellow-workmen in drink, his will, unfortunately, was overpowered, and he took from the mansion where he was working some articles of worth, for which he was accused, and afterwards sentenced to a term of imprisonment. When set at liberty he had the good fortune to be placed among some kind-hearted persons, vulgarly called *teetotallers;* and, from conscientious motives, signed the PLEDGE, now above twenty years ago. From that time to the present moment he has never experienced the overmastering desire which so often beset him in his drinking days—to take that which was not his own. Moreover, no pretext on earth could now entice him to taste of any liquor containing alcohol, feeling that, under its influence, he might again fall its victim. He holds an influential position in the town where he resides.

"I have known some ladies of good position in society, who, after a dinner or supper-party, and after having taken sundry glasses of wine, could not withstand the temptation of taking home any little article not their own, when the opportunity offered; and who, in their sober moments, have returned them, as if taken by mistake. We have many instances recorded in our police reports of gentlemen of position, under the influence of drink, committing thefts of the most paltry articles, afterwards returned to the owners by their friends, which can only be accounted for, psychologically, by the fact that the

LOSS OF MENTAL CLEARNESS.

"That alcohol, whether taken in large or small doses, immediately disturbs the natural functions of the mind and body, is now conceded by the most eminent physiologists. Dr. Brinton says: 'Mental acuteness, accuracy of conception, and delicacy of the senses, are all so far opposed by the action of alcohol, as that the maximum efforts of each are *incompatible* with the ingestion of any moderate quantity of fermented liquid. Indeed, there is scarcely any calling which demands skillful and exact effort of mind and body, or which requires the balanced exercise of many faculties, that does not illustrate this rule. The mathematician, the gambler, the metaphysician, the billiard-player, the author, the artist, the physician, would, if they could analyze their experience aright, generally concur in the statement, that *a single glass will often suffice to take*, so to speak, *the edge off both mind and body*, and to reduce their capacity to something below what is relatively their perfection of work.'

"Not long ago, a railway train was driven carelessly into one of the principal London stations, running into another train, killing, by the collision, six or seven persons, and injuring many others. From the evidence at the inquest, it appeared that the guard was reckoned sober, *only he had had two glasses of ale* with a friend at a previous station. Now, reasoning psychologically, these two glasses of ale had probably been instrumental in *taking off the edge* from his perceptions and prudence, and producing a carelessness or boldness of action which would not have occurred under the cooling, temperate influence of a beverage free from alcohol. Many persons have admitted to me that they were not the same after taking even one glass of ale or wine that they were before, and could not *thoroughly* trust themselves after they had taken this single glass."

IMPAIRMENT OF MEMORY.

An impairment of the memory is among the early symptoms of alcoholic derangement.

"This," says Dr. Richardson, "extends even to forgetfulness of the commonest things; to names of familiar persons, to dates, to duties of daily life. Strangely, too," he adds, "this failure, like that which indicates, in the aged, the era of second childishness and mere oblivion, does not extend to the things of the past, but is confined to events that are passing. On old memories the mind retains its power; on new ones it requires constant prompting and sustainment."

In this failure of memory nature gives a solemn warning that imminent peril is at hand. Well for the habitual drinker if he heed the warning. Should he not do so, symptoms of a more serious character will, in time, develop themselves, as the brain becomes more and more diseased, ending, it may be, in permanent insanity.

MENTAL AND MORAL DISEASES.

Of the mental and moral diseases which too often follow the regular drinking of alcohol, we have painful records in asylum reports, in medical testimony and in our daily observation and experience. These are so full and varied, and thrust so constantly on our attention, that the wonder is that men are not afraid to run the terrible risks involved even in what is called the moderate use of alcoholic beverages.

In 1872, a select committee of the House of Commons, appointed "to consider the best plan for the control and management of habitual drunkards," called upon some of the most eminent medical men in Great Britain to give their testimony in answer to a large number of questions, embracing every topic within the range of inquiry, from the pathology of inebriation to the practical usefulness of prohibitory laws. In this testimony much was said about the effect of alcoholic stimulation on the mental condition and moral character. One physician, Dr. James Crichton Brown, who, in ten years' experience as superintendent of lunatic asylums, has paid special attention to the relations of habitual drunkenness to insanity, having carefully examined five hundred cases, testified that alcohol, taken in excess, produced different forms of mental disease, of which he mentioned four classes : 1. *Mania a potu,* or alcoholic mania. 2. The monomania of suspicion. 3. Chronic alcoholism, characterized by failure of the memory and power of judgment, with partial paralysis —generally ending fatally. 4. Dypsomania, or an *irresistible* craving for alcoholic stimulants, occuring very frequently, paroxysmally, and with constant liability to periodical exacerbations, when the craving becomes altogether uncontrollable. Of this latter form of disease, he says: "This is invariably associated with a certain *impairment of the intellect, and of the affections and the moral powers.*"

Dr. Alexander Peddie, a physician of over thirty-seven years' practice in Edinburgh, gave, in his evidence, many remarkable instances of the moral perversions that followed continued drinking.

RELATION BETWEEN INSANITY AND DRUNKENNESS.

Dr. John Nugent said that his experience of twenty-six years among lunatics, led him to believe that there is a very close relation between the results of the abuse of alcohol and insanity. The population of Ireland had decreased, he said, two millions in twenty-five years, but there was the same amount of insanity now that there was before. He attributed this, in a great measure, to indulgence in drink.

Dr. Arthur Mitchell, Commissioner of Lunacy for Scotland, testified that the excessive use of alcohol caused a large amount of the lunacy, crime and pauperism of that country. In some men, he said, habitual drinking leads to other diseases than insanity, because the effect is always in the direction of the proclivity, but it is certain that there are many in whom there is a clear proclivity to insanity, *who would escape that dreadful consummation but for drinking; excessive drinking in many persons determining the insanity to which they are, at any rate, predisposed.* The children of drunkards, he further said, are in a larger proportion idiotic than other children, and in a larger proportion become themselves drunkards; they are also in a larger proportion liable to the ordinary forms of acquired insanity.

Dr. Winslow Forbes believed that in the habitual drunkard the whole nervous structure, and the brain especially, became poisoned by alcohol. All the mental symptoms which you see accompanying ordinary intoxication, he remarks, result from the poisonous effects of alcohol on the brain. It is the brain which is mainly effected. In temporary drunkenness, the brain becomes in an abnormal state of alimentation, and if this habit is persisted in for years, the nervous tissue itself becomes permeated with alcohol, and organic changes take place in the nervous tissues of the brain, producing *that frightful and dreadful chronic insanity which we see in lunatic asylums, traceable entirely to habits of intoxication.* A large percentage of frightful mental and brain disturbances can, he declared, be traced to the drunkenness of parents.

Dr. D. G. Dodge, late of the New York State Inebriate Asylum, who, with Dr. Joseph Parrish, gave testimony before the committee of the House of Commons, said, in one of his answers: "With the excessive use of alcohol, functional disorder will invariably appear, and no organ will be more seriously affected, and possibly impaired, than the brain. *This is shown in the inebriate by a weakened intellect, a general debility of the mental faculties,* a partial or total loss of self-respect, and a departure of the power of self-command; all of which, acting together, place the victim at the mercy of a depraved and morbid appetite, and make him utterly powerless, by his own unaided efforts, to secure his recovery from the disease which is destroying him." And he adds: "I am of opinion that there is a

GREAT SIMILARITY BETWEEN INEBRIETY AND INSANITY.

I am decidedly of opinion that the former has taken its place in the family of diseases as prominently as its twin-brother insanity; and, in my opinion, the day is not far distant when the pathology of the former will be as fully understood and as successfully treated as the latter, and even more successfully, since it is more within the reach and bounds of human control, which, wisely exercised and scientifically administered, may prevent curable inebriation from verging into possible incurable insanity."

GENERAL IMPAIRMENT OF THE FACULTIES.

In a more recent lecture than the one from which we have quoted so freely, Dr. Richardson, speaking of the action of alcohol on the mind, gives the following sad picture of its ravages:

"An analysis of the condition of the mind induced and maintained by the free daily use of alcohol as a drink, reveals a singular order of facts. The manifestation fails altogether to reveal the exaltation of any reasoning power in a useful or satisfactory direction. I have never met with an instance in which such a claim for alcohol has been made. On the contrary, confirmed alcoholics constantly say that for this or that work, requiring thought and attention, it is necessary to forego some of the usual potations in order to have a cool head for hard work.

"On the other side, the experience is overwhelmingly in favor of the observation that the use of

ALCOHOL SELLS THE REASONING POWERS,

make weak men and women the easy prey of the wicked and strong, and leads men and women who should know better into every grade of misery and vice. * * * If, then, alcohol enfeebles the reason, what part of the mental constitution does it exalt and excite? It excites and exalts those animal, organic, emotional centres of mind which, in the dual nature of man, so often cross and oppose that pure and abstract reasoning nature which lifts man above the lower animals, and rightly exercised, little lower than the angels.

IT EXCITES MAN'S WORST PASSIONS.

"Exciting these animal centres, it lets loose all the passions, and gives them more or less of unlicensed dominion over the man. It excites anger, and when it does not lead to this extreme, it keeps the mind fretful, irritable, dissatisfied and captious. * * * And if I were to take you through all the passions, love, hate, lust, envy, avarice and pride, I should but show you that alcohol ministers to them all; that, paralyzing the reason, it takes from off these passions that fine adjustment of reason, which places man above the lower animals. From the beginning to the end of its influence it subdues reason and sets the passions free. The analogies, physical and mental, are perfect. That which loosens the tension of the vessels which feed the body with due order and precision, and, thereby, lets loose the heart to violent excess and unbridled motion, loosens, also, the reason and lets loose the passion. In both instances, heart and head are, for a time, out of harmony; their balance broken. The man descends closer and closer to the lower animals. From the angels he glides farther and farther away.

A SAD AND TERRIBLE PICTURE.

"The *destructive* effects of alcohol on the human mind present, finally, the saddest picture of its influence. The most æsthetic artist can find no angel here. All is animal, and animal of the worst type. Memory irretrievably lost, words and very elements of speech forgotten or words displaced to have no meaning in them. Rage and anger persistent and mischievous, or remittent and impotent. Fear at every corner of life, distrust on every side, grief merged into blank despair, hopelessness into permanent melancholy. Surely no Pandemonium that ever poet dreamt of could equal that which would exist if all the drunkards of the world were driven into one mortal sphere.

"As I have moved among those who are physically stricken with alcohol, and have detected under the various disguises of name the fatal diseases, the pains and penalties it imposes on the body, the picture has been sufficiently cruel. But even that picture pales, as I conjure up, without any stretch of imagination, the devastations which the same agent inflicts on the mind. Forty per cent., the learned Superintendent of Colney Hatch, Dr. Sheppard, tells us, of those who were brought into that asylum in 1876, were so brought because of the direct or indirect effects of alcohol. If the facts of all the asylums were collected with equal care, the same tale would, I fear, be told. What need we further to show the destructive action on the human mind? The Pandemonium of drunkards; the grand transformation scene of that pantomime of drink which commences with moderation! Let it never more be forgotten by those who love their fellow-men until, through their efforts, it is closed forever."

We might go on, adding page after page of evidence, showing how alcohol curses the souls, as well as the bodies, of men; but enough has been educed to force conviction on the mind of every reader not already satisfied of its poisonous and destructive quality.

How light are all evils flowing from intemperance compared with those which it thus inflicts on man's higher nature. "What," says Dr. W. E. Channing, "is the great essential evil of intemperance? The reply is given, when I say, that intemperance is the

VOLUNTARY EXTINCTION OF REASON.

The great evil is inward or spiritual. The intemperate man divests himself, for a time, of his rational and moral nature, casts from himself self-consciousness and self-command, brings on frenzy, and by repetition of this insanity, prostrates more and more his rational and moral powers. He sins immediately and directly against the rational nature, that Divine principle which distinguishes between truth and falsehood, between right and wrong action, which distinguishes man from the brute. This is the essence of the vice, what constitutes its peculiar guilt and woe, and what should particularly impress and awaken those who are laboring for its suppression. Other evils of intemperance are light compared with this, and almost all flow from this; and it is right, it is to be desired that all other evils should be joined with and follow this. It is to be desired, when a man lifts a suicidal arm against his higher life, when he quenches reason and conscience, that he and all others should receive solemn, startling warning of the greatness of his guilt; that terrible outward calamities should bear witness to the inward ruin which he is working; that the handwriting of judgment and woe on his countenance, form and whole condition, should declare what a fearful thing it is for a man, "God's rational offspring, to renounce his reason, and become a brute."

CHAPTER V.

NOT A FOOD, AND VERY LIMITED IN ITS RANGE AS A MEDICINE.

THE use of alcohol as a medicine has been very large. If his patient was weak and nervous, the physician too often ordered wine or ale; or, not taking the trouble to refer his own case to a physician, the invalid prescribed these articles for himself. If there was a failure of appetite, its restoration was sought in the use of one or both of the above-named forms of alcohol; or, perhaps, adopting a more heroic treatment, the sufferer poured brandy or whisky into his weak and sensitive stomach. Protection from cold was sought in a draught of some alcoholic beverage, and relief from fatigue and exhaustion in the use of the same deleterious substance. Indeed, there is scarcely any form of bodily ailment or discomfort, or mental disturbance, for the relief of which a resort was not had to alcohol in some one of its many forms.

It is fair to say that, as a medicine, its consumption has far exceeded that of any other substance prescribed and taken for physical and mental derangements.

The inquiry, then, as to the true remedial value

of alcohol is one of the gravest import; and it is of interest to know that for some years past the medical profession has been giving this subject a careful and thorough investigation. The result is to be found in the brief declaration made by the Section on Medicine, of the

INTERNATIONAL MEDICAL CONGRESS,

which met in Philadelphia in 1876. This body was composed of about six hundred delegates, from Europe and America, among them, some of the ablest men in the profession. Realizing the importance of some expression in relation to the use of alcohol, medical and otherwise, from this Congress, the National Temperance Society laid before it, through its President, W. E. Dodge, and Secretary, J. N. Stearns, the following memorial:

"The National Temperance Society sends greeting, and respectfully invites from your distinguished body a public declaration to the effect that alcohol should be classed with other powerful drugs; that, when prescribed medicinally, it should be with conscientious caution and a sense of grave responsibility; that it is in no sense food to the human system; that its improper use is productive of a large amount of physical disease, tending to deteriorate the human race; and to recommend, as representatives of enlightened science, to your several nationalities, total abstinence from alcoholic beverages."

In response to this memorial, the president of

the society received from J. Ewing Mears, M. D., Secretary of the Section on Medicine, International Congress, the following official letter, under date of September 9th, 1876:

"DEAR SIR: I am instructed by the Section on Medicine, International Medical Congress, of 1876, to transmit to you, as the action of the Section, the following conclusions adopted by it with regard to the use of alcohol in medicine, the same being in reply to the communication sent by the National Temperance Society.

"1. Alcohol is not shown to have a definite food value by any of the usual methods of chemical analysis or physiological investigation.

"2. Its use as a medicine is chiefly that of a cardiac stimulant, and often admits of substitution.

"3. As a medicine, it is not well fitted for self-prescription by the laity, and the medical profession is not accountable for such administration, or for the enormous evils arising therefrom.

"4. The purity of alcoholic liquors is, in general, not as well assured as that of articles used for medicine should be. The various mixtures, when used as medicine, should have definite and known composition, and should not be interchanged promiscuously."

The reader will see in this no hesitating or half-way speech. The declaration is strong and clear, that, as a food, alcohol is not shown, when subjected to the usual method of chemical or physiological investigation, to have any food value; and that, as a medicine, its use is chiefly confined to a cardiac stimulant, and often admits of substitution.

A declaration like this, coming, as it does, from a body of medical men representing the most advanced ideas held by the profession, must have great weight with the people. But we do not propose resting on this declaration alone. As it was based on the results of chemical and physiological investigations, let us go back of the opinion expressed by the Medical Congress, and examine these results, in order that the ground of its opinion may become apparent.

There was presented to this Congress, by a distinguished physician of New Jersey, Dr. Ezra M. Hunt, a paper on "Alcohol as a Food and Medicine," in which the whole subject is examined in the light of the most recent and carefully-conducted experiments of English, French, German and American chemists and physiologists, and their conclusions, as well as those of the author of the paper, set forth in the plainest manner. This has since been published by the National Temperance Society, and should be read and carefully studied by every one who is seeking for accurate information on the important subject we are now considering. It is impossible for us to more than glance at the evidence brought forward in proof of the assertion that

ALCOHOL HAS NO FOOD VALUE,

and is exceedingly limited in its action as a remedial agent; and we, therefore, urge upon all who are interested in this subject, to possess themselves of Dr. Hunt's exhaustive treatise, and to study it carefully.

If the reader will refer to the quotation made by us in the second chapter from Dr. Henry Monroe, where the food value of any article is treated of, he will see it stated that "every kind of substance employed by man as food consists of sugar, starch, oil and glutinous matter, mingled together in various proportions; these are designed for the support of the animal frame. The glutinous principles of food—fibrine, albumen and casein—are employed to build up the structure; while the oil, starch and sugar are chiefly used to generate heat in the body."

Now, it is clear, that if alcohol is a food, it will be found to contain one or more of these substances. There must be in it either the nitrogenous elements found chiefly in meats, eggs, milk, vegetables and seeds, out of which animal tissue is built and waste repaired; or the carbonaceous elements found in fat, starch and sugar, in the consumption of which heat and force are evolved.

"The distinctness of these groups of foods," says Dr. Hunt, "and their relations to the tissue-producing and heat-evolving capacities of man, are so definite and so confirmed by experiments on animals and by manifold tests of scientific, physiological and clinical experience, that no attempt to discard the classification has prevailed. To draw so straight a line of demarcation as to limit the one entirely to tissue or cell production, and the other to heat and force production through ordinary combustion, and to deny any power of interchangeability under special demands or amid defective supply of one variety, is, indeed, untenable. This does not in the least invalidate the fact that we are able to use these as ascertained landmarks."

How these substances, when taken into the body, are assimilated, and how they generate force, are well known to the chemist and physiologist, who is able, in the light of well-ascertained laws, to determine whether alcohol does or does not possess a food value. For years, the ablest men in the medical profession have given this subject the most careful study, and have subjected alcohol to every known test and experiment, and the result is that it has been, by common consent, excluded from the class of tissue-building foods. "We have never," says Dr. Hunt, "seen but a single suggestion that it could so act, and this a promiscuous guess. One writer (Hammond) thinks it possible that it may 'somehow' enter into combination with the products of decay in tissues, and 'under certain circumstances might yield *their* nitrogen to the construction of new tissues.' No parallel in organic chemistry, nor any evidence in animal chemistry, can be found to surround this guess with the areola of a possible hypothesis."

Dr. Richardson says: "Alcohol contains no nitrogen; it has none of the qualities of structure-building foods; it is incapable of being transformed into any of them; it is, therefore, not a food in any sense of its being a constructive agent in building up the body." Dr. W. B. Carpenter says: "Alcohol cannot supply anything which is essential to the true nutrition of the tissues." Dr. Liebig says: "Beer, wine, spirits, etc., furnish no element capable of entering into the composition of the blood, muscular fibre, or any part which is the seat of the principle of life." Dr. Hammond, in his Tribune Lectures, in which he advocates the use of alcohol in certain cases, says: "It is not demonstrable that alcohol undergoes conversion into tissue." Cameron, in his Manuel of Hygiene, says: "There is nothing in alcohol with which any part of the body can be nourished." Dr. E. Smith, F. R. S., says: "Alcohol is not a true food. It interferes with alimentation." Dr. T. K. Chambers says: "It is clear that we must cease to regard alcohol, as in any sense, a food."

"Not detecting in this substance," says Dr. Hunt, "any tissue-making ingredients, nor in its breaking up any combinations, such as we are able to trace in the cell foods, nor any evidence either in the experience of physiologists or the trials of alimentarians, it is not wonderful that in it we should find neither the expectancy nor the realization of constructive power."

Not finding in alcohol anything out of which the body can be built up or its waste supplied, it is next to be examined as to its heat-producing quality.

ALCOHOL NOT A PRODUCER OF HEAT.

"The first usual test for a force-producing food," says Dr. Hunt, "and that to which other foods of that class respond, is the production of heat in the combination of oxygen therewith. This heat means vital force, and is, in no small degree, a measure of the comparative value of the so-called respiratory foods. * * * If we examine the fats, the starches and the sugars, we can trace and estimate the processes by which they evolve heat and are changed into vital force, and can weigh the capacities of different foods. We find that the consumption of carbon by union with oxygen is the law, that heat is the product, and that the legitimate result is force, while the result of the union of the hydrogen of the foods with oxygen is water. If alcohol comes at all under this class of foods, we rightly expect to find some of the evidences which attach to the hydrocarbons."

What, then, is the result of experiments in this direction? They have been conducted through long periods and with the greatest care, by men of the highest attainments in chemistry and physiology, and the result is given in these few words, by Dr.

H. R. Wood, Jr., in his Materi Medica. "No one has been able to detect in the blood any of the ordinary results of its oxidation." That is, no one has been able to find that alcohol has undergone combustion, like fat, or starch, or sugar, and so given heat to the body. On the contrary, it is now known and admitted by the medical profession that

ALCOHOL REDUCES THE TEMPERATURE OF THE BODY,

instead of increasing it; and it has even been used in fevers as an anti-pyretic. So uniform has been the testimony of physicians in Europe and this country as to the cooling effects of alcohol, that Dr. Wood says, in his Materia Medica, "that it does not seem worth while to occupy space with a discussion of the subject." Liebermeister, one of the most learned contributors to Zeimssen's Cyclopædia of the Practice of Medicine, 1875, says: "I long since convinced myself, by direct experiments, that alcohol, even in comparatively large doses, does not elevate the temperature of the body in either well or sick people." So well had this become known to Arctic voyagers, that, even before physiologists had demonstrated the fact that alcohol reduced, instead of increasing, the temperature of the body, they had learned that spirits lessened their power to withstand extreme cold. "In the Northern regions," says Edward Smith, "it was proved that the entire exclusion of spirits was necessary, in order to retain heat under these unfavorable conditions."

ALCOHOL DOES NOT GIVE STRENGTH.

If alcohol does not contain tissue-building material, nor give heat to the body, it cannot possibly add to its strength. "Every kind of power an animal can generate," says Dr. G. Budd, F. R. S., "the mechanical power of the muscles, the chemical (or digestive) power of the stomach, the intellectual power of the brain—accumulates *through the nutrition of the organ* on which it depends.' Dr. F. R. Lees, of Edinburgh, after discussing the question, and educing evidence, remarks: "From the very nature of things, it will now be seen how *impossible* it is that alcohol can be strengthening food of either kind. Since it cannot become a *part* of the body, it cannot consequently contribute to its cohesive, organic strength, or fixed power; and, since it comes out of the body just as it went in, it cannot, by its decomposition, generate *heat*-force."

Sir Benjamin Brodie says: "Stimulants do not create nervous power; they merely enable you, as it were, to *use up* that which is left, and then they leave you more in need of rest than before."

Baron Liebig, so far back as 1843, in his "Animal Chemistry," pointed out the fallacy of alcohol generating power. He says: "The circulation will appear accelerated at the expense of the force available for voluntary motion, but without the production of a greater amount of mechanical force." In his later "Letters," he again says: "Wine is quite superfluous to man, * * * it is constantly followed by the expenditure of power"—whereas, the real function of food is to give power. He adds: "These drinks promote the change of matter in the body, and are, consequently, attended by an inward loss of power, which ceases to be productive, because it is not employed in overcoming outward difficulties— *i. e.*, in working." In other words, this great chemist asserts that alcohol abstracts the power of the system from doing useful work in the field or workshop, in order to cleanse the house from the defilement of alcohol itself.

The late Dr. W. Brinton, Physician to St. Thomas', in his great work on Dietetics, says: "Careful observation leaves little doubt that a moderate dose of beer or wine would, in most cases, at once diminish the maximum weight which a healthy person could lift. Mental acuteness, accuracy of perception and delicacy of the senses are all so far opposed by alcohol, as that the maximum efforts of each are incompatible with the ingestion of any moderate quantity of fermented liquid. A single glass will often suffice to take the edge off both mind and body, and to reduce their capacity to something below their perfection of work."

Dr. F. R. Lees, F. S. A., writing on the subject of alcohol as a food, makes the following quotation from an essay on "Stimulating Drinks," published by Dr. H. R. Madden, as long ago as 1847: "Alcohol is not the natural stimulus to any of our organs, and hence, functions performed in consequence of its application, tend to debilitate the organ acted upon.

"Alcohol is incapable of being assimilated or converted into any organic proximate principle, and hence, cannot be considered nutritious.

"The strength experienced after the use of alcohol is not new strength added to the system, but is manifested by calling into exercise the nervous energy pre-existing.

"The ultimate exhausting effects of alcohol, owing to its stimulant properties, produce an unnatural susceptibility to morbid action in all the organs, and this, with the plethora superinduced, becomes a fertile source of disease.

"A person who habitually exerts himself to such an extent as to require the daily use of stimulants to ward off exhaustion, may be compared to a machine working under high pressure. He will become much more obnoxious to the causes of disease, and will certainly break down sooner than he would have done under more favorable circumstances.

"The more frequently alcohol is had recourse to for the purpose of overcoming feelings of debility, the more it will be required, and by constant repetition a period is at length reached when it cannot be foregone, unless reaction is simultaneously brought about by a temporary total change of the habits of life.

"Owing to the above facts, I conclude that the DAILY USE OF STIMULANTS IS INDEFENSIBLE UNDER ANY KNOWN CIRCUMSTANCES."

DRIVEN TO THE WALL.

Not finding that alcohol possesses any direct alimentary value, the medical advocates of its use have been driven to the assumption that it is a kind of secondary food, in that it has the power to delay the metamorphosis of tissue "By the metamorphosis of tissue is meant," says Dr. Hunt, "that change which is constantly going on in the system which involves a constant disintegration of material; a breaking up and avoiding of that which is no longer aliment, making room for that new supply which is to sustain life." Another medical writer, in referring to this metamorphosis, says: "The importance of this process to the maintenance of life is readily shown by the injurious effects which follow upon its disturbance. If the discharge of the excrementitious substances be in any way impeded or suspended, these substances accumulate either in the blood or tissues, or both. In consequence of this retention and accumulation they become poisonous, and rapidly produce a derangement of the vital functions. Their influence is principally exerted upon the nervous system, through which they produce most frequent irritability, disturbance of the special senses, delirium, insensibility, coma, and finally, death."

"This description," remarks Dr. Hunt, "seems almost intended for alcohol." He then says: "To claim alcohol as a food because it delays the metamorphosis of tissue, is to claim that it in some way suspends the normal conduct of the laws of assimilation and nutrition, of waste and repair. A leading advocate of alcohol (Hammond) thus illustrates it: 'Alcohol retards the destruction of the tissues. By this destruction, force is generated, muscles contract, thoughts are developed, organs secrete and excrete.' In other words, alcohol interferes with all these. No wonder the author 'is not clear' how it does this, and we are not clear how such delayed metamorphosis recuperates. To take an agent which is

NOT KNOWN TO BE IN ANY SENSE AN ORIGINATOR OF VITAL FORCE;

which is not known to have any of the usual power of foods, and use it on the double assumption that it delays metamorphosis of tissue, and that such delay is conservative of health, is to pass outside of the bounds of science into the land of remote possibilities, and confer the title of adjuster upon an agent whose agency is itself doubtful. * * * *

"Having failed to identify alcohol as a nitrogenous or non-nitrogenous food, not having found it amenable to any of the evidences by which the food-force of aliments is generally measured, it will not do for us to talk of benefit by delay of regressive metamorphosis unless such process is accompanied with something evidential of the fact—something scientifically descriptive of its mode of accomplishment in the case at hand, and unless it is shown to be practically desirable for alimentation.

"There can be no doubt that alcohol does cause

defects in the processes of elimination which are natural to the healthy body and which even in disease are often conservative of health. In the pent-in evils which pathology so often shows occurrent in the case of spirit-drinkers, in the vascular, fatty and fibroid degenerations which take place, in the accumulations of rheumatic and scrofulous tendencies, there is the strongest evidence that

ALCOHOL ACTS AS A DISTURBING ELEMENT

and is very prone to initiate serious disturbances amid the normal conduct both of organ and function.

"To assert that this interference is conservative in the midst of such a fearful accumulation of evidence as to result in quite the other direction, and that this kind of delay in tissue-change accumulates vital force, is as unscientific as it is paradoxical.

"Dickinson, in his able expose of the effects of alcohol, (*Lancet*, Nov., 1872,) confines himself to pathological facts. After recounting, with accuracy, the structural changes which it initiates, and the structural changes and consequent derangement and suspension of vital functions which it involves, he aptly terms it the 'genius of degeneration.'

"With abundant provision of indisputable foods, select that liquid which has failed to command the general assent of experts that it is a food at all, and because it is claimed to diminish some of the excretions, call that a delay of metamorphosis of tissue conservative of health! The ostrich may bury his head in the sand, but science will not close its eyes before such impalpable dust."

Speaking of this desperate effort to claim alcohol as a food, Dr. N. S. Davis well says: "It seems hardly possible that men of eminent attainments in the profession should so far forget one of the most fundamental and universally recognized laws of organic life as to promulgate the fallacy here stated. The fundamental law to which we allude is, that all vital phenomena are accompanied by, and dependent on, molecular or atomic changes; and whatever retards these retards the phenomena of life; whatever suspends these suspends life. Hence, to say that an agent which retards tissue metamorphosis is in any sense a food, is simply to pervert and misapply terms."

Well may the author of the paper from which we have quoted so freely, exclaim: "Strangest ot foods! most impalpable of aliments! defying all the research of animal chemistry, tasking all the ingenuity of experts in hypothetical explanations, registering its effects chiefly by functional disturbance and organic lesions, causing its very defenders as a food to stultify themselves when in fealty to facts they are compelled to disclose its destructions, and to find the only defense in that line of demarcation, more imaginary than the equator, more delusive than the mirage, between use and abuse."

That alcohol is not a food in any sense, has been fully shown; and now,

WHAT IS ITS VALUE AS A MEDICINE?

Our reply to this question will be brief. The reader has, already, the declaration of the International Medical Congress, that, as a medicine, the range of alcohol is limited and doubtful, and that its self-prescription by the laity should be utterly discountenanced by the profession. No physician who has made himself thoroughly acquainted with the effects of alcohol when introduced into the blood and brought in contact with the membranes, nerves and organs of the human body, would now venture to prescribe its free use to consumptives as was done a very few years ago.

"In the whole management of lung diseases," remarks Dr. Hunt, "with the exception of the few who can always be relied upon to befriend alcohol, other remedies have largely superseded all spirituous liquors. Its employment in stomach disease, once so popular, gets no encouragement, from a careful examination of its local and constitutional effects, as separated from the water, sugar and acids imbibed with it."

TYPHOID FEVER.

It is in typhoid fever that alcohol has been used, perhaps, most frequently by the profession; but this use is now restricted, and the administration made with great caution. Prof. A. L. Loomis, of New

York City, has published several lectures on the pathology and treatment of typhoid fever. Referring thereto, Dr. Hunt says: "No one in our country can speak more authoritatively, and as he has no radical views as to the exclusion of alcohol, it is worth while to notice the place to which he assigns it. In the milder cases he entirely excludes it. As a means of reducing temperature, he does not mention it, but relies on cold, quinine, and sometimes, digitalis and quinine." When, about the third week, signs of failure of heart-power begin to manifest themselves, and the use of some form of stimulant seems to be indicated, Dr. Loomis gives the most guarded advice as to their employment. "Never," he says, "give a patient stimulants simply because he has typhoid fever." And again, "Where there is reasonable doubt as to the propriety of giving or withholding stimulants, it is safer to withhold them." He then insists that, if stimulants are administered, the patient should be visited every two hours to watch their effects.

It will thus be seen how guarded has now become the use of alcohol as a cardiac stimulant in typhoid fevers, where it was once employed with an almost reckless freedom. Many practitioners have come to exclude it altogether, and to rely wholly on ammonia, ether and foods.

In Cameron's "Hygiene" is this sentence: "In candor, it must be admitted that many eminent physicians deny the efficacy of alcohol in the treatment of any kind of disease, *and some assert that it is worse than useless.*"

ACCUMULATIVE TESTIMONY.

Dr. Arnold Lees, F. L. S., in a recent paper on the "Use and Action of Alcohol in Disease," assumes "*that the old use of alcohol was not science, but a grave blunder.*" Prof. C. A. Parks says: "It is impossible not to feel that, so far, the progress of physiological inquiry renders the use of alcohol (in medicine) more and more doubtful." Dr. Anstie says: "If alcohol is to be administered at all for the *relief* of neuralgia, it should be given with as much precision, as to dose, as we should use in giving an acknowledged *deadly poison.*" Dr. F. T. Roberts, an eminent English physician, in advocating a guarded use of alcohol in typhoid fever, says: "Alcoholic stimulants are, by no means, always required, and their indiscriminate use may do a great deal of harm." In Asiatic cholera, brandy was formerly administered freely to patients when in the stage of collapse. The effect was injurious, instead of beneficial. "Again and again," says Prof. G. Johnson, "have I seen a patient grow colder, and his pulse diminish in volume and power, after a dose of brandy, and, apparently, as a direct result of the brandy." And Dr. Pidduck, of London, who used common salt in cholera treatment, says: "Of eighty-six cases in the stage of collapse, sixteen only proved fatal, and scarcely one would have died, *if I had been able to prevent them from taking brandy and laudanum.*" Dr. Collenette, of Guernsey, says: "For more than thirty years I have abandoned the use of all kinds of alcoholic drinks in my practice, and with such good results, that, were I sick, *nothing* would induce *me* to have resource to them—*they are but noxious depressants.*"

As a non-professional writer, we cannot go beyond the medical testimony which has been educed, and we now leave it with the reader. We could add many pages to this testimony, but such cumulative evidence would add but little to its force with the reader. If he is not yet convinced that alcohol has no food value, and that, as a medicine, its range is exceedingly limited, and always of doubtful administration, nothing further that we might be able to cite or say could have any influence with him.

CHAPTER VI.

THE GROWTH AND POWER OF APPETITE.

ONE fact attendant on habitual drinking stands out so prominently that none can call it in question. It is that of the steady growth of appetite. There are exceptions, as in the action of nearly every rule; but the almost invariable result of the habit we have mentioned, is, as we have said, a steady growth of appetite for the stimulant imbibed. That this is in consequence of certain morbid changes in the physical condition produced by the alcohol itself, will hardly be questioned by any one who has made himself acquainted with the various functional and organic derangements which invariably follow the continued introduction of this substance into the body.

But it is to the fact itself, not to its cause, that we now wish to direct the reader's attention. The man who is satisfied at first with a single glass of wine at dinner, finds, after awhile, that appetite asks for a little more; and, in time, a second glass is conceded. The increase of desire may be very slow, but it goes on surely until, in the end, a whole bottle will scarcely suffice, with far too many, to meet its imperious demands. It is the same in regard to the use of every other form of alcoholic drink.

Now, there are men so constituted that they are able, for a long series of years, or even for a whole lifetime, to hold this appetite within a certain limit of indulgence. To say "So far, and no farther." They suffer ultimately from physical ailments, which surely follow the prolonged contact of alcoholic poison with the delicate structures of the body, many of a painful character, and shorten the term of their natural lives; but still they are able to drink without an increase of appetite so great as to reach an overmastering degree. They do not become abandoned drunkards.

NO MAN SAFE WHO DRINKS.

But no man who begins the use of alcohol in any form can tell what, in the end, is going to be its effect on his body or mind. Thousands and tens of thousands, once wholly unconscious of danger from this source, go down yearly into drunkards' graves. There is no standard by which any one can measure the latent evil forces in his inherited nature. He may have from ancestors, near or remote, an unhealthy moral tendency, or physical diathesis, to which the peculiarly disturbing influence of alcohol will give the morbid condition in which it will find its disastrous life. That such results follow the use of alcohol in a large number of cases, is now a well-known fact in the history of inebriation. During the past few years, the subject of alcoholism, with the mental and moral causes leading thereto, have attracted a great deal of earnest attention. Physicians, superintendents of inebriate and lunatic asylums, prison-keepers, legislators and philanthropists have been observing and studying its many sad and terrible phases, and recording results and opinions. While differences are held on some points, as, for instance, whether drunkenness is a disease for which, after it has been established, the individual ceases to be responsible, and should be subject to restraint and treatment, as for lunacy or fever; a crime to be punished; or a sin to be repented of and healed by the Physician of souls, all agree that there is an inherited or acquired mental and nervous condition with many, which renders any use of alcohol exceedingly dangerous.

The point we wish to make with the reader is, that no man can possibly know, until he has used alcoholic drinks for a certain period of time, whether he has or has not this hereditary or acquired physical or mental condition; and that, if it should exist, a discovery of the fact may come too late.

Dr. D. G. Dodge, late Superintendent of the New York State Inebriate Asylum, speaking of the causes leading to intemperance, after stating his belief that it is a transmissible disease, like "scrofula, gout or consumption," says:

"There are men who have an organization, which may be termed an alcoholic idiosyncrasy; with them the latent desire for stimulants, if indulged, soon leads to habits of intemperance, and eventually to a morbid appetite, which has all the characteristics of a diseased condition of the system, which the patient, unassisted, is powerless to relieve—since the weakness of the will that led to the disease obstructs its removal.

"Again, we find in another class of persons, those who have had healthy parents, and have been educated and accustomed to good social influences, moral and social, but whose temperament and physical constitution are such, that, when they once indulge in the use of stimulants, which they find pleasurable, they continue to habitually indulge till they cease to be moderate, and become excessive drinkers. A depraved appetite is established, that leads them on slowly, but surely, to destruction."

A DANGEROUS DELUSION.

In this chapter, our chief purpose is to show the growth and awful power of an appetite which begins striving for the mastery the moment it is indulged, and against the encroachments of which no man who gives it any indulgence is absolutely safe. He who so regards himself is resting in a most dangerous delusion. So gradually does it increase, that few observe its steady accessions of strength until it has acquired the power of a master. Dr. George M. Burr, in a paper on the pathology of drunkenness, read before the "American Association for the Cure of Inebriates," says, in referring to the first indications of an appetite, which he considers one of the symptoms of a forming disease, says: "This early stage is marked by an occasional desire to drink, which recurs at shorter and shorter intervals, and a propensity, likewise, gradually increasing for a greater quantity at each time. This stage has long been believed to be one of voluntary indulgence, for which the subject of it was morally responsible. The drinker has been held as criminal for his occasional indulgence, and his example has been most severely censured. This habit, however, must be regarded as the first intimation of the approaching disease—the stage of invasion, precisely as sensations of *mal-aise* and chills usher in a febrile attack.

"It is by no means claimed that in this stage the subject is free from responsibility as regards the consequences of his acts, or that his case is to be looked upon as beyond all attempts at reclamation. Quite to the contrary. This is the stage for active interference. Restraint, prohibition, quarantine, anything may be resorted to, to arrest the farther advance of the disease. Instead of being taught that the habit of occasional drinking is merely a moral *lapsus* (not the most powerful restraining motive always), the subject of it should be made to understand that it is the commencement of a malady, which, if unchecked, will overwhelm him in ruin, and, compared with which, cholera and yellow fever are harmless. He should be impressed with the fact that the early stage is the one when recuperation is most easy—that the will then has not lost its power of control, and that the fatal propensity is not incurable. The duty of prevention, or avoidance, should be enforced with as much earnestness and vigor as we are required to carry out sanitary measures against the spread of small-pox or any infectious disease. The subject of inebriety may be justly held responsible, if he neglects all such efforts, and allows the disease to progress without a struggle to arrest it.

"The formative stage of inebriety continues for a longer or shorter period, when, as is well known, more frequent repetitions of the practice of drinking are to be observed. The impulse to drink grows stronger and stronger, the will-power is overthrown and the entire organism becomes subject to the fearful demands for stimulus. It is now that the stage of confirmed inebriation is formed, and *dypso-mania* fully established. The constant introduction of alcohol into the system, circulating with the fluids and permeating the tissues, adds fuel to the already enkindled flame, and intensifies the propensity to an irresistible degree. Nothing now satisfies short of complete intoxication, and, until the unhappy subject of the disease falls senseless and completely overcome, will he cease his efforts to gratify this most insatiable desire."

Dr. Alexander Peddie, of Edinburgh, who has given twenty years of study to this subject, remarked, in his testimony before a Committee of the House of Commons, that there seemed to be "a peculiar elective affinity for the action of alcohol on the nervous system after it had found its way through the circulation into the brain," by which the whole organism was disturbed, and the man rendered less able to resist morbid influences of any kind. He gave many striking instances of the growth and power of appetite, which had come under his professional notice, and of the ingenious devices and desperate resorts to which dypsomaniacs were driven in their efforts to satisfy their inordinate cravings. No consideration, temporal or spiritual, had any power to restrain their appetite, if, by any means, fair or foul, they could obtain alcoholic stimulants. To get this, he said, the unhappy subject of this terrible thirst " will tell the most shameful lies—for no truth is ever found in connection with the habitual drunkard's state. He never yet saw truth in relation to drink got out of one who was a dysomaniac—he has sufficient reason left to tell these untruths, and to understand his position, because people in that condition are seldom dead drunk; they are seldom in the condition of total stupidity; they have generally an eye open to their own affairs, and that which is the main business of their existence, namely, how to get drink. They will resort to the most ingenious, mean and degrading contrivances and practices to procure and conceal liquor, and this, too, while closely watched; and will succeed in deception, although fabulous quantities are daily swallowed."

Dr. John Nugent gives a case which came within his own knowledge, of a lady who had been

' A MOST EXEMPLARY NUN

for fifteen or twenty years. In consequence of her devotion to the poor, attending them in fevers, and like cases, it seemed necessary for her to take stimulants; these stimulants grew to be habitual, and she had been compelled, five or six times, to place herself in a private asylum. In three or four weeks after being let out, she would relapse, although she was believed to be under the strongest influences of religion, and of the most virtuous desires. There had been developed in her that disposition to drink which she was unable to overcome or control.

The power of this appetite, and the frightful moral perversions that often follow its indulgence are vividly portrayed in the following extract, from an address by Dr. Elisha Harris, of New York, in which he discusses the question of the criminality of drunkenness.

"Let the fact be noticed that such is the lethargy which alcoholism produces upon reason and conscience, that it is sometimes necessary to bring the offender to view his drunken indulgence as a crime. We have known a refined and influential citizen to be so startled at the fact that he wished to destroy the lives of all persons, even of his own family, who manifested unhappiness at his intemperance, that seeing this terrible criminality of his indulgence, instantly formed, and has forever kept, his resolutions of abstinence. We have known the hereditary dypsomaniac break from his destroyer, and when tempted in secret by the monstrous appetite, so grind his teeth and clinch his jaws in keeping his vows to taste not, that blood dripped from his mouth and cold sweat bathed his face. That man is a model of temperance and moral power to-day. And it was the consciousness of personal criminality that stimulated these successful conflicts with the morbid appetite and the powers of the alcohol disease that had fastened upon them. Shall we hesitate to hold ourselves, or to demand that communities shall hold every drunkard—not yet insane—responsible for every act of inebriety? Certainly, it is not cruel or unjust to deal thus with drunkenness. It is not the prison we open, but conscience."

The danger in which those stand who have an

INHERITED PREDISPOSITION TO DRINK,

is very great. Rev. I. Willett, Superintendent of the Inebriate's Home, Fort Hamilton, Kings County, New York, thus refers to this class, which is larger than many think: "There are a host of living men and women to be found who never drank, and who dare not drink, intoxicating liquors or beverages, because one or both of their parents were inebriates before they were born into the world; and, besides, a number of these have brothers or sisters who, having given way to the inherited appetite, are now passing downward on this descending sliding scale. The greater portion of them have already passed over the bounds of self-control, and the varied preliminary symptoms of melancholy, mania, paralysis, ideas of persecution, etc., etc., are developing. As to the question of responsibility, each case is either more or less doubtful, and can only be tested on its separate merits. There is, however, abundant evidence to prove that this predisposition to inebriety, even after long indulgence, can, by a skillful process of medication, accompanied by either voluntary or compulsory restraint, be subdued; and the counterbalancing physical and mental powers can at the same time be so strengthened and invigorated as in the future to enable the person to resist the temptations by which he may be surrounded. Yea, though the powers of reason may, for the time being, be dethroned, and lunacy be developed, these cases, in most instances, will yield to medical treatment where the surrounding conditions of restraint and careful nursing are supplemental.

"We have observed that in many instances the fact of the patient being convinced that he is an hereditary inebriate, has produced beneficial results. Summoning to his aid all the latent counterbalancing energies which he has at command, and clothing himself with this armor, he goes forth to war, throws up the fortifications of physical and mental restraint, repairs the breaches and inroads of diseased appetite, regains control of the citadel of the brain, and then, with shouts of triumph, he unfurls the banner of 'VICTORY!'"

Dr. Wood, of London, in his work on insanity, speaking on the subject of hereditary inebriety, says:

"Instances are sufficiently familiar, and several have occurred within my own personal knowledge, where the father, having died at any early age from the effects of intemperance, has left a son to be brought up by those who have severely suffered from his excesses, and have therefore the strongest motives to prevent, if possible, a repetition of such misery; every pains has been taken to enforce sobriety, and yet, notwithstanding all precautions, the habits of the father have become those of the son, who, never having seen him from infancy, could not have adopted them from imitation. Everything was done to encourage habits of temperance, but all to no purpose; the seeds of the disease had begun to germinate; a blind impulse led the doomed individual, by successive and rapid strides, along the same course which was fatal to the father, and which, ere long, terminated in his own destruction."

How great and fearful the power of an appetite which cannot only enslave and curse the man over which it gains control, but send its malign influence down to the second and third and fourth generations, sometimes to the absolute

EXTINGUISHMENT OF FAMILIES!

Morel, a Frenchman, gives the following as the result of his observation of the hereditary effects of drunkenness:

"*First generation:* Immorality, depravity, excess in the use of alcoholic liquors, moral debasement. *Second generation:* Hereditary drunkenness, paroxysms of mania, general paralysis. *Third generation:* Sobriety, hypochondria, melancholy, systematic ideas of being persecuted, homicidal tendencies. *Fourth generation:* Intelligence slightly developed, first accessions of mania at sixteen years of age, stupidity, subsequent idiocy and probable extinction of family."

Dr. T. D. Crothers, in an analysis of the hundred cases of inebriety received at the New York Inebriate Asylum, gives this result: "Inebriety inherited direct from parents was traced in twenty-one cases. In eleven of these the father drank alone, in six instances the mother drank, and in four cases both parents drank.

"In thirty-three cases inebriety was traced to ancestors more remote, as grandfather, grandmother, etc., etc., the collateral branches exhibiting both inebriety and insanity. In some instances a whole generation had been passed over, and the disorders of the grandparents appeared again.

"In twenty cases various neurosal disorders had been prominent in the family and its branches, of which neuralgia, chorea, hysteria, eccentricity, mania, epilepsy and inebriety, were most common.

"In some cases, a wonderful periodicity in the outbreak of these disorders was manifested.

"For instance, in one family, for two generations, inebriety appeared in seven out of twelve members, after they had passed forty, and ended fatally within ten years. In another, hysteria, chorea, epilepsy and mania, with drunkenness, came on soon after puberty, and seemed to deflect to other disorders, or exhaust itself before middle life. This occurred in eight out of fourteen, extending over two generations. In another instance, the descendants of three generations, and many of the collateral branches, developed inebriety, mental eccentricities, with other disorders bordering on mania, at about thirty-five years of age. In some cases this lasted only a few years, in others a lifetime."

And here let us say that in this matter of an inherited appetite there is a difference of views with some who believe that appetite is never transmitted but always acquired. This difference of view is more apparent than real. It is not the drunkard's appetite that is transmitted, but the bias or proclivity which renders the subject of such an inherited tendency more susceptible to exciting causes, and therefore in greater danger from the use of alcoholic drinks than others.

Dr. N. S. Davis, in an article in the *Washingtonian,* published at Chicago, presents the opposite view of the case. The following extract from this article is well worthy to be read and considered:

"If we should say that man is so constituted that he is capable of feeling weary, restless, despondent and anxious, and that he instinctively desires to be relieved of these unpleasant feelings, we should assert a self-evident fact. And we should thereby assert all the instincts or natural impulse there is in the matter. It is simply a desire to be relieved from unpleasant feelings, and does not, in the slightest degree, indicate or suggest any particular remedy. It no more actually suggests the idea of alcohol or opium than it does bread and water. But if, by accident, or by the experience of others, the individual has learned that his unpleasant feelings can be relieved, for the time being, by alcohol, opium or any other exhilarant, he not only uses the remedy himself, but perpetuates a knowledge of the same to others. It is in this way, and this only, that most of the nations and tribes of our race, have, much to their detriment, found a knowledge of some kind of intoxicant. The same explanation is applicable to the supposed 'constitutional susceptibility,' as a primary cause of intemperance. That some persons inherit a greater degree of nervous and organic susceptibility than others, and are, in consequence of this greater susceptibility, more readily affected by a given quantity of narcotic, anæsthetic or intoxicant, is undoubtedly true. And that such will

MORE READILY BECOME DRUNKARDS,

if they once commence to use intoxicating drinks, is also true. But that such persons, or any others, have the slightest inherent or constitutional taste or any longing for intoxicants, until they have acquired such taste or longing by actual use, we find no reliable proof. It is true that statistics appear to show that a larger proportion of the children of drunkards become themselves drunkards, than of children born of total abstainers. And hence the conclusion has been drawn that such children INHERITED the constitutional tendency to inebriation. But before we are justified in adopting such a conclusion, several other important facts must be ascertained.

"1st. We must know whether the mother, while nursing, used more or less constantly some kind of alcoholic beverage, by which the alcohol might have impregnated the milk in her breasts and thereby made its early impression on the tastes and longings of the child.

"2d. We must know whether the intemperate parents were in the habit of frequently giving alcoholic preparations to the children, either to relieve temporary ailments, or for the same reason that they drank it themselves. I am constrained to say, that from my own observation, extending over a period of forty years, and a field by no means limited, I am satisfied that nineteen out of every twenty persons who have been regarded as HEREDITARY inebriates have simply ACQUIRED the disposition to drink by one or both of the methods just mentioned, after birth."

The views here presented in no way lessen but really heighten the perils of moderate drinking. It is affirmed that some persons inherit a greater degree of nervous and organic susceptibility than others, and are, in consequence, more readily affected by a given quantity of narcotic, anæsthetic or intoxicant; *and that such " will more readily become drunkards if they commence to use intoxicating drinks."*

Be the cause of this

INHERITED NERVOUS SUSCEPTIBILITY

what it may, and it is far more general than is to be inferred from the admission just quoted, the fact stands forth as a solemn warning of the peril every man encounters in even the most moderate use of alcohol. Speaking of this matter, Dr. George M. Beard, who is not as sound on the liquor question as we could wish, says, in an article on the " Causes of the Recent Increase of Inebriety in America:" "As a means of prevention, abstinence from the *habit* of drinking is to be enforced. Such abstinence may not have been necessary for our fathers, but it is rendered necessary for a large body of the American people on account of our greater nervous susceptibility. It is possible to drink without being an habitual drinker, as it is possible to take chloral or opium without forming the habit of taking these substances. In certain countries and climates where the nervous system is strong and the temperature more equable than with us, in what I sometimes call the temperate belt of the world, including Spain, Italy, Southern France, Syria and Persia, the habitual use of wine rarely leads to drunkenness, and never, or almost never, to inebriety; but in the intemperate belt, where we live, and which includes Northern Europe and the United States, with a cold and violently changeable climate, the habit of drinking either wines or stronger liquors is liable to develop in some cases a habit of intemperance. Notably in our country, where nervous sensitiveness is seen in its extreme manifestations, the majority of brain-workers are not safe so long as they are in the habit of even moderate drinking. I admit that this was not the case one hundred years ago—and the reasons I have already given—it is not the case to-day in Continental Europe; even in England it is not so markedly the case as in the northern part of the United States. *For those individuals who inherit a tendency to inebriety, the only safe course is absolute abstinence, especially in early life.*"

In the same article, Dr. Baird remarks: "The number of those in this country who cannot bear tea, coffee or alcoholic liquors of any kind, is very large. There are many, especially in the Northern

States, who must forego coffee entirely, and use tea only with caution; either, in any excess, cause trembling nerves and sleepless nights. The susceptibility to alcohol is so marked, with many persons, that no pledges, and no medical advice, and no moral or legal influences are needed to keep them in the paths of temperance. *Such persons are warned by flushing of the face, or by headache, that alcohol, whatever it may be to others, or whatever it may have been to their ancestors, is poison to them.*"

But, in order to give a higher emphasis to precepts, admonition and medical testimony, we offer a single example of the enslaving power of appetite, when, to a predisposing hereditary tendency, the excitement of indulgence has been added. The facts of this case were communicated to us by a professional gentleman connected with one of our largest inebriate asylums, and we give them almost in his very words in which they were related.

A REMARKABLE CASE.

A clever, but dissipated actor married clandestinely a farmer's daughter in the State of New York. The parents of the girl would not recognize him as the husband of their child; rejecting him so utterly that he finally left the neighborhood. A son born of this marriage gave early evidence of great mental activity, and was regarded, in the college where he graduated, as almost a prodigy of learning. He carried off many prizes, and distinguished himself as a brilliant orator. Afterwards he went to Princeton and studied for the ministry. While there, it was discovered that he was secretly drinking. The faculty did everything in their power to help and restrain him; and his co-operation with them was earnest as to purpose, but not permanently availing. The nervous susceptibility inherited from his father responded with a morbid quickness to every exciting cause, and the moment wine or spirits touched the sense of smell or taste, he was seized with an almost irresistible desire to drink to excess, and too often yielded to its demands. For months he would abstain entirely; and then drink to intoxication in secret.

After graduating from Princeton he became pastor of a church in one of the largest cities of Western New York, where he remained for two years, distinguishing himself for his earnest work and fervid eloquence. But the appetite he had formed was imperious in its demands, and periodically became so strong that he lost the power of resistance. When these periodic assaults of appetite came, he would

LOCK HIMSELF IN HIS ROOM FOR DAYS

and satiate the fierce thirst, coming out sick and exhausted. It was impossible to conceal from his congregation the dreadful habit into which he had fallen, and ere two years had elapsed he was dismissed for drunkenness. He then went to one of the chief cities of the West, where he received a call, and was, for a time, distinguished as a preacher; but again he fell into disgrace and had to leave his charge. Two other churches called him to fill the office of pastor, but the same sad defections from sobriety followed. For a considerable time after this his friends lost sight of him. Then he was found in the streets of New York City by the president of the college from which he had first graduated, wretched and debased from drink, coatless and hatless. His old friend took him to a hotel, and then brought his case to the notice of the people at a prayer-meeting held in the evening at one of the churches. His case was immediately taken in hand and money raised to send him to the State Inebriate Asylum. After he had remained there for a year, he began to preach as a supply in a church a few miles distant, going on Saturday evening and returning on Monday morning; but always having an attendant with him, not daring to trust himself alone. This went on for nearly a whole year, when a revival sprang up in the church, which he conducted with great eloquence and fervor. After the second week of this new excitement, he began to lock himself up in his room after returning from the service, and could not be seen until the next morning. In the third week of the revival, the excitement of the meetings grew intense. After this he was only seen in the pulpit, where his air and manner were wild and thrilling. His friends at the asylum knew that he must be drinking, and while hesitating as to their wisest course, waited anxiously for the result. One day he was grandly eloquent. Such power in the pulpit had never been witnessed there before—his appeals were unequalled; but so wild and impassioned that some began to fear for his reason. At the close of this day's services, the chaplain of the institution of which he was an inmate, returned with him to the asylum, and on the way, told him frankly that he was deceiving the people—that his eloquent appeals came not from the power of he Holy Spirit, but from the excitement of drink; and that all farther conduct of the meetings must be left in other hands. On reaching the asylum he retired, greatly agitated, and soon after died from a stroke of apoplexy. In his room many empty bottles, which had contained brandy, were found; but the people outside remained in ignorance of the true cause of the marvelous eloquence which had so charmed and moved them.

We have already extended this chapter beyond the limit at first proposed. Our object has not only been to show the thoughtful and intelligent reader who uses alcoholic beverages, the great peril in which he stands, but to make apparent to every one, how insidious is the growth and how terrible the power of this appetite for intoxicants; an appetite which, if once established, is almost sure to rob its victim of honor, pity, tenderness and love; an appetite, whose indulgence too often transforms the man into a selfish demon. Think of it, all ye who dally with the treacherous cup; are not the risks you are running too great? Nay, considering your duties and your obligations, have you any right to run these risks?

And now that we have shown the curse of strong drink, let us see what agencies are at work in the abatement, prevention and cure of a disease that is undermining the health of whole nations, shortening the natural term of human life, and in our own country alone, sending over sixty thousand men and women annually into untimely graves.

CHAPTER VII.

MEANS OF CURE.

IS this disease, or vice, or sin, or crime of intemperance—call it by what name you will—increasing or diminishing? Has any impression been made upon it during the half-century in which there have been such earnest and untiring efforts to limit its encroachments on the health, prosperity, happiness and life of the people? What are the agencies of repression at work; how effective are they, and what is each doing?

These are questions full of momentous interest. Diseases of the body, if not cured, work a steady impairment of health, and bring pains and physical disabilities. If their assaults be upon nervous centres, or vital organs, the danger of paralysis or death becomes imminent. Now, as to this disease of intemperance, which is a social and moral as well as a physical disease, it is not to be concealed that it has invaded the common body of the people to an alarming degree, until, using the words of Holy Writ, "the whole head is sick and the whole heart faint." Nay, until, using a still stronger form of Scriptural illustration, "From the sole of the foot even unto the head, there is no soundness in it; but wounds and bruises and putrifying sores."

In this view, the inquiry as to increase or diminution, assumes the gravest importance. If, under all the agencies of cure and reform which have been in active operation during the past fifty years, no impression has been made upon this great evil which is so cursing the people, then is the case indeed desperate, if not hopeless. But if it appears that, under these varied agencies, there has been an arrest of the disease here, a limitation of its aggressive force there, its almost entire extirpation in certain cases, and a better public sentiment everywhere; then, indeed, may we take heart and say "God speed temperance work!" in all of its varied aspects.

HOPEFUL SIGNS.

And here, at the outset of our presentation of some of the leading agencies of reform and cure, let us say, that the evidence going to show that an impression has been made upon the disease is clear and indisputable; and that this impression is so marked as to give the strongest hope and assurance. In the face of prejudice, opposition, ridicule, persecution, obloquy and all manner of discouragements, the advocates of temperance have held steadily to their work these many years, and now the good results are seen on every hand. Contrast the public sentiment of to-day with that of twenty, thirty and forty years ago, and the progress becomes at once apparent. In few things is this so marked as in the changed attitude of the medical profession towards alcohol. One of the most dangerous, and, at the same time, one of the most securely intrenched of all our enemies, was the family doctor. Among his remedies and restoratives, wine, brandy, whisky and tonic ale all held a high place, and were administered more frequently, perhaps, than any other articles in the Materia Medica. The disease of his patients arrested by special remedies or broken by an effort of nature, he too often commenced the administration of alcohol in some one or more of its disguised and attractive forms, in order to give tone and stimulus to the stomach and nerves, and as a general vitalizer and restorative. The evil consequences growing out of this almost universal prescription of alcohol, were of the most lamentable character, and thousands and tens of thousands of men and women were betrayed into drunkenness. But to-day, you will not find a physician of any high repute in America or Europe who will give it to his patients, except in the most guarded manner and under the closest limitations; and he will not consent to any self-prescription whatever.

FRUITS OF TEMPERANCE WORK.

Is not this a great gain? And it has come as the result of temperance work and agitation, as Dr. Henry Monroe frankly admits in his lecture on the Physiological Action of Alcohol, where, after stating that his remarks would not partake of the character of a total abstinence lecture, but rather of a scientific inquiry into the mode of action of alcohol when introduced into the tissues of the body, he adds: "Nevertheless, I would not have it understood that I, in any way, disparage the moral efforts made by total abstainers who, years ago, amid good report and evil report, stood in the front of the battle to war against the multitude of evils occasioned by strong drink;—all praise be due to them for their noble and self-denying exertions! Had it not been for the successful labors of these moral giants in the great cause of temperance, presenting to the world in their own personal experiences many new and astounding physiological facts, *men of science would, probably, never have had their attention drawn to the topic.*"

Then, as a result of temperance work, we have a more restrictive legislation in many States, and prohibitory laws in New Hampshire, Vermont and Maine. In the State of Maine, a prohibitory law has been in operation for over twenty-six years; and so salutary has been the effect as seen in the

REDUCTION OF POVERTY, PAUPERISM AND CRIME,

that the Legislature, in January, 1877, added new and heavier penalties to the law, both Houses passing on the amendment without a dissenting voice. In all that State there is not, now, a single distillery or brewery in operation, nor a single open bar-room.

Forty years ago the pulpit was almost silent on the subject of intemperance and the liquor traffic; now, the church is fast arraying itself on the side of total abstinence and prohibition, and among its ministers are to be found many of our most active temperance workers.

Forty or fifty years ago, the etiquette of hospitality was violated if wine, or cordial, or brandy were not tendered. Nearly every sideboard had its display of decanters, well filled, and it was almost as much an offense for the guest to decline as for the host to omit the proffered glass. Even boys and girls were included in the custom; and tastes were acquired which led to drunkenness in after life. All this is changed now.

The curse of the liquor traffic is attracting, as never before, the attention of all civilized people; and national, State and local legislatures and governments are appointing commissions of inquiry, and gathering data and facts, with a view to its restriction.

And, more hopeful than all, signs are becoming more and more apparent that the people are everywhere awakening to a sense of the dangers that attend this traffic. Enlightenment is steadily progressing. Reason and judgment; common sense and prudence, are all coming to the aid of repression. Men see, as they never saw before, how utterly evil and destructive are the drinking habits of this and other nations; how they weaken the judgment and deprave the moral sense; how they not only take from every man who falls into them his ability to do his best in any pursuit or calling, but sow in his body the germs of diseases which will curse him in his later years and abridge their term.

Other evidences of the steady growth among the people of a sentiment adverse to drinking might be given. We see it in the almost feverish response that everywhere meets the strong appeals of temperance speakers, and in the more pronounced attitude taken by public and professional men.

JUDGES ON THE BENCH

and preachers from the pulpit alike lift their voices in condemnation. Grand juries repeat and repeat their presentations of liquor selling and liquor drinking as the fruitful source of more than two-thirds of the crimes and miseries that afflict the community; and prison reports add their painful emphasis to the warning of the inquest.

The people learn slowly, but they are learning. Until they *will* that this accursed traffic shall cease, it must go on with its sad and awful consequences. But the old will of the people has been debased by sensual indulgence. It is too weak to set itself against the appetite by which it has become enslaved. There must be a new will formed in the ground of enlightenment and intelligence; and then, out of knowing what is right and duty in regard to this great question of temperance and restriction, will come the will to do. And when we have this new will resting in the true enlightenment of the people, we shall have no impeded action. Whatever sets itself in opposition thereto must go down.

And for this the time is coming, though it may still be far off. Of its steady approach, the evidences are many and cheering. Meanwhile, we must work and wait. If we are not yet strong enough to drive out the enemy, we may limit his power, and do

THE WORK OF HEALING AND SAVING.

What, then, is being done in this work of healing and saving? Is there, in fact, any cure for the dreadful malady of drunkenness? Are men ever really saved from its curse? and, if so, how is it done, and what are the agencies employed?

Among the first of these to which we shall refer, is the pledge. As a means of reform and restriction, it has been used by temperance workers from the beginning, and still holds a prominent place. Seeing that only in a complete abstinence from intoxicating drinks was there any hope of rescue for the drunkard, or any security for the moderate drinker, it was felt that under a solemn pledge to wholly abstain from their use, large numbers of men would, from a sense of honor, self-respect or conscience, hold themselves free from touch or taste. In the case of moderate drinkers, with whom appetite is yet under control, the pledge has been of great value; but almost useless after appetite has gained the mastery.

In a simple pledge there is no element of self-control. If honor, self-respect or conscience, rallying to its support in the hour of temptation, be not stronger than appetite, it will be of no avail. And it too often happens that, with the poor inebriate, these have become blunted, or well-nigh extinguished. The consequence has been that where the pledge has been solely relied upon, the percentage of reform has been very small. As a first means of rescue, it is invaluable; because it is, on the part of him who takes it, a complete removal of himself from the sphere of temptation, and so long as he holds himself away from the touch and taste of liquor, he is safe. If the pledge will enable him to do this, then the pledge will save him. But it is well known, from sad experience, that only a few are saved by the pledge. The strength that saves must be something more than the external bond of a promise; it must come from within, and be grounded in a new and changed life, internally as well as externally. If the reformed man, after he takes his pledge, does not endeavor to lead a better moral life—does not keep himself away from old debasing associations—does not try, earnestly and persistently, to become, in all things,

A TRUER, PURER, NOBLER MAN,

then his pledge is only as a hoop, that any overstrain may break, and not an internal bond, holding in integrity all things from the centre to the circumference of his life.

So well is this now understood, that little reliance is had on the pledge in itself, though its use is still general. It is regarded as a first and most important step in the right direction. As the beginning of a true and earnest effort on the part of some unhappy soul to break the bonds of a fearful slavery. But few would think of leaving such a soul to the saving power of the pledge alone. If other help came not, the effort would be, except in rare cases, too surely, all in vain.

The need of something more reliable than a simple pledge has led to other means of reform and cure, each taking character and shape from the peculiar views of those who have adopted them. Inebriate Asylums and Reformatory Homes have been established in various parts of the country, and through their agency many who were once enslaved by drink are being restored to society and good citizenship. In what is popularly known as the "Gospel Temperance" movement, the weakness of the pledge, in itself, is recognized, and, "God being my helper," is declared to be the ultimate and only sure dependence.

It is through this abandonment of all trust in the pledge, beyond a few exceptional cases, that reformatory work rises to its true sphere and level of success. And we shall now endeavor to show what is being done in the work of curing drunkards, as well in asylums and Reformatory Homes, as by the so-called "Gospel" methods. In this we shall, as far as possible, let each of these important agencies speak for itself, explaining its own methods and giving its own results. All are accomplishing good in their special line of action; all are saving men from the curse of drink, and the public needs to be more generally advised of what they are doing.

CHAPTER VIII.

INEBRIATE ASYLUMS.

THE careful observation and study of inebriety by medical men, during the past twenty-five or thirty years, as well in private practice as in hospitals and prisons, has led them to regard it as, in many of its phases, a disease needing wise and careful treatment. To secure such treatment was seen to be almost impossible unless the subject of intemperance could be removed from old associations and influences, and placed under new conditions, in which there would be no enticement to drink, and where the means of moral and physical recovery could be judiciously applied. It was felt that, as a disease, the treatment of drunkenness, while its subject remained in the old atmosphere of temptation, was as difficult, if not impossible, as the treatment of a malarious fever in a miasmatic district. The result of this view was the establishment of Inebriate Asylums for voluntary or enforced seclusion, first in the United States, and afterwards in England and some of her dependencies.

In the beginning, these institutions did not have much favor with the public; and, as the earlier methods of treatment pursued therein were, for the most part, experimental, and based on a limited knowledge of the pathology of drunkenness, the beneficial results were not large. Still, the work went on, and the reports of cures made by the New York State Asylum, at Binghampton, the pioneer of these institutions, were sufficiently encouraging to lead to their establishment in other places; and there are now in this country as many as from twelve to fifteen public and private institutions for the treatment of drunkenness. Of these, the New York State Inebriate Asylum, at Binghamton; the Inebriate Home, at Fort Hamilton, Long Island; and the Home for Incurables, San Francisco, Cal., are the most prominent. At Hartford, Conn., the Walnut Hill Asylum has recently been opened for the treatment of inebriate and opium cases, under the care of Dr. T. D. Crothers. The Pinel Hospital, at Richmond, Va., chartered by the State, in 1876, is for the treatment of nervous and mental diseases, and for the reclamation of inebriates and opium-eaters. In Needham, Mass., is the Appleton Temporary Home, where a considerable number of inebriates are received every year.

Besides these, there are private institutions, in which dypsomaniac patients are received. The methods of treatment differ according to the views and experience of those having charge of these institutions. Up to this time a great deal of the treatment has been experimental; and there is still much difference of opinion among physicians and superintendents in regard to the best means of cure. But, on two important points, all are nearly in agreement. The first is in the necessity for an immediate and ABSOLUTE WITHDRAWAL OF ALL INTOXICANTS FROM THE PATIENT, no matter how long he may have used them; and the second in the necessity of his entire abstinence therefrom after leaving the institution. *The cure never places a man back where he was before he became subject to the disease; and he can never, after his recovery, taste even the milder forms of alcoholic beverage without being exposed to the most imminent danger of relapse.*

The great value of an asylum where the victim of intemperance can be placed for a time beyond the reach of alcohol is thus stated by Dr. Carpenter: "Vain is it to recall the motives for a better course of conduct, to one who is already familiar with them all, but is destitute of the will to act upon them; the seclusion of such persons from the reach of alcoholic liquors, for a sufficient length of time to *free the blood from its contamination, to restore the healthful nutrition of the brain and to enable the recovered mental vigor to be wisely directed, seems to afford the only prospect of reformation:* and this cannot be expected to be permanent, unless the patient determinately adopts and steadily acts on the resolution to abstain from that which, *if again indulged in, will be poison, alike to his body and to his mind.*"

In the study of inebriety and the causes leading thereto, much important information has been gathered by the superintendents and physicians connected with these establishments. Dr. D. G. Dodge, late Superintendent of the New York State Inebriate Asylum, read a paper before the American Association for the Cure of Inebriates, in 1876, on "Inebriate Asylums and their Management," in which are given the results of many years of study, observation and experience. Speaking of the causes leading to drunkenness, he says:

"Occupation has a powerful controlling influence in developing or warding off the disease. In-door life in all kinds of business, is a predisposing cause, from the fact that nearly the whole force of the stimulant is concentrated and expended upon the brain and nervous system. A proper amount of out-door exercise, or labor, tends to throw off the stimulus more rapidly through the various functional operations of the system. Occupation of all kinds, mental or muscular, assist the nervous system to retard or resist the action of stimulants—other conditions being equal. Want of employment, or voluntary idleness is the great nursery of this disease.

TOBACCO.

"*The use of tobacco predisposes the system to alcoholism*, and it has an effect upon the brain and nervous system similar to that of alcohol. The use of tobacco, if not prohibited, should be discouraged.

The treatment of inebriates can never be wholly successful until the use of tobacco in all forms is absolutely dispensed with.

"Statistics show that inebriety oftenest prevails between the *ages of thirty and forty-five. The habit seldom culminates until thirty,* the subject to this age generally being a *moderate drinker; later in life the system is unable to endure the strain of a continued course of dissipation.*

"Like all hereditary diseases, intemperance is transmitted from parent to child as much as scrofula, gout or consumption. It observes all the laws in transmitting disease. It sometimes overleaps one generation and appears in the succeeding, or it will miss even the third generation, and then reappear in all its former activity and violence. Hereditary inebriety, like all transmissible diseases, gives the least hope of permanent cure, and temporary relief is all that can generally be reasonably expected.

"Another class possesses an organization which may be termed an alcoholic idiosyncrasy; with them the latent desire for stimulants, if indulged, soon leads to habits of intemperance, and eventually to a morbid appetite, which has all the characteristics of a diseased condition of the system, which the patient, unassisted, is powerless to relieve, since the weakness of will that led to the disease obstructs its removal.

"The second class may be subdivided as follows: First, those who have had healthy and temperate parents, and have been educated and accustomed to good influences, moral and social, but whose temperament and physical constitution are such *that when they once indulge in the use of stimulants, which they find pleasurable, they continue to habitually indulge till they cease to be moderate, and become excessive drinkers. A depraved appetite is established that leads them on slowly, but surely, to destruction.*

"Temperaments have much to do with the formation of the habit of excessive drinking. Those of a nervous temperament are less likely to contract the habit, from the fact that they are acutely sensitive to danger, and avoid it while they have the power of self-control. On the other hand, those of a bilious, sanguine and lymphatic temperament, rush on, unmindful of the present, and soon become slaves to a depraved and morbid appetite, powerless to stay, or even to check their downward course."

As we cannot speak of the treatment pursued in inebriate asylums from personal observation, we know of no better way to give our readers correct impressions on the subject, than to quote still farther from Dr. Dodge. "For a better understanding," he says, "of the requisite discipline demanded in the way of remedial restraint of inebriates, we notice some of the results of chronic inebriation affecting more particularly the brain and nervous system—which, in addition to the necessary medical treatment, necessitates strict discipline to the successful management of these cases.

RESULTS OF CHRONIC INEBRIATION.

"We have *alcoholic epilepsy, alcoholic mania, delirium tremens, tremors, hallucinations, insomnia, vertigo, mental and muscular debility, impairment of vision, mental depression, paralysis, a partial or total loss of self-respect and a departure of the power of self-control.* Many minor difficulties arise from mere functional derangement of the brain and nervous system, which surely and rapidly disappear when the cause is removed."

The general rule, on the reception of a patient, is to cut off at once and altogether the use of alcohol in every form. "More," says the doctor, "can be done by diet and medicine, than can be obtained by a compromise in the moderate use of stimulants for a limited period." It is a mistake, he adds, to suppose "that any special danger arises from stopping the accustomed stimulus. Alcohol is a poison, and we should discontinue its use at once, as it can be done with safety and perfect impunity, except in rare cases."

To secure all the benefits to be derived from medical treatment, "we should have," says Dr. Dodge, "institutions for the reception of inebriates, where total abstinence can be rigidly, but judiciously enforced for a sufficient length of time, to test the curative powers of absolute restraint from all intoxicating drinks. When the craving for stimulants is irresistible, it is useless to make an attempt to reclaim and cure the drunkard, *unless the detention is compulsory*, and there is complete restraint from all spirituous or alcoholic stimulants."

REMOVAL FROM TEMPTATION.

In regard to the compulsory power that should inhere in asylums for the cure of drunkenness, there is little difference of opinion among those who have had experience in their management. They have more faith in time than in medicine, and think it as much the duty of the State to establish asylums for the treatment of drunkenness as for the treatment of insanity. "The length of time necessary to cure inebriation," says Dr. Dodge, "is a very important consideration. A habit covering five, ten, fifteen or twenty years, cannot be expected to be permanently eradicated in a week or a month. The fact that the excessive use of stimulants for a long period of time has caused a radical change, physically, mentally and morally, is not only the strongest possible proof that its entire absence is necessary, but, also, that it requires a liberal allowance of time to effect a return to a normal condition. The shortest period of continuous restraint and treatment, as a general rule, should not be less than six months in the most hopeful cases, and extending from one to two years with the less hopeful, and more especially for the class of periodical drinkers, and those with an hereditary tendency."

A well-directed inebriate asylum not only affords, says the same authority, "effectual removal of the patient from temptations and associations which surrounded him in the outer world, but by precept and example it teaches him that he can gain by his reformation, not the ability to drink moderately and with the least safety, *but the power to abstain altogether.* With the restraint imposed by the institution, and the self-restraint accepted on the part of the patient, are remedial agents from the moment he enters the asylum, growing stronger and more effective day by day, until finally he finds *total abstinence not only possible, but permanent.* With this much gained in the beginning, the asylum is prepared to assist in the cure by all the means and appliances at its command. With the co-operation of the patient, and such medicinal remedies and hygienic and sanitary measures as may be required, the most hopeful results may be confidently looked for.

THE HYGIENIC AND SANITARY MEASURES

consist in total abstinence from all alcoholic beverages; good nourishing diet; well ventilated rooms; pure, bracing air; mental rest, and proper bodily exercise. * * * Every patient should be required to conform to all rules and regulations which have for their object the improvement of his social, moral and religious condition. He must begin a different mode of life, by breaking up former habits and associations; driving from the mind the old companions of an intemperate life; forming new thoughts, new ideas and new and better habits, which necessitates a new life in every respect. This is the aim and object of the rules for the control and government of inebriates. To assist in this work, inebriate institutions should have stated religious services, and all the patients and officers should be required to attend them, unless excused by the medical officer in charge, for sickness, or other sufficient cause."

THE BINGHAMPTON ASYLUM.

Of all the inebriate asylums yet established, the one at Binghampton, New York, has been, so far, the most prominent. It is here that a large part of the experimental work has been done; and here, we believe, that the best results have been obtained. This asylum is a State Institution, and will accommodate one hundred and twenty patients. In all cases preference must be given to "indigent inebriates," who may be sent to the asylum by county officers, who are required to pay seven dollars a week for the medical attendance, board and washing, of each patient so sent. Whenever there are vacancies in the asylum, the superintendent can admit, under special agreement, such private patients as may seek admission, and who, in his opinion, promise reformation.

The building is situated on an eminence two hundred and fifty feet above the Susquehanna River, the scenery stretching far up and down the valley, having features of uncommon beauty and grandeur.

Each patient has a thoroughly warmed and ventilated room, which, from the peculiar situation of the house, commands a wide view of the adjoining country. The tables are supplied with a variety and abundance of good food, suitable in every respect to the wants of the patients, whose tastes and needs are carefully considered. Amusements of various kinds, including billiards, etc., are provided within the building, which afford pleasure and profit to the patients. Out-door pastimes, such as games of ball and croquet, and other invigorating sports, are encouraged and practised. The asylum grounds embrace over four hundred acres, part of which are in a state of cultivation. The remainder diversified in character, and partly consisting of forest.

Gentlemen who desire to place themselves under the care of the asylum, may enter it without any other formality than a compliance with such conditions as may be agreed upon between themselves and the superintendent. The price of admission varies according to location of rooms and attention required. Persons differ so widely in their circumstances and desires, that the scale of prices has been fixed at from ten to twenty-five dollars per week, which includes board, medical attendance, washing, etc. In all cases the price of board for three months must be paid in advance.

From one of the annual reports of this institution now before us, we learn that the number of patients treated during the year was three hundred and thirty-six, of whom one hundred and ninety-eight "were discharged with great hopes of permanent reformation." Fifty-eight were discharged unimproved. The largest number of patients in the asylum at one time was a hundred and five.

SAVING AND REFORMING INFLUENCES.

Of those discharged—two hundred and fifty-six in number—eighty-six were of a nervous temperament, ninety-eight sanguine and seventy-two bilious. In their habits, two hundred and thirty-four were social and twenty-two solitary. Out of the whole number, two hundred and forty-four used tobacco—only twelve being free from its use. Of these, one hundred and sixty had been constant and ninety-six periodical drinkers. Serious affliction, being unfortunate in business, love matters, prosperity, etc., were given as reasons for drinking by one hundred and two of the patients. One hundred and twenty-two had intemperate parents or ancestors. One hundred and forty were married men and one hundred and sixteen single. Their occupations were varied. Merchants, fifty-eight; clerks, thirty-five; lawyers, seventeen; book-keepers, sixteen; manufacturers, eight; bankers and brokers, eight; machinists, seven; mechanics, six; farmers, six; clergymen, five; editors and reporters, five, etc.

In regard to some of the special influences brought to bear upon the patients in this institution, we have the following. It is from a communication (in answer to a letter of inquiry) received by us from Dr. T. D. Crothers, formerly of Binghampton, but now superintendent of the new Walnut Hill Asylum, at Hartford, Connecticut: "You have failed to do us credit," he says, "in supposing that we do not use the spiritual forces in our treatment. We depend largely upon them. We have a regularly-appointed chaplain who lives in the building, and gives his entire time to the religious culture of the patients. Rev. Dr. Bush was with us eight years. He died a few months ago. He was very devoted to his work, and the good he did, both apparent to us and unknown, was beyond estimate. His correspondence was very extensive, and continued for years with patients and their families. He was the counselor and adviser of many persons who did not know him personally, but through patients. I have seen letters to him from patients in all conditions asking counsel, both on secular and spiritual matters; also the most heart-rending appeals and statements of fathers, mothers, wives and children, all of which he religiously answered. He urged that the great duty and obligation of every drunkard was to take care of his body; to build up all the physical, to avoid all danger, and take no risks or perils; that his only help and reliance were on *God and good health;* that with regular living and healthy surroundings, and a mind full of faith and hope in spiritual realities, the disorder would die out. Our new chaplain holds daily service, as usual, and spends much of his time among the patients. He lives in the building, pronounces grace at the table and is personally identified as a power to help men towards recovery. Quite a large number of patients become religious men here. Our work and its influences have a strong tendency this way. I believe in the force of a chaplain whose daily walk is with us; who, by example and precept, can win men to higher thoughts. He is the receptacle of secrets and much of the inner life of patients that physicians do not reach."

In another letter to us, Dr. Crothers says: "Every asylum that I know of is doing good work, and should be aided and encouraged by all means. The time has not come yet, nor the experience or study to any one man or asylum, necessary to build up a system of treatment to the exclusion of all others. We want many years of study by competent men, and the accumulated experience of many asylums before we can understand the first principles of that moral and physical disorder we call drunkenness.

TREATMENT.

"As to the treatment and the agents governing it, we recognize in every drunkard general debility and conditions of nerve and brain exhaustion, and a certain train of exciting causes which always end in drinking. Now, if we can teach these men the 'sources of danger,' and pledge them and point them to a higher power for help, we combine both spiritual and physical means. We believe that little can be expected from spiritual aids, or pledges, or resolves, unless the patient can so build up his physical as to sustain them. Give a man a healthy body and brainpower, and you can build up his spiritual life; but all attempts to cultivate a power that is crushed by diseased forces will be practically useless. Call it a vice or a disease, it matters not, the return to health must be along *the line of natural laws and means.* Some men will not feel any longing for drink unless they get in the centre of excitement, or violate some natural law, or neglect the common means of health. Now, teach them these exciting causes, and build up their health, and the pledge will not be difficult to keep. This asylum is a marvel. It is, to-day, successful. Other asylums are the same, and we feel that we are working in the line of laws that are fixed, though obscure."

DEEPLY INTERESTING CASES.

The records of this institution furnish cases of reform of the most deeply interesting character. Here are a few of them:

CASE No. 1. A Southern planter who had become a drunkard was brought to this asylum by his faithful colored man. In his fits of intoxication he fell into the extraordinary delusion that his devoted wife was unfaithful; and so exasperated did he become when seized by this insane delusion, that he often attempted her life. She was at last obliged to keep out of his way whenever he came under the influence of liquor. When sober, his memory of these hallucinations was sufficiently distinct to fill him with sorrow, shame and fear; for he sincerely loved his wife and knew her to be above reproach. After the war, during which he held the position of a general in the Southern army, he became very much reduced in his circumstances, lost heart and gave himself up to drink. The friends of his wife tried to prevail on her to abandon him; but she still clung to her husband, though her life was often in danger from his insane passion. Four years of this dreadful experience, in which she three times received serious personal injuries from his hands, and then the old home was broken up, and he went drifting from place to place, a human ship without a rudder on temptation's stormy sea; his unhappy wife following him, more or less, in secret, and often doing him service and securing his protection. In the spring of 1874, his faithful colored man brought him to the asylum at Binghampton, a perfect wreck. His wife came, also, and for three months boarded near the institution, and, without his knowledge, watched and prayed for him. After a few weeks' residence, the chaplain was able to lead his mind to the consideration of spiritual subjects, and to impress him with the value of religious faith and the power of prayer. He became, at length, deeply interested; read many religious books, and particularly the Bible. At the end of three months his wife came to see him, and their meeting was of a most affecting character. A year later, he left the asylum and went to a Western city, where he now resides—a prosperous and happy man.

CASE No. 2. A clergyman of fortune, position and education lost his daughter, and began to drink in order to drown his sorrow. It was in vain that his wife and friends opposed, remonstrated, implored and persuaded; he drank on, the appetite steadily increasing, until he became its slave. His congregation dismissed him; his wife died of a broken heart; he squandered his fortune; lost his friends, and, at last, became a street reporter for some of the New York papers, through means of which he picked up a scanty living. From bad to worse, he swept down rapidly, and, for some offense committed while drunk, was, at last, sent for three months to the State prison. On coming out, and returning to the city, he became a fish-peddler, but continued to drink desperately. One day he was picked up in the street in a state of dead intoxication and taken to the hospital, where he was recognized by the doctor, who had him sent to Binghampton as a county patient. Here he remained for over a year, submitting himself to the regime, and coming under the salutary influences of the institution, and making an earnest, prayerful and determined effort at reform. At the end of this period he left the asylum to enter upon the duties of a minister in the far

West; and to-day he is the president of a new college, and a devout and earnest man! He attributes his cure to the influence of the late chaplain, Rev. Mr. Bush, and to the new life he was able to lead under the protecting influences and sanitary regulations of the asylum. This is a meagre outline of a very remarkable case.

CASE No. 3. A poor farmer's boy acquired, while in the army, an inordinate appetite for drink. He was sent to the New York Inebriate Asylum, but was expelled because he made no effort to reform. Six months afterwards he joined a temperance society, and kept sober for a year; but fell, and was again sent to the asylum. This time he made an earnest effort, and remained at the asylum for seven months, when he was offered a situation in Chicago, which he accepted. For a year he held this place, then relapsed and came back to the asylum, where he stayed for over twelve months. At the end of that time he returned to Chicago and into his old situation. He is now a member of the firm, and an active temperance man, with every prospect of remaining so to the end of his life.

THE CARE AND TREATMENT OF DRUNKARDS.

The subject of the care and treatment of habitual drunkards is attracting more and more attention. They form so large a non-producing, and often vicious and dangerous class of half-insane men, that considerations of public and private weal demand the institution of some effective means for their reformation, control or restraint. Legislative aid has been invoked, and laws submitted and discussed; but, so far, beyond sentences of brief imprisonment in jails, asylums and houses of correction, but little has really been done for the prevention or cure of the worst evil that inflicts our own and other civilized nations. On the subject of every man's "liberty to get drunk," and waste his substance and abuse and beggar his family, the public mind is peculiarly sensitive and singularly averse to restrictive legislation. But a public sentiment favorable to such legislation is steadily gaining ground; and to the formation and growth of this sentiment, many leading and intelligent physicians, both in this country and Great Britain, who have given the subject of drunkenness as a disease long and careful attention, are lending all their influence. It is seen that a man who habitually gets drunk is dangerous to society, and needs control and restraint as much as if he were insane.

LEGISLATIVE CONTROL.

In 1875, a deputation, principally representative of the medical profession, urged upon the British Government the desirability of measures for the control and management of habitual drunkards. On presenting the memorial to the Secretary of State for the Home Department, Sir Thomas Watson, M.D., observed: "That during his very long professional life he had been incredulous respecting the reclamation of habitual drunkards; but his late experience had made him sanguine as to their cure, with a very considerable number of whom excessive drinking indulged in as a vice, developed itself into a most formidable bodily and mental disease."

In the early part of February, 1877, "A Bill to Facilitate the Control and Care of Habitual Drunkards," was introduced into the House of Commons. It is supposed to embody the latest and most practical methods of dealing legally with that class, and is of unusual interest from the fact that it was prepared under the direction of a society for the promotion of legislation for the cure of habitual drunkards, recently organized in London, in which are included some of the most learned, influential and scientific men of the Kingdom.

This bill provides for the establishment of retreats or asylums, public or private, into which drunkards may be admitted on their own application, or to which they may be sent by their friends, and where they can be held by law for a term not exceeding twelve months.

In the State of Connecticut, there is a law which may be regarded as embodying the most advanced legislation on this important subject. The first section is as follows:

"Whenever any person shall have become an habitual drunkard, a dypsomaniac, or so far addicted to the intemperate use of narcotics or stimulants as to have lost the power of self-control, the Court of Probate for the district in which such person resides, or has a legal domicil, shall, on application of a majority of the selectmen of the town where such person resides, or has a legal domicil, or of any relative of such person, make due inquiry, and if it shall find such person to have become an habitual drunkard, or so far addicted to the intemperate use of narcotics or stimulants as to have lost the power of self-control, then said court shall order such person to be taken to some inebriate asylum within this State, for treatment, care and custody, for a term not less than four months, and not more than twelve months; but if said person shall be found to be a dypsomaniac, said term of commitment shall be for the period of three years: *provided, however*, that the Court of Probate shall not in either case make such order without the certificate of at least two respectable practising physicians, after a personal examination, made within one week before the time of said application or said commitment, which certificate shall contain the opinion of said physicians that such person has become, as the case may be, a dypsomaniac, an habitual drunkard, or has, by reason of the intemperate use of narcotics or stimulants, lost the power of self-control, and requires the treatment, care and custody of some inebriate asylum, and shall be subscribed and sworn to by said physicians before an authority empowered to administer oaths."

LOSS TO THE STATE IN NOT ESTABLISHING ASYLUMS.

In a brief article in the *Quarterly Journal of Inebriety*, for 1877, Dr. Dodge thus emphasizes his views of the importance to the State of establishing asylums to which drunkards may be sent for treatment: "Every insane man who is sent to an asylum, is simply removed from doing harm, and well cared for, and rarely comes back to be a producer again. But inebriates (the hopeful class) promise immeasurably more in their recovery. They are, as inebriates, non-producers and centres of disease, bad sanitary and worse moral surroundings. All their career leads down to crime and poverty. The more drunkards, the more courts of law, and almshouses, and insane asylums, and greater the taxes. Statistics show that from fifty to sixty per cent. of crime is due to drunkenness; and we all know how large poverty is due to this cause. Drunkenness is alone responsible for from twenty to twenty-five per cent. of all our insane.

"We assert, and believe it can be proved, that reclaiming the drunkard is a greater gain to the State, practical and immediate, than any other charity.

"It is a low estimate to say it costs every county in the State three hundred dollars yearly to support a drunkard; that is, this amount, and more, is diverted from healthy channels of commerce, and is, practically, lost to the State. At an inebriate asylum, but little over that amount would, in a large majority of cases, restore them as active producers again.

"Figures cannot represent the actual loss to society, nor can we compute the gain from a single case cured and returned to normal life and usefulness. Inebriety is sapping the foundation of our Government, both State and National, and unless we can provide means adequate to check it, we shall leave a legacy of physical, moral and political disease to our descendants, that will ultimately wreck this country. Inebriate asylums will do much to check and relieve this evil."

We conclude this chapter, which is but an imperfect presentation of the work of our inebriate asylums, by a quotation from the *Quarterly Journal of Inebriety*, for September, 1877. This periodical is published under the auspices of "The American Association for the Cure of Inebriates." The editor, Dr. Crothers, says: "We publish in this number, reports of a large number of asylums from all parts of the country, indicating great prosperity and success, notwithstanding the depression of the times. Among the patients received at these asylums, broken-down merchants, bankers, business men, who are inebriates of recent date, and chronic cases that have been moderate drinkers for many years, seem to be more numerous. The explanation is found in the peculiar times in which so many of the business men are ruined, and the discharge of a class of employees whose uncertain habits and want of special fitness for their work make them less valuable. Both of these classes drift to the inebriate asylum, and, if not able to pay, finally go to insane hospitals and disappear.

"Another class of patients seem more prominent this year, namely, the hard-working professional and business men, who formerly went away to Europe, or some watering-place, with a retinue of servants; now they appear at our retreats, spend a few months, and go away much restored. The outlook was never more cheery than at present, the advent of several new asylums, and the increased usefulness of those in existence, with the constant agitation of the subject among medical men at home and abroad, are evidence of great promise for the future. Of the Journal we can only say that, as the organ of the American Association for the Cure of Inebriates, it will represent the broadest principles and studies which the experience of all asylums confirm, and independent of any personal interest, strive to present the subject of inebriety and its treatment in its most comprehensive sense."

CHAPTER IX.

REFORMATORY HOMES.

DIFFERING in some essential particulars from inebriate asylums or hospitals for the cure of drunkenness as a disease, are the institutions called "Homes." Their name indicates their character. It is now about twenty years since the first of these was established. It is located at 41 Waltham Street, Boston, in an elegant and commodious building recently erected, and is called the "Washingtonian Home." The superintendent is Dr. Albert Day. In 1863, another institution of this character came into existence in the city of Chicago. This is also called the "Washingtonian Home." It is situated in West Madison Street, opposite Union Park. The building is large and handsomely fitted up, and has accommodations for over one hundred inmates. Prof. D. Wilkins is the superintendent. In 1872 "The Franklin Reformatory Home," of Philadelphia, was established. It is located at Nos. 911, 913 and 915 Locust Street, in a well-arranged and thoroughly-furnished building, in which all the comforts of a home may be found, and can accommodate over seventy persons. Mr. John Graff is the superintendent.

As we have said, the name of these institutions indicates their character. They are not so much hospitals for the cure of a disease, as homes of refuge and safety, into which the poor inebriate, who has lost or destroyed his own home, with all its good and saving influences, may come and make a new effort, under the most favoring influences, to recover himself.

The success which has attended the work of the three institutions named above, has been of the most gratifying character. In the

WASHINGTONIAN HOME AT BOSTON,

drunkenness has been regarded as a malady, which may be cured through the application of remedial agencies that can be successfully employed only under certain conditions; and these are sought to be secured for the patient. The home and the hospital are, in a certain sense, united. "While we are treating inebriety as a disease, or a pathological condition," says the superintendent, in his last report, "there are those who regard it as a species of wickedness or diabolism, to be removed only by moral agencies. Both of these propositions are true in a certain sense. There is a difference between sin and evil, but the line of demarkation is, as yet, obscure, as much so as the line between the responsibility and irresponsibility of the inebriate."

Doubtless, the good work done in this excellent institution is due, in a large measure, to the moral and religious influences under which the inmates are brought. Nature is quick to repair physical waste and deterioration, when the exciting causes of disease are removed. The diseased body of the drunkard, as soon as it is relieved from the poisoning influence of alcohol, is restored, in a measure, to health. The brain is clear once more, and the moral faculties again able to act with reason and conscience. And here comes in the true work of the Home, which is the restoration of the man to a state of rational self-control; the quickening in his heart of old affections, and the revival of old and better desires and principles.

BENEFICIAL RESULTS.

"Among the beneficial results of our labor," says Dr. Day, "we see our patients developing a higher principle of respect for themselves and their friends. This, to us, is of great interest. We see indications convincing us that the mind, under our treatment, awakens to a consciousness of what it is, and what it is made for. We see man becoming to himself a higher object, and attaining to the conviction of the equal and indestructible of every being. In them we see the dawning of the great principle advocated by us continually, viz., That the individual is not made to be the instrument of others, but to govern himself by an inward law, and to advance towards his proper perfections; that he belongs to himself and to God, and to no human superior. In all our teachings we aim to purify and ennoble the character of our patients by promoting in them true virtue, strong temperance proclivities and a true piety; and to accomplish these ends we endeavor to stimulate their own exertions for a better knowledge of God, and for a determined self-control."

And again he says: "Almost every day we hear from some one who has been with us under treatment, who has been cured. Their struggles had been fierce, and the battle sometimes would seem to be against them; but, at last, they have claimed the victory. In my experience, I have found that so long as the victim of strong drink has the will, feeble as it may be, to put forth his efforts for a better life, and his constant struggle is in the right direction, he is almost sure to regain his will power, and succeed in overcoming the habit. By exercise, the will gains strength. The thorns in the flesh of our spiritual nature will be plucked out, the spiritual life will be developed, and our peace shall flow as the river. This condition we constantly invoke, and by all the means within our reach we try to stimulate the desire for a better life. I am pleased to say our efforts in this direction have not been in vain. For nearly twenty years we have been engaged in this work, and we have now more confidence in the means employed than at any other period. Situated, as we are, in the midst of a great city, with a Christian sympathy constantly active and co-operating with us, no one can remain in the institution without being the recipient of beneficial influences, the effect of which is salutary in the extreme. I am fully satisfied that the 'Washingtonian Home' is greatly indebted to these moral agencies for its success."

The following letter, received by us, from Otis Clapp, who has been for sixteen years president of the "Washingtonian Home," will give the reader a still clearer impression of the workings of that institution. It is in answer to one we wrote, asking for information about the institution in which he had been interested for so many years:

"BOSTON, August 9th, 1877.

"DEAR SIR:—Your letter is received, and I am glad to learn that your mind is directed to the subject of the curse and cure of drunkenness. This is one of the largest of human fields to work in. The 'Washingtonian Home' was commenced in a very humble way, in November, 1857. An act of incorporation was obtained from the State, March 26th, 1859.

"The institution has, therefore, been in existence nearly twenty years. My connection with it has been for eighteen years—sixteen years as president. During the period of its existence the whole number of patients has been five thousand three hundred and forty-eight. Of this number, the superintendent, Dr. Day, estimates the cured at one-half. Of the remainder, it is estimated that one-half, making one-quarter of the whole, are greatly improved.

"You say, 'I take the general ground, and urge it strongly upon the reader that, *without spiritual help—regeneration, in a word—there is, for the confirmed inebriate, but little hope, and no true safety.*'

"In this I fully concur. I believe in using all the agencies —medical, social, moral and religious—to bear upon the patient, and to encourage him to follow the 'straight and narrow way.' With this view, a morning service is held each day; a Sunday evening service at six o'clock, and every Friday evening a meeting, where patients relate their experience, and encourage each other in gaining power over the enemy. I have had much experience and abundant evidence that these meetings are of great value, for the reason that the patients are the principal speakers, and can do more to encourage each other than those outside of their own ranks. These meetings are usually attended by about equal numbers of both sexes, and, with fine music, can be kept up with interest indefinitely.

"It would be, in my judgment, a matter of wide economy for the intelligent citizens of every city, with twenty thousand or more inhabitants, to establish a home, or asylum for inebriates. Let those who favor sobriety in the community, take a part in it, and they will soon learn how to reach the class who needs assistance. A large, old-fashioned house can be leased at small expense, and the means raised by contributions of money and other necessary articles to start. The act of doing this will soon enable those engaged in the work to learn what the wants are, and how to meet them. It is only obeying the command, 'Go out into the highways and hedges and compel them to come in, that my house may be filled.' This is the Master's work, and those who hear this invitation, as well as those who accept it, will share in its blessings.

"Those who cultivate the spirit of ' love to God, and goodwill to their fellow-men,' will be surprised to see how much easier it is to *do* these things when they *try*, than when they only *think* about them.

"Much, of course, depends upon the superintendent, who needs to possess those genial qualities which readily win the confidence and good-will of patients, and which he readily turns to account, by encouraging them to use the means which the Creator has given them to co-operate in curing themselves. The means of cure are in the patient's own hands, and it is quite a gift to be able to make him see it."

THE WASHINGTONIAN HOME AT CHICAGO

is on the same plan, in all essential respects, with that of Boston; and the reports show about the same average of cures and beneficial results. How the patient is treated in this Home may be inferred from the following extract from an article on "The Cause, Effect and Cure of Inebriety," from the pen of Prof. D. Wilkins, the superintendent, which appeared in a late number of *The Quarterly Journal of Inebriety*. In answer to the question, How can we best save the poor drunkard, and restore him to his manhood, his family and society, he says:

"Money, friends, relatives and all have forsaken him, his hope blasted, his ambition gone, and he feels that no one has confidence in him, no one cares for him. In this condition he wends his way to an institution of reform, a penniless, homeless, degraded, lost and hopeless drunkard. Here is our subject, how shall we save him? He has come from the squalid dens, and lanes of filth, of misery, of want, of debauchery and death; no home, no sympathy and no kind words have greeted him, perhaps, for years. He is taken to the hospital. A few days pass, and he awakes from the stupidity of drink, and as he opens his eyes, what a change! He looks around, kind and gentle voices welcome him, his bed is clean and soft, the room beautiful, tasteful and pleasant in its arrangements, the superintendent, the physician, the steward and the inmates meet him with a smile and treat him as a brother. He is silent, lost in meditation. Thoughts of other days, of other years, pass through his mind in quick succession as the tears steal gently down his cheeks. He talks thus to himself: 'I am mistaken. *Somebody does care* for the drunkard. And if somebody cares for me, *I ought to care for myself.*' Here reform first commences. In a few days, when free, to some extent, from alcohol, he is admitted to the freedom of the institution. As he enters the reading-room, the library, the amusement, the gymnasium, dining-room and spacious halls, the conviction becomes stronger and stronger that somebody is interested in the inebriate, and he should be interested in himself. Then comes the lessons of the superintendent. He is taught that he cannot be reformed, but that he can reform himself. That God helps those only who help themselves. That he must ignore all boon companions of the cup as associates, all places where liquor is kept and sold, that, in order to reform himself, he must become a reformer, labor for the good of his brother; in short, he must shun every rivulet that leads him into the stream of intemperance, and as a cap-stone which completes the arch, that he must look to Him from whence cometh all grace and power to help in time of need.

"As he converses with those that are strong in experience, listens to the reading of the Holy Scriptures in the morning devotions, joins in the sweet songs of Zion and unites in unison with his brother inmates in saying the Lord's Prayer, as he hears the strong experiences in the public meetings and secret associations of those who have remained firm for one, two, three, and up to ten or fifteen years, little by little his confidence is strengthened, and almost before he is aware, the firm determination is formed and the resolve made, *I will drink no more.* As week after week, and month after month, glides pleasantly away, these resolutions become stronger and stronger, and by thus educating his intellect and strengthening his moral power, the once hopeless, disheartened and helpless one regains his former manhood and lost confidence, and becomes a moral, independent, reformed man. Perhaps the most difficult thing in this work of reform, is to convince our inmates that resolving to stop drinking, or even stopping drinking for the time being, is not reforming. Those admitted, generally, in about two weeks, under the direction of a skillful physician, and the nursing of a faithful steward, recover so as to sleep well and eat heartily, and their wills, seemingly, are as strong as ever. Feeling thus, they often leave the institution, sobered up, not reformed, and when the periodical time arrives, or temptation comes, they have no moral power to resist, and they rush back to habits of intoxication. They forget that the will is like a door on its hinges, with the animal desires, appetites, evil inclinations and passions attached to one side, leading them into trouble and making them unhappy, unless they are held by the strong power of the sense of moral right attached to the other side, and that for years they have been stifling and weakening this power, until its strength is almost, if not entirely, gone, and that the only way they can possibly strengthen it, independent of the grace of God, is by education, moral light and testing it under circumstances so favorable that it will not yield. It took years of disobedience to destroy the moral power, and it will take years of obedience to restore it again. The inebriate must be taught that he can refrain from drink only as he strengthens this moral power, and this requires time and trial. Here is just where we, as superintendents, or reformers, assume great responsibility. To understand just when to test, and how much temptation can be resisted by those under our charge, requires much wisdom and great experience."

From this extract the reader will learn something of the influences which are brought to bear upon the inmates of a home for the reformation of inebriates; and he will see how much reliance is placed on moral and religious agencies.

TESTIMONY OF THE REFORMED.

From the Chicago Home is issued a monthly paper called *The Washingtonian*, devoted to the interest of the institution and to temperance. In this appear many communications from those who are, or have been, inmates. We make a few selections from some of these, which will be read with interest:

"When I came into the Home, mind, memory, hope and energy were shattered. The only animating thought remaining to me was a misty speculation as to where the next drink was to come from. I had a kind of feeble perception that a few days more of the life I was leading must end my earthly career; but I didn't care. As to the 'hereafter'— that might take care of itself; I had no energy to make any provision for it.

"To-day, how different! A new man, utterly defiant of the devil and all 'his works and pomps,' I am ready and eager to take my place once more in the battle of life; atone for the miserable time gone by; to take again the place in the world I had forfeited, bearing ever in my breast the beautiful maxims of the German poet and philosopher, Schiller: 'Look not sorrowfully into the past; it comes not back again. Wisely improve the present; it is thine. Go forth to meet the shadowy future without fear, and with a manly heart.'"

Another writes: "I have been true and faithful to my promise, and have not touched or tampered with the curse since the first morning I entered the Home, ten months ago to-day, and, Mr. Superintendent, I shall never drink again as long as I live. My whole trust and hope is in God, who made me live, move and have my being; and as long as I trust in Him—and which I am thoroughly satisfied I always shall—I will be crowned with success in each and every good effort I make. * * * The day

I reached here, my little ones were out of town; but were telegraphed for at once. They came in the next morning, and, oh! how my heart rejoiced to see they knew and loved me. They came to my arms and threw their little arms around my neck, and hugged and kissed me until I wept with joy. They begged of me never to leave them again, and I never shall. My dear father, mother and all now wish me to stay with them, for they feel I can now be as great a comfort as I once, I might say, was a terror to them. Thank God, I can prove a comfort to them, and my daily life shall be such that they never can do without me. Praises be to God for His goodness and mercy to me, and for showing and guiding me in the straight path, that which leadeth, at last, to an everlasting life with Him and His redeemed in that great and glorious kingdom above."

Another writes, two years after leaving the Home: "In different places where I lived, I was generally a moving spirit in everything of a literary character, and, from a naturally social, convivial disposition, enjoyed the conversation and society of literary men over a glass of beer more than any other attraction that could have been presented. For years, this continued, I, all the time, an active spirit in whatever church I was a member of, and an active worker in whatever I engaged in, thereby always commanding a prominent position wherever I was. Thus matters progressed till I was about twenty-seven, and then I began to realize my position; but, alas, when it was too late. The kindly admonition of friends and my own intelligence began to tell me the story, and then how I struggled for months and months—a naturally sensitive nature only making me worse—till, at last, the conviction forced itself upon me that, for me there was no redemption, that I was bound, hand and foot, perfectly powerless, and then I was forced to accept the fact. My only desire then was to save those dear to me from any knowledge of the truth; for this reason I chose Chicago for my home. Not wishing to take my own life in my hands, I was simply waiting for the moment when, having gone lower and lower, it would, at last, please God to relieve me of my earthly sufferings. Oh! the mental agonies I endured! Too true is it that the drunkard carries his hell around with him. At any moment I was perfectly willing to die, perfectly willing to trust whatever might be before me in the other world, feeling it could be no worse. At last, by God's grace, I was directed to the 'Washingtonian Home,' and there, for the first time, I learned that I could be free; and in this knowledge lies the power of the Home. The Home took hold of me and bade me be a man, and directed me to God for help; and, at the same time, told me to work out my own salvation. Its teachings were not in vain; and to-day I can look up and ask God's blessing on you all for your kind labors. But for that Home, I should, to-day, have been filling a dishonored grave."

And another says: "It is now over five years since I applied to Mr. Drake for admission to the Home. I was then prostrated, both physically and mentally, to that degree that I had scarcely strength to drag myself along, or moral courage enough to look any decent man in the face. I was often assured that to quit whisky would kill me. I thought there was a probability of that; but, on the other hand, there was a certainty that to continue it would kill me. I resolved to make one more effort and die sober, for I never expected to live; had no hope of that. From the day I entered the Home I have been a changed man. The encouragement and counsel I received there, gave me strength to keep the resolution I had formed, and which I have kept to the present moment, viz: TO DRINK NO MORE! Ever since I left Chicago, I have held a respectable position; and now hold the principal position in a house of business, the doors of which I was forbidden to enter six years ago. I do not write this in any spirit of self-laudation, but simply to lay the honor where it belongs—at the door of the 'Washingtonian Home.'"

The following from the "experience" of one of the inmates of the Chicago "Home," will give the reader an idea of the true character of this and similar institutions, and of the way in which those who become inmates are treated. A lady who took an interest in the writer, had said to him, "You had better go to the Washingtonian Home." What followed is thus related:

HOW I WAS TREATED IN THE HOME.

"I looked at her in surprise. Send me to a reformatory? I told her that I did not think that I was sunk so low, or bound so fast in the coils of the 'worm of the still,' that it was necessary for me, a young man not yet entered into the prime of manhood, to be confined in a place designed for the cure of habitual drunkards. I had heard vague stories, but nothing definite concerning the Home, and thought that the question was an insult, but I did not reply to the question. All that night my thoughts would revert to the above question. My life past since I had become a devotee of the 'demon of strong drink,' passed in review before my mind. What had I gained? How improved? What had I obtained by it? And the answer was nothing. Then I asked myself, What had I lost by it? And the answer came to me with crushing force, everything that maketh life desirable. Starting out young in years into the busy highways of the world, with a good fortune, bright prospects and a host of friends to aid and cheer me on, I had lost ALL in my love for strong drink, and at times I thought and felt that I was a modern Ishmael.

"The lady, the next morning, again returned to the attack, and then, not thinking it an insult, but a benefit, to be conferred on me, I yielded a willing acquiescence. That same evening, with a slow step and aching head, I walked up Madison Street towards the Washingtonian Home, with thoughts that I would be considered by the officers of the institution as a sort of a felon, or, if not that, at least something very near akin to the brute, and it was with a sinking heart that I pushed open the main door and ascended the broad, easy stairs to the office. I asked if the superintendent was in, and the gentlemanly clerk at the desk told me that he was, and would be down immediately, meanwhile telling me to be seated. After the lapse of a few minutes, the superintendent, Mr. Wilkins, came into the office, his countenance beaming with benevolence. He took the card that I had brought with me, read it, and, turning round to where I sat, with a genial smile lighting up his countenance, with outstretched hand, greeted me most kindly and introduced me to the gentlemen present. I was dumbfounded, and it was with great difficulty that I restrained myself from shedding tears. It was the very opposite of the reception that I had pictured that I would receive, and I found that I was to be treated as a human being and not as a brute. With a smile, the superintendent addressed me again, and told me to follow him; and it was with a lighter heart and spirits that I ascended the second flight of stairs than the first, I can assure you. I was brought to the steward, who also greeted me most kindly, conversed with me a short time, fixed up some medicine for me and then took me into the hospital. By the word 'hospital,' dear reader, you must not take the usual definition of all that word implies, but in this case, take it as a moderate-sized room with eight or nine beds, covered with snow-white sheets and coverlids, and filled with air of the purest; no sickly smells or suffering pain to offend the most delicate.

"After a most refreshing night's rest—the first that I had had in three or four long, weary months—I arose, and for a few moments could not realize where I was, but memory came back, and I fell on my knees and gave thanks to God that I had fallen into the hands of the 'Good Samaritans.' After breakfast, I went with great diffidence into the common sitting-room, where there was about ten of the inmates sitting smoking, playing checkers, etc. I did not know how I would be received here, but as soon as I entered I was greeted most kindly and told to make myself at home. It seemed as if my cup was full and running over, and for a few moments I could scarcely speak, and I thought that the institution's motto must be founded on the Saviour's command to 'Love one another.'

"The first day I was not allowed to go down to the dining-room, I still being under the care of the hospital steward. The second day I was discharged from the hospital, assigned a most comfortable and cheerful furnished bed-room, and allowed the liberty of the whole building, and the day passed pleasantly. The next morning, at about six, I was awakened by the clangor of a bell shaken by a vigorous arm. Hurriedly dressing, I descended to the wash-room and performed my ablutions, and then waited for the next step. Half an hour having elapsed, the bell was rung a second time, and we all entered what is called the service-room. Shortly after Mr. Wilkins and his family entered; the superintendent read a chapter of the Bible, the inmates sung a hymn, accompanied on the organ by Miss Clara Wilkins; after a short prayer, the inmates marched in single file to the head of the room, where Mr. Wilkins stood, his kind face actually beaming, and with extended hand greeted every individual inmate. After leaving him we marched to the other side of the room, where we also received a cheery 'good morning,' and cordial grasp of the hand from the estimable and motherly wife of the superintendent. To describe one day is sufficient to picture the manner in which the inmates of the Home (and I sincerely believe that 'home' is the right designation for it) pass their time. I have never felt happier or more contented even in my most prosperous days than I have in these few short days that I have been an inmate of the Washingtonian Home."

In this institution, according to the last annual report, two thousand two hundred and fifty-two persons have been treated since it was opened. Of these, one thousand one hundred and eighteen, or over sixty per cent., are said to have remained sober, or nearly so, up to this time. During the last year two hundred and fifty-eight patients were under treatment (one-third free patients). Of these only thirty had relapsed, the others giving great promise of recovery.

The Philadelphia institution, known as the "FRANKLIN REFORMATORY HOME FOR INEBIATES," has been in existence over five years. It was organized in April, 1872. In this institution intemperance is not regarded as a disease, which may be cured through hygienic or medical treatment, but as *a sin, which must be repented of, resisted and overcome through the help of God*. In order to place the inebriate, who honestly desires to reform and lead a better life, under conditions most favorable to this work of inner reformation and true recovery, all the external associations and comforts of a pleasant home are provided, as with the two institutions whose record of good results has just been made. Its administrative work and home-life vary but little from that of the Homes in Boston and Chicago. But it is differenced from them and other institutions which have for their aim the cure of inebriety, in its rejection of the disease theory, and sole reliance on moral and spiritual agencies in the work of saving men from the curse of drink. It says to its inmates, this appetite for drink is not a disease that medicine can cure, or change, or eradicate. New sanitary conditions, removal from temptations, more favorable surroundings, congenial occupation, improved health, a higher self-respect, a sense of honor and responsibility, and the tenderness and strength of love for wife and children, may be powerful enough as motives to hold you always in the future above its enticements. But, trusting in these alone, you can never dwell in complete safety. You need a deeper work of cure than it is possible for you to obtain from any earthly physician. Only God can heal you of this infirmity.

A RELIGIOUS HOME.

While never undervaluing external influences, and always using the best means in their power to make their institution a home in all that the word implies, the managers have sought to make it distinctively something more—*a religious home.* They rely for restoration chiefly on the reforming and regenerating power of Divine grace. Until a man is brought under spiritual influences, they do not regard him as in safety; and the result of their work so far only confirms them in this view. They say, that in almost every case where an inmate has shown himself indifferent, or opposed to the religious influences of the Home, he has, on leaving it, relapsed, after a short period, into intemperance, while the men who have stood firm are those who have sought help from God, and given their lives to His service.

Under this view, which has never been lost sight of from the beginning, in the work of the "Franklin Home," and which is always urged upon those who seek its aid in their efforts to reform their lives, there has come to be in the institution a pervading sentiment favorable to a religions life as the only safe life, and all who are brought within the sphere of its influence soon become impressed with the fact. And it is regarded as one of the most hopeful of signs when the new inmate is drawn into accord with this sentiment, and as a most discouraging one if he sets himself in opposition thereto.

WHO ARE RECEIVED INTO "THE FRANKLIN HOME."

As in other institutions, the managers of this one have had to gain wisdom from experience. They have learned that there is a class of drinking men for whom efforts at recovery are almost useless; and from this class they rarely now take any one into the Home. Men of known vicious or criminal lives are not received. Nor are the friends of such as indulge in an occasional drunken debauch permitted to send them there for temporary seclusion. None are admitted but men of good character, in all but intemperance; and these must be sincere and earnest in their purpose to reform. The capacity of an institution in which the care, and service, and protection of a home can be given, is too small for mere experiment or waste of effort. There are too many who are anxious, through the means offered in a place like this, to break the chains of a debasing habit, and get back their lost manhood once more, to waste effort on the evil-minded and morally depraved, who only seek a temporary asylum and the opportunity for partial recovery, but with no purpose of becoming better men and better citizens. Apart from the fruitlessness of all attempts to permanently restore such men to sobriety, it has been found that their presence in the Home has had an injurious effect; some having been retarded in recovery through their influence, and others led away into vicious courses.

There is a chapel in the building, capable of holding over two hundred person In this, Divine worship is held every Sunday afternoon. A minister from some one of the churches is usually in attendance to preach and conduct the services. It rarely happens that the chapel is not well filled with present and former inmates of the Home, their wives, children and friends. Every evening, at half-past nine o'clock, there is family prayer in the chapel, and every Sunday afternoon the president, Mr. S. P. Godwin, has a class for Bible study and instruction in the same place. On Tuesday evenings there is a conversational temperance meeting; and on Thursday evening of each week the Godwin Association, organized for mutual help and encouragement, holds a meeting in the chapel.

USE OF TOBACCO DISCOURAGED.

The attending physician, Dr. Robert P. Harris, having given much thought and observation to the effects of tobacco on the physical system, and its connection with inebriety, discourages its use among the inmates, doing all in his power, by advice and admonition, to lead them to abandon a habit that not only disturbs and weakens the nervous forces, but too often produces that very condition of nervous exhaustion which leads the sufferer to resort to stimulation. In many cases where men, after leaving the "Home," have stood firm for a longer or shorter period of time, and then, relapsing into intemperance, have again sought its help in a new effort at reformation, he has been able to find the cause of their fall in an excessive use of tobacco.

Dr. Harris is well assured, from a long study of the connection between the use of tobacco and alcohol, that, in a very large number of cases tobacco has produced the nervous condition which led to inebriety. And he is satisfied that, if men who are seeking to break away from the slavery of drink, will give up their tobacco and their whisky at the same time, they will find the work easier, and their ability to stand by their good resolutions, far greater. See the next chapter for a clear and concise statement, from the pen of Dr. Harris, of the effects of tobacco, and the obstacles its use throws in the way of men who are trying to reform.

WHAT HAS BEEN ACCOMPLISHED.

The results of the work done in this "Home" are of the most satisfactory kind. From the fifth annual report, we learn that there have been received into the Home, since its commencement, seven hundred and forty-one persons. Of these, the report gives three hundred and fifty-four as reformed, and one hundred and three as benefited. Two hundred and ninety-seven were free patients.

WOMAN'S WORK IN THE HOME.

In the management of this Home there is, beside the board of directors, an auxiliary board of twenty-six lady managers, who supervise the work of the Home, and see to its orderly condition and the comfort of the inmates. Through visiting and relief committees the families of such of the inmates as need temporary care and assistance are seen, and such help and counsel given as may be required. An extract or two from the reports of this auxiliary board will not only give an idea of the religious influences of the institution, but of what is being done by the woman's branch of the work. Says the secretary, Mrs. E. M. Gregory, in her last annual report:

"The religious influence exerted by this institution by means of its Sunday evening services, its Bible class and its frequent temperance meetings, which are cordially open to all, is silently, but, we think, surely making itself felt among those brought within its reach, and establishing the highest and strongest bond among those whose natural ties are often unhappily severed by intemperance. We find whole families, long unused to any religious observance, now *regularly, for years,* accompanying the husband and father to this place of worship, and joining devoutly in the exercises.

"Especial emphasis is laid upon the doctrine that the only foundation for a thorough, enduring reformation is found in a radical change of heart, a preparation for the future life by a conscientious, persistent effort to lead a Christ-like life here.

"One result of this teaching is found in the fact that several 'of the inmates, not in the first pleasant excitement of their rescue from the immediate horrors of their condition, but after long and faithful observance of their pledge and constant attendance upon the religious instruction of the Home, have voluntarily and with solemn resolve united themselves to some Christian church, and are devoting a large share of their time and means to the work of bringing in their old companions to share this great salvation. When, in our visits among their families, we hear of those who formerly spent all their earnings at the saloon, bringing nothing but distress and terror into their homes, now walking the streets all day in search of work, without dinner themselves, because the 'wife and children need what little there is in the house;' and another, not only denying himself a reasonable share of the scanty food, but nursing a sick wife and taking entire care of the children and house, hastening out, when relieved awhile by a kindly neighbor, to do '*anything* to bring in a little money'—when we see changes like these, accompanied by patience and cheerfulness, and a growing sense of personal responsibility, we thankfully accept them as proofs of the genuineness of the work and hopefully look for its continuance."

TOUCHING INCIDENTS.

In a previous report, speaking of the visits made to the families of inmates, she says:

"In no case has a visit ever been received without expression of absolute pleasure, and especially gratitude, for 'what the Home has done for me and mine.'

"Although, unhappily, there are instances of men having, through stress of temptation, violated their pledges, it is believed that not one case has occurred of a family, once brought together through the influence of the Home, again being separated by the return to intemperance of the husband and father, and the results of their faithfulness are to be seen in the growing comfort and happiness of those dependent on them.

"An aged mother, not only bowed down with the weight of seventy years, but heart-sick with the 'hope deferred' of ever finding her intemperate son, heard of him at last, as rescued by the Home; and, being brought to the Sunday and evening services, met him there, 'clothed and in his right mind.' The tears streamed down her face, as she said: 'That man is forty years old, and I've been a widow ever since he was a baby, and I've wept over him often and often, and *to-day* I've shed tears enough to bathe him from head to foot, but, oh! thank the Lord! *these* are such *happy* tears!'

"Said one wife: 'Some days, these hard times, we have enough to eat, and some days we don't; but *all* the time I'm just as happy as I can be!

"'I wish you could see my children run, laughing, to the door when their father comes home. Oh! he is *another* man from what he was a year ago; he is so happy at home with us now, and always so patient and kind!

"'Do tell us if there isn't something—if it is ever so little—that we women can do for the Home; we *never* can forget what it has done for us!'

"Such words, heard again and again with every variety of expression, attests the sincerity of those who, in widely differing circumstances, perhaps, have yet this common bond, that through this instrumentality, they are rejoicing over a husband, a father, a son, 'which was dead, and is alive—was lost, and is found.'

"Surely, such proof of the intrinsic worth of a work like this, is beyond all expression—full of comfort and encouragement to persevere."

Again: "Through their instrumentality families long alienated and separated have been happily brought together. This branch of the ladies' work has been peculiarly blest; and their reward is rich in witnessing not only homes made happier through their labors, but hearts so melted by their personal kindness, and by the Gospel message which they carry, that husbands and wives, convicted of the sinfulness of their neglect of the great salvation, come forward to declare themselves soldiers of the cross, and unite with the Christian church."

THE TESTIMONY OF INMATES.

As the value of this and similar institutions is best seen in what they have done and are doing, we give two extracts from letters received from men who have been reformed through the agency of the "Home" in Philadelphia. In the first, the writer says:

"It has now been nearly two years since I left the Franklin Home. I had been a drinking man ten years, and it got such a hold on me that I could not resist taking it. I had tried a number of times to reform, and at one time, was in the Dashaway's Home, in California, where they steep everything in liquor, but when I came out I still had the desire to drink, and only kept from it for nine months. I again commenced, and kept sinking lower and lower, till I lost my friends, and felt there was no hope for me. On the 31st day of May, 1873, I came to the Franklin Home, and have never tasted intoxicating liquor since, which is the longest time I was ever without it since I commenced to drink. I feel now that I will never drink again, as I do not associate with drinking men, or go to places where liquor is sold. It was so different at the Home from anything I had ever met or heard of, that I went away with more strength to resist than ever before. When I came to the Home I could not get a position in Philadelphia, nobody having confidence in me. Since then I have been engaged as foreman in a manufacturing establishment, by the very man that had discharged me several times for drinking, and have been with him a year. I feel more happy and contented now than any time in ten years past, and if I had a friend who I found this was taking hold of, I would bring him to the Home, for I believe any one that is sincere can be reformed, and I would recommend any man that needs and desires to reform to go to the Home, as I did."

AFTER FIVE YEARS.

Writing to Mr. Samuel P. Godwin, President of the Franklin Home, an old inmate, five years after his reformation, says: "I received your kind letter and recognized in it the challenge of the ever-watchful sentinel, 'How goes the night, brother?' I answer back, 'All is well.' I am delighted to hear of the continued success of 'my second mother,' the Home, and the Association, my brothers; and I thank God, who is encouraging you all in your efforts for fallen men, by showing you the ripening fruits of your labor—efforts and labors that are inspired by a love of God that enables you to see in every fallen man the soul made like unto *His* own image. The Home and all its workers, its principles, the endless and untiring efforts made, challenge the wonder and admiration of every Christian heart. Its grand results will admit of but one explanation, that 'It is God's work.' We, the reclaimed, can never give expression to the grateful emotions of our hearts. We can only let our lives be its best eulogy. We hope to vindicate in the future, as we have in the past, (by adhering to its principles) the great Christian truth, the grace of God is all-powerful, all-saving. *Oh! what has not the Home done for us all!* It sought us amid temptations, misery and sorrow, and took us into its warm and fond embrace, clearing away the debris that intemperance and misfortune had piled up, tearing down all false theories of disease and seizing our convictions. It reached down into our hearts by its admirable practical mode of imparting its principles, impressing all its lessons with the examples of living, active men, who, through its aid, accepting its teachings and practicing them, have become reformed men—in a word, conquerors of self. By its love, fostering care and ever-watchful solicitude for us, it has awakened the lessons of love and faith learned at a dear mother's knee in childhood, which, if forgotten for a time, were never entirely dead, and required but just such an influence to warm them into life. It enables me to say to you now, at the end of five years, I have been a total abstinence man for that time, and by and with the help of God, I will die that."

But enough has been educed to show the importance of this and other "Homes" for the recovery of inebriates, and to direct public attention to their great value. Those already established should be liberally sustained by the communities in which they are located, and similar institutions should be organized and put in operation in all the larger cities of the Union. Thousands of outcast, helpless, perishing men, who, but for the fatal habits they have acquired, would be good and useful citizens, might, if this were done, be every year restored to themselves, their families and to society. If we cannot, as yet, stay the curse that is upon our land, let us do all in our power to heal what has been hurt, and to restore what has been lost.

In every truly reformed man, the temperance cause gains a new and valuable recruit. The great army that is to do successful battle with the destroying enemy that is abroad in the land, will come chiefly from the ranks of those who have felt the crush of his iron heel. So we gain strength with every prisoner that is rescued from the enemy; for every such rescued man will hate this enemy with an undying hatred, and so long as he maintains his integrity, stand fronting him in the field.

Dr. Harris, the attending physician of the "Franklin Reformatory Home," whose long experience and careful observation enable him to speak intelligently as to the causes which lead to relapses among reformed men, has kindly furnished us with the following suggestions as to the dangers that beset their way. The doctor has done a good service in this. To be forewarned is to be forearmed. We are also indebted to him for the chapter on "Tobacco as an Incitant to the Use of Alcoholic Stimulant," which immediately follows this one, and which was especially prepared by him for the present volume.

DANGERS THAT BESET THE REFORMED INEBRIATE.

BY DR. R. P. HARRIS.

"*Come, take a drink.*"—How pernicious is this treating generosity of the inebriate, and how important to the reformed to be firm in declining his invitation. To hesitate, is, in most cases, to yield.

Old companions.—These should be avoided, and made to understand that their company is not congenial; and new and safe ones should be selected.

Attacks of sickness.—A quondam inebriate should never employ a physician who drinks, and should always tell his medical attendant that he cannot take any medicine containing alcohol. It is very unsafe to resort to essence of ginger, paregoric, spirits of lavender or burnt brandy, and friends very injudiciously, sometimes, recommend remedies that are dangerous in the extreme. We saw one man driven into insanity by his employer recommending him a preparation of rhubarb, in Jamaica spirits, which he took with many misgivings, because, six years before he had been a drunkard. The old appetite was revived in full force at once. Diarrhœa can be much better treated without tinctures and essences than with them, as proved by the large experience of the Franklin Home, where they are never prescribed.

Bad company of either sex.—Remember what is said of the strange woman in Proverbs v., 3-12; and the advice given in the first Psalm. Lust has driven to drunkenness and death many a promising case of reform.

Entering a tavern.—It is never safe to buy a cigar, take a glass of lemonade, eat a plate of oysters or even drink water at a bar where liquors are sold. The temptation, and revival of old associations, are too much for weak human nature to withstand.

Politics, military organizations, etc.—Many a man has been made a drunkard by the war, or by becoming an active politician. Associations of men leading to excitement of any kind stimulate them to invite each other to drink as a social custom. Former inebriates should avoid all forms of excitement. Said a former politician, who has not drank for five years: "If I was to go back to politics, and allow matters to take their natural course, I should soon drift again into drunkenness."

"*Idleness*," says the French proverb, "is the mother of all vices;" hence the advantage and importance of being actively employed.

Working in communities.—There are no men more inclined to drunkenness than shoemakers, hatters and those in machine shops. Shoemakers are especially difficult to reform, as they incite each other to drink, and club together and send out for beer or whisky.

Use of excessive quantities of pepper, mustard and horse-radish.—No person can use biting condiments to the same degree as drunkards; and reformed men must largely moderate their allowance, if they expect to keep their appetite under for something stronger. Tavern-keepers understand that salt and peppery articles, furnished gratis for lunch, will pay back principal and profit in the amount they induce men to drink.

Loss of money or death in the family.—These are among the most severe of all the trials to be encountered by the reformed drunkard. Hazardous ventures in stocks or business are dangerous in the extreme. Without the grace of God in the heart, and the strength that it gives in times of depression of spirits under severe trial, there are few reformed men who can bear, with any safety, the loss of a wife or very dear child. Thousands who have, for the time, abandoned the habit have returned to it to drown, in unconsciousness, their feeling of loss; hence the great and vital importance of an entire change of heart to enable a man to go to his faith for consolation, and to look to God for help in times of trial and temptation.

CHAPTER X.

TOBACCO AS AN INCITANT TO THE USE OF ALCOHOLIC STIMULANTS, AND AN OBSTACLE IN THE WAY OF A PERMANENT REFORMATION.

BY DR. R. P. HARRIS, PHYSICIAN OF THE "FRANKLIN REFORMATORY HOME."

WHEN we consider the almost universal use of tobacco, especially in the form of smoking, among our male population, it is not to be wondered at that this powerful poison has come to be regarded as an innocent and almost necessary vegetable production, not to be used as food exactly, but greatly allied to it as an article of daily consumption. Few stop to reason about its properties or effects; they remember, perhaps, how sick they were made by the first chew or smoke, but this having long passed, believe that as their systems have become accustomed, *apparently*, to the poison, it cannot be doing them any real injury. When we reflect that tobacco contains from one to nearly seven per cent. of *nicotine*—one of the most powerful vegetable poisons known—a few drops of which are sufficient to destroy life, it is not difficult to perceive that this faith in the *innocence* begotten of use must be fallacious. We have met with instances where the poisonous effects of tobacco were manifest after every smoke, even where the attempt to accustom the system to its use had been persevered in for many years; and yet the men never realized what was the matter with them, until they had, under medical advice, ceased to use the drug.

Before the discovery of anæsthetics, tobacco was used as a remedy to produce relaxation in cases of strangulated hernia; and although very cautiously administered in the form of tea, or smoke per rectum, proved fatal in many instances. As little as twelve grains in six ounces of water having thus acted; and from half a drachm to two drachms in a number of instances. When men chew as high as a pound and a quarter of strong navy tobacco a week, or three packages of fine-cut in a day, it must certainly tell upon them sooner or later; or even in much less quantity.

If men used tobacco in moderation, there would be much less objection to it, if it was not so intimately

ASSOCIATED WITH THE HABIT OF DRINKING.

This is recognized by the trade, in the fact that we see many tobacco stores as the entrance to drinking saloons. Ninety-three per cent. of the men who have been admitted to the Franklin Reformatory Home used tobacco, and eighty per cent. of them chewed it. There may be possibly as high as ninety-three per cent. of male adults who smoke, but eighty per cent. of chewers is undoubtedly a large proportion as compared with those in the same ranks of society who do not drink.

Although the poisonous symptoms of tobacco are, in a great degree, the same in different persons at the inception of the habit, the effects vary materially in after years according to the quantity and variety used, the form employed and the habits and temperament of the user. One man will chew a paper a week, another four, many use one a day, and a few from one and a half to three a day, besides smoking. Occasionally, but very rarely, we find a man who limits himself to one cigar a day, a number allow themselves but three, but of later years even these are moderate compared with those who use eight, ten or more.

There are many men who, for years, preserve a robust, hale appearance under both tobacco and whisky, who are, notwithstanding their apparent health, steadily laying the foundation of diseased heart, or

DERANGEMENT OF THE DIGESTIVE ORGANS

or nervous system from the former, or an organic fatal disease of the liver or kidneys from the latter.

Healthy-looking men are often rejected by examiners of life insurance companies because of irregular and intermittent action of the heart from tobacco; and equally robust subjects are forced to abandon the habit because of tremors, vertigo or a peculiar form of dyspepsia. We have known men who died from the use of tobacco, and others who met a like fate from whisky, who were never fully in the state denominated drunk. Men may earn a hobnail liver and dropsy by the constant, steady use of alcoholic drink taken systematically, so as always to keep within the limits of intoxication; or they may, in the same way, get a diabetes or Bright's disease.

Abundant testimony in regard to the effects of tobacco in creating an appetite for strong drink has been given by the inmates of the Franklin Home. In a few exceptional cases the use of tobacco does not appear to create any sense of thirst; and this is specially the case with the smokers who do not spit when smoking. Some men seem to be free from any alcoholic craving when using tobacco, and say that when they commence to drink they give up the drug for the time being. These are exceptional cases, for excess in drinking generally leads to an excess in the use of tobacco, often to double the amount ordinarily employed. We have often been told by moderate drinkers, that they frequently

FELT A DESIRE FOR A LITTLE WHISKY AFTER A SMOKE,

and they have confessed that they were only saved from a habit of drinking to excess by the fact that they had no innate fondness for alcoholic stimulation. Unfortunately, there is a large and increasing class of men who, finding that water does not, but that alcohol does, relieve the dryness of throat and diseased thirst resulting from tobacco, are led, little by little, into the habit of using whisky to excess. Such men, after, it may be, a long abstinence, are not unfrequently led back into their old habits by an attack of nervousness, resulting from a temporary excessive use of tobacco, and a feeling that all that is wanting to relieve this is a glass of whisky, which being taken, at once determines a debauch of long or short duration, according to the habits and character of the party. Many a *so-called periodical drinker* fixes the return of his period by an act of this kind, and with such cases it is all-important to their permanent reformation, that they should cease entirely and forever from the use of tobacco. We have, in a few instances, prevailed upon men to do this, but in a large majority of cases, where they have admitted the connection between the two habits, in their own person, or volunteered to tell how much tobacco had acted in forming and keeping up their appetite for whisky, they have failed in being able to sum up sufficient resolution to abandon the use of the drug, saying that they felt the importance of the step, and would be glad to be able to give it up, but that the habit was

TEN TIMES AS DIFFICULT TO CONQUER AS THAT OF WHISKY-DRINKING.

All that we have been able to accomplish in such cases has been to check the excessive use. We have repeatedly assured men, after a careful examination of their peculiar cases, that they would certainly drink again unless they gave up their tobacco, and have seen this opinion verified, because they took no heed to the warning. We have also been gratified in a few instances by hearing a man say that he felt confident that he could never have accomplished his reformation as he had done, if he had not taken the advice given him about abandoning his tobacco. In contrast with the men of weak purpose, we have to admire one who had resolution enough to break off the three habits of opium-eating, whisky-drinking and tobacco-chewing—no trifling matter—when the first was of ten and the last of more than thirty years' duration.

We have been repeatedly asked which was the most injurious, smoking or chewing, and have replied, that everything depended upon the amount of nicotine absorbed in the process, and the loss to the system in the saliva spit out. Men have died from the direct effect of excessive smoking, and quite recently a death in a child was reported from the result of blowing soap-bubbles with an old wooden pipe. We have known a little boy to vomit from drawing air a few times through the empty meerschaum pipe of his German teacher. The smoking of two pipes as the first essay, very nearly caused the death of a young man, whose case was reported by Dr. Marshall Hall.

The least poisonous tobaccos are those of Syria and Turkey, but the cigarettes made of them in the

East and imported into this country are said to be impregnated with opium. Virginia tobacco, for the pipe or chewing, contains a large percentage of nicotine, and the former is often impregnated with foreign matters, recognizable by the choking effect of the smoke when inhaled, or by the removal of the epithelium (outer skin) of the tongue at the point under the end of the pipe-stem.

If we fail in our efforts to reform the tobacco habit, the next best thing to do, is to show men what the nature and capabilities of the poison are, and endeavor to persuade them to use the milder varieties and in a moderate quantity.

ONE OF THE GREAT CURSES OF THE RISING GENERATION

is the passion for imitating and acquiring the evil habits of men, under an impression that it hastens their approach to manhood. Weak, frail, delicate boys, with inherited tendencies to disease, who should, by all means, never use tobacco, or anything injurious, are often as obstinately bent upon learning to smoke, in spite of medical advice, as those in whom a moderate use would be far less objectionable. A recent observer, in examining into the cases of thirty-eight boys who had formed the habit of using tobacco, found that twenty-seven of them had also a fondness for alcoholic stimulants. A large proportion of the Franklin Home inmates attribute their habit of drinking to the effects of company; many commenced in the army, and many were induced to drink at first by invitation. If smoking was a solitary habit, it would be less likely to lead to drinking; but the same companionship, and habits of treating prevail, as in the saloon, and the step from the *estaminet* to the bar-room under invitation, is an easy one, where the diseased thirst, so often induced by tobacco, favors the movement to treat.

We have no prejudice against tobacco, other than what would naturally arise in the mind from a careful examination of the effects of the poison in hundreds of cases. We have seen large, hale-looking men forced in time to abandon, although very reluctantly, the use of tobacco in every form; and the most bitter enemy we have ever met to the *vile weed*, as he termed it, was a physician, who had been forced to give up chewing on account of the state of his heart, after years of indulgence. We have seen many such instances, and, in one case, the abandonment of the habit entirely cured a dyspepsia of twenty-eight years' standing.

CHAPTER XI.

THE WOMAN'S CRUSADE.

FOR every one saved through the agency of inebriate asylums and reformatory homes, hundreds are lost and hundreds added yearly to the great army of drunkards. Good and useful as such institutions are, they do not meet the desperate exigencies of the case. Something of wider reach and quicker application is demanded. What shall it be? In prohibition many look for the means by which the curse of drunkenness is to be abated. But, while we wait for a public sentiment strong enough to determine legislation, sixty thousand unhappy beings are yearly consigned to drunkards' graves.

What have temperance men accomplished in the fifty years during which they have so earnestly opposed the drinking usages of society and the traffic in alcoholic drinks? And what have they done for the prevention and cure of drunkenness? In limiting the use of intoxicants, in restricting the liquor traffic and in giving a right direction to public sentiment, they have done a great and good work; but their efforts to reclaim the fallen drunkard have met with sad discouragements. In the work of prevention, much has been accomplished; in the work of cure, alas! how little. The appetite once formed, and the unhappy victim finds himself under the control of a power from which he can rarely get free. Pledges, new associations, better and more favorable surroundings, all are tried, and many are saved; but the number of the saved are few in comparison with those who, after a season of sobriety, fall back into their old ways.

In all these many years of untiring efforts to lift up and save the fallen, what sad disappointments have met our earnest and devoted temperance workers. From how many fields, which seemed full of a rich promise, have they gathered only a meagre harvest. But still they have worked on, gaining strength from defeat and disappointment; for they knew that the cause in which they were engaged was the cause of God and humanity, and that in the end it must prevail.

Meantime, the bitter, half-despairing cry, "O Lord, how long!" was going up from the lips of broken-hearted wives and mothers all over the land, and year by year this cry grew deeper and more desperate. All hope in man was failing from their hearts. They saw restrictive legislation here and there, and even prohibition; but, except in a few cases, no removal of the curse; for behind law, usage, prejudice, interest and appetite the traffic stood intrenched and held its seat of power.

At last, in the waning years of the first century of our nation's existence, their failing hope in man died utterly, and with another and deeper and more despairing cry, the women of our land sent up their voices to God. Not now saying "O Lord, how long!" but "Lord, come to our help against the mighty!"

What followed is history. The first result of this utter abandonment of all hope in moral suasion or legal force, and of a turning to God in prayer and faith, was that strange, intense, impulsive movement known as the "Woman's Crusade."

BEGINNING OF THE CRUSADE.

Let us briefly give the story of its initiation late in the month of December, 1873. Dr. Dio Lewis, in a lecture which he had been engaged to deliver at Hillsboro, Ohio, related how, forty years before, his pious mother, the wife of a drunkard, who was struggling to feed, clothe and educate her five helpless children, went, with other women who had a similar sorrow with her own, to the tavern-keeper who sold their husbands drink, and, kneeling down in his bar-room, prayed with and for him, and besought him to abandon a business that was cursing his neighbors and bringing want and suffering into their homes. Their prayers and entreaties prevailed. After telling this story of his mother, the lecturer asked all the women present who were willing to follow her example to rise, and in response, nearly the entire audience arose. A meeting was then called for the next morning, to be held in the Presbyterian church.

Dr. Lewis was a guest at the old mansion of Ex-Governor Trimble, father of Mrs. E. J. Thompson, a most cultivated, devoted Christian woman, mother of eight children. She was not present at the lecture, but "prepared," as she writes, "as those who watch for the morning, for the first gray light upon this dark night of sorrow. Few comments were made in our house," she continues, "upon this new line of policy until after breakfast the next morning, when, just as we gathered about the hearth-stone, my daughter Mary said, very gently: 'Mother, will you go the meeting this morning?' Hesitatingly I replied: 'I don't know yet what I shall do.' My husband, fully appreciating the responsibility of the moment, said: 'Children, let us leave your mother alone; for you know where she goes with all vexed questions;' and pointing to the old family Bible, left the room. The awful responsibility of the step that I must needs next take was wonderfully relieved by thought of the 'cloudy pillar' and 'parted waters' of the past; hence, with confidence, I was about turning my eye of faith 'up to the hills,' from whence had come my help, when, in response to a gentle tap at my door, I met my dear Mary, who, with her Bible in hand and tearful eyes, said: 'Mother, I opened to Psalm cxlvi., and I believe it is for you.' She withdrew and I sat down to read the wonderful message from God. As I read what I had so often read before, the Spirit so strangely 'took of the things of God,' and showed me new meanings, I no longer hesitated, but, in the strength thus imparted, started to the scene of action.

"Upon entering the church, I was startled to find myself chosen as leader. The old Bible was taken down from the desk, and Psalm cxlvi. read. Mrs. General McDowell, by request, led in prayer, and, although she had never before heard her own voice in a public prayer, on this occasion 'the tongue of fire' sat upon her, and all were deeply affected. Mrs. Cowden, our Methodist minister's wife, was then requested to sing to a familiar air—

> "'Give to the winds thy fears!
> Hope, and be undismayed;
> God hears thy sighs and counts thy tears:
> He will lift up thy head.'

And while thus engaged, the women (seventy-five in number) fell in line, two and two, and proceeded first to the drug stores and then to the hotels and saloons."

Thus began this memorable Crusade, which was maintained in Hillsboro for over six months, during which time the saloons were visited almost daily.

Within two days, the women of Washington Court-House, a neighboring town, felt the inspiration of their sisters, and inaugurated the movement there. A description of what was done at this place will afford the reader a clear impression of the way in which the "Crusaders" worked, and the results that followed their efforts. We quote from the account given by Mrs. M. V. Ustick:

"After an hour of prayer, forty-four women filed slowly and solemnly down the aisle and started forth upon their strange mission, with fear and trembling, while the male portion of the audience remained at church to pray from the success of this new undertaking; the tolling of the church-bell keeping time to the solemn march of the women, as they wended their way to the first drug store on the list (the number of places within the city limits where intoxicating drinks were sold was fourteen—eleven saloons and three drug stores). Here, as in every place, they entered singing, every woman taking up the sacred strain as she crossed the threshold. This was followed by the reading of the appeal and prayer, and then earnest pleading to desist from their soul-destroying traffic and to sign the dealers' pledge. Thus, all the day long, going from place to place, without stopping even for dinner or lunch, till five o'clock, meeting with no marked success; but invariably courtesy was extended to them.

"The next day an increased number of women went forth, leaving the men in the church to pray all day long. On this day the contest really began, and at the first place the doors were found locked. With hearts full of compassion, the women knelt in the snow upon the pavement to plead for the Divine influence upon the heart of the liquor-dealer, and there held their first street prayer-meeting. The Sabbath was devoted to a union mass-meeting. Monday, December 29th, is one long to be remembered in Washington as the day on which occurred the first surrender ever made by a liquor-dealer of his stock of liquors of every kind and variety to the women, in answer to their prayers and entreaties, and by them poured into the street. Nearly a thousand men, women and children witnessed the mingling of beer, ale, wine and whisky, as they filled the gutters and were drunk up by the earth, while bells were ringing, men and boys shouting, and women singing and praying to God, who had given the victory.

"On the fourth day, the campaign reached its height; the town being filled with visitors from all parts of the country and adjoining villages. Another public surrender and another pouring into the street of a larger stock of liquors than on the day before, and more intense excitement and enthusiasm. In eight days all the saloons, eleven in number, had been closed, and the three drug stores pledged to sell only on prescription.

"Early in the third week the discouraging intelligence came that a new man had taken out license to sell liquor in one of the deserted saloons, and that he was backed by a whisky house in Cincinnati to the amount of five thousand dollars to break down this movement. On Wednesday, 14th of January, the whisky was unloaded at his room. About forty women were on the ground and followed the liquor in, and remained holding an uninterrupted prayer-meeting all day and until eleven o'clock at night. The next day—bitterly cold—was spent in the same place and manner, without fire or chairs, two hours of that time the women being locked in, while the proprietor was off attending a trial. On the following day, the coldest of the winter of 1874, the women were locked out, and remained on the street holding religious services all day long. Next morning a tabernacle was built in the street just in front of the house, and was occupied for the double purpose of watching and praying through the day; but before night the sheriff closed the saloon, and the proprietor surrendered. A short time afterwards, on a dying bed, this four-day's liquor-dealer sent for some of these women, telling them their songs and prayers had never ceased to ring in his ears, and urging them to pray again in his behalf; so he passed away."

From this beginning the new temperance movement increased and spread with a marvelous rapidity. The incidents attendant on the progress of the "Crusade" were often of a novel and exciting character. Such an interference with their business was not to be tolerated by the liquor men; and they soon began to organize for defense and retaliation. They not only had the law on their side, but in many cases, the administrators of the law. Yet it often happened, in consequence of their reckless violations of statutes made to limit and regulate the traffic, that dealers found themselves without standing in the courts, or entangled in the meshes of the very laws they had invoked for protection.

In the smaller towns the movement was, for a time, almost irresistible; and in many of them the drink traffic ceased altogether. But when it struck the larger cities, it met with impediments, against which it beat violently for awhile, but without the force to bear them down. Our space will not permit us to more than glance at some of the incidents attendant on this singular crusade. The excitement that followed its inauguration in the large city of Cleveland was intense. It is thus described by Mrs. Sarah K. Bolton in her history of the Woman's Crusade, to which we have already referred:

HOW THE CRUSADERS WERE TREATED.

"The question was constantly asked: 'Will the women of a conservative city of one hundred and fifty thousand go upon the street as a praying-band?' The liquor-dealers said: 'Send committees of two or three and we will talk with them; but coming in a body to pray with us brands our business as disreputable.' The time came when the Master seemed to call for a mightier power to bear upon the liquor traffic, and a company of heroic women, many of them the wives of prominent clergymen, led by Mrs. W. A. Ingham, said: 'Here am I; the Lord's will be done.'

"On the third day of the street work, the whisky and beer interest seemed to have awakened to a full consciousness of the situation. Drinkers, dealers and roughs gathered in large numbers on the street to wait for the praying women. A mob, headed by an organization of brewers, rushed upon them, kicking them, striking them with their fists and hitting them with brickbats. The women were locked in a store away from the infuriated mob, who, on the arrival of a stronger body of police, were dispersed, cursing and yelling as they went. The next day, taking their lives in their hands, a larger company of women went out, and somewhat similar scenes were enacted. Meantime, public meetings, called in the churches, were so crowded that standing room could not be found. The clergy, as one man, came to the front. Business men left their stores and shops, ministers their studies, and a thousand manly men went out to defend the praying women. The military companies were ordered to be in readiness, resting on their arms; the police force was increased, and the liquor interest soon made to feel that the city was not under its control. The mob never again tried its power. For three months, with scarcely a day's exception, the praying-bands, sometimes with twenty in each, working in various parts of the city; sometimes with five hundred, quietly and silently, two by two, forming a procession over a quarter of a mile in length, followed by scores in carriages, who could not bear the long walks, went from saloon to saloon, holding services where the proprietors were willing, and in warehouses which were thrown open to them, or in vacant lots near by, when they were unwilling.

* * * Men took off their hats, and often wept as the long procession went by. Little children gathered close to the singers, and catching the words, sang them months afterwards in their dingy hovels. Haggard women bent their heads as they murmured with unutterable sadness, 'You've come too late to save my boy or my husband.' Many saloon-keepers gave up their business and never resumed it. Many who had lost all hope because of the appetite which bound them, heard from woman's lips the glad tidings of freedom in Christ, and accepted the liberty of the Gospel."

In many other places the crusaders met with violence from exasperated liquor-dealers and their brutish associates. A pail of cold water was thrown into the face of a woman in Clyde, Ohio, as she knelt praying in front of a saloon. Dirty water was thrown by pailfuls over the women at Norwalk. At Columbus, a saloon-keeper assaulted one of the praying-band, injuring her seriously. In Cincinnati, forty-three women were arrested by the authorities for praying in the street and lodged in jail. In Bellefontaine, a large liquor-dealer declared that if the praying-band visited him he would use powder and lead; but the women, undeterred by his threat, sang and prayed in front of his saloon every day for a week, in spite of the insults and noisy interferences of himself and customers. At the end of that time the man made his appearance at a mass-meeting and signed the pledge; and on the following Sunday attended church for the first time in five years.

DECLINE OF THE CRUSADING SPIRIT.

From Ohio the excitement soon spread to other Western States, and then passed east and south, until it was felt in nearly every State in the Union; but it did not gain force by extension. To the sober, second-thought of those who had, in singleness of heart, self-consecration and trust in God, thrown themselves into this work because they believed that they were drawn of the Spirit, came the perception of other, better and more orderly ways of accomplishing the good they sought. If God were, indeed, with them—if it was His Divine work of saving human souls upon which they had entered, He would lead them into the right ways, if they were but willing to walk therein. Of this there came to them a deep assurance; and in the great calm that fell after the rush and excitement and wild confusion of that first movement against the enemy, they heard the voice of God calling to them still. And, as they hearkened, waiting to be led, and willing to obey, light came, and they saw more clearly. Not by swift, impetuous impulse, but through organization and slow progression was the victory to be won.

In the language of Frances E. Willard, in her history of "The Woman's National Christian Temperance Union," to be found in the Centennial temperance volume: "The women who went forth by an impulse sudden, irresistible, divine, to pray in the saloons, became convinced, as weeks and months passed by, that theirs was to be no easily-won victory. The enemy was rich beyond their power to comprehend. He had upon his side the majesty of the law, the trickery of politics and the leagued strength of that almost invincible pair— appetite, avarice. He was persistent, too, as fate; determined to fight it out on that line to the last dollar of his enormous treasure-house and the last ounce of his power. But these women of the Crusade believed in God, and in themselves as among His appointed instruments to destroy the rum-power in America. They loved Christ's cause; they loved the native land that had been so mindful of them; they loved their sweet and sacred homes; and so it came about that, though they had gone forth only as skirmishers, they soon fell into line of battle; though they had ignorantly hoped to take the enemy by a sudden assault, they buckled on the armor for the long campaign. The woman's praying-bands, earnest, impetuous, inspired, became the woman's temperance unions, firm, patient, persevering. The praying-bands were without leadership, save that which inevitably results from 'the survival of the fittest;' the woman's unions are regularly officered in the usual way. They first wrought their grand pioneer work in sublime indifference to prescribed forms of procedure—'so say we all of us' being the spirit of 'motions' often made, seconded and carried by the chair, while the assembled women nodded their earnest acquiescence; the second are possessed of good, strong constitutions (with by-laws annexed), and follow the order of business with a dutiful regard to parliamentary usage. In the first, women who had never lifted up their voices in their own church prayer-meetings stood before thousands and 'spoke as they were moved;' in the second, these same women with added experience, and a host of others who have since enlisted, impress the public thought and conscience by utterances carefully considered. The praying-bands, hoping for immediate victory, pressed their members into incessant service; the woman's unions, aware that the battle is to be a long one, ask only for such help as can be given consistently with other duties."

As the result of this intelligent effort at effective organization by the women who inaugurated and were prominent in the "Crusade," we have "The Woman's National Christian Temperance Union," with its auxiliary and local unions in nearly every State; one of the most efficient agencies in the practical work of temperance reform which the country has yet seen.

CHAPTER XII.

THE WOMAN'S NATIONAL CHRISTIAN TEMPERANCE UNION.

DURING the summer of 1874, when the reaction which had checked the "Crusade" was recognized as something permanent by the more thoughtful and observant of the women who had been engaged in it, they paused for deliberation, and took counsel together. Great victories had been won in the brief season during which they were masters of the field; and now that the enemy had rallied his forces, and intrenched himself behind law, public opinion, politics and the State, should they weakly give up the contest? Not so. They had discovered wherein the weakness, as well as the strength, of their enemy lay, and had come into a new perception of their own powers and resources.

ORGANIZATION.

The first step taken was to call conventions in the various States where the Crusade had been active. These were attended by delegates chosen by the local praying-bands. The result was the organization, in some of the States, of what were known as "Temperance Leagues." Afterwards the word "Unions" was substituted for Leagues. Having organized by States, the next thing was to have a National Union. In August of that year, the first National Sunday-School Assembly was held at Chautauqua Lake, near Buffalo, New York. Many of the most earnest workers in the temperance Crusade, from different parts of the United States, and from the various denominations of Christians, were present, and the conviction was general that steps should at once be taken towards forming a National League, in order to make permanent the work that had already been done. After much deliberation, a committee of organization was appointed, consisting of a woman from each State. This committee issued a circular letter, asking the various Woman's Temperance Leagues to hold meetings, for the purpose of electing one woman from each Congressional district as a delegate to a National Convention, to be held in November, at Cleveland, Ohio. A single paragraph from this circular will show the spirit that animated the call.

"It is hardly necessary to remind those who have worked so nobly in the grand temperance uprising that in union and organization are its success and permanence, and the consequent redemption of this land from the curse of intemperance. In the name of our Master—in behalf of the thousands of women who suffer from this terrible evil, we call upon all to unite in an earnest, continued effort to hold the ground already won, and move onward together to a complete victory over the foes we fight."

Delegates representing sixteen States were present at the convention, which held its first session in Cleveland, commencing on the 18th of November, 1874, and lasting for three days. Prominent among its members were active leaders of the Crusade, but, besides these, says Miss Willard, "there were present many thoughtful and gifted women, whose hearts had been stirred by the great movement, though until now they had lacked the opportunity to identify themselves with it. Mrs. Jennie F. Willing presided over the convention, which was one of the most earnest and enthusiastic ever held. A constitution was adopted, also a plan of organization intended to reach every hamlet, town and city in the land. There was a declaration of principles, of which Christianity alone could have furnished the animus. An appeal to the women of our country was provided for; another to the girls of America; a third to lands beyond the sea; a memorial to Congress was ordered, and a deputation to carry it appointed; a National temperance paper, to be edited and published by women, was agreed upon, also a financial plan, asking for a cent a week from members; and last, not least, was appointed a special committee on temperance work among the children. Four large mass-meetings were held during the convention, all of them addressed by women. Mrs. Annie Wittenmyer, of Philadelphia, was elected president; Miss Frances E. Willard, of Chicago, corresponding secretary; Mrs. Mary C. Johnson, of Brooklyn, recording secretary; Mrs. Mary A. Ingham, of Cleveland, treasurer, with one vice-president from each State represented in the convention."

The spirit of this assembly of workers is shown in the closing resolution, which it adopted unanimously:

"*Resolved*, That, recognizing the fact that our cause is, and is to be, combated by mighty, determined and relentless forces, we will, trusting in Him who is the Prince of Peace, meet argument with argument, misjudgment with patience, denunciation with kindness, and all our difficulties and dangers with prayer."

FIRST YEAR'S WORK.

During the first year six State organizations were added to the number represented in the beginning, including scores of local unions. A monthly paper was established; a deputation of women sent to Congress with a memorial, to which hundreds of thousands of signatures had been obtained, asking for inquiry and legislation in regard to the liquor traffic; a manual of "Hints and Helps," concerning methods of temperance work, prepared and issued; and other agencies of reform, and for the extermination of the liquor traffic, set in motion.

The reports from State Unions, made to the first annual meeting, held in Cincinnati, November, 1875, were, in most cases, highly encouraging. In Ohio, a large number of local unions were formed, nearly two hundred friendly inns established, while reading-rooms, juvenile societies and young people's leagues were reported as multiplying all over the State. Indiana showed effective work in the same direction; so did Illinois. In both of these States many local unions, reform clubs and juvenile organizations came into existence, while the work of temperance agitation was carried on with untiring vigor. Iowa reported fifty local unions, eleven juvenile societies, seven reform clubs and six coffee-houses and reading-rooms. But, how better can we sum up the results of this year's work, and how better give a clear idea of the new forces which were coming into the field under the leadership of women, than by giving an extract from the first annual report of the corresponding secretary, Miss Frances E. Willard:

"Briefly to recapitulate, bringing out salient features, Maine has given, since the Crusade, the idea of the temperance camp-meeting, which, though not original with us, has been rendered effective largely through the efforts of our own workers. Connecticut influences elections, has availed itself of petitions and given us the best form on record. New York has kept alive the visitation of saloons, and proved, what may we never forget, that this is always practicable, if conducted wisely. In the relief and rescue branches of our work, the Empire State is perhaps without a rival. The women of

Pennsylvania have bearded the gubernatorial lion in his den, and the Hartranft veto had the added sin of women's prayers and tears denied. Maryland and the District of Columbia prove that the North must look to her laurels when the South is free to enter on our work. As for Ohio, as Daniel Webster said of the old Bay State, 'There she stands; look at her!'—foremost among leaders in the new Crusade. Michigan is working bravely amid discouragements. Illinois has given us the most promising phase of our juvenile work, and leads off in reform clubs. Our best organized States are Ohio, Indiana, New York, Pennsylvania and Iowa. By reason of their multiplied conventions of State, district and county, their numerous auxilaries, their petitions and their juvenile work, Ohio and Indiana bear off the palm, and stand as the banner States of our Union up to this time, each of them having as many as two hundred and fifty auxiliaries.

"Our review develops the fact that of the forty-seven States and Territories forming the United States, twenty-two States have formed temperance unions auxiliary to the Woman's National Union. Of the twenty-five not yet organized, twelve are Southern States and eight are Territories; while of the remaining five, three are about to organize State unions, and have already flourishing local unions. So, that, without exaggeration, we may say we have fairly entered into the land to possess it. To bring about this vast result of organization, and to maintain it, there have been held (not to mention conventions of districts and counties, the name of which is legion,) forty-five State conventions of women, almost all within the last year.

"The number of written communications sent out during the year from our Western office to women in every State in the Union, is nearly five thousand. This is exclusive of 'documents,' which have gone by the bushel from the Eastern and Western offices, and also of the incessant correspondence of our president. Either president or secretary has spoken in nearly every State in which our organization exists. During the summer months, conventions, camp-meetings and local auxiliaries in large numbers have been addressed by officers of our National and State Unions in all of the Eastern and Middle and in many of the Western States. Noteworthy in our history for the year, is the monster petition circulated in nearly every State, presented to Congress on our behalf by Senator Morton, of Indiana, and defended in an eloquent speech before the Finance Committee by our president."

THE SECOND YEAR'S WORK.

The second annual meeting of the "Woman's National Christian Temperance Union" was held in Newark, N. J., in October, 1876. From the reports made to this meeting, we take the following interesting statements, showing how actively the work, for which this great National Association was organized, has been prosecuted.

Twenty-two State unions were represented at this meeting, and local unions were reported as having been formed for the first time in Tennessee, Louisiana and Arkansas, preparatory to State organizations. An International Temperance Convention of women had been held in the Academy of Music, Philadelphia, from which resulted an International Woman's Temperance Union. A summary of the work of the year says:

"In almost every organized State, the request of our National Committee that ministerial, medical and educational associations be asked to declare their position in relation to temperance reform has been complied with. In every instance, the ladies have been courteously received, and in no case has the declaration of opinion been adverse, and in many, most hopeful to our cause. The letter of Mrs. Wittenmyer to the International Medical Convention recently held in Philadelphia, secured the important declaration against alcohol made by that body.

"In February, our president, accompanied by Mrs. Mary R. Denman, President of New Jersey W. T. U., made a trip to Kentucky, Tennessee and Louisiana, in the endeavor to enlist our Southern sisters in the temperance work. Large meetings were addressed and several local unions organized.

"In the month of May thirty-six temperance meetings were held in the State of Ohio, by the corresponding secretary, who has also made a trip through Michigan, and spoken in all the Eastern, Middle and several of the Western States since the last meeting.

"Our recording secretary, Mrs. Mary C. Johnson, has visited Great Britian, by invitation of Christian women there, for the purpose of introducing our Gospel work. Going in the spirit of the Crusade, Mrs. Johnson's labors have awakened an earnest spirit of inquiry and activity among the thoughtful and comparatively leisure class. During her six months' absence in England and Ireland, she addressed one hundred and twenty-one audiences and conducted forty prayer-meetings.

"'Mother Stewart,' of Ohio, has also visited England and Scotland this year, under the auspices of the Good Templars, and much good has resulted from her labors.

"Our union has circulated the petition to Congress for a Commission of Inquiry into the costs and results of the liquor traffic in America, and to the Centennial Commissioners praying them not to allow the sale of intoxicants on the Exposition grounds. The desired Commission of Inquiry has been ordered by the Senate in response to the wish of the united temperance societies of the land, but the subject did not come before the House at the last session.

"Our paper has constantly increased in its hold upon the local unions, whose devotion to its interests augurs well for its future success.

"The number of documents scattered among our auxiliaries cannot be accurately stated, but is not less than twelve or fifteen thousand, and the correspondence of the officers by letter and postal-card, will not fall short of the same estimate. To correct misapprehensions, it should, perhaps, be stated that no officer of the National Union has received a dollar for services or traveling expenses during the year."

A WORKING ORGANIZATION.

To meet annually in convention and pass resolutions and make promises is one thing; to do practical and effective work all through the year is quite another. And it is just here that this new temperance organization exhibits its power. The women whom it represents are very much in earnest and mean work. What they resolve to do, if clearly seen to be in the right direction, will hardly fail for lack of effort. In their plan of work, one branch particularly embraces the children. If the rising generation can not only be pledged to abstinence, but so carefully instructed in regard to the sin and evil of intemperance, and their duty, when they become men and women, to make war upon the liquor traffic, and to discountenance all form of social drinking, then an immense gain will be had for the cause in the next generation, when the boys and girls of to-day will hold the ballots, make the laws, give direction to public sentiment and determine the usages of society.

LOOKING AFTER THE CHILDREN.

To what extent, then, are the State and local unions looking after the children? Writing, as we now are, before the third annual meeting of the National Union, and, therefore, without a general report of the year's work before us, we are unable to give a statement in full of the important temperance work which has been done with and for the rising generation. But, from official and other reliable sources of information, we are in possession of facts of a most gratifying character. In the State of Minnesota, as the result of woman's efforts, they have had for several years a "Sunday-School Temperance League," and their last annual report gives seventeen thousand as the number of children already "pledged to abstain from all intoxicants as a beverage." Says their report for 1877, "We have carried the work into sixty-one new schools, held sixty-three anniversary meetings and temperance concerts, instigated about one thousand addresses in the Sunday-schools, secured six thousand six hundred and seventy-four signers to our pledges, and one thousand and fifteen to our constitution."

In most of the larger towns throughout the United States where active local unions exist, juvenile unions, bands of hope or temperance associations by some other name, have been formed among the children. These have, in many cases, a large membership; often as high as from five to six hundred. In Rockford, Ill., the juvenile union numbers over eight hundred boys and as many girls. The pledge taken by these children includes, in some localities, tobacco and profanity as well as intoxicants.

THE WORK OF REFORM AND RESCUE.

In the work of reform and rescue, the State and local unions are very active, especially in the larger towns and cities. In the smaller towns, religious temperance meetings are held weekly, and in the larger cities, daily, and sometimes twice a day. Chicago has as many as eighteen meetings every week. In Chapters XIX. and XX. of the first part of this volume, we have described at length, and from personal observation, the way in which these temperance prayer-meetings are generally conducted, and the means used for lifting up and saving the poor drunkard.

What are known as "Reform Clubs," have grown out of the efforts made of these praying women, to hold in safety the men whom they have been able to rescue. These clubs are numerous in New England and the Western States, and have a large membership, which is composed exclusively of reformed men. The common platform upon which they all stand is: 1. Total abstinence. 2. Reliance upon God's help in all things. 3. Missionary work to induce others to sign the pledge. In Newark, N. J., there is a club with a membership of over six hundred reformed men, nearly all of whom have been rescued in the past three years, through the efforts of the Woman's Christian Temperance Union of that city.

In an interview with Mrs. Wittenmyer, President of the National Union, who had received reports of the third year's work from the various unions, we learned that, after deducting from the returns all who were known to have broken the pledge, ten thousand remained as the number reported to have been saved during the year, and who were still standing in the strength which God had given them. The larger part of these rescued men had united themselves with the church, and were earnestly endeavoring to lead Christian lives.

KEEPING ALIVE A SENTIMENT ADVERSE TO THE LIQUOR TRAFFIC.

Another and most important branch of the work of the " Woman's Christian Temperance Union," is that of arousing, keeping alive and intensifying a sentiment adverse to the liquor traffic. So long as the State and National Governments give the sanction of law to this traffic, they find their efforts to save the fallen, utterly unavailing in far too many instances. In an appeal made by the women of the State Union to the voters of Massachusetts, under date of August 15th, 1877, the curse of this traffic is exhibited in words of solemn earnestness. The document is strong and convincing, yet temperate and respectful. We copy it entire as presenting arguments and considerations which every humane and

Christian voter in the land should lay deeply to heart:

"The Woman's Christian Temperance Union comes to you with a solemn and earnest appeal.

"Our mission is the redemption of the Commonwealth from the curse of intemperance. During the past year we have labored incessantly for this end, and have expended nearly twenty thousand dollars in efforts to rescue the perishing, and to educate public sentiment in favor of total abstinence.

"In this work we have met numerous obstacles— the apathy of the people, the inherited and depraved appetites of drunkards, and the perilous social customs of the day, which are indorsed by the practice of many otherwise excellent people. Worse than all these combined is the influence of the licensed dram-shop. We can arouse the indifferent to action; we can enkindle in the drunkard aspirations for a better life than that of debauchery; we hope, in time, by constant agitation, to change the social customs of the day. But against the influence of the licensed dram-shop we are powerless. We have no ability to cope with this most formidable enemy of virtue, prosperity and good order.

"A long and bitter experience compels us to say that the most untiring efforts to reclaim the drunkard have, in many instances, proved unavailing, because his demoralized will has been powerless to resist the temptations placed in his path by the sanction of the State.

"Worse, if possible, even than this—the licensed dram-shop is instrumental in creating a new generation of drunkards. For thither resort our young men, the future hope of the country, who speedily fall before the seductions of the place, their habits of sobriety are subverted, their moral sense is blunted, their will palsied, and they drift rapidly into the appalling condition of habitual drunkenness. The licensed dram-shops are recruiting offices, where another army of drunkards is enlisted, to fill the ranks depleted by dishonored deaths—and the great Commonwealth extends over them the ægis of its protection, indorsing them by the sanction of law. The people of Massachusetts drink annually twenty-five million dollars' worth of intoxicating liquors. *Only God can furnish the statistics of sorrow, poverty, disease, vice and crime, begotten by this fearful consumption of strong drink.*

"Under these discouraging circumstances, men of Massachusetts, we appeal to you! The licensed dram-shop is the creature of political action. We are wholly destitute of political power, by which it must be overthrown. Anguished by the peril of fathers and brothers, husbands and sons, we appeal to you to make good the oft-repeated assertion that the men of the State represent and protect the women of the State at the ballot-box. We beseech you to make earnest efforts to secure the repeal of the license law at the next election, and the enactment of a law prohibiting the sale of intoxicating liquors as a beverage.

"We are sure we speak the sentiment of the Christian people of this State, and of all who stand for morality, thrift, virtue and good order, when we say that the great State of Massachusetts should not take sides with the drunkard-maker against his victim. If either is to be protected by law, it should be the drunkard, since he is the weaker, rather than the rumseller, who persistently blocks the pathway of reform.

"We know that we utter the voice of the majority of the women of the State when we plead the cause of prohibition—and the women of Massachusetts outnumbers its men by more than sixty thousand. It is women who are the greatest sufferers from the licensed dram-shops of the community—and we pray you, therefore, voters of Massachusetts, to take such action that the law which protects these drinking shops may be blotted from the statute book at the next election."

This appeal from the Christian women of Massachusetts is signed by Mrs. Mary A. Livermore, President, and Mrs. L. B. Barrett, Secretary of the State branch of the Woman's National Temperance Union, and shows the animating spirit of that body. No one can read it without a new impression of the wickedness of a traffic that curses everything it touches.

But not alone in Massachusetts are the women of

the "Union" using their efforts to shape public opinion and influence the ballot. In all the States where unions exist, this part of the work is steadily prosecuted; and it cannot be long ere its good results will become manifest at the polls in a steadily increasing anti-license vote, and, ultimately in the ranging of State after State with Maine, Vermont and New Hampshire on the side of prohibition.

INFLUENCE ON THE MEDICAL PROFESSION.

In still another direction important gains have been realized. But for the efforts of the Woman's National and State Temperance Unions we should scarcely have had the declaration of the International Medical Congress of 1876, adverse to the use of alcohol as food or medicine. Early in their work, the women of the "Union," seeing how largely the medical prescription of alcohol was hurting the cause of temperance, and being in possession of the latest results of chemical and physiological investigation in regard to its specific action on the body, sent delegations to various State medical associations at their annual meetings, urging them to pass resolutions defining its true status as a food or a medicine and discouraging its use in the profession. With most of these medical associations they found a respectful hearing; and their presentation of the matter had the effect of drawing to the subject the attention of a large number of medical men who had not, from old prejudices, or in consequence of their absorption in professional duties, given careful attention to the later results of scientific investigation. As a consequence, many physicians who had been in the habit of ordering alcoholic stimulants for weak or convalescent patients, gave up the practice entirely; while those who still resorted to their use, deemed it safest to be more guarded in their administration than heretofore.

ACTION OF THE INTERNATIONAL MEDICAL CONGRESS.

But the crowning result of this effort to induce the medical profession to limit or abandon the prescription of alcohol, came when the International Congress, one of the largest and ablest medical bodies ever convened, made, through its "Section on Medicine," the brief, but clear and unequivocal declaration already given in a previous chapter, and at once and forever laid upon alcohol the ban of the profession.

Official communications were addressed to this body by the National Temperance Society, through its president, Hon. Wm. E. Dodge, by the Woman's Christian Temperance Union, through its president, Mrs. Annie Wittenmyer, and by the New York Friends' Temperance Union, asking from it a declaration as to the true character of alcohol and its value in medicine.

The following is the full text of the memorial of the Woman's Christian Temperance Union:

" *To the Chairman and Members of the International Medical Congress:*

"HONORED SIRS:—I take the liberty, as a representative of the Woman's National Christian Temperance Union of the United States, to call your attention to the relation of the medical use of alcohol to the prevalence of that fearful scourge, *intemperance*.

"The distinguished Dr. Mussey said, many years ago: 'So long as alcohol retains a place among sick patients, so long there will be drunkards.'

"Dr. Rush wrote strongly against its use as early as 1790. And at one time the College of Physicians at Philadelphia memorialized Congress in favor of restraining the use of distilled liquors, because, as they claimed, they were 'destructive of life, health and the faculties of the mind.'

"'A Medical Declaration,' published in London, December, 1872, asserts that 'it is believed that the inconsiderate prescription of alcoholic liquids by medical men for their patients has given rise, in many instances, to the formation of intemperate habits.' This manifesto was signed by over two hundred and fifty of the leading medical men of the United Kingdom. When the nature and effects of alcohol were little known, it was thought to be invaluable as a medicine. But in the light of recent scientific investigations, its claims have been challenged and its value denied.

"We are aware that the question of the medical

use of alcohol has not been fully decided, and that there is a difference of opinion among the ablest medical writers. But we notice that as the discussion and investigation goes on, and the new facts are brought out, its value as a remedial agent is depreciated.

"A great many claims have been brought forward in its favor, but one by one they have gone down under the severe scrutiny of scientific research, until only a few points are left in doubt. In view of this, and the *startling fact* that tens of thousands die annually from its baneful effects, we earnestly urge you to give the subject a careful examination.

"You have made the study of the physical nature of man your life-work, and you are the trusted advisers of the people in all matters pertaining to the treatment of diseases and the preservation of life and health.

"You are, therefore, in a position to instruct and warn the masses in regard to its indiscriminate use, either as a medicine or a beverage.

"We feel sure that, true to your professional honor, and the grave responsibilities of your distinguished position, you will search out and give us the facts, whatever they may be.

"If you should appoint a standing committee from your own number, of practical scientific men, who would give time and thought to this question, it would be very gratifying to the *one hundred thousand* women I represent, and most acceptable to the general public.

"I am, with high considerations of respect,
 "Your obed't servant,
  "ANNIE WITTENMYER,
 "*Pres't W. Nat. Chris. Temp. Union.*
"*Philadelphia, Sept. 6th,* 1876."

How was this memorial received? Scarcely had it been presented ere a member moved that it be laid on the table without reading; but ere the vote could be taken the voice of another member rose clear and strong in the question whether that body could afford to treat a hundred thousand American women with such a discourtesy! And the motion to lay on the table was lost.

A vote to refer to the "Section on Medicine" was largely carried; and to that section the petitioners took their case, and were not only accorded a gracious and respectful hearing, but, after a full discussion of the subject, a declaration against the use of alcohol, as a substance both hurtful and dangerous—possessing no food value whatever, and as a medicine, being exceedingly limited in its range. All the points in reply were passed upon unanimously by the section to which the matter was referred, and afterwards by the Congress in full session, with but a single dissenting vote, and the result officially communicated to the president of the Woman's Christian Temperance Union. An official notification of the action of the Congress was also sent to Hon. Wm. E. Dodge, president of the National Temperance Society.

Other aspects of the work of this young and vigorous organization might be given; but enough has been presented to show that its agency in temperance reform is already far-reaching and powerful; and to give assurance that if the spirit which has influenced and directed its counsels so wisely from the beginning, can be maintained, it will achieve still greater and more important victories for the cause of temperance.

CHAPTER XIII.

REFORM CLUBS.

THESE differ in some aspects from most of the associations which, prior to their organization, had for their object the reformation of men who had fallen into habits of drunkenness. The distinguishing characteristics of the reform club is its religious spirit, its dependence upon God and its reliance upon prayer.

The first movement in this direction was made in Gardiner, Maine, in January, 1872, by Mr. I. K. Osgood. He says of himself that in fifteen years he had run down from a moderate and fashionable drinker of wine, to a constant and immoderate drinker of the vilest spirits; and from the condition of a respectable business man to one of misery and destitution. Coming back to his wretched home late one night, he saw through the window his poor wife sitting lonely and sorrowful, waiting for his return. The sight touched his heart and caused him to reflect, and then to resolve, that God being his helper he would never drink again. That resolution he found himself able, by God's help, to keep. A few months later he began the work of trying to reform others. His first effort was with a lawyer, an old friend, who was as much reduced by drink as he had been. After much entreaty, this man consented to break off drinking and sign the pledge. Mr. Osgood then drew up the following call for a meeting which both signed: "REFORMERS' MEETING.—There will be a meeting of reformed drinkers at City Hall, Gardiner, on Friday evening, January 19th, at seven o'clock. A cordial invitation is extended to all occasional drinkers, constant drinkers, hard drinkers and young men who are tempted to drink. Come and hear what rum has done for us."

A crowd came to the City Hall. The two men addressed the meeting with great earnestness, and then offered the pledge, which was signed by eight of their old drinking companions. These organized themselves into a reform club, which soon reached a hundred members, all of whom had been men of intemperate habits. The movement soon attracted attention in other places, especially among drinking men, and clubs multiplied rapidly throughout the State. In a few months, the aggregate membership reached nearly twenty thousand. In June of the following year, Mr. Osgood began his work in Massachusetts, under the auspices of the Massachusetts Temperance Alliance, organizing about forty clubs, one of which, in Haverill, numbered over three thousand members. In New Hampshire and Vermont, many clubs were organized by Mr. Osgood and some of his converts.

DR. HENRY A. REYNOLDS.

Another effective worker in the field is Dr. Henry A. Reynolds, of Bangor, Maine, where he was born in 1839. In 1863, he graduated from the Medical College of Harvard University, and was assistant surgeon in the First Maine Regiment, heavy artillery, during two years of the war, receiving an honorable discharge. He then entered upon the practice of medicine in his native city, and continued therein until 1874. But he had inherited a taste for strong drink, through the indulgence of which he became its abject slave. After many efforts at reform which proved of no avail, he resolved to look to Almighty God, and ask for strength to overcome his dreadful appetite. About this time there was, in the city of Bangor, a band of Christian women who met frequently to pray for the salvation of the intemperate. At one of their meetings, the doctor presented himself—it was two days after he had knelt alone in his office and prayed to God for help—and publicly signed the pledge.

Sympathy for those who were in the dreadful slough from which he had been lifted, soon began stirring in his heart, and he sought, by various methods, to influence and save them. After working for several months, with only partial success, it became evident, that for sure and permanent work, there must be organization, and he conceived the plan of a reform club made up exclusively of those who had been drinking men; believing, as he did, that there must exist between two men who had once been intemperate, a sympathy which could not exist between a man who has, and one who has never, drank to excess. As soon as this matter became clear to him, Dr. Reynolds, by notice in a daily paper, invited the drinking men of the city to meet him at a certain place. Eleven men responded to the call, and the Bangor Reform Club, the first of its kind, was organized, September 10th, 1874, with Dr. Henry A. Reynolds as president. The motto of the new organization was, "Dare to do Right." Filled with the true missionary spirit, this little band held other meetings, and did their utmost to bring in new members, and so successful were their efforts, that in a few weeks their membership swelled to hundreds, and the whole city was in a state of excitement over the new and strange work which had been inaugurated.

From Bangor, the excitement soon spread through the State. Dr. Reynolds, believing that God had called him to the work of saving men from intemperance and leading them to Christ, gave up his profession and threw himself into the work of preaching temperance and organizing reform clubs. Within a year forty-five thousand reformed men were gathered into clubs in the State of Maine. In August, 1875, at a meeting of the National Christian Temperance Camp-Meeting Association, held at Old Orchard, Maine, where temperance workers from all parts of the country had congregated, the president of the Woman's Christian Temperance Union of Salem, Massachusetts, learned of the great work of reform progressing in Maine under the leadership of Dr. Reynolds, and invited him to introduce his work in Massachusetts by holding a series of meetings in Salem during the month of September. So the work began in the Old Bay State, and within a year, forty thousand men of that Commonwealth, who had been habitual drinkers, were organized into reform clubs.

FORMATION OF CLUBS.

The method pursued by Dr. Reynolds in the formation of these clubs is very simple. There is a constitution with by-laws, to which the following pledge is prefixed: "Having seen and felt the evils of intemperance, therefore, Resolved, That we, the undersigned, for our own good and the good of the world in which we live, do hereby promise and engage, with the help of Almighty God, to abstain from buying, selling or using alcoholic or malt beverages, wine and cider included." Article III. of the constitution gives the qualification for membership: "All male persons of the age of eighteen or upwards, who have been in the habit of using intoxicating liquor to a greater or less extent, are eligible to membership in this club." After organizing a club of persons who have been addicted to drink, Dr. Reynolds appeals to the Christian women of the locality to throw around them the shield of their care and sympathy, and urges upon the people at large the necessity of upholding and encouraging them in every possible way.

The meetings of the clubs are held at least once during the week, in the evenings; and on Sunday afternoons or evenings, the clubs, with the Woman's Christian Temperance Unions, hold public religious temperance meetings, which are often crowded to overflowing. The order of exercises at these public meetings consist of prayer, reading of Scripture and brief addresses by reformed men, interspersed with the singing of such hymns as "Rock of Ages," "Hold the Fort," "I Need Thee Every Hour," etc. Brief addresses are the rule, and a hymn is usually sung between each address.

The badge worn by members of these reformed clubs is a red ribbon. Their motto is "Dare to do Right."

One of the first fruits of the establishment of a reform club in any locality, is an increase in church attendance, and a decrease in the tax rate. In many towns where they exist, liquor-selling has become unprofitable, and liquor-drinking a custom that hurts a man's social standing.

From the East, Dr. Reynolds extended his labors into the West, where his work has been chiefly confined to the State of Michigan. In a letter to the *Union*, the organ of the Woman's Christian Temperance Union, under date of July, 1877, the aspect and results of Dr. Reynolds's work in that State are thus referred to by a correspondent from Evanston: "His plan is to take a State and settle down in it 'to stay' until it capitulates to the red-ribbon pledge. None but men over eighteen years of age are allowed to sign this pledge. Eighty thousand men in Michigan, to-day, wear the ribbon, which is a token of their signature—all of them have been drinking men. 'None others need apply' as members of Dr. Reynolds's Reform Clubs. His method is to speak in a general way to the public on the evening of his arrival—his meetings being held in a hall and thoroughly announced. The next afternoon, the doctor addresses women, chiefly from the medical point of view. If they have not a W. T. U. he organizes one. The second night he talks to the public generally again, and organizes his club, then goes on his way, and leaves the town rejoicing. The doctor is thoroughly business-like and methodical. There is no doubt about his securing, in every State he visits, the same results as in Michigan, for his ability is marked, his experience growing, his sincerity complete and all his work is 'begun, continued and ended' in a firm reliance upon God."

To give an idea of the excitement created by the presence of Dr. Reynolds in any community, and of the results of his efforts to reclaim intemperate men, we copy the following brief reference to his work in the spring of 1877:

"It is impossible to give figures, for there are additions every day of hundreds in the State, and the climax of enthusiasm is by no means reached in any town while Dr. Reynolds is there.

"In Jackson, Sabbath evening, February 11th, two months after the organization of the club, Union Hall was so packed that the galleries settled and were cleared, and hundreds could not gain admittance.

"As the result of ten days' work in Saginaw Valley—at the three cities—(Bay City, Saginaw City and East Saginaw), the clubs number about three thousand men.

"From there, Dr. Reynolds went to Lansing, our capital, and at the first signing, two hundred and forty-five joined the club, which is far up in the hundreds now.

"The last and greatest victory is Detroit. Slow, critical, conservative, staid, not-any-shams-for-me Detroit.

"Friday and Saturday nights there were crowded houses. Sabbath afternoon, two thousand five hundred *men* together, and a club of three hundred and forty-five formed. Sabbath evening, no room could hold the people, and the club reached nearly nine hundred. It is safe to say to-day that a thousand men in the city of Detroit are wearing the red ribbon.

"Dr. Reynolds has done another grand work, and that is in bringing up the W. C. T. Unions. Everywhere this follows, churches are packed with women. Dr. Reynolds tells them how they can help the men and their families, and they fall into line by the hundreds. Three hundred have enlisted in Bay City, four hundred in Lansing, two hundred in East Saginaw, and so on, all over the State."

The establishment of reform clubs has been more general in New England and the Western States than in other parts of the country, though their organization in some of the Middle States has been attended with marked success. Vermont has a large number of clubs, the membership ranging from one hundred to fifteen hundred.

FRANCIS MURPHY.

The work of Francis Murphy, which has been attended with such remarkable fervors of excitement in nearly every community where he has labored, is not so definite in its purpose, nor so closely organized, nor so permanent in its results as that of Dr. Reynolds. He draws vast assemblies, and obtains large numbers of signers to his pledge, which reads:

"With malice towards none and charity for all, I, the undersigned, do pledge my word and honor, God helping me, to abstain from all intoxicating liquors as a beverage, and that I will, by all honorable means, encourage others to abstain."

An Irishman by birth, and full of the warm impulse and quick enthusiasm of his people, he has thrown himself into the work of temperance reform with an earnestness that commands a hearing, and with an ardor of appeal and solicitation that is, for the time, almost irresistible.

In the fall of 1869, Francis Murphy found himself in the cell of a prison in the city of Portland, Maine, to which he had been committed for drunkenness. He had been a liquor-seller, commencing the work as a sober man with a good character, and ending it in ruin to himself and family, and with the curse of the drunkard's appetite upon him. A Christian gentleman, Captain Cyrus Sturdevant, had obtained permission of the authorities to visit the jail and talk and pray with the prisoners. This brought him into personal contact with Mr. Murphy, who was not only deeply humiliated at the disgrace into which his intemperate life had brought him, but almost in despair. He tells the story of this part of his life with a moving eloquence. Capt. Sturdevant, after some solicitation, induced him to leave his cell one Sunday morning and attend religious services with the prisoners. He was in a state of mind to be deeply impressed by these services, and the result was a solemn resolution to walk, with God's help, in a new and better way. While yet a prisoner, he began his work of trying to save men from the curse of drink, and to lead them to enter upon a religious life; and his influence with his fellow-prisoners was very marked and for good. On leaving the jail, he began at once his efforts to rescue others from the slavery from which he had escaped. His first appearance as a lecturer was in the city of Portland. The effort was well received by the audience, and at its close he found himself an object of special interest. From this time, he gave himself almost wholly to the cause of temperance. After working for a time in Portland, and assisting in the organization of a reform club, he extended his efforts to other parts of the State of Maine, and afterwards to New Hampshire and the adjoining States, in which he labored for nearly three years with marked and often extraordinary success. From New England, Mr. Murphy went, on invitation, to the West, and was very active there, especially in Iowa and Illinois, in which States he aroused the people, and was instrumental in the organization of large numbers of local societies and reform clubs.

In the winter of 1876-7, his work in Pittsburgh was attended with remarkable results; over sixty thousand signatures were obtained to his pledge, and over five hundred saloons in Allegheny and neighboring counties closed their doors for want of patronage. The succeeding spring and summer Mr. Murphy spent in Philadelphia, where the excitement was almost as great as it had been in Pittsburgh. But, as in the last-named city, too large a portion of the harvest which had been reaped was left to perish on the ground for lack of the means, or the will, to gather and garner it. The real substantial and enduring work here has been that of the Woman's Christian Temperance Union; which not only held its meetings daily during the exciting time of the Murphy meetings, but has held them daily ever since, keeping, all the while, hand and heart upon the men who are trying in earnest to reform, and helping, encouraging and protecting them by all the means in their power.

Mr. Murphy continues to work in various parts of the country, attracting large audiences wherever he appears, and leading thousands to sign his pledge. He has done and is still doing good service in the cause to which he is so earnestly devoting himself.

CHAPTER XIV.

GOSPEL TEMPERANCE.

AS we have seen in the chapters on the "Crusade," the "Woman's Christian Temperance Union," and the "Reform Clubs," this new temperance movement, which has attained in the last few years such large dimensions, has in it many of the features of a religious revival. On this account, and to distinguish it from all preceding efforts to break down the liquor traffic and save the drunkard, it has been called a Gospel temperance movement. Its chief reliance with many has been on prayer and faith, as agencies by which the mighty power of God could be so determined as not only to save the drunkard from the curse of his debasing appetite, but to so move and act upon the liquor-seller as to lead him to abandon his accursed traffic.

THE VALUE OF PRAYER AND FAITH ALONE.

At the commencement of this movement, which took the form of what is known as the "Woman's Crusade," the power of prayer seemed for awhile to be an almost irresistible force. Thousands and tens of thousands of men were, as they felt assured in their hearts, freed in an instant of time from an appetite which had been growing and strengthening for years, until it held complete mastery over them; and this in answer to the prayer of faith. And hundreds of saloon and tavern-keepers abandoned their evil work, because, as was believed, God, in answer to the prayers of pious men and women, had turned upon them the influences of His Holy Spirit, and constrained them to this abandonment.

For awhile this power of prayer was regarded as the force that was to break down the liquor traffic, and rescue the people from the curse of appetite. If prayer were persistent enough, and faith strong enough, God would come to the rescue, overthrow the enemy, and redeem and save the wretched victims he was holding in such cruel bondage. But, as time moved on, and the enemy, whose ranks were at first thrown into confusion, rallied his forces and held himself secure against renewed attack, there came a doubt in the minds of many as to the value of prayer and faith as the sole agency by which the rule of the demon of intemperance was to be overthrown; and the same doubt came as to the power of prayer and faith alone to work the removal of an appetite for drink, when it was found by sad experience that of the thousands of men who signed the pledge under religious excitement, and made public declaration that, through faith in Christ, they had been healed of their infirmity, only a few were able to stand in the hour of temptation; and these stood fast because they rested in no vain security. They knew, from an inner conviction, that appetite had not been destroyed; and that, in some unguarded moment, it would spring upon and endeavor to enslave them again. But, with God's help, they had resolved to hold it in check. Humbly they looked to Him for strength—meantime watching, as well as praying—to fight and overcome when their hour of trial and darkness came. So they stood ever on guard; and God gave them the strength they asked for, and victory after victory, until their enemy was under their feet; not dead, but held there by the power which is given to every one who will use it against the enemies of his soul.

PRAYER SUPPLEMENTED BY ORGANIZED WORK.

Not so much dependence on prayer and faith now as on organized work in the natural plane of means and forces. This came as an orderly sequence, and gave to the cause of Gospel temperance a surer foundation to rest upon, and a larger promise of success. There was no turning away from God; no weakness of faith in His Divine power and readiness to save; but clearer light as to His ways with man, and as to how He is able to save, to the uttermost, all who come unto Him. The instances going to show that men were not cured of the appetite for strong drink in a moment of time by prayer and faith, were too many and too sorrowful not to force this conviction upon the mind of every thoughtful and observant Christian man and woman. And, so, even while many sincere and self-devoted workers in this cause still hold to the view that God can, and will, if the faith be strong enough, change a man in an instant of time, and with no co-operation of his own beyond this act of faith, from vileness to purity—from a love of evil to a love of good—the sounder, safer and more Scriptural doctrine that, if a man would be saved from the enemies of his soul, he must fight and overcome them in the strength which God gives to all who will ask and receive, is the one now more generally preached to reformed men; and, as a result, the number of those who stand fast in the new life to which they have attained, is steadily increasing.

THE APPETITE FOR DRINK NOT TAKEN AWAY IN A MOMENT.

Still, far too widely in this Gospel work of saving fallen men from the power of appetite, is the delusive idea held out that if a man will "give his heart to Christ," as it is called; that is, pray humbly, sincerely and in faith to have his sins forgiven, and his soul purified from all evil by an application of Divine grace; God will, in answer to this prayer alone, and in an instant of time, take away the appetite for drink which has been for years gradually gaining the mastery over him. We have heard a man declare, in the presence of an assemblage of men who had been slaves to drink, and who were seeking for a way of escape, that God had, in answer to his prayers, destroyed in a moment the appetite which had long held him in a close bondage; and that, if they would come to Him and give Him their hearts, He would work in them the same miracle of spiritual healing. As we listened to his confident speech, we felt how great was the danger in which he himself stood, and how much better it would have been for his hearers if he had kept silent.

HOW MANY ARE REALLY SAVED.

Facts are solid things, and weigh heavily in the scale of argument. They are not always pleasant to look at; but it is weakness to ignore them. Let us take a few facts in connection with this Gospel temperance work. The first of these came to our knowledge while we were revolving the contents of this chapter, and before we had commenced writing it. A leading temperance worker, who was an active participant in the Murphy movement, and who holds that there is for the confirmed drunkard no hope or safety but in the power of religion, stated to us that during the Moody and Sankey revival in Philadelphia, something over two hundred drunken men were reclaimed and converted; changed in heart, as it was declared, and "*saved*" by the power of God. These were gathered together on a certain evening in one of the churches, and the gentleman to whom we have referred was among those who addressed them. The poor, weak, and in too many instances, friendless and homeless men were talked to, and then committed to God in prayer. They had His grace in their hearts—had been "saved" through prayer and faith—and would He not care for, protect and defend them?

Alas, for the sequel! Of all these two hundred converted and "saved" men, who had, in a moment of time, been changed from servants of sensuality and sin into children of God, their souls made "whiter than snow," not over five or six can to-day be found in the ranks of sober men!

In and around Pittsburgh, during the religious temperance revival which, under Francis Murphy, wrought such marvels in that city and neighborhood, over fifty thousand signatures were obtained to the pledge, the signers, in a large number of cases, professing faith in Christ, and having an inner assurance, as they believed, that He would keep them, by the power of His grace, from again falling into the sin and misery of intemperance. But, to-day, only a small proportionate number can be found out of this great multitude who are standing fast by their profession. A like result has followed the great Gospel work of Mr. Murphy in Philadelphia. Of the thirty or forty thousand who signed the pledge and professed to be saved through faith in Christ, the number of men who have been rescued from drunkenness can scarcely be counted by hundreds; and of these the large proportion owe their salvation to the natural safeguards and orderly external conditions which were brought to the aid of spiritual resolve and spiritual forces.

When the excitement of these great revivals was over, and the contagious enthusiasm had died away, and men fell back into their old ways, amid old surroundings and temptations, each alone in the house of his own real life, then came

THE TRIAL AND THE TEST,

and it was found that to depend on grace alone, and the inner change it had effected in answer to prayer, was to rest, too often, in a vain security. The new convert was the same as to the essential evil quality of his life as before his conversion—or turning round to go the other way—and if he stood still where he had turned, and did not, in a new life of practical obedience to Divine laws, walk forward in the Heavenly road, his conversion would avail him nothing. Not that he was left alone by God to stand or fall as he might. No human heart ever felt even the faintest motions of that Divine pity, and compassion, and yearning to save his lost and perishing children, which is felt by our Heavenly Father, who is very love itself. But He cannot save humanity by destroying it, and this destruction would take place the moment he touched man's freedom to choose between good and evil. Of his own will, man has turned away from God; and of his own will he must return to Him if ever he return at all. The way of return has been opened and made plain, and God is forever calling and entreating His poor, wandering ones to come back, and offering them strength to walk, and weapons to fight, and armor for defense. But He cannot walk for them, nor fight for them, nor defend them unless they put on the armor His mercy supplies. They must, of themselves, using the strength He gives them, walk in the Heavenly way; and with the sword of Divine truth He places in their hands, do battle with the enemies of their souls. There is no other means of attaining Heaven. This strength to walk and fight and overcome, is the Divine grace that saves. It is the free gift of our Lord and Saviour Jesus Christ; the very power of God unto salvation.

THE DIVINE GRACE THAT SAVES.

It is by the application of this Divine grace that men are saved from their sins and from the power of hell. But they can never receive it as passive subjects. They must take it and apply it in and of themselves, and use it as if it were their own; yet never forgetting that it is the gift of God, and never ceasing to acknowledge and thank Him for His infinite goodness and mercy in teaching their "hands to war;" in "girding" them "with strength unto the battle," and in giving them a "lamp unto their feet and a light unto their path," so that they may walk in safety.

If salvation were of grace alone, as so many teach in this Gospel temperance work, what need of "sword," or "armor," or a "lamp unto the feet?" for if, in answer to prayer and faith, a man's evil nature is instantly changed, he is no longer subject to temptation, and cannot, therefore, enter into combat with evil; and if God lift him out of the darkness of his carnal nature into the light of regeneration solely in answer to prayer, what need of any lamp unto his feet or light unto his path? He is no longer a pilgrim and a wayfarer, journeying heavenward through an enemy's land.

We press this subject on the reader's attention, because so much of success or failure in this great Gospel temperance work depends on a right understanding of spiritual laws and a true comprehension of the means of salvation. Holding, as we do, that, for the thousands and hundreds of thousands of unhappy and wretched men and women in our land who have become the almost helpless slaves of an appetite which is rarely, if ever, wholly destroyed, no true succor lies in anything but Divine grace and help, we feel that a great responsibility rests with all who, in the providence of God, have been drawn into this work.

Referring to the loose, and we cannot help saying hurtful teachings of too many temperance revivalists, Rev. Charles I. Warren, writing in the New York *Christian Advocate*, says:

"Religious conversion, all are agreed, is the first necessity for all men, and especially for inebriates, as the surest hope of a real and permanent reformation of life. And intemperate men, especially those who become demented rather than demonized, it is well known, are always easily moved by religious influences, even when so drunk that they would wisely be deemed incompetent to execute a will for the disposal of earthly property, and incapable of giving testimony in a court of law.

"Yet, this idea of a spiritual renovation of the heart, while the head is too intoxicated to apprehend a moral obligation, is almost beyond rational belief. It is difficult to conceive that any man, in such a state of voluntarily-induced imbecility, too drunk to hold intelligent converse with men, can be competent to transact business with God, to receive and answer those calls from the Holy Spirit that decide the eternal destinies of the soul."

And he adds: "We judge instinctively that all men, intemperate or sober, must work out their own salvation with fear, while God works in them to will and to do."

This is the key-note to the whole subject of spiritual regeneration. It is active co-operation; work, conflict, victory; and this down on the sphere of common life, and in the midst of temptation—not out of the world, but "in the world;" not something done in and for a man while he waits in prayer on God, but after he has fought his battle with some enemy of his soul, and overcome in the strength which God has given him in answer to prayer. Only they who have fought and conquered can possess the land and dwell there in safety.

AN UNSOUND AND DANGEROUS DOCTRINE.

In a meeting at which we were present, and where from one to two hundred reformed men were gathered for religious worship, and for help and counsel, the hymn commencing

> "Prone to wander, Lord I feel it,"

was sung. At its close, a man rose from his seat and entered his protest against the singing of that hymn any more. It is not true, he said, that the man whom God has converted feels any proneness to wander. He had had the grace of God in his soul for—we don't remember how many years—and he could testify that the desire to wander from God's commandments had been wholly removed. He, therefore, repeated his protest against the use of a hymn containing a sentiment so dishonorable to a truly saved Christian. As he sat down, a very young man arose and added the weight of his testimony to the assertion of his older Christian brother. He also, in answer to prayer, as he confidently asserted, had attained unto that higher life which is not only free from sin, but from even the desire to wander from the ways of holiness.

As we looked into and read the faces of these two men, we sighed for what we saw therein, and pitied them for the peril in which they stood. But our greater concern was for the poor, weak, almost helpless ones we saw around us, and for the effect of this delusive error which had been so needlessly thrown into their minds. If any of them should rest in the belief that they, too, had, by the grace of God, been wholly set free from the bondage of sin; that the appetite for drink and the lust of all evil had been extinguished, and their proneness to wander from God taken away in simple answer to prayer, then would their danger, we felt, be so imminent as to leave but little room for hope of their standing in the new life. A stumbling-block had been laid in their way over which they must almost surely fall.

We are writing for the help and safety of men for whom there is but little or no hope of rescue from the depths of evil and sensuality into which they have fallen, except in a truly religious life; not a life of mere faith and sentiment and fancied holiness, but of earnest conflict and daily right living. A life in which not only intemperance is to be shunned as a sin against God, but every impure and evil desire of the heart, and every thought and purpose of wrong to the neighbor. And, believing as we do, that God's grace and power can only be given to those who will take it as active subjects—not mere passive recipients—and by using it as if it were their own, avail themselves of its purifying and regenerating influence, we can do no less than question and reject any doctine that even seems to give a different impression, as delusive and exceedingly dangerous.

To make Gospel temperance the true power of God unto the salvation of intemperate men, we must have in it, and with it, the Gospel of conflict with evil, the Gospel of daily right living, the Gospel of love to the neighbor and the Gospel of common sense. And these are coming more and more into the work, which is widening and increasing, and every year adding thousands upon thousands to the number of those who are saved from the curse of drink.

CHAPTER XV.

TEMPERANCE COFFEE-HOUSES AND FRIENDLY INNS.

THE cure of a drunkard is always attended with peculiar difficulties. The cost is often great. Sometimes cure is found to be impossible. A hundred may be protected from the ravages of intemperance at the cost of saving one who has fallen a victim to the terrible malady. "An ounce of prevention is worth a pound of cure."

While so much is being done to reform and save the drunkard, the work of prevention has not been forgotten. Great good has been accomplished in this direction through the spread of total-abstinence principles. In this the various temperance organizations have done much, and especially with the rising generation. But, so long as men are licensed by the State to sell intoxicating drinks, the net of the tempter is spread on every hand, and thousands of the weak and unwary are yearly drawn therein and betrayed to their ruin. In our great cities a large number of men who have to do business at points remote from their dwellings, are exposed to special temptations. The down-town lunch-room and dining-room have, in most cases, their drinking-bars; or, if no bar is visible, the bill of fare offers, in too many cases, any kind of intoxicating beverage that may be desired. Thousands of men are, in consequence, yearly led away from sobriety.

Seeing this, efforts have been made during the past few years to establish cheap temperance coffee-houses, where workingmen and others may get a good noonday lunch, or a morning and evening meal at a trifling cost. In all cases, these have been found of great service to the cause of temperance. A pint mug of excellent coffee, with sugar and milk, and a large, sweet roll, costing five cents, are found to make a far better and healthier lunch than the highly-seasoned hashes and scraps called "free lunches," which must be washed down by a five or ten-cent glass of liquor.

THE EXPERIMENT IN PHILADELPHIA.

The success which has attended the establishment of cheap temperance coffee-houses in this city (Philadelphia), is quite remarkable. In the fall of 1874, Joshua L. Baily, one of our active, clear-headed merchants, who had been for many years an earnest temperance man, determined to give the cheap coffee-house experiment a fair trial, cost what it might; for he saw that if it could be made successful, it would be a powerful agency in the work of prevention. He began in a modest way, taking a small store at the corner of Market and Fifteenth Streets, and fitting it up in a neat and attractive manner. With a few pounds of coffee, and a few dozens of rolls, the place was opened, the single attendant, a woman, acting the double part of cook and waiter. For five cents a pint mug of the best Java coffee, with milk and sugar, and a good-sized roll, were furnished.

From the very start "The Workingmen's Central Coffee-House," as Mr. Baily called it, was successful. In the immediate neighborhood five hundred workmen were employed on the city buildings, and opposite stood the Pennsylvania Railroad freight depot, to which came daily about the same number of men—draymen, teamsters and others. It took but a few days to so crowd the new coffee-room at the usual lunching time as to require an additional assistant. From day to day the business went on increasing, until more help and larger accommodations became necessary. Soon a complete kitchen had to be built in the basement, and the adjoining store added, in order to meet the steadily-enlarging demands upon the new establishment. The fame of the good coffee, which was better than most people found at home, spread far and near, and larger and larger numbers of clerks, workingmen and others, turned their steps daily, at lunch time, towards the Central Coffee-House. It was so much better than the poor stuff served in most of the eating-houses; and, with the sweet roll added, so much better than the free lunch and glass of beer or whisky with which too many had been accustomed to regale themselves.

SIGNAL SUCCESS.

Steadily swelled the tide of custom. Within a year a third store, adjoining, was added. But the enlarged premises soon proved inadequate to the accommodation of the still-increasing crowd.

At this writing "The Central" is from six to seven times larger than when first opened; and there lunch in its rooms, daily, nearly two thousand persons. One room has been fitted up for ladies exclusively, in which from forty to fifty can lunch at one time.

But Mr. Baily looked beyond the cheap coffee and rolls by which he was able to keep so many away from bar-rooms and restaurants where liquor was sold. He believed in other influences and safeguards. And to this end, and at his own cost, he fitted up the various rooms over the seven stores extending along Market Street from Fifteenth to Broad, in which the coffee-rooms are located, and set them apart for various uses. Here is a lecture-hall, capable of seating four hundred persons; a free reading-room, well warmed and lighted and supplied with the best daily newspapers, American and English illustrated publications, and the standard periodicals; besides four other rooms that will hold from seventy to one hundred persons, which are used for various meeting purposes, all in connection with temperance. Five regular services are held in the lecture-room every week, viz.: "Bible Reading," on Sunday afternoon; "Temperance Experience meeting," on Monday evening; "Prayer and Praise meeting," Tuesday evening; "Gospel Temperance meeting," on Thursday evening; and "Youths' Temperance meeting," Friday evening. These meetings are often crowded, and, like the coffee-rooms below, attract audiences made up from every rank in society. At many of these meetings, Mr. Baily presides in person.

Encouraged by the success of this first effort, Mr. Baily opened another cheap coffee-house in the very centre of the wholesale trade of the city, where thousands of clerks, workingmen and merchants were in the habit of resorting for lunch or dinner to the restaurants and bar-rooms in the neighborhood. This, located at No. 31 South Fourth Street, he called "The Model Coffee-House."

CROWDED FROM THE FIRST.

From the first it was crowded even to an uncomfortable extent. The demands of its patrons soon rendered larger quarters a necessity. A new building was erected specially adapted to the purpose, many novel features being introduced which a twelvemonth's experience had suggested.

The *new* "Model" opened June 1st, 1876. Many persons thought it was too large, and that it would never be filled. But it was thronged on the day of opening, and on every day since the demands upon it have been fully up to its capacity. The number lunching here daily is about three thousand.

In the establishment of the coffee-houses there were, of course, many mistakes, the results of inexperience. Many things had to be unlearned as well as many learned. But mistakes were promptly corrected. With the growth of the work, ability to provide for it seemed to keep pace, and modifications in the management were adopted as necessity dictated. Not much was anticipated at the commencement beyond furnishing a mug of coffee and a roll of bread, but it soon became apparent that something more than this was needed. To meet this necessity, the coffee-house bill of fare was greatly extended, and now quite a variety of nutritious and substantial dishes are provided, and each at the uniform price of *five cents*. The main feature—the coffee—is, however, preserved. A full pint mug of the best Java (equal to two ordinary cups) with pure, rich milk and white sugar, and two ounces of either wheat or brown bread, all for *five cents*, is the every-day lunch of many a man who, but for this provision, would be found in the dram shop.

No dish, as we have said, costs over five cents, which is the standard price the year round, whatever the fluctuations of markets may be. In addition to the bread and coffee already mentioned for five cents, the bill of fare comprises puddings of rice, tapioca and corn starch, baked apples dressed with sugar and milk, all sorts of pies (half a pie being given for a portion), mushes of cracked wheat, corn and oatmeal, dumplings, eggs, potatoes, beans, ham, corned beef, liver, "scrapple," sausage, custards, soups, pickles and, in season, fresh fruits. Of bread, there are Boston and Philadelphia brown, wheat, Philadelphia and Vienna rolls. A pint glass of milk with a roll, costs five cents; butter three cents, and extra rolls one cent each; so that for ten or fifteen cents a man gets a full luncheon, as every portion of food is equal to a large saucer heaped.

These establishments require, of course, the most methodical, orderly and careful management, with capable matrons at the head of each, and a steward or superintendent to make intelligent purchases. At the "Model Coffee-House," there are nearly fifty employees, and, excepting three or four men, they are girls and women. The upper rooms of the building are for the lodgings, offices, laundry and drawing-room, for the use of the employees. The girls, who are mostly of country birth and training, are thus furnished with a good and safe home, where they have books and music, large and well-furnished chambers, a good table—they dine at one family table in their own dining-room—and have their washing and ironing done in the house. They are required to be neat and tidy in appearance, respectable and discreet in character and manner.

THE GOOD DONE.

The good that is done through an instrumentality like this can never be fully known. Of those who are drawn into paths of safety, we do not so often hear as of those who are led astray. But enough is already known of the good done by these two coffee-houses to give large encouragement for their establishment in other localities and other cities. Hundreds of young men who had fallen into the dangerous habit of taking a glass of beer every day with their lunch, now take a fragrant cup of coffee instead, and find themselves better for the change; hundreds more who had begun to feel the insidious encroachments of appetite, have been able to get out of the way of temptation.

The question that naturally arises with all who look practically at this matter is, whether there is any profit in the business of keeping a cheap temperance coffee-house? Can a pint of coffee, with sugar, milk and a two-ounce roll of bread, be furnished for five cents and leave any margin for profit? Mr. Baily's experiment has proved that it can.

FRIENDLY INNS.

But not alone in Philadelphia is the cheap coffee-house to be found. There are hundreds of them in our various towns and cities, though none on so large a scale as here; and they are rapidly multiplying and doing good. "The Friendly Inn," and "The Holly-Tree Inn," are places somewhat similar in character, but partaking more of the nature of an "inn" than a simple eating-house. These have, usually, a pleasant parlor, with light, and warmth, and books, into which any one may come and pass the evening, instead of drifting into a saloon, and where cheap meals and lodgings can be had if needed. In Cleveland, Ohio, Christian temperance work, which is very large and effective, is carried on almost entirely in connection with "Friendly Inns," of which there are five. A chapel, reading-room, sleeping apartments and a cheap restaurant are maintained in connection with each of these inns. The women engaged in the cause of Gospel temperance in that city regard them as most valuable auxiliaries to the spiritual work in which they are engaged. In a large number of cases, they have been the direct means of bringing men in whom few traces of goodness could at first be discerned in such contact with religious influences as to win them over to a better life.

CHAPTER XVI.

TEMPERANCE LITERATURE.

THE greatest and most effective agency in any work of enlightenment and reform is the press. By it the advanced thinker and Christian philanthropist is able to speak to the whole people, and to instruct, persuade and influence them. He can address the reason and conscience of thousands, and even of hundreds of thousands of people to whom he could never find access in any other way, and so turn their minds to the right consideration of questions of social interest in regard to which they had been, from old prejudices or habits of thinking, in doubt or grievous error.

No cause has been more largely indebted to the press than that of temperance reform. From the very beginning of agitation on the subject of this reform, the press has been used with great efficiency; and to-day, the literature of temperance is a force of such magnitude and power, that it is moving whole nations, and compelling Parliaments, Chambers of Deputies and Houses of Congress to consider the claims of a question which, if presented fifty years ago, would have been treated, in these grave assemblages, with levity or contempt.

For many years after the reform movement began in this country, the press was used with marked effect. But as most of the books, pamphlets and tracts which were issued came through individual enterprise, the editions were often small and the prices high; and as the sale of such publications was limited, and the profit, if any, light, the efforts to create a broad and comprehensive temperance literature met with but feeble encouragement. But in 1865, a convention was called to meet at Saratoga to consider the subject of a national organization so comprehensive and practical that all the friends of temperance in religious denominations and temperance organizations could unite therein for common work. Out of this convention grew the

NATIONAL TEMPERANCE SOCIETY AND PUBLICATION HOUSE,

which began, at once, the creation of a temperance literature worthy of the great cause it represented. The president of this society is Hon. William E. Dodge, of New York. The vice-presidents are ninety-two in number, and include some of the most distinguished men in the country; clergymen, jurists, statesmen, and private citizens eminent for their public spirit and philanthropy. It has now been in existence some twelve years. Let us see what it has done in that time for temperance literature and the direction and growth of a public sentiment adverse to the liquor traffic. We let the efficient corresponding secretary and publishing agent, J. N. Stearns, speak for the association he so ably represents. Its rooms are at No. 58 Reade Street, New York. Referring to the initial work of the society, "It was resolved," says Mr. Stearns, "that the publishing agent should keep 'all the temperance literature of the day.' This was found to consist of less than a dozen different publications in print, and these of no special value. All the plates of valuable works before in existence were either shipped across the water or melted up and destroyed. The society commenced at once to create a literature of its own, but found it was not the work of a moment. The first publication outside of its monthly paper, was a four-page tract by Rev. T. L. Cuyler, D.D., in February, 1866, entitled 'A Shot at the Decanter,' of which about two hundred thousand copies have been published.

FIRST BOOK PUBLISHED.

"The first book was published in May of the same year, entitled, 'Scripture Testimony against Intoxicating Wine.' Prizes were offered for the best tracts and books, and the best talent in the land sought and solicited to aid in giving light upon every phase of the question. The result has been that an immense mass of manuscripts have been received, examined, assorted, some approved and many rejected, and the list of publications has gone on steadily increasing, until in the eleven years it amounts to four hundred and fifty varieties upon every branch of the temperance question. There were over twenty separate so-called secret temperance societies, each with a different ritual and constitution, with subordinate organizations scattered all over the land. These contained probably about one million of members. Then there were churches, open societies, State temperance unions, etc., each operating independently and with no common bond of union. Some were for moral suasion alone, others for political action, while others were for both united. The great need for some national organization which should be a common centre and ground of union, a medium of communication between all, and to aid, strengthen and benefit every existing organization and denomination, was felt all over the land.

"This society was organized to supply such a need. It is both a society and a publication house. The need and demand came from every quarter for facts, statistics, arguments and appeals upon every phase of the question, in neat, cheap and compact form, which could be sent everywhere and used by everybody. Public opinion had settled down against us, and light was needed to arouse it to right action. The pulpit and the platform were to be supplemented by the press, which, henceforth, was to be used in this great and rapidly strengthening cause, as in every other, to reach the individuals and homes of every portion of the land.

AFTER TWELVE YEARS.

"Twelve years have passed—years of anxious preparation and toil, of seed-planting and sowing, and they have been improved. This society now publishes books and tracts upon the moral, economical, physiological, political, financial, religious, medical and social phases of the reform. We have the writings of over two hundred different persons in almost every walk and station in life. We already have a literature of no mean character. Its influence is not only felt in every State and Territory in the land, but in every country on the globe.

* * * * * * * *

"Among the early publications of the society were those printed upon 'The Adulteration of Liquors,' 'The Physiological Action of Alcohol,' 'Alcohol: Its Nature and Effects,' 'Alcohol: Its Place and Power,' 'Is Alcohol Food?' 'Text-Book of Temperance,' etc., followed later by 'Bacchus Dethroned,' 'The Medical Use of Alcohol,' 'Is Alcohol a Neccessary of Life?' 'Our Wasted Resources,' 'On Alcohol,' 'Prohibition does Prohibit,' 'Fruits of the Liquor Traffic,' 'The Throne of Iniquity,' 'Suppression of the Liquor Traffic,' 'Alcohol as a Food and Medicine,' etc.

"The truths of these books and pamphlets, which have been reproduced in a thousand ways in sermons, addresses, newspapers, etc., have already permeated the community to such an extent as to bear much fruit."

In the creation of a literature for children, the society early issued *The Youths' Temperance Banner*, a paper for Sunday-schools. This has attained a circulation of nearly one hundred and fifty thousand copies monthly. It has also created a Sunday-school temperance library, which numbers already as many as seventy bound volumes; editions of which reaching in the aggregate to one hundred and eighty-three thousand five hundred and seventy-six volumes have already been sold. The society also publishes a monthly paper called the *National Temperance Advocate*, which has a wide circulation.

REMARKABLE GROWTH OF TEMPERANCE LITERATURE.

The number of books, pamphlets and tracts which have been issued by the National Temperance Society during the twelve years of its existence, is four hundred and sixty, some of them large and important volumes.

To this extraordinary production and growth of temperance literature in the past twelve years are the people indebted for that advanced public sentiment which is to-day gathering such force and will.

And here, let us say, in behalf of a society which has done such grand and noble work, that from the very outset it has had to struggle with pucuniary difficulties.

Referring to the difficulties and embarrassments with which the society has had to contend from the beginning, the secretary says:

"The early financial struggles of the society are known only to a very few persons. It was deemed best by the majority of the board not to let the public know our poverty. Looking back over the eleven years of severe struggles, pecuniary embarrassments, unexpected difficulties, anxious days, toiling, wearisome nights, with hopes of relief dashed at almost every turn, surrounded by the indifference of friends, and with the violent opposition of enemies, we can only wonder that the society has breasted the storm and is saved from a complete and total wreck. * * * This society never was endowed, never had a working capital, never has been the recipient of contributions from churches or of systematic donations from individuals. It never has had a day of relief from financial embarrassment since its organization; and yet there never has been a day but that the sum of ten thousand dollars would have lifted it out of its embarrassments and started it with a buoyant heart on towards the accomplishment of its mission."

And he adds: "Notwithstanding all these constant and ever-pressing financial embarrassments, the society has never faltered for one moment, but has gone steadily on doing its appointed work, exploring new fields, and developing both old and new truths and documents and principles, and it stands to-day the strongest and most solid and substantial bulwark against intemperance in the land."

A MOST IMPORTANT AGENCY.

As the most important of all the agencies now used for the suppression of the liquor traffic, and as the efficient ally of all let us rally to the support of our great publication house and see that it has ampler means for the work in which it is engaged. There are hundreds of thousands of men and women in our land who are happy and prosperous to-day because of what this society has done in the last twelve years to create a sentiment adverse to the traffic and to the drinking usages of society. Its work is so silent and unobtrusive in comparison with that of many other efficient, but more limited instrumentalities, that we are apt to lose sight of its claims, and to fail in giving an adequate support to the very power, which is, in a large measure, the source of power to all the rest.

If we would war successfully with our strong and defiant enemy, we must look to it that the literature of temperance does not languish. We are not making it half as efficient as it might be. Here we have a thoroughly organized publication house, with capable and active agents, which, if the means were placed at its disposal, could flood the country with books, pamphlets and tracts by millions every year; and we leave it to struggle with embarrassments, and to halting and crippled work. This is not well. Our literature is our right arm in this great conflict, and only in the degree that we strengthen this arm will we be successful in our pursuit of victory.

CHAPTER XVII.

LICENSE A FAILURE AND A DISGRACE.

FOR over two hundred years in this country, and for a much longer period of time in Great Britain and some of the countries of Continental Europe, attempts have been made to protect the people against the evils of intemperance by restrictive liquor laws. But as these laws were permissive and not prohibitory, the evil was not restrained. Nay, its larger growth came as the natural consequence of such laws, for they not only gave to a few men in every community the right to live and grow rich by doing all in their power to increase the evil, but threw around them the protection of the State; so leaving the people powerless in their hands.

HISTORY OF LICENSE IN MASSACHUSETTS.

The history of all restrictive laws which have stopped short of absolute prohibition, is a history of the saddest of failures, and shows that to license an evil is to increase its power.

Judge Robert C. Pitman, in his "Alcohol and the State," an exceedingly valuable discussion of the "Problem of Law as Applied to the Liquor Traffic," gives an instructive history of the license laws of

Massachusetts from early colonial times down to the year 1877. The experience of Massachusetts is that of every other community, State or nation, which has sought to repress drunkenness and its attendant evils by the enactment of license laws; and we ask the reader's earnest and candid consideration of the facts we shall here present.

As early as 1636, an effort was made in the Old Colony to lessen intemperance by the passage of a restrictive law, declaring "That none be suffered to retail wine, strong water or beer, either within doors or without, except in inns or victualing-houses allowed." That this law did not lessen the evil of drunkenness is plain from the fact that, in 1646, in the preamble to a new liquor law it was declared by the Massachusetts colony that, "Forasmuch as drunkenness is a vice to be abhorred of all nations, especially of those who hold out and profess the Gospel of Christ, and seeing *any strict law will not prevail unless the cause be taken away*, it is, therefore, ordered by this Court,"—What? Entire prohibition of the sale of intoxicating drinks? No. Only, "That no merchant, cooper or any other person whatever, shall, after the first day of the first month, sell any wine under one-quarter of a cask, neither by quart, gallon or any other measure, *but only such taverners as are licensed to sell by the gallon.*" And in order still further to protect and encourage the publican in his vested and exclusive right, it was further enacted that, "Any *taverners* or other persons who shall inform against any transgressor, shall have one-half of the fines for his *encouragement.*" This law contained a section which forbids any person licensed "to sell strong waters, or any private housekeeper to permit any person to sit drinking or tippling strong waters, wine or strong beer in their houses."

THE EVIL STILL INCREASING.

Still the evil of drunkenness went on increasing under the license system, until in 1692, we find in a preamble to certain more stringent laws for the regulation of the traffic, this sad confession: "And forasmuch as the ancient, true and principal use of inns, taverns, ale-houses, victualing-houses and other houses for common entertainment is for receipt, relief and lodging of travelers and strangers, and the refreshment of persons on lawful business. * * * And not for entertainment and harboring of lewd or idle people to spend or consume their time or money there; therefore, *to prevent the mischief and great disorders happening daily by abuse of such houses,* It is further enacted," etc.—not prohibition of the sale; but further restrictions and penalties. How far these restrictions and penalties were effective, appears from the statue of 1695, in the preamble of which is a complaint that divers persons who had obtained license to sell liquor to be taken away and not drunk in their houses, did, notwithstanding, "give entertainment to persons to sit drinking and tippling there," while others who "*have no license at all* are yet so hardy as to run upon the law," to the " great increase of drunkenness and other debaucheries."

These colonial fathers, in their efforts to lessen the evil of drinking by restrictive license, for which a fee to the State was required, opened a door for the unlicensed dram-shop, which was then, as it is now, one of the worst forms of the liquor traffic, because it is in the hands of more unscrupulous persons, too many of whom are of the lowest and vilest class, and whose tippling-houses are dens of crime and infamy as well as drunkenness.

How this was in the colony of Massachusetts under license in 1695 is seen above, and further appears in this recital taken from the statute to further limit the spread of drunkenness, wherein it refers to "divers *ill-disposed and indigent persons, the pains and penalties in the laws already made not regarding,* who are so hardy *as to presume to sell and retail* strong beer, ale, cider, sherry wine, rum or other strong liquors or mixed drinks, and *to keep common tippling-houses*, thereby harboring and entertaining apprentices, Indians, negroes and other idle and dissolute persons, tending to the ruin and impoverishment of families, and all impieties and debaucheries, and *if detected are unable to pay their fine.*" All such were sentenced to the whipping-post.

Three years later, the curse of the licensed traffic had so augmented that another effort was made for its regulation by the enactment of a new and more comprehensive law entitled, "An Act for the Inspecting and *Suppressing of Disorders* in Licensed Houses."

WORSE AND WORSE.

How successful the good people of Massachusetts were in holding in check and regulating the evil which they had clothed with power by license, appears in the preamble to a new Act passed in 1711, "For reclaiming the over great number of licensed houses, many of which are chiefly used for revelling and tippling, and become *nurseries of intemperance and debauchery*, indulged by the masters and keepers of the same for the sake of gain."

So it went on, from bad to worse, under the Colonial Government, until 1787, when the State constitution was adopted. To what a frightful magnitude the evil of drunkenness, provided for and fostered by license, had grown, appears from an entry in the diary of John Adams, under date of February 29th, 1760, in which he says that few things were "so fruitful of destructive evils" as "licensed houses." They had become, he declares, "the eternal haunts of loose, disorderly people of the town, which renders them offensive and unfit for the entertainment of any traveler of the least delicacy." * * * "Young people are tempted to waste their time and money, and to acquire habits of intemperance and idleness, that we often see reduce many to beggary and vice, and lead some of them, at least, to prison and the gallows."

In entering upon her career as a State, Massachusetts continued the license system, laying upon it many prudent restrictions, all of which were of no avail, for the testimony is complete as to the steady increase of drunkenness, crime and debauchery.

TESTIMONY OF JOHN ADAMS.

Writing to Mr. Rush in 1811, John Adams says: "Fifty-three years ago I was fired with a zeal, amounting to enthusiasm, against ardent spirits, the multiplication of taverns, retailers, dram-shops and tippling-houses. Grieved to the heart to see the number of idlers, thieves, sots and consumptive patients made for the physicians in these infamous seminaries, I applied to the Court of Sessions, procured a Committee of Inspection and Inquiry, reduced the number of licensed houses, etc., *but I only acquired the reputation of a hypocrite and an ambitious demagogue by it.* The number of licensed houses was soon reinstated; drams, grog and sotting were not diminished, *and remain to this day as deplorable as ever.*"

OPENING A WIDER DOOR.

In 1816, so demoralized had the sentiment of the people become, and so strong the liquor interest of the State, that the saving provision in the license laws, which limited the sale of liquor to inns and taverns, was repealed, and licenses were granted to common victualers, "who shall not be required to furnish accommodations" for travelers; and also to confectioners on the same terms as to inn-keepers; that is, to sell and to be drunk on the premises. This change in the license laws of Massachusetts was declared, by Judge Aldrich, in 1867, to be "one of the most fruitful sources of crime and vice that ever existed in this Commonwealth."

Up to as late as 1832, attempts were continued to patch up and amend the license laws of the State; after that they were left, for a time, to do their evil work, all efforts to make them anything but promoters of drunkenness, crime and poverty being regarded as fruitless.

"Miserable in principle," says Judge Pitman, "license laws were found no less inefficient in practice." Meantime, the battle against the liquor traffic had been going on in various parts of the State. In 1835, a law was secured by which the office of county commissioner (the licensing authority) was made an elective office; heretofore it had been held by appointment. This gave the people of each county a local control over the liquor question, and in the very first year the counties of Plymouth and Bristol elected boards committed to the policy of no license. Other counties followed this good example; and to bar all questions of the right to refuse every license by a county, the power was expressly conferred by a law passed in 1837.

A CHANGE FOR THE BETTER.

The good results were immediately apparent in all places where license to sell intoxicating drinks was refused. After a thorough investigation of the matter, the Judiciary Committee of the Legislature reported the evidence to be " perfectly incontrovertable, that the good order and the physical and moral welfare of the community had been promoted by refusing to license the sale of ardent spirits; and that although the laws have been and are violated to some extent in different places, the practice soon becomes disreputable and hides itself from the public eye by shrinking into obscure and dark places; that noisy and tumultuous assemblies in the streets and public quarrels cease where license is refused; *and that pauperism has very rapidly diminished from the same cause.*"

An attempt to prohibit entirely the retail liquor traffic was made in 1838, by the passage of what was known as the "Fifteen-Gallon Law," which forbade the sale of spirituous liquors in a less quantity than fifteen gallons, which had to be "carried away all at one time;" except by apothecaries and practicing physicians, who might sell for use in the arts and for medicinal purposes.

But this law remained in operation only a year and a half; when, in concession to the liquor interest of the State, which had been strong enough to precipitate a political revolution and get its own men in the legislature, it was repealed.

"But the State," says Judge Pitman, "while the memory of license was fresh, was not to fall again under its sway. The struggle for local prohibition was at once renewed, and in a few years license had ceased throughout the Commonwealth. The statement may surprise many; but I have the authority of the city clerk of Boston for saying, that 'no licenses for the sale of intoxicating liquors were granted in Boston between 1841 and 1852.' * * * And so the chapter of license was apparently closed. It had not only had its 'day,' but its centuries in court; and the well-nigh unanimous verdict was: '*disgrace—failure.*'"

So strong was this conviction in the minds of the people of Massachusetts, that Governor Bullock, in 1861, while acting as chairman of the Judiciary Committee of the House, gave it expression in these notable words: "It may be taken as the solemnly declared judgment of the people of the Commonwealth, that the principle of licensing the traffic in intoxicating drinks as a beverage, *and thus giving legal sanction to that which is regarded in itself as an evil, is no longer admissible in morals or in legislation.*"

THE LIQUOR POWER IN THE ASCENDANT AGAIN.

But in 1868, adverse influences prevailed, and after all her sad and disgraceful experience, Massachusetts abandoned her prohibition of the traffic and went back to license again; but the evil consequences began to show themselves so quickly that the law was repealed in less than a year.

Governor Claflin, in his message to the legislature in January, 1869, thus speaks of the effect of the new license law: "The increase of drunkenness and crime during the last six months, as compared with the same period of 1867, is very marked and decisive as to the operation of the law. *The State prisons, jails and houses of correction are being rapidly filled*, and will soon require enlarged accommodation if the commitments continue to increase as they have since the present law went in force."

While the chaplain of the State prison in his annual report for 1868, says: "The prison never was so full as at the present time. If the rapidly increasing tide of intemperance, so greatly swollen by the present wretched license law, is suffered to rush on unchecked, there will be a fearful increase of crime, and the State must soon extend the limits of the prison, or create another."

This law was repealed, as we have seen. A year of its bitter fruit was enough for the people.

SUBMITTING AGAIN TO THE YOKE.

But, strange to say, after all she has suffered from license laws, the old Bay State has again submitted to the yoke, and is once more in the hands of the great liquor interest. In 1874, she drifted out from the safe harbor of prohibition, and we find her, to-day, on the stormy and storm-wrecked sea of license. A miserable attempt has been made by the friends of this law to show that its action has been salutory in Boston, the headquarters of the liquor power, in the diminution of dram-shops and arrests for drunkenness. Water may run up hill in Boston; but it obeys the law of gravitation in other places. We leave the reader to draw his own conclusions from this extract from the report of the License Commissioners of that city, made February 1st, 1877: "It must be admitted that the business of liquor-selling in this city is, to a very large extent, in the hands of *irresponsible men and women*, whose idea of a license law ends with the simple matter of paying a certain sum, the amount making but little difference to them, *provided they are left to do as they please after pagment.* Besides the saloons and bar-rooms, which are open publicly, the traffic in small grocery stores, in cellars and in dwelling-houses, in some parts of the city, *is almost astounding. The Sunday trade is enormous, and it seems as if there were not hours enough in the whole round of twenty-four, or days enough in the entire week to satisfy the dealers.*"

The experience of Massachusetts is, as we have already said, the experience of every community, State or nation in which an effort has been made to abridge the evils of intemperance by licensing the dram-shop.

And to whom and to what class of citizens does the State accord, under license, the privilege of making gain out of the people's loss? For whom is every interest in the nation taxed and every industry hurt? For whom are the houses of the poor made poorer; and the supply of bread diminished? For whom are a crime-assaulted and pauper-ridden people driven to build jails and poor-houses, and insane asylums, and maintain courts and juries and a vast army of police, at the cost of millions of dollars every year?

For great benefactors to whom the nation owes a debt of gratitude? For men who are engaged in great industrial or commercial enterprises? Promoters of education? leaders in the great march of civilization? Even if this were so, better not to have accepted the service than pay for it at so fearful a cost.

Who and what are these men?—this great privileged class? Let us see. In Boston, we have the testimony of the License Commissioners that liquor-selling is in the hands of "irresponsible men and women," who pay a license for the privilege of doing "as they please after payment." And for the maintenance of these "irresponsible" men and women in their right to corrupt and degrade the people, a forced tax is laid on every bit of property and every interest in the great city of Boston! What was the tax on tea to this? And yet, Boston patiently submits!

Is it better in New York, Philadelphia, Baltimore, Cincinnati, Chicago or any other of our large cities? Not a whit! In some it is worse, even, than in the capital of the old Bay State. In one of these last-mentioned cities, where, under the license system so dear to politicians, and for which they are chiefly responsible, between seven and eight thousand places in which liquor is sold at retail exist, an effort was made in 1876 to ascertain the character and antecedents of every person engaged in dram-selling. We are not able to say how carefully or thoroughly the investigation was pursued, but it was in the hands of those who meant that it should be complete and accurate. One fact elicited was, that the proportion of native-born citizens to the whole number engaged in the business was less than one-sixth. Another was, that over six thousand of these dram-sellers belonged to the criminal class, and had suffered imprisonment, some for extended terms in the State prison. And another was, that nearly four thousand of the drinking-places which had been established under the fostering care of State license laws were houses of ill-fame as well! Comment is unnecessary.

We cannot lessen the evil nor abate the curse of drunkenness so long as we license a traffic, which, from its essential hostility to all the best interests of society, naturally falls into the hands of our worst citizens, who persistently violate every salutary and restrictive feature in the laws which give their trade a recognized existence.

What then? Is there any remedy short of Prohibition? We believe not.

CHAPTER XVIII.

PROHIBITION.

IT has taken nearly half a century to convince the people that only in total abstinence lies any hope of cure for the drunkard. When this doctrine was first announced, its advocates met with opposition, ridicule and even insult. Now it has almost universal acceptance. The effort to hold an inebriate's appetite in check by any restriction that included license, has, in all cases, proved so signal a failure, that the "letting down," or "tapering off" process has been wholly abandoned in inebriate asylums. There is no hope, as we have said, but in complete abstinence.

NO REMEDY BUT PROHIBITION.

Is there any other means of cure for national drunkenness? The remedy of license has been found as valueless for the whole people as restriction for the individual. Appetite, when once depraved, becomes, in the individual, lawless, exacting and unscrupulous; not hesitating to trample on duty, justice, humanity and every public and private virtue. It will keep no faith; it will hold to no pledge, however solemnly taken. It must be wholly denied or it will be wholly master.

As in the individual, so in the nation, State or community. Appetite loses nothing by aggregation; nor are the laws of its action changed. If not denied by prohibition in the State, as by total abstinence in the individual, it will continue to entail upon the people loss and ruin and unutterable woes. License, restrictive permission, tax, all will be vain in the future as they have been in the past. There is no hope, no help, no refuge in anything but *Prohibition!*

And here we art met by two questions, fairly and honestly asked. First. Is prohibition right in the abstract as a legislative measure? Second. Can prohibitory laws be enforced, and will they cure the evil of drunkenness?

First, as to the question of legislative action. Can the State forbid the sale of intoxicating drinks as a beverage without violating the natural right of certain citizens, engaged in the manufacture and sale of these articles, to supply them to customers who wish to purchase?

We answer, that no man has a natural right to do wrong; that is, to engage in any pursuit by which he makes gain out of loss and injury to his neighbor. The essential principle of government is the well-being of the people. It guarantees to the weak, security against the strong; it punishes evil-doers, and seeks to protect its citizens from the evil effects of that unscrupulous selfishness in the individual which would trample on the rights of all the rest in its pursuit of money or power.

Now, if it can be shown that the liquor traffic is a good thing; that it benefits the people; makes them more prosperous and happy; improves their health; promotes education and encourages virtue, then its right to exist in the community has been established. Or, even if the good claimed for it be only negative instead of positive, its right must still be unquestioned. But what if it works evil and only evil in the State? What if it blights and curses every neighborhood, and town, and city, and nation in which it exists; laying heavy taxes upon the people that it may live and flourish, crippling all industries; corrupting the morals of the people; enticing the young from virtue; filling jails, and poor-houses, and asylums with a great army of criminals, paupers and insane men and women, yearly extinguishing the light in thousands of happy homes? What then?

Does this fruit of the liquor traffic establish its right to existence and to the protection of law? Let the reader answer the question for himself. That it entails all of these evils, and many more, upon the community, cannot and will not be denied. That it does any good, cannot be shown. Fairly, then, it has no right to existence in any government established for the good of the people; and in suppressing it, no wrong can be done.

PROHIBITION NOT UNCONSTITUTIONAL.

How the question of prohibition is regarded by the highest legal authority in the United States will appear from the following opinions officially given by four of the Justices of our Supreme Court. They are expressed in no doubtful or hesitating form of speech:

Chief Justice Taney said: "If any State deems the retail and internal traffic in ardent spirits injurious to its citizens, and calculated to produce idleness, vice or debauchery, I see nothing in the Constitution of the United States to prevent it from regulating or restraining the traffic, or from prohibiting it altogether, if it thinks proper."—[5 Howard, 577.]

Hon. Justice McLean said: "A license to sell is a matter of police and revenue within the power of the State."—[5 Ibid., 589.] "If the foreign article be injurious to the health and morals of the community, a State may prohibit the sale of it."

Hon. Justice Catron said: "If the State has the power of restraint by license to any extent, she may go to the length of prohibiting sales altogether."—[5 Ibid., 611.]

Hon. Justice Grier said: "It is not necessary to array the appalling statistics of misery, pauperism and crime which have their origin in the use and abuse of ardent spirits. The police power, which is exclusively in the State, is competent to the correction of these great evils, and all measures of restraint or prohibition necessary to effect that purpose are within the scope of that authority."—[Ibid., 532.]

That the State has a clear right to prohibit the

sale of intoxicating drinks, because this sale not only hurts all other interests, but destroys the health and degrades the morals of the people, has been fully shown.

The question next to be considered is, Can prohibitory laws be enforced? and if so, will they remove from the people the curse of drunkenness?

CAN PROHIBITORY LAWS BE ENFORCED?

As to the complete enforcement of any salutory law, that depends mainly on the public sentiment regarding it, and on the organized strength of its opposers. If the common sentiment of the people were in favor of every man's liberty to steal whatever he could lay his hands on, it would be found very difficult to convict a rogue, no matter how clearly expressed the law against stealing. A single thief in the jury-box could defeat the ends of justice. A hundred loop-holes for escape can always be found in the provisions of a law with which the majority of the people are not in sympathy. Indeed, it often happens that such loop-holes are provided by the law-makers themselves; and this is especially true in too many of the laws made for the suppression of the liquor trade.

Is this an argument against the enactment of laws to protect the people from great wrongs—especially the weaker and more helpless ones? To the half-hearted, the indifferent and the pusillanimous—yes! But with brave, true men, who have at heart the best interests of humanity, this can only intensify opposition to wrong, and give strength for new efforts to destroy its power. These have an undying faith in the ultimate victory of good over evil, and mean, so far as they are concerned, that the battle shall continue until that victory is won.

Judge Pitman has eloquently expressed this sentiment in the closing pages of his recent work, to which we have more than once referred. Speaking of those who distrust the practicability of securing such legislation as will effectually destroy the liquor trade, he says: "They are appalled at the power of the traffic. They see that it has uncounted wealth at its command; that it is organized and unscrupulous; that it has the support of fierce appetite behind it and the alliance of every evil lust; that it is able to bribe or intimidate the great political parties. All this is true; but still it is not to be the final victor. It has all the elemental moral forces of the human race against it, and though their working be slow, and their rate of progress dependent on human energy and fidelity, the ultimate result is as certain as the action of the law of gravity in the material universe. Wealth may be against us.; rank may affect to despise us; but the light whose dawn makes a new morning in the world, rarely shines from palace or crown, but from the manger and the cross. Before the aroused consciences of the people, wielding the indomitable will of a State, the destroyers of soul and body shall go down forever."

THE VALUE OF PROHIBITORY LAWS WHEN ENFORCED.

It remains now to show how far prohibitory laws, when enforced, have secured the end for which they were created. On this point, the evidence is clear and satisfactory. In Vermont, a prohibitory law has existed for over twenty-three years. In some parts of the State it is rigidly enforced; in others with less severity. Judge Peck, of the Supreme Court says: "The law has had an effect upon our customs, and has done away with that of treating and promiscuous drinking. * * * *In attending court for ten years, I do not remember to have seen a drunken man.*" In St. Johnsbury, where there is a population of five thousand, the law has been strictly enforced; and the testimony in regard to the town is this: "There is no bar, no dram-shop, no poor, and no policeman walks the streets. It is the workingman's paradise."

Connecticut enacted a prohibitory law in 1854. In 1855, Governor Dutton said, in his annual message to the General Assembly: "There is scarcely an open grog-shop in the State, the jails are fast becoming tenantless, and a delightful air of security is everywhere enjoyed."

In Meriden, the chaplain of the reform school testified that "crime had diminished seventy-five per cent." In New London, the jail was tenantless. In Norwich, the jails and almshouses were reported "as almost empty." But in 1873, the liquor influence was strong enough in the legislature to substitute license for prohibition. The consequence was an immediate increase of drunkenness and crime. Two years afterwards, the Secretary of State declared that "there was a greater increase of crime in one year under license than in seven years under prohibition."

Vineland, New Jersey, has a population of ten thousand. Absolute prohibition is the law of that community. One constable, who is also overseer of the poor, is sufficient to maintain public order. In 1875, his annual report says: "We have practically no debt. * * * The police expenses of Vineland amount to seventy-five dollars a year, the sum paid to me, and our poor expenses are a mere trifle."

In Potter County, Pennsylvania, there has been a prohibitory law for many years. Hon. John S. Mann says: "Its effect, as regards crime, is marked and conspicuous. *Our jail is without inmates, except the sheriff*, for more than half the time."

Other instances of local prohibition in this country could be given, but these are sufficient.

Bessbrook, a town in Ireland of four thousand inhabitants, has no liquor-shop, and whisky and strong drink are strictly prohibited. *There is no poor-house, pawn-shop or police-station.* The town is entirely free from strife, discord or disturbance.

In the county of Tyrone, Ireland, no drinking house is allowed. In 1870, Right Hon. Claude Hamilton said: "At present there is not a single policeman in that district. The poor-rates are half what they were before, and the magistrates testify to the great absence of crime."

In many parts of England and Scotland there is local prohibition, and the uniform testimony as to the absence of pauperism and crime is as unequivocal as that given above.

THE MAINE LAW—ITS COMPLETE VINDICATION.

But it is to the State of Maine, where a prohibitory law has existed for over a quarter of a century, and where prohibition has been put to the severest tests, that we must look for the more decisive proofs of success or failure.

On the evidence which Maine furnishes, the advocates of legal suppression are content to rest their case. In order to get a brief, but thoroughly accurate and reliable history of the Maine law, we addressed a letter to Hon. Neal Dow, of Portland, Maine, asking him to furnish us, for this volume, with the facts and evidence by which our readers could for themselves judge whether the law were a dead letter, as some asserted, or effective and salutory. In reply, Mr. Dow has kindly furnished us with the following deeply interesting and important communication:

TESTIMONY OF HON. NEAL DOW.

PORTLAND, October 12th, 1877.

T. S. ARTHUR, ESQ.:

Dear Sir—I will gladly furnish you with a brief history of the Maine Law, and a statement of its operation and effects in

Maine, in the hope that the wide circulation of the work you have in preparation may serve to correct the mistaken notion that prevails, to the effect that the law has failed of any useful result, and that the liquor traffic is carried on as extensively in Maine as ever it had been, with all its baleful effects upon the moral and material interests of the State.

In the old time the people of Maine were as much addicted to the use of strong drinks as those of any other part of the country; and the effects of this shocking habit were seen everywhere in shabby buildings, neglected farms and in wide-spread poverty. There were, in this State, magnificent forests of the best pine timber in the world. The manufacture of this timber into "lumber" of various descriptions, and the sale of it, were the leading industries of Maine. The products of our vast forests were sent chiefly to the West India Islands, and the returns were mostly in rum and in molasses, to be converted into rum by our own distilleries, of which there were many among us, in various parts of the State—seven of them in this city, running night and day. This rum, almost the whole of it, whether imported or home-made, was consumed among our own people. It was sent in the way of trade and in exchange for "lumber" into every part of our territory; not a town or village, or rural district escaped, however remote or thinly populated it might be.

The result of this was, that almost the entire value of all this vast industry went down the throats of our people in the shape of rum, either imported or home-made. I have heard men say who had been extensively engaged in this lumber trade, that Maine is not a dollar the richer, and never was, on account of this immense business; but that the people were poorer in consequence of it, and more miserable than they would have been if the pine forests had been swept away by a great conflagration.

The effects of this course of trade were seen everywhere throughout the State. In scarcely any part of it was there any evidence of business prosperity or thrift, but, generally, there was abundant evidence of poverty, untidiness and decay. In the lumbering towns and villages, where the innumerable saw-mills were, the greatest bustle and activity prevailed. The air resounded with the loud noises coming from these mills. Night and day they were "run," never ceasing until the "logs" were "worked up." Relays of hands were employed at all these lumbering centres, so that the saw-mills never stopped even for an hour during "the season," except for some occasional repairs. All these men drank rum; a quart a day per man was a moderate quantity; but a great many of them required two quarts a day. The result of this was, that the entire wages of the men were consumed in drink, except a meagre share that went to the miserable wives and children at home.

Everywhere throughout the State the results of this way of life was to be seen—in the general poverty of the people, and in the shabbiness of all their surroundings. But some persons conceived the idea that all this evil was not necessary and inevitable; that it came from the liquor traffic, which might be prohibited and suppressed, as lottery-tickets, gambling-houses and impure books and pictures had already been. And they devoted themselves constantly and industriously to the work of correcting the public opinion of the people as to the liquor traffic by demonstrating to them that this trade was in deadly hostility to every interest of the State, while no good came from it, nor could come from it, to State or people.

This educational work was carried on persistently for years; meetings were held by these persons in every little country-church and town-house, and in every little wayside school-house, where the farmers and their wives and children assembled at the call of these missionaries, to listen to their burning denunciation of the liquor traffic, which lived only by spreading poverty, pauperism, suffering, insanity, crime and premature death broadcast over the State. The result of this teaching was, that the public opinion of the State became thoroughly changed as to the character of the liquor traffic and its relation to the public prosperity and welfare.

When we thought the time had come for it, we demanded of the Legislature that the law of "license," then upon the statute books, which represented the public opinion of the old time, should be changed for a law of prohibition, representing the improved public opinion of the present time; and, after two unsuccessful attempts to procure such a law, we obtained what we desired, an act of absolute prohibition to the manufacture and sale of strong drink—a measure for which we had labored long and industriously for many years.

At the time of the enactment of this statute, now known as the MAINE LAW. the world over, the liquor traffic was carried on extensively in the State, wholesale and retail, precisely as it is now in New York, New Jersey, Pennsylvania and in every other State where that trade is licensed and protected by the law. The Maine Law went into operation immediately upon its approval by the Governor, and by its provisions, liquors kept for sale everywhere, all over the State, were liable to be seized, forfeited and destroyed, and the owners to be punished by fine and imprisonment. The municipal authorities of the cities and towns allowed the dealers a reasonable time to send away their stocks of liquors to other States and countries, where their sale was permitted by the law.

The liquor-traders availed themselves of this forbearance of the authorities, and did generally send their stock of liquors out of the State. The open sale of liquors came instantly to an end throughout all our territory, and where it continued, it was done secretly, as other things are done in violation of law. The manufacture of intoxicating liquors was entirely stopped, so that in all the State there was absolutely none produced, except cider, which might be made and used for vinegar.

The effect of this policy of prohibition to the liquor traffic was speedily visible in our work-houses, jails and houses of corrections. The jail of Cumberland County, the most populous of the State, had been badly over-crowded, but within four months of the enactment of the law there were but five prisoners in it, three of whom were liquor-sellers, put in for violation of the law. The jails of Penobscot; Kennebec, Franklin, Oxford and York were absolutely empty. The inmates of the work-houses were greatly reduced in number, and in some of the smaller towns pauperism ceased entirely.

But, during all this time, in every part of the country, reports were industriously circulated that the law was inoperative for good, and that liquors were sold in Maine as freely and in as large quantities as before the law. These false statements were industriously and persistently made everywhere by those interested in the liquor trade, and by those impelled by appetite or passion. It is sufficient for me to say here that the Maine Law, from the first, has been as faithfully executed as our other criminal laws have been, though there has been, at certain times, and in certain localities, considerable complicity with the violators of it, on the part of many officers of the law, so that the Legislature has at last provided heavy penalties for the punishment of prosecuting officers, justices of the peace and judges of municipal and police courts, in case of failure in their duty. I am glad to be able to say that the judges of our higher courts have, from the first, been true to their duty in the administration of this law, as of all others.

In much the larger part of Maine, in all the rural districts, in the villages and smaller towns, the liquor traffic is absolutely unknown; no such thing as a liquor-shop exists there, either open or secret. The traffic lingers secretly only in the larger towns and cities, where it leads a precarious and troubled life—only among the lowest and vilest part of our foreign population. Nowhere in the State is there any visible sign of this horrible trade. The penalties of the law, as they now stand, are sufficient to extinguish the traffic in all the small towns, and to drive it into dens and dark corners in the larger towns. The people of Maine now regard this trade as living, where it exists at all, only on the misery and wretchedness of the community. They speak of it everywhere, in the press, on the platform, and in legislative halls, as the gigantic crime of crimes, and we mean to treat it as such by the law.

For some years after the enactment of the law, it entered largely into the politics of the State. Candidates were nominated by one party or the other with reference to their proclivities for rum or their hostility to it, and the people were determined in their votes, one way or the other, by this consideration.

Now, the policy of prohibition, with penalties stringent enough to be effective, has become as firmly settled in this State as that of universal education or the vote by ballot. The Republican party, in its annual conventions, during all these years, has affirmed, unanimously, its "adhesion to prohibition and the vigorous enforcement of laws to that end;" and the Democratic party, in its annual convention of this year, rejected, by an immense majority, and with enthusiastic cheers, a resolution, proposed from the floor, in favor of "license."

The original Maine Law was enacted by a vote in the House of eighty-six to forty, and in the Senate by eighteen to ten. There have been several subsequent liquor laws, all in the direction of greater stringency; and the Legislature of this year enacted an additional law, with penalties much more stringent than any which had preceded it, without a dissenting vote. No one can mistake the significance of this fact, it was an unanimous affirmation of adhesion to the policy of prohibition, after a steady trial of it and experience of its results for more than a quarter of a century. And, since that time, the people have passed upon it at the late annual election by an approval of the policy and of the men who favor it—by an immense majority. If it be conceded that the people of Maine possess an ordinary share of intelligence and common sense, this result would be impossible, unless the effect of prohibition had been beneficial to the State and to them.

While we were earnestly at work in bringing up the public opinion of the State to the point of demanding the prohibition of the liquor traffic, as a more important political and social question than any other or all others, I was startled at hearing a gentleman of the town of Raymond declare that in his town the people consumed in strong drink its entire valuation in every period of eighteen years, eight months and twenty-five days! "Here are the figures," he said; "I know the quantity of liquor brought into the town annually. I am so situated that I am able to state this accurately, beyond all possibility of doubt, except that liquors may be brought here by other than the ordinary mode of transportation without my knowledge; but the quantities stated in this paper (which he held in his hand), and their cost are within my knowledge." This was part of a speech to his fellow-townsmen, and his statement was admitted to be true. Now, there is not a drop of liquor sold in that town, and there has not been any sold there for many years. This statement may strike us at first blush to be tremendously exaggerated, that the people of any locality should consume in strong drink the entire value of its real estate and personal property in every period of less than twenty years. But let us examine it.

We learn from the Bureau of Statistics that the annual liquor bill of the United States is seven hundred millions of dollars. This does not include the enormous quantity of "crooked whisky," which has been put upon the market with or without the knowledge, consent, assent or complicity of our public officers, from the highest to the lowest. The drink bill of the United Kingdom, with a population smaller than ours, is more than this by many millions. This valuation—seven hundred millions of dollars—is the price, by the quantity, taken from the figures as they come into the public office, while the cost to the consumers is vastly greater. Now, this sum, with annual compound interest for ten years, amounts to the enormous figure of eight billions nine hundred and forty-four millions one hundred and forty-one thousands of dollars—almost nine thousand millions of dollars! For twenty years the amount is twenty-five billions two hundred and forty-five millions six hundred and eighty-one thousands of dollars. Twenty-five thousand two hundred and forty-five millions of dollars and more; actually as much, within a fraction, as the entire value of the personal and landed property of the United States! My friend of Raymond may well be credited in the statement made to his fellow-townsmen.

Now, as the result of the Maine Law, in Maine, the wealth and prosperity of the people have greatly increased. This can be seen in every part of the State, and is obvious to the most casual observer, who knew what Maine was before the law of prohibition, and knows what it has been since and down to the present time. Evidences of industry, enterprise and thrift everywhere, instead of the general poverty, unthrift and shabness of the old rum-time.

The share of Maine, of the National drink bill, would be about thirteen millions of dollars, and but for the Maine Law, we should be consuming our full proportion; but now I feel myself fully warranted in saying that we do not expend in that way one-tenth of that sum. A mayor of the city of Portland, in a message to the City Council, said: "The quantity of liquor now sold is not one-fiftieth part as much as it was before the enactment of the law." The difference, whatever it may be, between the sum we should waste in strong drink, but for the law, and that which we actually squander in that way, we have in our pockets, in our savings banks and in our business, so that Maine has suffered far less, financially, during this crisis, than any other part of the country.

I have said the drink bill of Maine, but for prohibition, would be about thirteen millions of dollars annually, in proportion to that of the whole country. Now, this sum, with annual compound interest at six per cent., in ten years will amount to one hundred and seventy millions three hundred and nineteen thousand five hundred and twenty-eight dollars, and in twenty years to four hundred and sixty-three millions eight hundred and fifty-four thousand four hundred and twenty dollars—more than twice the entire valuation of the State, by the estimate made in 1870, which was two hundred and twenty-four millions eight hundred and twenty-two thousand nine hundred and thirteen dollars. There was a reason then for the fact, that in the old rum-time the people of Maine were poor and unthrifty in every way—and for that other fact, that now they are prosperous and flourishing, with a better business than that of any other State, proportionately.

Notwithstanding the fact that in Portland a great conflagration destroyed ten millions of dollars in 1866, burned down half the town, and turned ten thousand people out of doors, the prosperity of the city has been steadily on the increase. Its valuation, in 1860, was twenty-one millions eight hundred and sixty-six thousand dollars, and in 1870, twenty-nine millions four hundred and thirty-nine thousand two hundred and fifty-seven dollars. In the last year the increase in valuation, in spite of the hard times, was four hundred and eighty thousand dollars, while Boston, with free rum, has lost more than eight millions, and New York and Brooklyn has experienced an immense depreciation.

I think I have said enough to satisfy every intelligent, unprejudiced man that the absolute prohibition and suppression of the liquor traffic has been in the highest interest of our State and people. I am, very truly, yours,

NEAL DOW.

And here we close our discussion of the most important of all the social questions that are to-day before the people; and in doing so, declare it as our solemn conviction, that until the liquor traffic is abolished, and the evils with which it curses the people, removed, all efforts at moral reforms must languish, and the church find impediments in her way which cannot be removed. The CURSE is upon us, and there is but one CURE; *Total Abstinence,* by the help of God, for the individual, and *Prohibition* for the State.

www.ingramcontent.com/pod-product-compliance
Lightning Source LLC
Chambersburg PA
CBHW021218300426
44111CB00007B/350